GPU Pro 360

Guide to 3D Engine Design

GPU Pro 360

Guide to 3D Engine Design

Edited by Wolfgang Engel

CRC Press
Taylor & Francis Group
Boca Raton London New York

CRC Press is an imprint of the
Taylor & Francis Group, an **informa** business

AN A K PETERS BOOK

CRC Press
Taylor & Francis Group
6000 Broken Sound Parkway NW, Suite 300
Boca Raton, FL 33487-2742

International Standard Book Number-13: 978-0-8153-9075-6 (Paperback)
International Standard Book Number-13: 978-0-8153-9079-4 (Hardback)

Library of Congress Cataloging-in-Publication Data

Names: Engel, Wolfgang F., editor.
Title: GPU pro 360 guide to 3D engine design / [edited by] Wolfgang Engel.
Description: First edition. | Boca Raton, FL : CRC Press/Taylor & Francis Group, 2018. | Includes bibliographical references and index.
Identifiers: LCCN 2018020471| ISBN 9780815390756 (pbk. : acid-free paper) |
   ISBN 9780815390794 (hardback : acid-free paper)
Subjects: LCSH: Computer graphics. | Graphics processing units--Programming.
| Graphics processing units--Design and construction. | Three-dimensional modeling.
Classification: LCC T385 .G688778 2018 | DDC 006.6/93--dc23
LC record available at https://lccn.loc.gov/2018020471

Visit the eResources: www.crcpress.com/9780815390756

Visit the Taylor & Francis Web site at
http://www.taylorandfrancis.com

and the CRC Press Web site at
http://www.crcpress.com

Contents

Introduction

This book targets the design of a renderer. A renderer is a very complex software module that requires attention to a lot of details. The requirements and attention also vary greatly on different hardware platforms. The chapters here cover various aspects of engine design, such as quality and optimization, in addition to high-level architecture.

The chapter "Multi-Fragment Effects on the GPU Using Bucket Sort" covers a technique on how to render order-independent transparency by utilizing a bucket sort system. Traditionally, pixels or fragments are processed in depth order rather than rasterization order and modern GPUs are optimized to capture the nearest and furthest fragment per pixel in each geometry pass. Depth peeling offers a simple and robust solution by peeling off one layer per pass, but rasterizing depth data multiple times leads to performance bottlenecks. Newer approaches like the K-buffer approach capture fragments in a single pass but suffer from read-modify-write (RMW hazards). This chapter presents a method that utilizes a bucket array per pixel that is allocated using MRT as the storage. It is more efficient than classical depth peeling while offering good visual results.

The next chapter, "Parallelized Light Pre-Pass Rendering with the Cell Broadband Engine," demonstrates the efficient implementation of a light pre-pass / deferred lighting engine on the PS3 platform. Distributing the workload of rendering many lights over the SPE and GPU requires some intricate knowledge of the platform and software engineering skills that are covered in the chapter.

In Stephen Hill and Daniel Collin's chapter "Practical, Dynamic Visibility for Games," the authors introduce methods for determining per-object visibility, taking into account occlusion by other objects. The chapter provides invaluable and inspiring experience from published AAA titles, showing excellent gains that are otherwise lost without this system.

Next, Eric Penner presents "Shader Amortization Using Pixel Quad Message Passing." In this chapter, he analyzes one particular aspect of modern programmable hardware: the pixel derivative instructions and pixel quad rasterization. The chapter identifies a new level at which optimizations can be performed, and applies this method to achieve results such as 4×4 percentage closer filtering (PCF) using only one texture fetch, and 2×2 bilateral up-sampling using only one or two texture fetches.

On the topic of crowd rendering, the chapter "A Rendering Pipeline for Real-Time Crowds," by Benjamín Hernández and Isaac Rudomin, describes a detailed system for simulating and rendering large numbers of different characters on the GPU, making use of optimizations such as culling and LOD-selection to improve performance of the system.

Pascal Gautron, Jean-Eudes Marvie, and Gaël Sourimant present us with the chapter, "Z^3 Culling," in which the authors suggest a novel method to optimize depth testing over the Z-buffer algorithm. The new technique adds two "depth buffers" to keep the early-Z culling optimization even on objects drawn with states that prevent early-Z culling (such as alpha testing).

Next, Dzmitry Malyshau brings his experience of designing a quaternion-based 3D engine in his chapter, "Quaternion-Based Rendering Pipeline." Malyshau shows the benefits of using quaternions in place of transformation matrices in various steps of the rendering pipeline based on his experience of a real-world 3D-engine implementation.

In the chapter, "Implementing a Directionally Adaptive Edge AA Filter Using DirectX 11," Matthew Johnson improves upon the box antialiasing filter using a postprocessing technique that calculates a best fit gradient line along the direction of candidate primitive edges to construct a filter that gives a better representation of edge information in the scene, and thus higher quality antialiased edges.

Donald Revie describes the high-level architecture of a 3D engine in the chapter "Designing a Data-Driven Renderer." The design aims to bridge the gap between the logical simulation at the core of most game engines and the strictly ordered stream of commands required to render a frame through a graphics API. The solution focuses on providing a flexible data-driven foundation on which to build a rendering pipeline, making minimal assumptions about the exact rendering style used.

Next, Donald Revie brings his experience of engine design in his chapter "An Aspect-Based Engine Architecture." Aspect-based engines apply the principles of component design and object-oriented programming (OOP) on an engine level by constructing the engine using modules. Such architecture is well suited to small or distributed teams who cannot afford to establish a dedicated structure to design and manage all the elements of their engine but would still like to take advantage of the benefits that developing their own technology provides. The highly modular nature allows for changes in development direction or the accommodation of multiple projects with widely varying requirements.

In the chapter "Kinect Programming with Direct3D 11," Jason Zink provides a walkthrough into this emerging technology by explaining the hardware and software aspects of the Kinect device. The chapter seeks to provide the theoretical underpinnings needed to use the visual and skeletal data streams of the Kinect, and it also provides practical methods for processing and using this data with the Direct3D 11 API. In addition, it explores how this data can be used in real-time rendering scenarios to provide novel interaction systems.

Homam Bahnassi and Wessam Bahnassi present a description of a full pipeline for implementing structural damage to characters and other environmental objects in the chapter "A Pipeline for Authored Structural Damage." The chapter covers details for a full pipeline from mesh authoring to displaying pixels on the screen, with qualities including artist-friendliness, efficiency, and flexibility.

Next, Peter Sikachev, Vladimir Egorov, and Sergey Makeev share their experience using quaternions in an MMORPG game engine. Their chapter, "Quaternions Revisited," illustrates the use of quaternions for multiple purposes in order to replace bulky 3×3 rotation and tangent space matrices throughout the entire engine, most notably affecting aspects such as normal mapping, generic transforms, instancing, skinning, and morph targets. The chapter shows the performance and memory savings attributable to the authors' findings.

Fabrice Robinet, Rémi Arnaud, Tony Parisi, and Patrick Cozzi present the chapter "glTF: Designing an Open-Standard Runtime Asset Format." This chapter introduces work by the COLLADA Working Group in the Khronos Group to provide a bridge between interchange asset formats and the OpenGL-based runtime graphics APIs (e.g., WebGL and OpenGL ES). The design of the glTF open-standard transmission-format is described, along with open-source content pipeline tools involved in converting COLLADA to glTF and REST-based cloud services.

Bartosz Chodorowski and Wojciech Sterna present the chapter "Managing Transformations in Hierarchy," which provides a study on this basic 3D engine component. In addition to presenting the theory, it describes and addresses some of the issues found in common implementations of the transformation hierarchy system. It also describes how to achieve some useful operations within this system such as re-parenting nodes and global positioning.

Holger Gruen examines the benefits of a block-wise linear memory layout for binary 3D grids in the chapter "Block-Wise Linear Binary Grids for Fast Ray-Casting Operations." This memory layout allows mapping a number of volumetric intersection algorithms to binary AND operations. Bulk-testing a subportion of the voxel grid against a volumetric stencil becomes possible. The chapter presents various use cases for this memory layout optimization.

Michael Delva, Julien Hamaide, and Ramses Ladlani present the chapter "Semantic-Based Shader Generation Using Shader Shaker." This chapter offers one solution for developing and efficiently maintaining shader permutations across multiple target platforms. The proposed technique produces shaders automatically from a set of handwritten code fragments, each responsible for a single feature. This particular version of the proven divide-and-conquer methodology differs in the way the fragments are being linked together by using a path-finding algorithm to compute a complete data flow through shader fragments from the initial vertex attributes to the final pixel shader output.

Shannon Woods, Nicolas Capens, Jamie Madill, and Geoff Lang present the chapter "ANGLE: Bringing OpenGL ES to the Desktop." ANGLE is a portable, open-source, hardware-accelerated implementation of OpenGL ES 2.0 used by software like Google Chrome. The chapter provides a close insight on the Direct3D 11 backend implementation of ANGLE along with how certain challenges were handled, in addition to recommended practices for application developers using ANGLE.

Homam and Wessam Bahnassi describe a new real-time particle simulation method that works by capturing simulation results from DCC tools and then replaying them in real time on the GPU at a low cost while maintaining the flexibility of adding interactive elements to those simulations. Their technique "Interactive Cinematic Particles" has been applied successfully in the game *Hyper Void*, which runs at 60 fps even on the Playstation 3 console.

Krzysztof Narkowicz presents the chapter "Real-Time BC6H Compression on GPU." The chapter describes a simple real-time BC6H compression algorithm, one which can be implemented on GPU entirely with practical performance figures. Such a technique can be very useful for optimizing rendering of dynamic HDR textures such as environment cubemaps.

The next chapter by Gustavo Bastos Nunes is "A 3D Visualization Tool Used for Test Automation in the Forza Series." The tool introduced automatically analyzes a mesh for bad holes and normal data and gives the manual tester an easy semantic view of what are likely to be bugs and what are by-design data. The tool was used during the entire production cycle of *Forza Motorsport 5* and *Forza: Horizon 2* by Turn 10 Studios and Playground Games, saving several hundred hours of manual testing and increasing trust in shipping the game with collision meshes in a perfect state.

Finally, Takahiro Harada presents the chapter "Semi-Static Load Balancing for Low-Latency Ray Tracing on Heterogeneous Multiple GPUs," which describes a low-latency ray tracing system for multiple GPUs with nonuniform compute powers. To realize the goal, a semi-static load balancing method is proposed that uses rendering statistics of the previous frame to compute work distribution for the next frame. The proposed method does not assume uniform sampling density on the framebuffer, thus it is applicable for a problem with an irregular sampling pattern. The method is not only applicable for a multi-GPU environment, but it can be used to distribute compute workload on GPUs and a CPU as well.

Web Materials

Example programs and source code to accompany some of the chapters are available on the CRC Press website: go to https://www.crcpress.com/9780815390756 and click on the "Downloads" tab.

The directory structure follows the book structure by using the chapter numbers as the name of the subdirectory.

General System Requirements

The material presented in this book was originally published between 2010 and 2016, and the most recent developments have the following system requirements:

- The DirectX June 2010 SDK (the latest SDK is installed with Visual Studio 2012).

- DirectX 11 or DirectX 12 capable GPUs are required to run the examples. The chapter will mention the exact requirement.

- The OS should be Microsoft Windows 10, following the requirement of DirectX 11 or 12 capable GPUs.

- Visual Studio C++ 2012 (some examples might require older versions).

- 2GB RAM or more.

- The latest GPU driver.

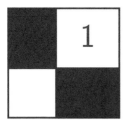

Multi-Fragment Effects on the GPU Using Bucket Sort

Meng-Cheng Huang, Fang Liu, Xue-Hui Liu, and En-Hua Wu

1.1 Introduction

Efficient rendering of multi-fragment effects has long been a great challenge in computer graphics, which always require to process fragments in depth order rather than rasterization order. The major problem is that modern GPUs are optimized only to capture the nearest or furthest fragment per pixel each geometry pass. The classical depth peeling algorithm [Mammen 89, Everitt 01] provides a simple but robust solution by peeling off one layer per pass, but multi-rasterizations will lead to performance bottleneck for large-scale scene with high complexity. The k-buffer [Bavoil et al. 07, Liu et al. 06] captures k fragments in a single pass but suffers from serious read-modify-write(RMW) hazards.

This chapter presents a fast approximation method for efficient rendering of multi-fragment effects via bucket sort on GPU. In particular, a bucket array of size K is allocated per pixel location using MRT as storage, and the depth range of each pixel is consequently divided into K subintervals. During rasterization, fragments within the kth ($k = 0, 1, \cdots, K - 1$) subinterval will be routed to the kth bucket by a bucket sort. Collisions will happen when multiple fragments are routed to the same bucket, which can be alleviated by multi-pass approach or an adaptive scheme. Our algorithm shows great speedup to the classical depth peeling with visually faithful results, especially for large scenes with high complexity.

1.2   Design of Bucket Array

The bucket array can be constructed as a fixed size buffer per pixel location in GPU memory, thus the MRT buffers turn out to be a natural candidate. Since modern GPUs can afford at most eight MRTs with internal pixel format of GL_RGBA32F_ARB, the size of our bucket array can reach up to 32, which is often enough for most common applications.

The default REPLACE blending of the MRTs will introduce two problems. First, when multiple fragments are trying to update the bucket array on the same pixel location concurrently, the number of the operations on that location and the order in which they occur is undefined, and only one of them is guaranteed to succeed. Thus they will produce unpredictable results under concurrent writes. Second, modern GPUs have not yet supported independent update of arbitrary channels of MRT buffers. The update of a specific channel of the MRT buffers will result in all the remaining channels being overwritten by the default value zero simultaneously. As a result, the whole bucket array will hold at most one depth value at any time.

Fortunately, these problems can be solved via the 32-bit floating-point MAX/ MIN blending operation, which is available on recent commodity NVIDIA GeForce 8 or its ATI equivalents. Take the MAX blending operation as an example, which performs a comparison between the source and the destination values of each channel of MRTs, and keeps the greater one of each pair. This atomic operation guarantees all the read, modify, write operations to the same pixel location will be serialized and performed without interference from each other, thus completely avoiding the first problem of RMW hazards.

The second problem can be solved by initializing each bucket of the bucket array to zero. When updating a certain bucket, if the original value in the bucket is zero, the update will always succeed since the normalized depth values are always greater than or equal to zero; otherwise, the greater one will survive the comparison. As for other buckets, we implicitly update them simultaneously by the default value zero so that their original values are always greater and can be kept unchanged. When multiple fragments are routed to the same bucket, i.e., a collision happens, the MAX blending operation assures that the maximum depth value will win all the tests and finally stay in the bucket. MIN blending is performed in a similar way except initializing each bucket and explicitly updating the other buckets by one. The MAX/MIN blending operation enables us to update a specific bucket independently, and guarantees correct results free of RMW hazards. Since the default update value for each channel of the MRT is zero, we prefer to utilize MAX blending in our implementation for simplicity.

1.3   The Algorithm

The depth value of each fragment is normalized into a range [0,1], but for most pixels, the geometry only occupies a small subrange. Thus a bounding box or a coarse visual hull can be first rendered to approximate the depth range [zNear, zFar] per pixel in the same way as dual depth peeling [Bavoil and Myers 08]. During rasterization, the consecutive buckets per pixel are bind into 16 pairs and the depth range are divided into 16 corresponding subintervals uniformly. We then perform the dual depth peeling within each subinterval concurrently. For a fragment with depth value d_f, the corresponding bucket pair index k can be computed as follows:

$$k = \text{floor}\left(\frac{16 \times (d_f - z\text{Near})}{z\text{Far} - z\text{Near}}\right).$$

Then the kth pair of buckets will be updated by $(1 - d_f, d_f)$ and the rest pairs by $(0, 0)$. When the first geometry pass is over, the minimum and maximum depth values within the kth subinterval can be obtained from the kth pair of buckets, i.e.,

$$\text{dmin}_k^1 = 1 - \max_{d_f \in [d_k, d_{k+1})} (1 - d_f), \quad \text{dmax}_k^1 = \max_{d_f \in [d_k, d_{k+1})} (d_f).$$

It is obvious that these fragments in the consecutive depth intervals are in correct depth ordering:

$$\text{dmin}_0^1 \leq \text{dmax}_0^1 \leq \text{dmin}_1^1 \leq \text{dmax}_1^1 \leq \cdots \leq \text{dmin}_{15}^1 \leq \text{dmax}_{15}^1.$$

If there is no fragment within the kth subinterval, both dmax_k^1 and dmin_k^1 will remain the initial value 0 and can be omitted. While if there is only one fragment within the kth subinterval, dmax_k^1 and dmin_k^1 will be equal and one of them can be eliminated. In a following fullscreen pass, the bucket array will be sequentially accessed as eight input textures to retrieve the sorted fragments for post-processing.

For applications that need other fragment attributes, taking order independent transparency as an example, we can pack the RGBA8 color into a 32-bit positive floating-point using the Cg function *pack_4ubyte*. The alpha channel will be halved and mapped to the highest byte to ensure the positivity of the packed floating-point. We then divide the depth range into 32 subintervals corresponding to the 32 buckets and capture the packed colors instead of the depth values in a similar way. In post-processing, we can unpack the floating-point colors to RGBA8 and double the alpha channel for blending.

1.4   Multi-Pass Approach

The algorithm turns out to be a good approximation for uniformly distributed scenes with few collisions. But for non-uniform ones, collisions will happen more frequently especially on the silhouette or details of the model with noticeable artifacts. The algorithm can be extended to a multi-pass approach for better results. In the second geometry pass, we allocate a new bucket array for each pixel and the bucket array captured in the first pass will be taken as eight input textures. For a fragment within the kth subinterval, if its depth value d_f satisfies condition $d_f \geq \mathrm{dmax}_k^1$ or $d_f \leq \mathrm{dmin}_k^1$, it must have been captured in the previous pass, thus can be simply discarded. When the second pass is over, the second minimal and maximum depth values dmin_k^2 and dmax_k^2 in the kth subinterval can be retrieved from the kth pair of buckets similarly. The depth values captured in these two passes are naturally in correct ordering:

$$\mathrm{dmin}_0^1 \leq \mathrm{dmin}_0^2 \leq \mathrm{dmax}_0^2 \leq \mathrm{dmax}_0^1 \leq \mathrm{dmin}_1^1 \leq \mathrm{dmin}_1^2 \leq \mathrm{dmax}_1^2,$$

$$\leq \mathrm{dmax}_1^1 \leq \cdots \leq \mathrm{dmin}_{15}^1 \leq \mathrm{dmin}_{15}^2 \leq \mathrm{dmax}_{15}^2 \leq \mathrm{dmax}_{15}^1.$$

During post-processing, both bucket arrays can be passed to the pixel shader as input textures and accessed for rendering of multi-fragment effects.

Theoretically, we can obtain accurate results by enabling the occlusion query and looping in the same way until all the fragments have been captured. However, the sparse layout of depth values in the bucket arrays will lead to memory exhaustion especially for non-uniform scenes and high screen resolutions. Artifacts may also arise due to the inconsistency between the packed attribute ordering and the correct depth ordering. We instead propose a more robust scheme to alleviate these problems at the cost of an additional geometry pass, namely adaptive bucket depth peeling. The details will be described as follows.

1.5   The Adaptive Scheme

The uniform division of the depth range may result in some buckets overloaded while the rest idle for non-uniform scenes. Ideally, we prefer to adapt the division of subintervals to the distribution of the fragments per pixel, so that there is only one fragment falling into each subinterval. The one-to-one correspondence between fragments and subintervals will assure only one fragment for each bucket, thus can avoid the collisions.

Inspired by the image histogram equalization, we define a depth histogram as an auxiliary array with each entry indicating the number of fragments falling into the corresponding depth subinterval, thus is a probability distribution of the geometry. We allocate eight MRT buffers with pixel format GL_RGBA32UI_EXT as our depth histogram. Considering each channel of the MRT as a vector of 32 bits, the depth histogram can be cast to a bit array of size 4*8*32=1024, with each bit as a binary counter for fragments. Meanwhile, the depth range is divided into 1024 corresponding subintervals: $[d_k, d_{k+1}), d_k = z\text{Near} + \frac{k}{1024}(z\text{Far} - z\text{Near}), k = 0, 1, \cdots, 1023$. The depth range is always on a magnitude of 10^{-1}, so the subintervals will be on a magnitude of 10^{-4}, which are often small enough to distinguish almost any two close layers. As a result, there is at most one fragment within each subinterval on most occasions, thus a binary counter for each entry of the depth histogram will be sufficient most of the time.

Similarly, we begin by approximating the depth range per pixel by rendering the bounding box of the scene in an initial pass. In the first geometry pass, an incoming fragment within the kth subinterval will set the kth bit of the depth histogram to one using the OpenGL's 32-bit logic operation GR_OR. After the first pass, each bit of the histogram will indicate the presence of fragments in that subinterval or not. A simplified example with depth complexity $N = 8$ (the maximum number of layers of the scene at all viewing angles) is

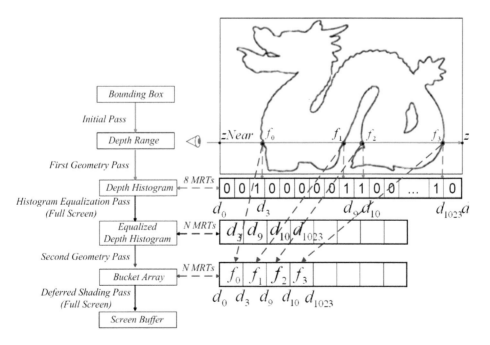

Figure 1.1. An example of adaptive bucket depth peeling. The red arrows indicate the operations in the first geometry pass and the blue arrows indicate the operations in the second geometry pass.

```
void main(  float4   wpos : WPOS,
            uniform samplerRECT depthRange,

            //Output histogram as eight MRTs.
            out unsigned int4  color0 : COLOR0,
            out unsigned int4  color1 : COLOR1,
            ......
            out unsigned int4  color7 : COLOR7 )
{
  float z = wpos.z;
  float4 range = texRECT(depthRange, wpos.xy);

  float zNear = 1 - range.x;
  float zFar = range.y;

  int k = floor( 1024 * ( z-zNear)/(zFar-zNear) );
  int i = k >> 5;
  int j = k & 0x1F;

  unsigned int SetBit = 0x80000000 >> j;

  if(i==0) color0 = unsigned int4(SetBit,0,0,0);
  else if(i==1) color0 = unsigned int4(0,SetBit,0,0);
  else if(i==2) color0 = unsigned int4(0,0,SetBit,0);
  ......
  else if(i==30) color7 = unsigned int4(0,0,SetBit,0);
  else color7 = unsigned int4(0,0,0,SetBit);
}
```

Listing 1.1. The pixel shader in the first geometry pass.

shown in Figure 1.1. Suppose at a certain pixel location, the eye ray intersects the scene generating four fragments $f_0 - f_3$ within four different subintervals $[d_2, d_3], [d_8, d_9], [d_9, d_{10}], [d_{1022}, d_{1023}]$. They will set the 3rd, 9th, 10th, and the 1023rd bit of the depth histogram to 1 in the first geometry pass. The code snippet Listing 1.1 shows the pixel shader in the first geometry pass.

The depth histogram is equalized in a following fullscreen pass. For scenes with depth complexity N less than 32, the histogram is passed into the pixel shader as eight input textures, and new floating-point MRT buffers with N channels will be allocated as an equalized histogram for output. We can consecutively obtain the jth bit of the ith $(i, j = 0, 1, 2, \cdots, 31)$ channel of the input depth histogram. If the bit is zero, it means that there is no fragment falling into the kth $(k = i * 32 + j)$ depth subinterval, thus can be simply skipped over; otherwise, there is at least one fragment within that subinterval, so we store the corresponding upper bound d_{k+1} consecutively into the equalized histogram for output. As for the example in Figure 1.1, two MRT buffers with eight channels will be allocated as the equalized histogram, and the upper bounds d_3, d_9, d_{10}, and d_{1023} will be stored into it in the equalization pass. The code snippet Listing 1.2 shows the pixel shader in the histogram equalization pass.

```
void main( float4   wpos : WPOS,
           uniform samplerRECT depthRange,
           //Input histogram as eight textures.
           usamplerRECT fbcolor0,
           usamplerRECT fbcolor1,
           ......
           usamplerRECT fbcolor7,
           //Output equalized histogram as eight MRTs.
           out float4 color0 : COLOR0,
           out float4 color1 : COLOR1,
           ......
           out float4 color7 : COLOR7 )
{
  float4 range = texRECT(depthRange, wpos.xy);
  float zFar = range.y;  if( zFar == 0 ) discard;
  float zNear = 1 - range.x;

  unsigned int4 fb0 =   texRECT(fbcolor0, wpos.xy);
  unsigned int4 fb1 =   texRECT(fbcolor0, wpos.xy);
  ......
  unsigned int4 fb7 =   texRECT(fbcolor7, wpos.xy);

  // Discard pixels that are not rendered.
  if( any( fb0|fb1|fb2|fb3|fb4|fb5|fb6|fb7 ) == 0 ) discard;

  unsigned int Histogram[32];
  Histogram[0]=fb0.x; Histogram[1]=fb0.y;
  Histogram[2]=fb0.z; Histogram[3]=fb0.w;
  ......
  Histogram[30]=fb7.z; Histogram[31]=fb7.w;

  float EquHis[32]; // Equalized histogram
  float coeff = (zFar - zNear) / 1024.0;
  int HisIndex = 1, EquHisIndex= 0;

  for(int i = 0; i < 32; i++, HisIndex += 32)
  {
    unsigned int remainded = Histogram[i];
    // End the inner loop when the remained bits are all zero.
    for(int k = HisIndex; remainded != 0; k++, remainded <<= 1)
    {
      if(remainded >= 0x80000000)
      {
        // The $k$th bit of the histogram has been set to one,
        // so store the upper bound of the $k$th subinterval.
        EquHis[EquHisIndex++] = k * coeff + zNear;
      }
    }
```

```
    }
    color0 = float4(EquHis[0],EquHis[1],EquHis[2],EquHis[3]);
    color1 = float4(EquHis[4],EquHis[5],EquHis[6],EquHis[7]);
    ......
    color7 = float4(EquHis[28],EquHis[29],EquHis[30],EquHis[31]);
}
```

Listing 1.2. The pixel shader of the histogram equalization pass.

We perform the bucket sort in the second geometry pass. The equalized histogram is passed to the pixel shader as input textures and a new bucket array of the same size N is allocated as output for each pixel. The upper bounds in the input equalized histogram will redivide the depth range into non-uniform subintervals with almost one-to-one correspondence between fragments and subintervals. As a result, there will be only one fragment falling into each bucket on most occasions; thus collisions can be reduced substantially. During rasterization, each incoming fragment with a depth value d_f will search the input equalized histogram (denoted as EquHis for short). If it belongs to the kth subinterval, i.e., it satisfies conditions $d_f \geq \text{EquHis}[k-1]$ and $d_f < \text{EquHis}[k]$, it will be routed to the kth bucket. In the end, the fragments are consecutively stored in the output bucket array, so our adaptive scheme will be memory efficient. The bucket array will then be passed to the fragment shader of a fullscreen deferred shading pass as textures for post-processing. As for our example in Figure 1.1, the upper bounds in the equalized histogram redivide the depth range into 4 subintervals: $[0, d_3), [d_3, d_9), [d_9, d_{10}), [d_{10}, d_{1023}]$. Fragment f_0 is within the first subinterval $[0, d_3)$, so it is routed to the first bucket. Fragment f_1 is within the second subinterval $[d_3, d_9)$, and is routed to the second bucket, and so on. After the second geometry pass, all of the four fragments are stored in the bucket array for further applications.

This adaptive scheme can reduce the collisions substantially, but collisions might still happen when two close layers of the model generate two fragments with a distance less than 10^{-4}, especially on the silhouette or details of the model. These fragments are routed to the same bucket and merged into one layer, thus resulting in artifacts. In practice, we can further reduce collisions by binding the buckets into pairs and performing dual depth peeling within each non-empty subinterval. Theoretically, the multi-pass approach can be resorted to for better results.

For applications that need multiple fragment attributes, the one-to-one correspondence between fragments and subintervals can assure the attributes consistency, so we can bind consecutive buckets into groups and update each group by the attributes simultaneously.

For scenes with more than 32 layers, we can handle the remaining layers by scanning over the remaining part of the histogram in a new fullscreen pass to get another batch of 32 nonzero bits. We then equalize it and pass the equalized histogram to the next geometry pass to route the fragments between layer 32 and 64 into corresponding buckets in the same way, and so on, until all the fragments have been captured.

1.6 Applications

Many multi-fragment effects can benefit from our algorithm and gain high performance in comparison to the previous methods. To demonstrate the results, we took several typical ones as examples. Frame rates are measured at 512×512 resolution on an NVIDIA 8800 GTX graphics card with driver 175.16 and Intel Duo Core 2.4G Hz with 3GB memory.

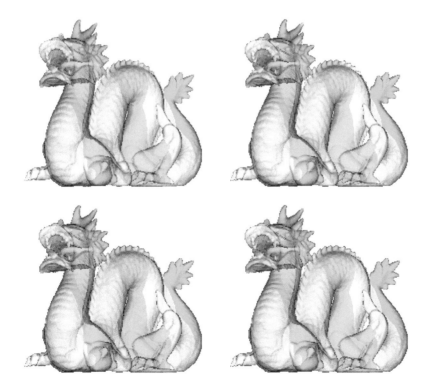

Figure 1.2. Transparent effect on Stanford Dragon (871K triangles). The left top is rendered by BDP (256fps); the right top is by BDP2 (128fps); the left bottom is by ADP (106fps); and the right bottom is the ground truth generated by DP (24fps).

1.6.1   Transparent Effect

Figure 1.2 shows the order independent transparent effect on Stanford Dragon rendered by our bucket depth peeling with a single pass (BDP) and its two-pass extension (BDP2) and the adaptive bucket depth peeling (ADP) in comparison to the classical depth peeling (DP). The differences between the results of our algorithm and the ground truth genertated by DP are visually unnoticeable, so one pass would be a good approximation when performance is more crucial.

1.6.2   Translucent Effect

The translucent effect can be rendered accounting only for absorption and ignoring reflection [NVIDIA 05]. The ambient term I_a can be computed using

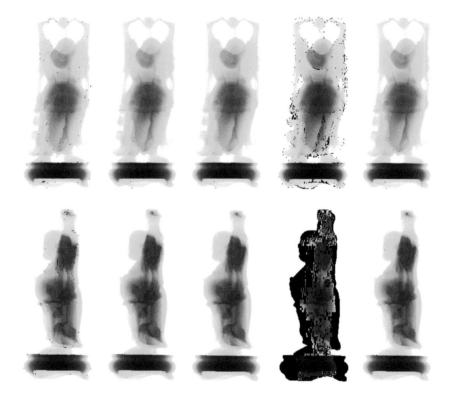

Figure 1.3. Translucent effect on the Buddha model (1,087K triangles). The first column is rendered by BDP (212fps); the second and third are by BDP2 and ADP (106fps); the third is by the k-buffer of 16 layers without modifications (183fps); and the last one is the ground truth generated by DP (20fps).

Beer-Lambert's law: $I_a = \exp(-\sigma_t l)$, where σ is the absorption coefficient and l is the accumulated distance that light travels through the material, which can be approximated by accumulating the thickness between every two successive layers of the model per pixel. As a result, the translucent effect is quite sensitive to errors. Figure 1.3 shows the translucent effect on the Buddha model using different methods. Experimental results show that for k-buffer the RMW hazards are more severe on the side views with more layers, while in contrast, the single pass BDP provides a good approximation and the two-pass approach or the adaptive scheme is preferred for better visual quality.

1.6.3 Fresnel's Effect

Taking into account the attenuation of rays, Schlick's approximation can be used for fast calculation of Fresnel's transmittance of each fragment: $Ft = 1 - (1 - \cos(\theta))^5$. Figure 1.4 shows the results of Fresnel's effect rendered by ADP. In the second geometry pass, we transform the normal into eye space and pack it into a positive floating-point using the Cg function `pack_4byte`. The buckets are bind into pairs and each pair will be updated by the packed normal and the depth value simultaneously. In the deferred shading pass, the ambient term of each pixel can be obtained using Beer-Lambert's law. For a certain pixel, the eye direction can be restored by transforming the fragment position from the screen space back to the the eye space. We then unpack the normal of each fragment and perform a dot product with the eye direction to get the incident angle θ on that

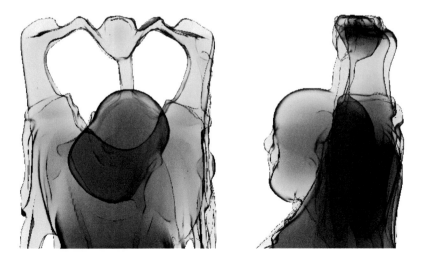

Figure 1.4. Fresnel's effect on the Buddha model (1,087K triangles) rendered by ADP.

surface. In the end, Fresnel's transmittance of each fragment can be computed and multiplied together as the final attenuating factor to the ambient term on that pixel location. The code snippet Listing 1.3 shows the pixel shader for the deferred shading of the Fresnel's effect.

More applications such as constructive solid geometry (CSG), depth of field, shadow maps, refraction, and volume rendering will also benefit from our algorithms greatly in a similar way.

```
// Restore the eye-space position of the fragment from the depth
// value.
float3 TexToEye(float2 pixelCoord, float eye_z,float2 focusLen)
{
    pixelCoord.xy -= float2(0.5, 0.5);
    pixelCoord.xy /= float2(0.5, 0.5);
    float2 eye_xy = (pixelCoord.xy / focusLen) * eye_z;
    return float3(eye_xy, eye_z);
}

void main(  float4 pixleCoordinate : TEXCOORD0,
            float4 wpos            : WPOS,
            uniform float2 focusLength,//Focus length of camera
            //Input bucket array as eight textures.
            uniform samplerRECT fbcolor0,
            uniform samplerRECT fbcolor1,
            ......
            uniform samplerRECT fbcolor7,
            out float4 color : COLOR)
{
  float4 fb0 = texRECT(fbcolor0, wpos.xy);
  float4 fb1 = texRECT(fbcolor1, wpos.xy);
  ......
  float4 fb7 = texRECT(fbcolor7, wpos.xy);

  unsigned int DepthNormal[32]; //Depth value and packed normal
  DepthNormal[0]=fb0.x; DepthNormal[1]=fb0.y;
  DepthNormal[2]=fb0.z; DepthNormal[3]=fb0.w;
  ......
  DepthNormal[30]=fb7.z; DepthNormal[31]=fb7.w;

  float thickness = 0;
  float x = -1;
  float coeff = 1.0; //The final attenuating factor

  for(int i=0;i<32;i+=2)
  {
    if( DepthNormal[i] > 0 )
    {
      float z = DepthNormal[i];
      thickness += x*z; //Accumulating the thickness
      x = -x;
      //Unpack eye-space normal N.
```

```
      float3 N = normalize(unpack_4byte(DepthNormal[i+1]).xyz);
      //Compute eye-space position P and incident direction I.
      float3 P = TexToEye(pixleCoordinate.xy,z,focusLength);
      float3 I = normalize(P);
      float cosTheta = abs(dot(I,N));   //Incident angle
      coeff *= (1-pow(1.0-cosTheta,5));//Fresnel's transmittance
    }
  }
  if( thickness == 0 ) discard;
  float4 jade = float4(0.14,0.8,0.11,1.0) * 8;
  color = exp(-30*thickness) * jade * coeff;
}
```

Listing 1.3. The pixel shader for rendering of Fresnel's effect.

1.7 Conclusions

This chapter presents a novel framework of bucket depth peeling, the first linear algorithm for rendering multi-fragment effects via bucket sort on GPU. Experiment results show great speedup to classical depth peeling with faithful results, especially for large-scale scenes with high depth complexity.

The main disadvantages are the approximate nature of the algorithm and the large memory overhead. In the future, we are interested in forming more efficient schemes to reduce collisions further more. In addition, the memory problem might be alleviated by composing the fragments within each bucket per pass, and finally composing all the buckets after done.

Bibliography

[Bavoil and Myers 08] Louis Bavoil and Kevin Myers. "Order Independent Transparency with Dual Depth Peeling." Technical report, NVIDIA Corporation, 2008.

[Bavoil et al. 07] Louis Bavoil, Steven P. Callahan, Aaron Lefohn, Jo ao L. D. Comba, and Cláudio T. Silva. "Multi-Fragment Effects on the GPU Using the k-Buffer." In *Proceedings of the 2007 Symposium on Interactive 3D Graphics and Games*, pp. 97–104, 2007.

[Everitt 01] Cass Everitt. "Interactive Order-Independent Transparency." Technical report, NVIDIA Corporation, 2001. Available at http://developer.nvidia.com/object/Interactive_Order_Transparency.html.

[Liu et al. 06] Bao-Quan Liu, Li-Yi Wei, and Ying-Qing Xu. "Multi-Layer Depth Peeling via Fragment Sort." Technical report, Microsoft Research Asia, 2006.

[Mammen 89] Abraham Mammen. "Transparency and Antialiasing Algorithms Implemented with the Virtual Pixel Maps Technique." *IEEE Computer Graphics and Applications* 9:4 (1989), 43–55.

[NVIDIA 05] NVIDIA. "GPU Programming Exposed: the Naked Truth Behind NVIDIA's Demos." Technical report, NVIDIA Corporation, 2005.

Parallelized Light Pre-Pass Rendering with the Cell Broadband Engine

Steven Tovey and Stephen McAuley

The light pre-pass renderer [Engel 08, Engel 09, Engel 09a] is becoming an ever more popular choice of rendering architecture for modern real-time applications that have extensive dynamic lighting requirements. In this chapter we introduce and describe techniques that can be used to accelerate the real-time lighting of an arbitrary three-dimensional scene on the Cell Broadband Engine without adding any additional frames of latency to the target application. The techniques described in this chapter were developed for the forthcoming PLAYSTATION3 version of *Blur* (see Figure 2.1), slated for release in 2010.[1]

2.1 Introduction

As GPUs have become more powerful, people have sought to use them for purposes other than graphics. This has opened an area of research called GPGPU (General Purpose GPU), which even major graphics card manufacturers are embracing. For example, all NVIDIA GeForce GPUs now support PhysX technology, which enables physics calculations to be performed on the GPU.

However, much less has been made of the opposite phenomenon—with the increase in speed and number of CPUs in a system, it is becoming feasible on some architectures to move certain graphics calculations from the GPU back onto the

---

[1] "PlayStation," "PLAYSTATION," and the "PS" family logo are registered trademarks, and "Cell Broadband Engine" is a trademark of Sony Computer Entertainment Inc. The "Blu-ray Disc" and "Blu-ray Disc" logos are trademarks. Screenshots of *Blur* appear courtesy of Activision Blizzard Inc. and Bizarre Creations Ltd.

CPU. Forthcoming hardware such as Intel's Larrabee even combines both components [Seiler 08], which will certainly lead to CPU-based approaches to previously GPU-only problems becoming more popular. Today, one such architecture is the PLAYSTATION3 where the powerful Cell Broadband Engine was designed from the outset to support the GPU in its processing activities [Shippy 09].

This paper expands upon the work of Swoboda in [Swoboda 09] and explains how the Cell Broadband Engine can be used to calculate lighting within the context of a light pre-pass rendering engine.

2.2 Light Pre-Pass Rendering

A recent problem in computer graphics has been how to construct a renderer that can handle many dynamic lights in a scene. Traditional forward rendering does not perform well with multiple lights. For example, if a pixel shader is written for up to four point lights, then only four point lights can be drawn (and no spotlights). We could either increase the number of pixel shader combinations to handle as many cases as possible, or we could render the geometry multiple times, once more for each additional light. Neither of these solutions is desirable as they increase the number of state changes and draw calls to uncontrollable levels.

A popular solution to this problem is to use a deferred renderer, which uses an idea first introduced in [Deering 88]. Instead of writing out fully lit pixels from the pixel shader, we instead write out information about the surface into a *G-Buffer*, which would include depth, normal, and material information. An example G-buffer format is shown in Figure 2.2.

Figure 2.1. A screenshot from the forthcoming *Blur*.

R (8bit)	G (8bit)	B (8bit)	α (8bit)	
Depth 24bpp			Stencil	**DS**
Lighting Accumulation RGB			Intensity	**RT0**
Normal X (fp16)		Normal Y (fp16)		**RT1**
Motion Vectors XY		Spec Power	Spec Inten	**RT2**
Diffuse Albedo RGB			Sun Occ.	**RT3**

Figure 2.2. An example G-Buffer format from a deferred rendering engine (after [Valient 07]).

We then additively blend the lights into the scene, using the information provided in the G-Buffer. Thus many lights can be rendered, without additional geometry cost or shader permutations. In addition, by rendering closed volumes for each light, we can ensure that only calculations for pixels directly affected by a light are carried out. However, with deferred rendering, all materials must use the same lighting equation, and can only vary by the properties stored in the G-Buffer. There are also huge memory bandwidth costs to rendering to (and reading from) so many buffers, which increases with MSAA.

In order to solve these problems, Engel suggested the light pre-pass renderer, first online in [Engel 08] and then later published in [Engel 09], although a similar idea had been recently used in games such as *Uncharted: Drake's Fortune* [Balestra 08]. Instead of rendering out the entire G-Buffer, the light pre-pass renderer stores depth and normals in one or two render targets. The lighting phase is then performed, with the properties of all lights accumulated into a lighting buffer. The scene is then rendered for a second time, sampling the lighting buffer to determine the lighting on that pixel.

Using a *Blinn-Phong lighting model* means that the red, green, and blue channels of the lighting buffer store the diffuse calculation, while we can fit a specular term in the alpha channel, the details of which are described in [Engel 09]. This means that unlike a deferred renderer, different materials can handle the lighting values differently. This increased flexibility, combined with reduced memory bandwidth costs, has seen the light pre-pass renderer quickly increase in popularity and is now in use in many recent games on a variety of hardware platforms.

Yet the deferred renderer and light pre-pass renderer share the fact that lighting is performed in image space, and as such requires little to no rasterization. This makes the lighting pass an ideal candidate to move from the GPU back onto the CPU. Swoboda first demonstrated this method with a deferred renderer on the PLAYSTATION3 and Cell Broadband Engine in [Swoboda 09], and now we expand upon his work and apply similar techniques to the light pre-pass renderer.

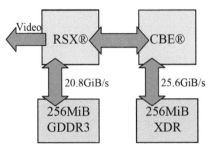

Figure 2.3. The PLAYSTATION3 architecture. (Illustration after [Möller 08, Perthuis 06]).

2.3 The PLAYSTATION3 and the CBE

Sony Computer Entertainment released the PLAYSTATION3 in 2006. It contains the Cell Broadband Engine, which was developed jointly by Sony Computer Entertainment, Toshiba Inc., and IBM Corp. [Shippy 09, Möller 08, IBM 08]. The cell is the central processing unit (CPU) of the PLAYSTATION3. In addition to the cell chip, the PLAYSTATION3 also has a GPU, the reality synthesizer (RSX). The RSX was developed by NVIDIA Corporation and is essentially a modified GeForce7800 [Möller 08]. A high-level view of the architecture can be found in Figure 2.3.

Inside the Cell chip one can find two distinctly different types of processor. There is the PowerPC Processing Element (PPE) and eight[2] pure SIMD processors [Möller 08] known as Synergistic Processing Elements (SPEs) all of which are connected by a high speed, token-ring bus known as the *element interconnect bus* (EIB; see Figure 2.4). The techniques introduced and described in this paper are chiefly concerned with the usage of the SPEs and as such further discussion of the PPE has been omitted.

One interesting quirk of the SPE is that it does not directly have access to the main address space, and instead has its own internal memory known as the *local store*. The local store on current implementations of the CBE is 256KB in size. The memory is unified, untranslatable, and unprotected [Bader 07, IBM 08] and must contain the SPE's program code, call stack, and any data that it may happen to be processing. To load or store data from or to the main address space a programmer must explicitly use the memory flow controller (MFC). Each SPE has its own MFC which is capable of queuing up to sixteen Direct Memory Accesses (DMAs) [IBM 08].

---

[2]One of the eight SPEs is locked out to increase chip yield and another is reserved by the Sony's Cell OS. Applications running on the PLAYSTATION3 actually have six SPEs to take advantage of.

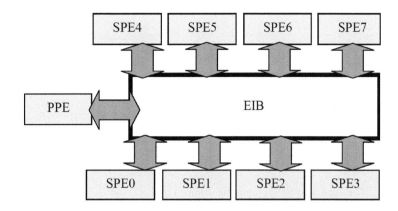

Figure 2.4. The Cell Broadband Engine (after [IBM 08]).

As the SPU ISA operates primarily on SIMD vector operands, both fixed-point and floating-point [IBM 09], it is very well equipped to process large quantities of vectorised data. It has a very large register file (4KB) which is helpful to hide the latencies of pipelined and unrolled loops, and while the local store is relatively small in capacity, it is usually sufficient to allow a programmer is able to hide the large latency of main memory accesses[3] through effective multi-buffering. Code that is to efficiently execute on the SPE should be written to play to the SPE's strengths.

A more in-depth discussion of the PLAYSTATION3 and the Cell Broadband Engine is out of the scope of this paper, interested readers can refer to IBM's website for more in depth details about the Cell chip [IBM 09], and Möller, Haines and Hoffman describe some of the PLAYSTATION3 architecture in [Möller 08].

2.4 GPU/SPE Synchronization

As the number of processors in our target platforms becomes ever greater, the need to automate the scheduling of work being carried out by these processing elements also becomes greater. This has continued to the point where game development teams now build their games and technology around the concept of the job scheduler [Capcom 06]. Our engine is no exception to this trend and the solution we propose for GPU/SPE interprocessor communication relies on close integration with such technology. It is for this reason we believe our solution to be a robust and viable solution to the problem of RSX/SPE communication that many others can easily foster into their existing scheduling frameworks.

---

[3]As one might expect, linear access patterns fair significantly better than random access.

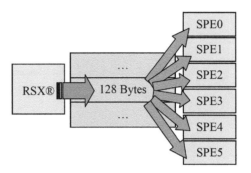

Figure 2.5. The RSX and SPE communication. The RSX writes a 128 byte value when the normal/depth buffer is available for processing. The SPEs poll the same location to know when to begin their work.

In order to perform fragment shading on the SPE without introducing unwanted latency into the rendering pipeline there needs to be a certain amount of interprocessor communication between the GPU and SPEs. This section discusses the approach we used in achieving this synchronization.

Each SPE has several memory mapped I/O (MMIO) registers it can use for interprocessor communication with other SPEs or the PPU. However, these are unfortunately not trivially writable from the RSX. An alternative approach is required in order to have the RSX signal the SPEs that the rendering of the normal/depth buffer is complete and that they can now begin their work, without having the desired SPE programs spinning on all six of the available SPEs wasting valuable processing time.

When adding a job to our job scheduler it is optionally given an address in RSX-mapped memory upon which the job is dependent. When the scheduler is pulling the next job from the job queue it polls this address to ensure that it is written to a known value by the RSX. If this is not the case, the job is skipped and the next one fetched from the queue and processed, if the location in memory is written however, then our job is free to run. This dependency is visualized in Figure 2.5.

The problem of ensuring that the GPU waits for the light buffer to be available from the SPEs is solved by a technique that is well-known to PLAYSTATION3 developers, but unfortunately we cannot disclose it here; interested developers can consult Sony's official development support website.

It is desirable for the RSX to continue doing useful work in parallel with the SPEs performing the lighting calculations. In *Blur* we are fortunate in that we have a number of additional views that are rendered which do not rely on the lighting buffer, for example, planar reflections and a rear-view mirror (in

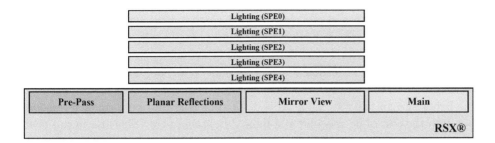

Figure 2.6. The RSX continues to do useful work as the SPEs calculate the dynamic lighting for our scene.

other applications these might also include the rendering of a shadow buffer). This is shown in Figure 2.6. If no useful work can be performed on the RSX, it may be possible (depending on your memory budget and the requirements of your application) to perform the lighting calculations one frame latent as in [Swoboda 09], this approach also has the added benefit of reducing the likelihood of stalling the RSX.

2.5   The Pre-Pass

To begin the lighting pre-pass we must first construct the normal and depth buffers. We store view space normals in an 8:8:8:8 format, and since we are able to read from the depth buffer on our chosen hardware, we have no need for a separate target for the depth. We chose to perform our lighting in view space as we find it faster compared with world space.

Next we render the relevant solid and alpha-test geometry into the buffers. We only render the geometry affected by the lights—we cull all draw calls against the bounding spheres of the lights and also bring in the far clip plane (note that a simple sphere test is not sufficient, since we also need to render near objects that occlude the light spheres). These methods of culling reduce the cost of drawing the pre-pass geometry by approximately half.

When rendering the scene, we enable stencil writes with a reference value of 0xFF. The stencil buffer is cleared to 0x00 beforehand, which gives us the relevant region of the screen masked out in the stencil buffer. Whether rendering lights on the RSX or the SPE, this enables us to use the early stencil to ensure that we only light relevant pixels.

We do not currently render the pre-pass or the light buffers with MSAA. This has a number of disadvantages, including some lighting artifacts around the edges of objects, and the loss of the ability to use the depth buffer as a depth pre-pass with the main scene (which we render with MSAA). However, we found the artifacts minimal, and the extra cost of rendering the light pre-pass MSAA outweighed the saving from having a depth pre-pass. This is still an area we wish to return to in the future.

Once we have the normal and depth buffers, we are able to perform the lighting. Currently, we use the Lambert diffuse model for our lights, and render the lights into an 8:8:8:8 buffer. This is for simplicity and performance reasons, but with the cost of no specular and limited lighting range. This also means that the alpha channel of the lighting buffer is unused. Some ideas for its use are explained in Section 2.9.

We maintain a GPU implementation of our lighting model for reference and for other platforms. First, the stencil test is set to "equals" with a reference value of 0xFF, so we only render to pixels marked in the stencil buffer. Then, the lights are rendered, with point lights and spot lights using two very different methods.

Point lights are rendered as in [Balestra 08]: the frame buffer is split into tiles, and we gather lists of lights (up to a maximum of eight) that affect each tile. We then render each tile using a shader corresponding to its number of lights. This method saves on fill rate, enabling us to perform the reconstruction of view space position and normal from our normal and depth buffers only once per pixel, no matter the number of point lights.

Spot lights use the more standard method of rendering bounding volumes of the lights: in this case, cones. We render front faces, unless we are inside the volume, in which case we render back faces.

We further optimize the lighting code by making use of the depth bounds test, when it is available on the target hardware. The depth bounds test compares the depth buffer value at the current fragment's coordinates to a given minimum and maximum depth value. If the stored depth value is outside the given range, then the fragment is discarded. When drawing either a tile of point lights, or a spot light volume, we set the depth bounds range to be the minimum and maximum depth extents of the light (or lights, in case of the point lights).

This gives us a fast, optimized GPU implementation of our lighting model. However, it is still a significant percentage of our frame rendering time, and its image space nature makes it a perfect candidate to offload from the GPU onto the SPEs.

2.6   The Lighting SPE Program

This section describes in detail the SPE program that performs our lighting calculations. In order to try to contextualize each subsection, we have included Figure 2.7, which shows the high-level structure of the SPE program as a whole.

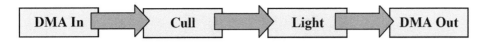

Figure 2.7. The high-level flow of our SPE lighting program.

2.6.1 The Atomic Tile Arbiter

Due to the relatively large memory footprint of a 720p frame buffer; the limitations imposed by the size of an SPE's local store; and the internal format of a surface created by PLAYSTATION3's RSX, our lighting SPE program works on *tiles* of the frame buffer, 64×64 pixels in size, as shown in Figure 2.8. Thus, there is a need to keep track of which tile is free to bring in to local store for processing. The simplest and most concurrent way we found of achieving this was by way of an atomically incremented tile index which resides in main memory. It should be noted that the SPE and RSX are only able to *efficiently* cooperate on the processing of resources that are placed into correctly mapped main memory.

For efficiency (and to avoid contention for the cache line) the tile index is aligned to a 128 byte boundary and padded to 128 bytes in size to exactly match the cache line width of the SPEs atomic unit (ATO) [IBM 08, IBM07]. The effective address (EA) of the tile is given by the product of the tile index and the total size of a single tile summed with the address of the beginning of the frame buffer, as in Equation (2.1). For our chosen tile size, the resulting effective address always falls on a 16 byte boundary since our tile size is itself a 16 byte multiple.

$$\text{tile}_{\text{address}_i} = \text{tile}_{\text{index}_i} \times \text{tile}_{\text{size}} + \text{tile}_{\text{address}_0}. \tag{2.1}$$

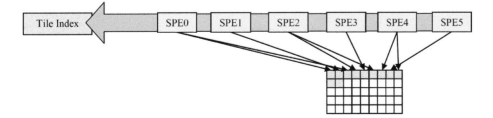

Figure 2.8. Each SPE assigns itself a task by atomically incrementing a tile index held in main memory.

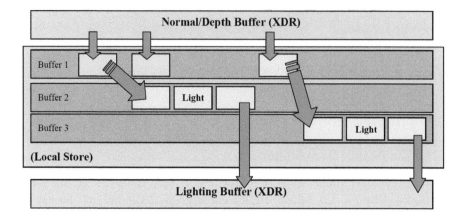

Figure 2.9. The triple-buffering strategy in our lighting SPE program.

2.6.2 Multi-Buffering

Multi-buffering is a must for almost all SPE programs that process any significant volume of data [Bader 07] and our lighting program is no exception. In our implementation we use triple buffering to minimize the latency of accesses to the normal/depth buffer in main memory. Each buffer in the triple buffer has enough space to support a single unit of work (i.e., a single tile of the frame buffer). The first of the buffers in our triple buffer is used as the target for inbound DMA, it utilizes its own tag group and DMA into this buffer are initiated as soon as the tile decoding process[4] on the previous tile has completed. The second and third buffers are used as the output targets for the decoding process. In addition to this, they act as scratch memory for the lighting calculations and are the source of the outgoing DMA from the running SPE program back to the light buffer in main memory.[5] This is achieved by using the two buffers alternately in order to allow outgoing DMA to complete, asynchronously, the tile decoding and lighting of the next tile. A high level view of our multi-buffering strategy is depicted in Figure 2.9.

The multi-buffering system described here works so effectively that our SPE program spends an average of $2\mu s$ per frame waiting for data to be transferred to and from main memory, with the bulk of this delay being introduced early in the program's execution as one should expect.

---

[4]For information on how to decode, Sony PLAYSTATION3 developers can consult the RSX User's Manual.

[5]We do not currently encode the lighting results; please see further work for more information.

2.6.3 Light Gathering and Culling

When the incoming DMAs for the normal buffer and depth-stencil buffer tiles have completed, we can begin processing. Before we light, we first gather the lights that affect a given tile. We do this by constructing a view frustum for each tile and culling the bounding spheres of the lights against the frustum. In addition, we also cull against the stencil buffer. This is a vital optimization as it minimizes the work done in the expensive lighting phase.

In order to perform the culling and the lighting, we actually work on *sub-tiles* of the frame buffer tile, 32×16 pixels in size. Culling over a smaller region is more effective, and we found sub-tiles of the above size to be optimal in our case.

Next we iterate over the depth-stencil tile to collect the minimum and maximum depth values and the minimum and maximum stencil values for each sub-tile. The depth values will form the near and far clip planes of our sub-tile's view frustum and the stencil values allow us to do a stencil test akin to the early-stencil hardware on a GPU.

In Section 2.5 we described how we write `0xFF` into the stencil buffer when rendering the pre-pass buffers: hence any pixels with a stencil of `0x00` we do not wish to light. However, we do not stencil on a per-pixel basis, but instead skip the lighting on a sub-tile if the maximum stencil value is equal to `0x00` (hence it is `0x00` across the entire sub-tile).

Once a sub-tile has passed the stencil test, we construct its view frustum. Knowing the screen-space position of the corners of the sub-tile, using values from the projection matrix we can construct its position in view-space space, at a fixed distance of one meter from the camera (see Equation (2.5)). Multiplication by the minimum and maximum view-space depth values then gives us the eight vertices of the frustum, from which we can construct the frustum's six planes (see Equation (2.4) for how to construct view-space z from a depth buffer value).

We then construct separate lists of point lights and spot lights that intersect this view frustum. The bounding sphere of each light is tested against each frustum plane, with successful point lights added to a point light list, and successful spot lights added to a spot light list: see Equation (2.2).

$$p_x l_x + p_y + p_z l_z \leq l_{\text{radius}}. \tag{2.2}$$

If no lights are gathered, then the sub-tile follows the same path as one which fails the stencil test—the lighting is skipped and we output zero to the frame buffer. However, if at least one light does affect the sub-tile, then the lists of point lights and spot lights are passed into our lighting function to perform the most important part of the work.

2.6.4 Point Lights

The SPE program used for lighting is written in C and makes heavy use of SPE-specific language extensions. We made the choice early on to favor the si-style of intrinsic over the higher-level spu-style. This is due to a closer mapping to the underlying opcodes generated by the compiler [Acton08].

Lighting code is an excellent candidate for both software pipelining and loop unrolling; our lighting is performed on batches of 16 pixels at a time. We found that 16 pixels gave us a very small number of wasted cycles per iteration of our lighting loops while still allowing us to fit everything we needed into the 4KB (128×16 byte) register file.[6] The large numbers of independent instructions that result from lighting a relatively large set of pixels mean that the latency caused by dependent instructions closely following one another is almost completely eliminated and overall performance is massively increased (limited only by the number of issued instructions). Non-dependent instructions are interleaved with one another. The results are used some time later when they are available: this well-known optimization technique also has the side effect of improving the balance of instructions over the odd and even execution pipelines because there are a greater number of suitable, non-dependent instructions that can occupy a single fetch group in the synergistic execute unit (SXU). We found that we were able to achieve approximately three times the pixel throughput from batching pixels into groups of 16 over our earlier attempts, which loosely mimicked RSX quads by lighting smaller groups of four pixels:

$$[(\text{point})] \downarrow \text{value} = \text{sat}(\hat{n} \cdot \hat{l}) \times \text{sat}(1 - \frac{[(\|l\|)]^\top 2}{r^\top 2}). \tag{2.3}$$

Before any lighting can begin it is important to reconstruct the correct input to our lighting equation expressed in Equation (2.3). Equation (2.4) demonstrates how to reconstruct the z component of the view-space position of a pixel given its depth buffer value and the near and far planes of the view frustum:

$$Z_{\text{view}} = \left(Z_{\text{val}} \times \left(Z_{\text{far}}^{-1} - Z_{\text{near}}^{-1}\right) + Z_{\text{near}}^{-1}\right)^{-1}. \tag{2.4}$$

Calculating the x- and y-components of the view-space position is equally trivial when given the x- and y-coordinates of the pixel in screen-space and the view projection matrix. This is shown by Equation (2.5).

$$xy_{\text{view}} = \left(xy_{\text{screen}} \times \left(\frac{1}{[\text{width}, \text{height}]} \times [2, -2]\right) + [-1, 1]\right) \times$$
$$\left[vp_{0,0}^{-1}, vp_{1,1}^{-1}\right] \times z_{\text{view}}. \tag{2.5}$$

---

[6]Any more pixels in a single loop in our implementation would risk causing registers to be spilled.

```
// HLSL saturate, clamp to [0..1].
qword x = si_cfltu(q, 0x20);
qword y = si_cuflt(x, 0x20);
```

Listing 2.1. Saturate a `qword` in two odd pipeline instructions.

In HLSL/Cg shaders it is quite common to use the saturate intrinsic function to clamp values to a [0..1] range. To achieve this on the SPE, there is a clever trick that we feel is certainly worthy of mention here. Day et al. introduced the fast saturate/clamp technique, which uses the SPU's floating-point conversion instructions in order to achieve clamping of a floating-point value to a variety of different ranges. This depends on the combination of scale bias operands issued with the instructions [Day 08]. In a pipelined loop, such as our lighting loop, instruction count is oftentimes the overriding determinant of the code's execution speed and as such we are able to employ this trick to great effect. Listing 2.1 demonstrates this technique.

One interesting difference between the GPU implementation of our lighting and the SPE implementation is the switch from the default *array of structures* (AoS) data layout on the GPU, to the transposed, SIMD-friendly *structure of arrays* (SoA)[7] data layout on the SPE. The difference in format of the data is illustrated below in Figure 2.10. By storing, loading and shuffling data into a SoA layout we are able to perform our lighting calculations much more optimally on the SPEs. A pleasant side effect of the switch is that the resulting C code becomes much more scalar-like in appearance, making it easier for other programmers to follow [Bader 07].

The SPE is only equipped to deal with 16 byte aligned writes and reads to and from its local store [Bader 07, IBM 08, IBM 08a]. The targets from all load and store operations first undergo a logical "and" with the LSLR register (set to `0x3ffff` for current implementations of the CBE) before the SPU Store and Load unit (SLS) fetches or writes the address [IBM 08, IBM 08a]. Writing scalar

Figure 2.10. Shuffling an AoS into a SoA.

---

[7]SOA organization is also known as "parallel-array."

```
qword c0          = si_cfltu(dif0, 0x20);
qword c1          = si_cfltu(dif1, 0x20);
qword c2          = si_cfltu(dif2, 0x20);
qword c3          = si_cfltu(dif3, 0x20);
      dif         = si_ila(0x8000);
qword scale       = si_ilh(0xff00);
      dif0        = si_mpyhhau(c0, scale, dif);
      dif1        = si_mpyhhau(c1, scale, dif);
      dif2        = si_mpyhhau(c2, scale, dif);
      dif3        = si_mpyhhau(c3, scale, dif);
const vector unsigned char _shuf_uint =
  { 0xc0, 0x00, 0x04, 0x08,
    0xc0, 0x10, 0x14, 0x18,
    0xc0, 0x00, 0x04, 0x08,
    0xc0, 0x10, 0x14, 0x18 };
qword s_uint      = (const qword)_shuf_uint;
qword base_addr   = si_from_ptr(result);
qword p0_01       = si_shufb(dif0, dif1, s_uint);
qword p0_02       = si_shufb(dif2, dif3, s_uint);
qword p0          = si_selb(p0_01, p0_02, m_00ff);
                    si_stqd(pixel0, base_addr, 0x00);
```

Listing 2.2. Pixels are converted from their floating-point representations into 32 bit values, batched into 16 byte chunks, and stored.

values is achieved by way of a load-shuffle-store pattern. It is therefore desirable to perform loads and stores on 16 byte boundaries only. As our program required a lot of four byte loads from our normal/depth buffer and a lot of similarly sized writes to our light buffer we ended up batching these loads and stores into 16 byte chunks in order to eliminate the overhead of the additional code that would be required if we were to perform these operations on a pixel-by-pixel basis. This proved to deliver a significant performance increase, especially in the case of storing where nearly all pipeline bubbles were eliminated. We present a portion of our pixel writing code in Listing 2.2 for a single four pixel block.

2.6.5 Spot Lights

In the interest of completeness we present the mathematics used for our, regular spotlights in Equation (2.6).

$$\text{spot}_{\text{value}} = \text{sat}\left(\hat{n} \cdot \hat{l}\right) \times \text{sat}\left(1 - \frac{\|l\|^z}{r^z}\right) \times \text{sat}\left(\frac{\hat{d} \cdot \hat{l} - \cos\frac{\phi}{2}}{\cos\frac{\theta}{2} - \cos\frac{\phi}{2}}\right). \qquad (2.6)$$

Note that this is the same as the equation for the point lights, with an additional term at the end. The direction of the light is d (as opposed to l, which is the direction from the light to the point), θ is the angle of the inner cone and φ is the angle of the outer cone. However, we store their cosines on the light rather than calculating them every time. All lighting values for both point and spot lights are summed for each pixel, yielding Equation (2.7).

$$\text{pixel}_{\text{final}} = \text{sat} \left(\begin{array}{c} \sum_{i=0}^{\text{point}_{\text{count}}} \left[\text{point}_{\text{value}_i} \times \text{point}_{\text{color}_i} \right] + \\ \sum_{i=0}^{\text{spot}_{\text{count}}} \left[\text{spot}_{\text{value}_i} \times \text{spot}_{\text{color}_i} \right] \end{array} \right) \qquad (2.7)$$

2.7   The Main Pass

When the SPEs have finished calculating the light buffer, they then signal to the RSX that the main pass can be rendered. As mentioned above, the synchronization at this stage is very important—we do not want to be reading from an incomplete light buffer. To composite the light buffer with the main scene, we read it as a texture in the pixel shaders. However, as not every pixel in our scene receives light from our pre-pass (see above, we only render geometry into the pre-pass that receives light), we use two shader techniques in the scene: one which samples from the light buffer, and one which does not. For the former technique, each pixel looks up its lighting in the light buffer using its screen-space coordinate, and then composites the light value as a diffuse light, as shown in Equation (2.8).

$$\text{light}_{\text{diffuse}} = \text{surface}_{\text{albedo}} \times \text{light}_{\text{buffer}}. \qquad (2.8)$$

It might be tempting to simply additively or multiplicatively blend the lighting buffer over the scene, but as can be seen above, that method will result in incorrect lighting. This is due to the presence of additional static lighting in our scene.

It is also possible to read from the normal buffer in the main pass. This means that reading from normal maps and converting from tangent space to view (or world) space only happens once. However, this also means that the low precision of the normals stored in the pre-pass becomes more noticeable (only eight bits per component). For this reason and others we did not use this option.

At the end of rendering we have a scene with many dynamic lights rendered using the Cell Broadband Engine. Not only does this open up exciting new possibilities for our rendering engine, but it does so with minimal GPU cost, with a large amount of work performed on the CPU.

2.8   Conclusion

We have presented a method which splits the work of light pre-pass rendering between the RSX and the SPEs on the Cell Broadband Engine. We use the strengths of both components to our advantage: the rasterization performance of the RSX to render the pre-pass geometry, and the vector maths performance of the SPEs to calculate the lighting buffer. By parallelizing the lighting calculation on the SPEs with some other rendering on the RSX (for instance, a dynamic cube map), the lighting becomes *free* and thus this can be a major GPU optimization. Even without the added bonus of parallelization, we found that in some cases, five SPEs running carefully crafted programs could outperform the RSX when performing lighting calculations.

As new architectures emerge we believe there will be increasing opportunities to take processing load off the GPU and place it back onto the CPU. It remains to be seen how things will pan out when the two are combined in Intel's Larrabee [Seiler 08], but on the Cell Broadband Engine we offer that the GPU can be massively accelerated in cases such as deferred lighting or light pre-pass rendering by writing a custom CPU implementation that executes on the SPEs.

2.9   Further Work

There are many improvements that could be done to techniques we describe. Firstly, we currently omit specular from our lighting model. We propose either writing out specular to a separate lighting buffer or placing a monochrome specular term in the alpha channel of the lighting buffer as in [Engel 09]. Material properties could be controlled by adding a specular power in the alpha channel of the normal buffer. Another problem is that our lighting is currently LDR, as it is stored in an 8:8:8:8 integer format. One option is moving to a 16:16:16:16 float, but Wilson suggests instead using the CIE Luv color space [Wilson 09]. Using this method, we can still use an 8:8:8:8 buffer, but with the luminance part of the color using 16 bits. This technique has problems on the GPU, as additive blending of lights on top of each other no longer works. But in the SPE program we have no such problem and thus this becomes more feasible; if one wished to implement a more GPU-friendly technique, then diffuse light intensity could also be stored in the alpha channel as in [Valient 07].

Both of the previous suggestions involve making use of the currently unused alpha channel in the lighting buffer. While there are certainly many possible uses for this byte, one idea we are currently investigating is storing the amount of fog for each pixel. We believe this could be especially beneficial for more expensive fogging equations, for instance, if height fog is being used. This is an example of *adding value* to the SPE program [Swoboda 09a].

Figure 2.11. Another screenshot from *Blur*.

Given the amount of work already being done, including processing the entire normal and depth buffers, there is extra rendering work that could be done in the SPE program. One simple example is performing a down-sample of the depth buffer to a quarter resolution—this could be output asynchronously through the MFC, adding little overhead to the SPE program, and would be useful for many reduced resolution effects such as motion blur, soft particles, occlusion culling, and even screen-space ambient occlusion. It would be possible to reduce the amount of processing on the normal depth buffers by combining the view-space normals and depth into a single 32-bit buffer. By encoding the x- and y-components of the normal into the first two channels (or by converting them to spherical coordinates), and packing linear view-space depth into the remaining 16 bits. This halves the amount of data needed by our SPE program. In fact, this approach is the method we chose for the final version of *Blur* (see Figure 2.11).

Finally, it is our intention to remove the decoding of the buffers altogether and perform lighting on encoded normal/depth buffers, this has several advantages. The decoding process can be replaced with a simple pass over all the pixels in the frame buffer tile, which should yield a minor increase in overall lighting performance together with saving the memory required for the lighting buffer. However, this extra performance and improved memory footprint come at the cost of added mathematical complexity, as deriving the view-space position of pixels becomes non-trivial. This is due to the need to take into account the effects of the encoded buffer's format on the final view-space position of the pixel.

2.10 Acknowledgments

First and foremost we would like to extend our unending thanks to Matt Swoboda of SCEE R&D for laying the groundwork for our continuing efforts and for his suggestions for our implementation. We would also like to thank Colin Hughes of SCEE R&D for his help and suggestions with optimizations.

We also extend our thanks to all the supremely talented individuals that form the Core Technologies Team at Bizarre Creations Ltd., especially to Ian Wilson, Paul Malin, Lloyd Wright, Ed Clay, Jose Sanchez, Charlie Birtwistle, Jan van Valburg, Kier Storey, Fengyun Lu, Jason Denton, Dave Hampson, Chris Cookson and Richard Thomas.

Bibliography

[Acton 08] M. Acton and E. Christensen. "Insomniac's SPU Best Practices." Game Developers Conference, 2008. Available at http://www.insomniacgames.com/tech/articles/0208/files/insomniac_ spu_programming_gdc08.ppt.

[Bader 07] D. A. Bader. "Cell Programming Tips & Techniques." Available at http://www.cc.gatech.edu/~bader/CellProgramming.html, 2007.

[Balestra 08] C. Balestra and P. Engstad. "The Technology of Uncharted: Drake's Fortune." Game Developers Conference, 2008. Available at http://www.naughtydog.com.

[Capcom 06] Capcom Inc. "The MT Framework." Available at http://game. watch .impress.co.jp/docs/20070131/3dlp.htm, 2006.

[Day 08] M. Day and J. Garrett. "Faster SPU Clamp." http://www .insomniacgames.com/tech/articles/0308/faster_spu_clamp.php, 2008.

[Deering 88] M. Deering. "The Triangle Processor and Normal Vector Shader: A VLSI System for High Performance Graphics." ACM SIGGRAPH Computer Graphics 22:4 (1988), 21–30.

[Engel 08] W. Engel. "Light Pre-Pass Renderer." *Diary of a Graphics Programmer.* http://diaryofagraphicsprogrammer.blogspot.com/2008/03/light-pre-pass-renderer.html, 2008.

[Engel 08a] W. Engel. "Designing a Renderer for Multiple Lights: The Light
    Pre-Pass Renderer." In *ShaderX7*, edited by Wolfgang Engel, pp. 655–66.
    Boston: Charles River Media, 2008.

[Engel 09] W. Engel. "The Light Pre-Pass Renderer Mach III." To appear in
    proceedings of ACM SIGGRAPH09, 2009.

[IBM 08] "Cell Broadband Engine Programming Handbook Version 1.11." Tech-
    ncial Report, IBM Corporation, 2008. Available at https://www-01.ibm.
    com/chips/techlib/techlib.nsf.

[IBM 08a] "Synergistic Processing Unit Instruction Set Architecture." Techni-
    cal Report, IBM Corporation, 2008. Available at https://www-01.ibm.com/
    chips/techlib/techlib.nsf/techdocs.

[IBM 09] "The Cell Project at IBM." *IBM*. Available at http://researchweb
    .watson.ibm.com/cell/home.html, 2009.

[Möller 08] T. Akenine-Möller, E. Haines, and N. Hoffman. "Real-Time Render-
    ing." Third edition. Natick, MA: A K Peters, 2008.

[Perthuis 06] C. Perthuis. "Introduction to the Graphics Pipeline of the PS3."
    Presented at Eurographics, Vienna, Austria, September 4–8, 2006.

[Seiler 08] L. Seiler, D. Carmean, E. Sprangle, T. Forsyth, M. Abrash, P. Dubey,
    S. Junkins, A. Lake, J. Sugerman, R. Cavin, R. Espasa, E. Grochowski,
    T. Juni, and P. Hanrahan. "Larabee: A Many Core X86 Architecture for
    Visual Computing." *ACM Transactions on Graphics* 27:3 (2008).

[Shippy 09] D. Shippy and M. Phipps. *The Race for a New Games Machine:
    Creating the Chips inside the New Xbox360 & the Playstation 3.* New York:
    Citadel Press, 2009.

[Swoboda 09] M. Swoboda, "Deferred Lighting and Post Processing on
    PLAYSTATION3." Presented at Game Developers Conference, San Fran-
    cisco, March 23–27 2009. Available at http://www.technology.scee.net/files/
    presentations/gdc2009/DeferredLightingandPostProcessingonPS3.ppt.

[Swoboda 09a] M. Swoboda. Correspondance with author, 2009.

[Valient 07] M. Valient, "Deferred Rendering in Killzone 2." Develop Confer-
    ence, Brighton, July 2007. Available at http://www.dimension3.sk/mambo/
    Download-document/Deferred-Rendering-In-Killzone.php.

[Wilson 09] P. Wilson, "Light Pre-Pass Renderer: Using the CIE Luv Color
    Space." In *ShaderX7*, edited by Wolfgang Engel, pp. 667–77. Boston: Charles
    River Media, 2008.

3

Practical, Dynamic Visibility
for Games
Stephen Hill and Daniel Collin

3.1 Introduction

With the complexity and interactivity of game worlds on the rise, the need for efficient dynamic visibility is becoming increasingly important.

This chapter covers two complementary approaches to visibility determination that have shipped in recent AAA titles across Xbox 360, PS3, and PC: *Splinter Cell Conviction* and *Battlefield: Bad Company 1 & 2*.

These solutions should be of broad interest, since they are capable of handling completely dynamic environments consisting of a large number of objects, with low overhead, straightforward implementations, and only a modest impact on asset authoring.

Before we describe our approaches in detail, it is important to understand what motivated their development, through the lens of existing techniques that are more commonly employed in games.

3.2 Surveying the Field

Static potentially visible sets (PVSs) is an approach popularized by the Quake engine [Abrash 96] and is still in common use today, in part because of its low runtime cost. Put simply, the world is discretized in some way (BSP, grid, etc.) and the binary visibility from each sector (leaf node, cell, or cluster, respectively) to all other sectors is precomputed and stored. At runtime, given the current sector containing the camera, determining the set of potentially visible objects becomes a simple matter of retrieving the potentially visible sectors (and by extension, their associated objects) and performing frustum culling.

One major drawback of using PVS by itself is that any destructible or moving objects (e.g., doors) typically have to be treated as nonoccluding from the perspective of visibility determination. This naturally produces over inclusion—in addition to that coming from sector-to-sector visibility—and can therefore constrain level-design choices in order to avoid pathological situations.

Another disadvantage stems from the fact that a PVS database can be extremely time consuming to precompute,[1] which may in turn disrupt or slow production.

Portals are another approach that can complement or replace static PVS. Here, sectors are connected via convex openings or "portals" and the view frustum is progressively clipped against them [Akenine-Möller et al. 08], while objects are simultaneously gathered and tested against the active subfrustum.

Since clipping happens at runtime, the state of portals can be modified to handle a subset of dynamic changes to the world, such as a door closing or opening. But, even though portals can ameliorate some of the limitations of a static PVS solution, they are still best suited to indoor environments, with corridors, windows, and doorways providing natural opportunities to constrain and clip the view frustum.

Antiportals are a related technique for handling localized or dynamic occlusion whereby, instead of constraining visibility, convex shapes are used to occlude (cull away) objects behind them with respect to the player. Though antiportals can be effective in open areas, one can employ only a limited number in any given frame, for performance reasons. Similarly, occluder fusion—culling from the combined effect of several antiportals—is typically not viable, due to the much higher cost of inclusion testing against concave volumes.

In recent years, hardware occlusion queries (OQs) have become another popular tool for visibility determination [Soininen 08]. The canonical approach involves rendering the depth of a subset (or a simplified representation) of the scene—the occluders—and then rasterizing (without depth writes) the bounds of objects, or groups of objects. The associated draw calls are bracketed by a query, which instructs the GPU to count pixels passing the depth test. If a query returns that no pixels passed, then those objects can be skipped in subsequent rendering passes for that camera.

This technique has several advantages over those previously discussed: it is applicable to a wider range of environments, it trivially adapts to changes in the world (occluders can even deform), and it handles occluder fusion effortlessly, by nature of z-buffer-based testing. In contrast, whereas both static PVS and portals can handle dynamic objects, too, via sector relocation, those objects cannot themselves occlude in general.

3.3 Query Quandaries

On paper OQs are an attractive approach, but personal experience has uncovered a number of severe drawbacks, which render them unsuitable for the afore-

---

[1]On the order of 10 hours, in some cases [Hastings 07].

mentioned titles. We will now outline the problems encountered with occlusion queries.

3.3.1 Batching

First, though OQs can be batched in the sense that more than one can be issued at a time [Soininen 08]—thereby avoiding lock-step CPU-GPU synchronization— one cannot batch several bounds into a single draw call with individual query counters. This is a pity, since CPU overhead alone can limit the number of tests to several hundred per frame on current-generation consoles, which may be fine if OQs are used to supplement another visibility approach [Hastings 07], but is less than ideal otherwise.

3.3.2 Latency

To overcome latency, and as a general means of scaling OQs up to large environments, a hierarchy can be employed [Bittner et al. 09]. By grouping, via a bounding volume hierarchy (BVH) or octree for instance, tests can be performed progressively, based on parent results, with sets of objects typically rejected earlier.

However, this dependency chain generally implies more CPU-GPU synchronization within a frame since, at the time of this writing, only the CPU can issue queries.[2] Hiding latency perfectly in this instance can be tricky and may require overlapping *query* and *real* rendering work, which implies redundant state changes in addition to a more complicated renderer design.

3.3.3 Popping

By compromising on correctness, one can opt instead to defer checking the results of OQs until the next frame—so called latent queries [Soininen 08]—which practically eliminates synchronization penalties, while avoiding the potential added burden of interleaved rendering. Unfortunately, the major downside of this strategy is that it typically leads to objects "popping" due to incorrect visibility classification [Soininen 08]. Figure 3.1 shows two cases where this can occur. First, the camera tracks back to reveal object A in Frame 1, but A was classified as outside of the frustum in Frame 0. Second, object B moves out from behind an occluder in Frame 1 but was previously occluded in Frame 0.

Such artifacts can be reduced by extruding object-bounding volumes,[3] similarly padding the view frustum, or even eroding occluders. However, these fixes come with their own processing overhead, which can make eliminating all sources of artifacts practically impossible.

---

[2]Predicated rendering is one indirect and limited alternative on Xbox 360.

[3]A more accurate extrusion should take into account rotational as well as spatial velocity, as with continuous collision detection [Redon et al. 02].

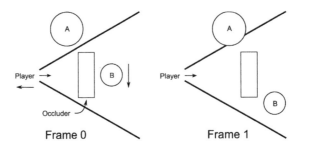

Figure 3.1. Camera or object movement can lead to popping with latent queries.

Sudden changes such as camera cuts are also problematic with latent queries, potentially leading to either a visibility or processing spike [Hastings 07] to avoid rampant popping. As such, it may be preferable to simply skip rendering for a frame and only process visibility updates behind the scenes.

3.3.4   GPU Overhead

The GPU is a precious resource and a common bottleneck in games, as we seek to maximize visual fidelity for a given target frame rate. Therefore, a visibility solution that relies heavily on GPU processing is less than ideal, particularly on modern consoles where multiple CPU cores or SPUs are available. While it is true to say that OQs should be issued only when there is an overall GPU saving [Soininen 08], this cannot be guaranteed in general and we would ideally like to dedicate as much GPU muscle as possible to direct rendering.

3.3.5   Variable Costs

A final disadvantage with OQs is that the cost of testing an object is roughly proportional to its size on screen, which typically does not reflect its true rendering cost. While one can, for instance, choose to always render objects with high screen-space coverage to avoid this penalty, it is a less viable strategy when working with a hierarchy.

Even if one develops a more sophisticated oracle [Bittner et al. 09] to normalize performance, this can come at the cost of reduced culling effectiveness. Furthermore, a hierarchy requires additional CPU overhead when objects move, or parts become visible or occluded. As with queries, the per-frame update cost can be bounded by distributing work over multiple frames, but this can similarly compromise culling.

Ideally we would like to avoid these kinds of unfortunate trade-offs, especially when major changes to the environment occur; although leveraging coherency can be a great way to reduce the average per-frame processing time, it should not exacerbate worst-case performance!

3.4 Wish List

Ideally we would like to take the strengths of OQs but reduce or eliminate the negatives. Here is our wish list:

These first items are already taken into account with OQs:

- no precomputation

- general applicability

- cccluder fusion

Here is a list of improvements we would like to achieve:

- low latency

- reduced CPU-GPU dependency

- no reliance on coherency

- bounded, high performance

- simple, unified solution

In summary, we would like to be able to handle a wide range of dynamic scenes with the minimum of fuss and no less than great performance. Essentially, we *want it all* and in the case of *Splinter Cell Conviction*—as you will now learn—we wanted it *yesterday*!

3.5 *Conviction* Solution

One of the initial technical goals of *Splinter Cell Conviction* was to support dense environments with plenty of clutter and where, in some situations, only localized occlusion could be exploited.

We initially switched from PVS visibility to OQs because of these requirements, but having battled for a long time with the drawbacks outlined earlier, and becoming increasingly frustrated by mounting implementation complexity, hacks, and failed work-arounds, we started to look for alternatives. Unfortunately, by this point we had little time and few resources to dedicate to switching solutions yet again.

Luckily for us, [Shopf et al. 08] provided a guiding light, by demonstrating that the hierarchical Z-buffer (HZB) [Greene et al. 93] could be implemented efficiently on modern GPUs—albeit via DX10—as part of an AMD demo. The demo largely validated that the HZB was a viable option for games, whereas we had previously been skeptical, even with a previous proof of concept by [Décoret 05].

Most importantly, it immediately addressed all of our requirements, particularly with respect to implementation simplicity and bounded performance. In fact, the elegance of this approach cannot be understated, comparing favorably with the illusory simplicity of OQs, but without any of the associated limitations or management complexity in practice.

3.5.1 The Process

The steps of the process are detailed here.

Render occluder depth. As with OQs, we first render the depth of a subset of the scene, this time to a render target texture, which will later be used for visibility testing, but in a slightly different way than before.

For *Conviction*, these occluders were typically artist authored[4] for performance reasons, although any object could be optionally flagged as an occluder by an artist.

Create a depth hierarchy. The resulting depth buffer is then used to create a depth hierarchy or z-pyramid, as in [Greene et al. 93]. This step is analogous to generating a mipmap chain for a texture, but instead of successive, weighted down-sampling from each level to the next, we take the maximum depth of sets of four texels to form each new texel, as in Figure 3.2.

This step also takes place on the GPU, as a series of quad passes, reading from one level and writing to the next. To simplify the process, we restrict the visibility resolution to a power of two, in order to avoid the additional logic of [Shopf et al. 08]. Figure 3.3 shows an example HZB generated in this way.

In practice, we render at 512×256,[5] since this seems to strike a good balance between accuracy and speed. This could theoretically result in false occlusion for objects of 2×2 pixels or less at native resolution, but since we contribution-cull small objects anyway, this has not proven to be a problem for us.

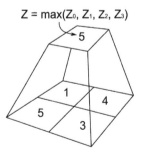

$$Z = \max(Z_0, Z_1, Z_2, Z_3)$$

Figure 3.2. Generating successive levels of the HZB.

---

[4]These are often a simplified version of the union of several adjoining, structural meshes.

[5]This is approximately a quarter of the resolution of our main camera in single-player mode.

Figure 3.3. The resulting depth hierarchy. Note that the sky in the distance increasingly dominates at coarser levels.

Test object bounds. We pack object bounds (world-space AABBs) into a dynamic point-list vertex buffer and issue the tests as a single draw call. For each point, we determine, in the vertex shader, the screen-space extents of the object by transforming and projecting the bounds (see Figure 3.4). From this, we calculate the finest mip level of the hierarchy that covers these extents with a fixed number of texels or fewer and also the minimum, projected depth of the object (see Listing 3.1).

```
//Contains the dimensions of the viewport.
//In this case x = 512, y = 256
float2 cViewport;

OUTPUT main(INPUT input)
{
    OUTPUT output;

    bool visible = !FrustumCull(input.center, input.extents);

    // Transform/project AABB to screen-space
    float min_z;
    float4 sbox;
    GetScreenBounds(input.center, input.extents, min_z, sbox);

    // Calculate HZB level
    float4 sbox_vp = sbox*cViewport.xyxy;
    float2 size = sbox_vp.zw - sbox_vp.xy;
    float level = ceil(log2(max(size.x, size.y)));
```

```
        output.pos = input.pos;
        output.sbox = sbox;
        output.data = float4(level, min_z, visible, 0);

        return output;
}
```

Listing 3.1. HZB query vertex shader.

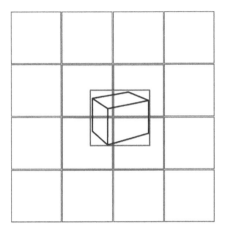

Figure 3.4. The object's world-space AABB (blue), screen extents (green) and overlapping HZB texels (orange).

This depth, plus the UVs (sbox is the screen-space AABB) and mip level for HZB lookup are then passed to the pixel shader. Here we test for visibility by comparing the depth against the overlapping HZB texels and write out 1 or 0 as appropriate (see Listing 3.2).

```
sampler2D sHZB : register(s0);

float4 main(INPUT input) : COLOR0
{
    float4 sbox = input.sbox;
    float level = input.data.x;
    float min_z = input.data.y;
    bool visible = input.data.z;

    float4 samples;
    samples.x = tex2Dlod(sHZB, float4(sbox.xy, 0, level)).x;
    samples.y = tex2Dlod(sHZB, float4(sbox.zy, 0, level)).x;
```

```
        samples.z = tex2Dlod(sHZB, float4(sbox.xw, 0, level)).x;
        samples.w = tex2Dlod(sHZB, float4(sbox.zw, 0, level)).x;

        float max_z = max4(samples);

        // Modulate culling with depth test result
        visible *= min_z <= max_z;

        return visible;
}
```

Listing 3.2. HZB query pixel shader.

In practice, we chose to use 4×4 HZB depth comparisons in contrast to the simpler example code above, since this balanced ALU instructions and texture lookups on the Xbox 360.

Also note that we perform world-space frustum testing and screen-bound generation separately. While the two can be combined as in [Blinn 96], we found that we got better code generation by performing them separately and could add additional planes to the frustum test when processing visibility for mirrors.

It is also possible to improve on the mip level selection for situations when an object covers fewer texels.

Process the results. Finally, the results are read back to the CPU via MemExport on Xbox 360. On PC, under DX9, we instead emulate DX10 stream-out by rendering with a point size of one to an off-screen render-target, followed by a copy to system memory via `GetRenderTargetData`.

3.5.2   Tradeoffs

By using a fixed number of lookups instead of rasterization, the performance of the visibility tests is highly predictable for a given number of objects. That said, this bounded performance comes at the cost of reduced accuracy for objects that are large on screen.

On the other hand, this approach can be viewed as probabilistic: large objects are, on average, more likely to be visible anyway, so performing more work (in the form of rasterization with OQs) is counter-productive. Instead, with HZB testing, accuracy is distributed proportionally. This proved to be a particularly good fit for us, given that we wanted a lot of relatively small clutter objects, for which instancing was not appropriate for various reasons.

We also benefited from the high granularity afforded by a query per object, whereas wholly OQ-based methods require some degree of aggregation in order to be efficient, leading to reduced accuracy and more variable performance. This became clear in our own analysis when we switched to HZB visibility from OQs. We started off with a 2×2 depth-test configuration, and even that out-performed hand-placed occlusion query volumes, both in terms of performance and amount of culling. Essentially, what we lost in terms of occlusion accuracy, we gained back in being able to test objects individually.

Point rendering with a vertex buffer was chosen primarily for ease of development because vertex buffers offered the convenience of heterogeneous data structures. However, a more efficient option could be to render a single quad and fetch object information from one or more textures instead. Not only would this ensure better pixel-quad utilization on some hardware, but it would also play to the strength of GPUs with a nonunified shader architecture such as the PS3's RSX, where the bulk of the shader hardware is dedicated to pixel processing.

3.5.3 Performance

Table 3.1 represents typical numbers seen in PIX on Xbox 360, for a single camera with around 22000 objects, all of which are processed in each each frame.

Pass	Time (ms)
Occlusion	0.06
Resolve	0.04
HZB Generation	0.10
HZB Queries	0.32
Total	**0.52**

Table 3.1. Performance timings.

3.5.4 Extensions

Once you have a system like this in place, it becomes easy to piggy-back related work that could otherwise take up significant CPU time compared with the GPU, which barely breaks a sweat. Contribution fading/culling, texture streaming and LOD selection, for instance, can all be determined based on each object's screen extents,[6] with results returned in additional bits.

On Xbox 360, we can also bin objects into multiple tiles ourselves, thereby avoiding the added complexity and restrictions that come with using the predicated tiling API, not to mention the extra latency and memory overhead when double-buffering the command buffer.

Finally, there is no reason to limit visibility processing to meshes. We also test and cull lights, particle systems, ambient occlusion volumes [Hill 10], and dynamic decals.

---

[6]We choose to use the object's bounding sphere for rotational invariance.

3.5.5 Shadow Caster Culling

We also extend our system to accelerate shadow-map rendering, with a two-pass technique initially inspired by [Lloyd et al. 04], but with a more straightforward approach. For instance, we do not slice up the view frustum and test subregions as they do. This is primarily because we are not using shadow volumes for rendering and therefore are not aiming to minimize fill-rate[7]—only the number of casters—for CPU and vertex transform savings. Development time and ease of GPU implementation are also factors.

In the first pass, we test caster visibility from the light's point of view, in exactly the same way that we do for a regular camera: via another HZB. If a given caster is visible, we write out the active shaft bounds, which are formed from the 2D light-space extents, the caster's minimum depth, and the maximum depth from the HZB (see Listing 3.3), otherwise it is culled as before:

```
float3 shaft_min = float3(input.sbox.xy, min_z)
float3 shaft_max = float3(input.sbox.zw, max_z)
```

Figure 3.5 shows this in action for a parallel light source. Here, caster C is fully behind an occluder,[8] so it can be culled away since it will not contribute to the shadow map.

In the second pass, we transform these shafts into camera space and test their visibility from the player's point of view via the existing player camera HZB—again just like regular objects. Here, since the shafts of A and B have been clamped to the occluder underneath, they are not visible either.

```
// Use the lower level if we only touch <= 2 texels
// in both dimensions

float level_new = max(level - 1, 0);
float2 scale = pow(2, -level_new);

float2 a = floor(sbox_vp.xy*scale);
float2 b = ceil(sbox_vp.zw*scale);

float2 dims = b - a;

if (dims.x <= 2 && dims.y <= 2)
    level = level_new;
```

Listing 3.3. HZB level refinement.

---

[7]But we could adapt this type of testing to cull more. See Section 3.7.

[8]Occluders used for shadow culling always cast shadows.

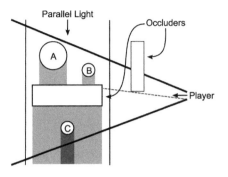

Figure 3.5. Two-pass shadow visibility.

Conceptually, we are exploiting the redundancy of shadow-volume overlap across two viewpoints in order to reduce our set of potential casters.

3.5.6 Summary

To reiterate, this entire process takes place as a series of GPU passes; the CPU is involved only in dispatching the draw calls and processing the results at the end.

In retrospect, a CPU solution could have also worked well as an alternative, but we found the small amount of extra GPU processing to be well within our budget. Additionally, we were able to leverage fixed-function rasterization hardware, stream processing, and a mature HLSL compiler, all with literally man-years of optimization effort behind them. In contrast to the simple shaders listed earlier, a hand-optimized VMX software rasterizer would have taken significantly longer to develop and would have been harder to extend.

If you already have a PVS or portal visibility system, there can still be significant benefits to performing HZB processing as an additional step. In the first place, either system can act as an initial high-level cull, thus reducing the number of HZB queries. In the case of portals, the "narrow-phase" subfrusta testing could also be shifted to the GPU. Indeed, from our own experience, moving basic frustum testing to the GPU alone was a significant performance improvement over VMX tests on the CPU. Finally, in the case of BSP-based PVS, the faces could be preconverted to a number of large-scale occluders for direct rendering.

3.6 *Battlefield* Solution

When developing the game (*Battlefield: Bad Company 1*) using our new in-house Frostbite engine for the first time, we knew that we needed a solution for removing objects occluded by others. We discussed many methods, but it all came down to a list of things that we wanted the system to have:

- must be fully dynamic, since the environment—both objects and terrain— can deform

- low GPU overhead

- results accessible from the CPU, so we can skip updating certain aspects of occluded objects, such as animation

After reading about Warhawk's approach [Woodard 07] based on software rasterization on SPUs, we decided to try a similar approach since we had spare processing power available on the CPU side. The resulting implementation was subsequently rolled out across all of our target platforms (PlayStation 3, Xbox 360, and PC), but we will focus in particular on the details of the PS3 version.

At a high level, the steps involved are very similar to those used for *Conviction*: a software occlusion rasterizer renders low polygon meshes to a z-buffer, against which occluders are tested to determine if they are visible or not.

In reality, the work is broken down into a number of stages, which are job-scheduled in turn across several SPUs. We will now describe these in detail.

3.6.1 The Process

Occluder triangle setup. This stage goes through all occluders in the world space (a flat array) in preparation for rasterization:

1. Each job grabs a mesh from the array using `InterlockedIncrement`.

2. The job checks if the mesh is inside the frustum. If it is not, it continues to the next one (Step 1).

3. If the mesh is fully inside the frustum, its triangles are immediately appended to an output array (also interlocked and shared between the jobs).

4. If the mesh was not fully inside, its triangles are clipped before being added.

Terrain triangle setup. This is effectively the same as the previous stage, except that it generates and adds conservative triangles for the terrain[9] to the array.

Occluder render. This is the stage that actually rasterizes the triangles. Each SPU job has its own z-buffer (256×114) and grabs 16 triangles at a time from the triangle array generated previously.

When the jobs are finished getting triangles from the triangle array, they will each try to lock a shared mutex. The first one will simply DMA its z-buffer to main memory, unlock the mutex, and exit so that the next job can start running.

As the mutex gets unlocked, the next job will now merge its own buffer with the one in main memory and send back the result, and so on. (*Note*: There are

---

[9]As the terrain can deform, these must be regenerated.

several ways to improve on this and make it faster. We could, for example, DMA directly from each SPU.)

Frustum cull. This stage performs frustum versus sphere/bounding box (BB) checks on all meshes in the world—typically between 10,000 and 15,000—and builds an array for the next stage. The implementation traverses a tree of spheres (prebuilt by our pipeline) and at each leaf we do bounding-box testing if the sphere is not fully inside.

Occlusion cull. Finally, this is where visibility testing against the z-buffer happens. We first project the bounding box of the mesh to screen-space and calculate its 2D area. If this is smaller than a certain value—determined on a per-mesh basis—it will be immediately discarded (i.e, contribution culled).

Then, for the actual test against the z-buffer, we take the minimum distance from the camera to the bounding box and compare it against the z-buffer over the whole screen-space rectangle. This falls somewhere between the approach of [Woodard 07]—which actually rasterizes occluders—and that of *Conviction* in terms of accuracy.

Performance The timings reflect best-case parallelism over five SPUs and were measured in a typical scene (see Table 3.2). In practice, workloads between SPU jobs will vary slightly and may be intermixed with other jobs, so the overall time for visibility processing will be higher in practice.

In this case we rasterized around 6000 occluder triangles (we normally observe 3000 to 5000), and performed around 3000 occlusion tests after frustum and extent culling.

Stage	Time/SPU (ms)
Triangle Setup	0.4
Rasterization	1.0
Frustum Cull	0.6
Occlusion Cull	0.3
Total	**2.3**

Table 3.2. Performance timings.

3.7 Future Development

3.7.1 Tools

Although artist-authored occluders are generally a good idea for performance reasons (particularly so with a software rasterizer), we encountered a couple of notable problems with this strategy on *Conviction*. First, with a large team and therefore a number of people making changes to a particular map, there were a few cases where modifications to the layout of visual meshes would not be applied to the associated occluders. Even with the blueprint of a map largely locked down, cosmetic changes sometimes introduced significant errors and these tended to occur right at the end of testing when production was most stretched!

Second, some artists had a tendency to think of modeling occluders in the same way as collision meshes—when, in fact, occluders should always be flush with, or inside of, the visual meshes they represent—or they did not feel that a small inaccuracy would be that important. This simply was not the case: time and again, testers would uncover these problems, particularly in "scope mode" where the reduced field of view can magnify these subtle differences up to half of the screen, causing large chunks of the world to disappear.

These errors would also show up as "shadow acne" due to the requirement that shadow occluders—those used for culling casters during shadow map visibility— had to cast shadows themselves. Sometimes, it would have made more sense to have just used these visual meshes directly as occluders, instead of creating separate occluder meshes.

Though checks can be added in the editor to uncover a lot of these issues, another option could be to automatically weld together, simplify, and chunk up existing visual meshes flagged by artists.

At the root of it all, the primary concern is correctness; there is no such thing as "pretty looking" visibility, so one could argue that it is not the best use of an artist's time to be modeling occluders if we can generate them automatically for the most part, particularly if a human element can introduce errors. This is definitely something we would like to put to the test, going forward.

3.7.2 Optimizations

One trivial optimization for the GPU solution would be to add a pre-pass, testing a coarse subdivision of the scene (e.g., regular grid) to perform an earlier, high-level cull—just like in *Battlefield*, but using the occlusion system too. We chose not to do this since performance was already within our budget, but it would certainly allow the approach to scale up to larger environments (e.g., "open world").

Additionally, a less accurate *object-level* pre-pass (for instance, four HZB samples using the bounding sphere, as with [Shopf et al. 08]) could lead to a speed up wherever there is a reasonable amount of occlusion (which by necessity is a common case). Equally, a finer-grained final pass (e.g., 8×8 HZB samples) could improve culling of larger occluders.

In a similar vein, another easy win for the SPU version would be using a hierarchical z-buffer either for early rejection or as a replacement for a complete loop over the screen bounds. As earlier numbers showed, however, the main hotspot performance-wise is occluder rasterization. In that instance we might

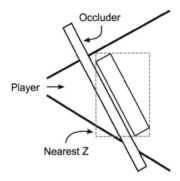

Figure 3.6. A single screen-space z-value for occluders can lead to conservative acceptance in some cases.

gain again, this time from *hierarchical* rasterization as in [Abrash 09], although at the cost of increased implementation complexity. Frustum culling could also be sped up by switching to a different data structure (e.g., grid) to improve load balancing on SPUs as well as memory access patterns.

Although the accuracy-performance trade-off from the HZB was almost always beneficial for *Conviction*, we did encounter a couple of instances where we could have profited from better culling of large, structural geometry. We believe that the biggest factor here was the lack of varying z over the occluder (see Figure 3.6) when testing against the HZB, not the number of tests (beyond 4×4) or the base resolution.

On Xbox 360, we investigated hardware-rasterizing occluder bounds as a proof-of-concept for overcoming this, but we ran out of time and there were some performance pitfalls with MemExport. We hope to pick up where we left off in the future.

Conviction's shadow-caster culling proved to be a significant optimization for cascaded shadow maps. One potential avenue of future development would be to try to adapt the idea of frustum subdivision coupled with caster-receiver intersection testing, as presented in [Diamond 10], with similarities to [Lloyd et al. 04]. [Eisemann and Décoret 06] and [Décoret 05] also build on the latter.

We would also like to extend culling to local shadow lights. As we already cache casters per shadow light (the cache is updated on object or light movement), we could directly evaluate shadow visibility for this subset of the scene. This would avoid the higher fixed overhead of processing all objects in the map as we do for the main view or shadow cascades, which is important since we can have up to eight active shadow lights per camera. These updates could happen either every frame or whenever the list changes.

3.7.3 Future Hardware

The jury is out on exactly what sort of future we face when it comes to the convergence of increasingly multi-core CPUs and more programmable GPUs and when, or indeed if, it will happen. Larrabee is an interesting example, showing that even fixed-function rasterization hardware is potentially on the way out [Abrash 09] and, while a CPU solution could be considered a safe long-term bet, the most efficient method going forward may be closer to the way hardware works than a traditional scan-line approach.

[Andersson 10] describes two possible future scenarios for visibility processing: either a progression of the GPU approach we already described, but with lower latency, or having the ability for the GPU to feed itself commands. A killer application for the latter could be shadow-map rendering, where visibility (as earlier) and subsequent draw calls would happen entirely on the GPU, thereby avoiding any CPU synchronization, processing, and dispatch. This is almost possible today and potentially so on current consoles, but existing APIs are a roadblock.

3.7.4 General Observations

In *Conviction*, although arbitrary occlusion tests could be issued by the main thread (to accelerate other systems, in much the same way as in *Battlefield*), we had to restrict their use in the end due to the need for deterministic behavior during co-operative play. This was primarily an issue for PC as we could not ensure matching results between GPUs from different IHVs, or indeed across generations from the same vendor. For the next title, we hope to find other applications for exploiting our system so this will not be a problem.

Were we to generate a min/max depth hierarchy, we could also return more information about the state of occlusion, which may open up more applications. By testing the z-range of objects, we can determine one or more states: Completely visible or occluded (all tests pass conclusively), partially occluded (tests pass conclusively as fully visible or occluded), potentially occluded (some tests are inclusive, i.e., z-range overlap with the HZB).

3.8 Conclusion

Whatever the future, experimenting with solutions like these is a good investment; in our experience, we gained significantly from employing these fast yet straightforward visibility systems, both in development and production terms.

The GPU implementation in particular is trivial to add (demonstrated by the fact that our initial version was developed and integrated in a matter of days) and comes with a very reasonable overhead.

3.9   Acknowledgments

We would like to thank Don Williamson, Steven Tovey, Nick Darnell, Christian Desautels, and Brian Karis, for their insightful feedback and correspondence, as well as the authors of all cited papers and presentations, for considerable inspiration.

Bibliography

[Abrash 96] Michael Abrash. "Inside Quake: Visible-Surface Determination." *Dr. Dobb's Sourcebook* Jan/Feb (1996), 41–45.

[Abrash 09] Michael Abrash. "Rasterization on Larrabee." In *Game Deveoper's Conference*, 2009.

[Akenine-Möller et al. 08] Tomas Akenine-Möller, Eric Haines, and Naty Hoffman. *Real-Time Rendering*, Third edition. Natick, MA: A K Peters, 2008.

[Andersson 10] Johan Andersson. "Parallel Futures of a Game Engine v2.0." In *STHLM Game Developer Forum*, 2010.

[Bittner et al. 09] Jiří Bittner, Oliver Mattausch, and Michael Wimmer. "Game Engine Friendly Occlusion Culling." In *ShaderX⁷*, pp. 637–653. Hingham, MA: Charles River Media, 2009.

[Blinn 96] Jim Blinn. "Calculating Screen Coverage." *IEEE CG&A* 16:3 (1996), 84–88.

[Décoret 05] Xavier Décoret. "N-Buffers for Efficient Depth Map Query." *Computer Graphics Forum (Eurographics)* 24:3 (2005), 8 pp.

[Diamand 10] Ben Diamand. "Shadows in *God of War III*." In *Game Developer's Conference*, 2010.

[Eisemann and Décoret 06] Elmar Eisemann and Xavier Décoret. "Fast Scene Voxelization and Applications." In *Proceedings of the 2006 Symposium on Interactive 3D Graphics and Games, I3D '06*, pp. 71–78. New York: ACM, 2006.

[Greene et al. 93] Ned Greene, Michael Kass, and Gavin Miller. "Hierarchical Z-buffer Visibility." In *Proceedings of the 20th Annual Conference on Computer Graphics and Interactive Techniques, SIGGRAPH '93*, pp. 231–238. New York: ACM, 1993.

[Hastings 07] Al Hastings. "Occlusion Systems." http://www.insomniacgames.com/research_dev/articles/2007/1500779, 2007.

[Hill 10] Stephen Hill. "Rendering with Conviction." In *Game Developer's Conference*, 2010.

[Lloyd et al. 04] Brandon Lloyd, Jeremy Wendt, Naga Govindaraju, and Dinesh Manocha. "CC Shadow Volumes." In *ACM SIGGRAPH 2004 Sketches, SIGGRAPH '04*, p. 146. New York: ACM, 2004.

[Redon et al. 02] Stephane Redon, Abderrahmane Kheddar, and Sabine Coquillart. "Fast Continuous Collision Detection between Rigid Bodies." *Computer Graphics Forum* 21:3 (2002), 279–288.

[Shopf et al. 08] Jeremy Shopf, Joshua Barczak, Christopher Oat, and Natalya Tatarchuk. In *ACM SIGGRAPH 2008 Classes*, *SIGGRAPH '08*, pp. 52–101. New York: ACM, 2008.

[Soininen 08] Teppo Soininen. "Visibility Optimization for Games." Gamefest, 2008. Microsoft Download Center, Available at http://www.microsoft.com/downloads/en /details.aspx?FamilyId=B9B33C7D-5CFE-4893-A877-5F0880322AA0& displaylang =en, 2008.

[Woodard 07] Bruce Woodard. "SPU Occlusion Culling." In *SCEA PS3 Graphics Seminar*, 2007.

4

Shader Amortization Using Pixel Quad Message Passing
Eric Penner

4.1 Introduction

Algorithmic optimization and level of detail are very pervasive topics in real-time rendering. With each rendering problem comes the question of the acceptable amount of approximation error and the quality vs. performance trade-off of increasing or decreasing approximation error. Programmable hardware pipelines play one of the largest roles in how we optimize rendering algorithms because they dictate where we can add algorithmic modification via programmable shaders.

In this chapter we analyze one particular aspect of modern programmable hardware—the pixel derivative instructions and pixel quad rasterization—and we identify a new level at which optimizations can be performed. Our work demonstrates how values calculated in one pixel can be passed to neighboring pixels in the frame buffer allowing us to amortize the cost of expensive shading operations. By amortizing costs in this manner we can reduce texture fetches and/or arithmetic operations by factors of two to sixteen times. Examples in this chapter include 4×4 percentage closer filtering (PCF) using only one texture fetch, and 2×2 bilateral upsampling using only one or two texture fetches. Our approach works using a technique we call pixel quad amortization (PQA). Although our approach already works on a large set of existing hardware, we propose some standards and extensions for future hardware pipelines, or software pipelines, to make it ubiquitous and more efficient.

4.2 Background and Related Work

As the performance of programmable graphics hardware increases exponentially, there has been a steady increase in the complexity of real-time rendering applications, often expressed as the number of arithmetic operations and texture accesses required to shade each pixel. In response to increasing complexity, much recent research and development effort has focused on methods to reduce pixel processing workload. This includes techniques for simplifying shaders [Olano et al. 03], reusing data from previous frames [Zhu et al. 05, Nehab et al. 07] , or by simply using lower resolutions within a single frame.

One of the first upsampling approaches, known as dynamic video resizing [Montrym et al. 97], dynamically adjusts resolution based on performance, followed by simple bilinear or nearest-neighbor upsampling to a full-resolution frame. While this is effective for controlling pixel workload, artifacts are very noticeable in the upsampled frame. More recent techniques apply geometry-aware upsampling such as the joint bilateral filter [Tomasi and Manduchi 98] from either fixed size [Ren et al. 06] or dynamically resized [Yang et al. 08] frame buffers. What all of these techniques have in common is the requirement of an extra low-resolution pass, followed by upsampling. Our approach differs in that we are able to perform operations at two separate resolutions natively, in the same pass on existing hardware.

4.3   Pixel Derivatives and Pixel Quads

Before describing our technique, it is important to understand a few details of how modern graphics hardware works with respect to texture mapping, and why the pixel shader partial-derivative instructions exist. The need for partial derivatives arises from the simple problem of texture mapping a triangle. As a triangle becomes smaller on screen, one screen pixel will cover many texels, resulting in harsh aliasing unless the texture is adequately sampled. This issue is typically solved in graphics hardware with mipmapping, but a method is needed to compute which mipmap level to use.

Partial derivatives relate the infinitesimal change in one variable to the infinitesimal change in another variable at a particular location. Pixel shader partial derivatives refer to the rate of change of a shader value with respect to the screen-space x- and y-axes. When applied to texture coordinates, this can tell us how fast a texture coordinate is changing on the screen, and thus what mipmap level we should use. Before dependent texture fetches, derivatives could potentially be computed analytically, based on homogeneous barycentric texture coordinates calculated from three triangle vertices. However, dependent texture fetches can depend on arbitrary calculations including data from another texture; thus, no analytic solution exists for these cases.

The only solution remaining is to compute pixel shader derivatives discretely by looking at the value of a texture coordinate in neighboring screen pixels and computing the difference between them. Computing derivatives in this manner is called *forward differencing* or *backward differencing*, depending on whether you look at the pixel in front of or behind the current pixel, to compute the derivative. For example, in a row of pixels p, $p[i+1] - p[i]$ is a forward difference while $p[i] - p[i-1]$ is a backward difference. Both of these typical schemes fail for parallel graphics hardware however, as they imply a dependency on the order in which pixels are computed. To solve this issue, modern hardware rasterizes triangles in quads, or 2×2 blocks of pixels, and uses custom derivative calculations that depend only on the values within a quad.

Unfortunately, neither the location of quads, nor derivatives within quads, nor even the use of pixel quads, is standardized by modern graphics APIs. Instead these details are left up to the vendor to implement as long as some form of derivative is provided. Since no documentation was provided, we turned to experimentation to determine exactly how derivatives are calculated on modern hardware. Not surprisingly, the implementations we found were exactly what one would expect, given the constraints. First and foremost, on all the hardware we tested, pixel quads have always been stationary in the same locations within the

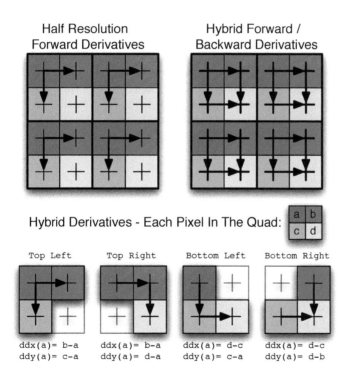

Figure 4.1. Derivative calculations used in practice in modern hardware. We found derivatives were either calculated at half-resolution using forward differencing, or using a hybrid of forward and backward differencing. In the hybrid case we have broken out each pixel's derivatives.

frame buffer; they are essentially double width pixels. Second, we found only two approaches to computing derivatives within these quads, as illustrated in Figure 4.1.

Interestingly, Shader Model 5 in Direct3D 11 has both *coarse* and *fine* versions of the derivative instructions, likely exposing the trade-offs of these two approaches to the developer. Half-resolution derivatives always return the same value within a quad, allowing for optimized texture sampling in some cases, while hybrid derivatives have the potential to provide slightly more accurate results.

It is important to note at this point that although derivative instructions were created to assist with texture mapping, they are not reserved for computing derivatives of texture coordinates. You can use the derivative instructions to calculate the derivative of *any value* in a shader. One obvious question that arises is, what happens when a triangle does not cover all the pixels in a given quad, or if some pixels in a quad are rejected by the depth test? Another question is, how does graphics hardware synchronize all the seemingly independent shader programs such that derivatives can be calculated anywhere? The answer is that in the real shader processing core the "loop" over all the pixels in a triangle is unrolled into blocks of at least four pixels. So all quad pixels are always calculated in lockstep and in parallel, likely even sharing the same set of real hardware registers. The shader program will execute for all the pixels in a quad even if only one pixel is actually needed. In the event that a quad pixel falls outside of a triangle, the values passed down from the vertices are extrapolated using the triangle's homogenous coordinates.

4.4   Pixel Quad Message Passing

Now that we have described pixel quads and why they exist in modern hardware, we turn to how we use them to our advantage. The obvious question is: Can some shaders, or some calculations within shaders, execute at the pixel quad level instead of the pixel level? If a graphics API were to theoretically support a "quad shader" it would lead to another dilemma for parallelism; we would essentially need another pipeline stage. For example, if the hardware was optimized for running 16 shaders in parallel, it would need to cache the output of 16 pixel quad shaders as input to 64 pixels shaders.

What might be a better compromise, and what we found we can already do with today's hardware, is to share values between the pixels in a given quad, but still execute a shader at the pixel level. If we choose problems that have inherent symmetries and are divisible into four identical operations, we can actually use the same pixel shader instructions to perform different "jobs" in each pixel, and then share the values in the quad. Now it should be clear why the derivative instructions are so important. They rely on the difference between two pixels, and thus can be used as a mechanism to share values between pixels, with some simple arithmetic. We utilize the derivative instructions as message-passing instructions.

4.5   PQA Initialization

In the case of hybrid forward- and backward-differencing, each derivative is simply the positive or negative difference of the current pixel's value with the vertical/horizontal adjacent pixel. With this knowledge, it is easy to calculate what an adjacent pixel's value is. We simply subtract or add the derivative to the current pixel's value, based on the pixel's location in the quad. As an example, for the pixel in the quad in Figure 4.1(top left), we have

$$a + ddx(a) = a + (b - a) = b.$$

For the top-right pixel, we have

$$b - ddx(b) = b - (b - a) = a.$$

So to generically pass a value v horizontally within a quad and get the horizontal neighbor h, we compute

$$h = v - \text{sign}_x * ddx(v),$$

where sign_x denotes the sign of x in the quadrant of the current pixel within a quad. Although we can not access the pixel diagonally across from the current pixel directly, we can determine the horizontal neighbor followed by the vertical neighbor of that value. An example that computes all three neighbors is as follows:

```
//Gather four float4s
void QuadGather2x2(float4 value,
                   out float4 horz,
                   out float4 vert,
                   out float4 diag)
{
    horz = value + ddx(value) * QuadVector.z; //Horizontal
    vert = value + ddy(value) * QuadVector.w; //Vertical
    diag = vert  + ddx(vert)  * QuadVector.z; //Diagonal
}
```

If we need to gather only one or two values instead of a full `float4` vector, we can optimize this calculation down to as little as two MAD instructions and two derivative instructions:

```
//Gather four floats into one float4
float QuadGather2x2 (float value)
{
    float4 r = value;
    r.y  = r.x  + ddx(r.x)  * QuadVector.z; //Horizontal
    r.zw = r.xy + ddy(r.xy) * QuadVector.w; //Vertical /
        Diagonal
    return r;
}
```

In both of these examples we used the variable `QuadVector`. Figure 4.2 illustrates the value of `QuadVector` for each pixel in a quad. Most of the optimizations we perform in this chapter rely on this vector and one other variable called `QuadSelect`. `QuadVector` is used to divide two-dimensional symmetric problems into four parts, while `QuadSelect` is used to choose between two values based on the current pixel's quadrant.

The following code demonstrates one way to calculate `QuadVector` and `QuadSelect` from a pixel's screen coordinates. The negated/flipped values are also useful and are stored in z/w components.

```
void InitQuad(float2 screenCoord)
{
    //This assumes screenCoord contains an integer pixel
        coordinate
    ScreenCoord = screenCoord;
    QuadVector = frac(screenCoord.xy*0.5).xyxy;
    QuadVector = QuadVector*float4(4,4,-4,-4) + float4(-1,-1,1,1)
        ;
    QuadSelect = saturate(QuadVector);
}
```

While it takes a few instructions to initialize communication within a quad, this will allow us to amortize the cost of several costly shading operations. First, however, we will identify a few drawbacks and limitations when using PQA.

4.6   Limitations of PQA

There are a number of limitations to pixel quad amortization that become immediately apparent. First and foremost, pixel quad message passing works only on hardware that uses hybrid forward and backward derivatives as illustrated in Figure 4.2. When half-resolution derivatives are used, the derivative instructions never touch the bottom-right pixel in the quad. There is no way to communicate that pixel's value to the other pixels in the quad in that case, thus hybrid derivative support needs to be detected based on the graphics card. Appendix A

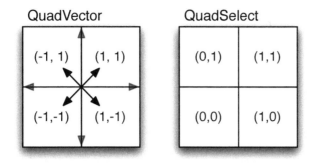

Figure 4.2. To initialize PQA we calculate two simple values for each pixel. `QuadVector` contains the x/y sign of the pixel within it's quad and is used to perform symmetric operations while `QuadSelect` is used to choose between values based on the pixel's location in the quad.

provides a list of hardware that supports hybrid derivatives at the time this chapter was written. It is also possible that a hardware vendor could change the way the derivative instructions work, breaking this functionality. Although this seems very unlikely, it is easy enough to write a detection routine to test which type of derivatives are used.

The second problem that becomes immediately apparent is that there is no interpolation between quads as there would be from a pre-rendered half-resolution buffer. Thus, if we output the same value for an entire quad, it will resemble unfiltered point sampling from a half-resolution frame buffer. This may be acceptable in certain situations, but if we want higher quality results, we still need to compute unique values for each pixel. Our ability to produce pleasing results really depends on the specific problem.

The third problem is that quad-level calculations work effectively only in the current triangle's domain. For example, we can use pixel quad amortization to accelerate PCF shadow-map sampling in forward rendering, but not nearly as easily in deferred rendering. This is because in the deferred case the quads being rendered are not in object space; thus, a pixel quad may straddle a depth discontinuity, creating a large gap in shadow space. In forward rendering, the entire quad will project into a contiguous location in shadow space, which is what we rely on to amortize costs effectively.

Although there are a number of drawbacks to PQA, we found we could solve these issues for several common graphics problems and still achieve large performance gains. In the following sections we will discuss how to optimize PCF, bilateral upsampling, and basic convolution and blurring with PQA.

4.7   Cross Bilateral Sampling

The cross bilateral filter has been popularized as a means to provide geometry-aware upsampling. If a screen-space buffer is blurred or upsampled using a simple bilinear filter, the features in the low-resolution buffer will bleed across depth boundaries, creating artifacts. The basic idea behind the bilateral filter is to modify the reconstruction kernel to avoid integrating across depth or normal boundaries in the scene. This is achieved by storing a depth and/or normal for each low-resolution sample and assigning filter weight according to not only the distance in screen space to each sample, but also distance in depth and/or normal space. Bilateral filters usually use Gaussian weighting functions in both depth and screen space, however [Yang et al. 08] proposed to use a simple tent function in screen space, mimicking the effect of a bilinear upsample and therefore requiring only four depth/image samples. No matter what type of weighting function is used, the filter weight is accumulated such that the sample can be normalized by the total accumulated weight:

$$
c_i^H = \frac{\Sigma c_j^L f(\hat{x}_i, x_j) g(|z_i^H - z_j^L|)}{\Sigma f(\hat{x}_i, x_j) g(|z_i^H - z_j^L|)}
$$

In this example $f()$ is the normal linear filtering weight while $g()$ is a Gaussian falloff based on the difference in depth between the high-resolution and low-resolution depths. One disadvantage of bilateral upsampling is its cost compared with simple bilinear filtering. While a bilinear upsample requires only one hardware filtered sample, a bilateral upsample will require at minimum four point samples and four depth samples. This cost is incurred at the high resolution, thus it often partially defeats the purpose of performing calculations at a lower resolution in the first place. Obviously, if the calculation costs less than eight samples, it will be less expensive to just compute the value at the high resolution.

The bilateral filter is one example where PQA works without any of the drawbacks mentioned in the previous section. Since bilateral upsampling occurs in screen space, we can set up our low-resolution buffer such that all the pixels in the same high-resolution quad will share the same low-resolution samples. All that is needed then is to share the samples across the quad and let each pixel perform the bilateral filter independently. Here is an example for a 2X upsample of a low-resolution AO texture. To optimize this further to only one sample, the depth can be packed into extra channels of the AO texture.

```
//Gather quad horizontal / vertical / diagonal samples
float2 AO_D, AO_D_H, AO_D_V, AO_D_D;
AO_D.x = tex2D( lowResDepthSampler , coord ).x;
AO_D.y = tex2D( lowResAOSampler    , coord ).x;
QuadGather2x2( AO_D, AO_D_H, AO_D_V, AO_D_D );
```

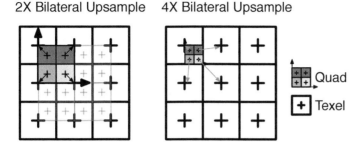

Figure 4.3. Bilateral upsampling from a half-resolution or quarter-resolution buffer. All quad pixels utilize the same four low-resolution samples. We can therefore perform a bilateral upsample with only one or two texture fetches and two derivative instructions, instead of eight texture fetches.

The bilateral upsample can then be performed as usual for each pixel, with the caveat that tent weights will need to flip to compensate for the samples being flipped in each pixel. A similar approach can be taken for a 4X upsample, or for bilateral blurring operations at any resolution. One extra thing to note is that the low-resolution buffer is shifted half a pixel (see Figure 4.3).

4.8 Convolution and Blurring

Convolution and blurring operations can also be accelerated using PQA. Although we are performing calculations at the pixel quad level, we would not want our result to be output at half-resolution or we might as well simply output a truly half-resolution texture! Thankfully, because we can share results at any point in the shader, we can customize the message delivered to other pixels in the quad in order to perform unique blurs for each pixel. The following code illustrates a 3×3 blur with four samples, while Figure 4.4 illustrates this process for a 5×5 blur using nine samples:

```
//Populate messages for neighbors
float4 m = 0;
m.rgba+= tex2D(imageSampler, coord ).x;
m.rb   += tex2D(imageSampler,coord+QuadVector*
           float2(TEXEL_SIZE.x,0)).x;
m.rg   += tex2D(imageSampler,coord+QuadVector*
           float2(TEXEL_SIZE.y,0)).x;
m.r    += tex2D(imageSampler,coord+QuadVector*
           float2(TEXEL_SIZE.xy )).x;
```

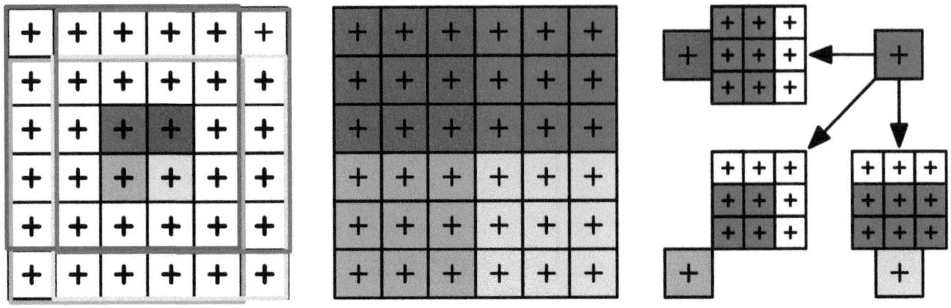

Figure 4.4. Illustration of a 5×5 blur using PQA. The blur kernel footprint of four pixels in a quad (left). Samples taken by each pixel in the quad (middle). Uniquely weighted messages from the red pixel to other pixels in the quad (right).

```
//Gather messages
float4 h, v, d;
QuadGather2x2( m, h, v, d );

//Weight results for 3x3 blur
float4 result = dot(float4(4,2,2,1) / 9.0 ,
                    float4(m.x,h.g,v.b,d.w) );
```

Unfortunately, though we can gather more samples, it becomes cumbersome to apply unique weights for more complicated filters, especially when bilinear filtering is also applied to increase the kernel width. In our example it would also take several QuadGather operations for a multiple channel texture. While this can be optimized significantly by separating vertical and horizontal messages, we recommend this approach primarily for performing nonseparable and/or nonlinear blurring operations on one or two channel data. In the case that only approximate results are required, we discuss a gradient approximation to support bilinear filtering in Section 4.9.

In the case of Direct3D 11 hardware, it should be noted that PQA should not be used for simple image blurring. In this case DirectCompute or OpenCL can achieve much better performance by applying the same idea in a compute shader. For example, one could output in quad-sized groups of pixels, or even output an entire row of quads in one shader. For this reason PQA should be used only during geometry rasterization on hardware that supports compute shaders. PQA will remain a valid technique in these cases since rasterization is only a semi-parallelizable task.

4.9 Percentage Closer Filtering

Percentage closer filtering refers to filtering in which a nonlinear operation is required before the filter can take place. In graphics, PCF usually refers to shadow-map filtering, where the nonlinear operation is a depth comparison. A naive N × N PCF filter looks something like this:

```
for( int i = 0; i < N; i++ )
for( int j = 0; j < N; j++ )
{
    shad += ShadowSample(Map, Coord,
                SM_TEXEL * float2( i-(N/2.0-0.5),j-(N/2.0-0.5)
                    ) );
}
shad /= (N*N);
```

Many graphics cards support native bilinear PCF filtering, and this section assumes we have at least bilinear PCF support. Some more recent graphics cards support fetching four depth values at once, allowing the user to arbitrarily filter them in the shader. Since utilizing bilinear PCF is more difficult in our case, but is supported on a much wider set of hardware, we will focus on using bilinear PCF. Extensions to `Gather` instructions can further improve results.

Since we cannot access the result of each pixel when using bilinear PCF, we start by applying an approach from [Sigg and Hadwiger 05, Gruen 10], which uses bilinear samples to build efficient larger filters. This involves using sample offsets such that each bilinear sample fetches four uniquely weighted samples. In the most simple case, where we want equal weights, this simply means placing a bilinear PCF sample in the middle of the four texels we want:

```
//Fraction of a pixel
float2 a = frac(Coord.xy * SM_SIZE - 0.5 );

//Negative/Positive offsets to compute equal weights
float4 Offset = a.xyxy * -(SM_TEXEL) +
                    float4(-0.5,-0.5,1.5,1.5)*SM_TEXEL;
float4 taps;
    taps.x = ShadowSample( Map, Coord, Offset.xw  );
    taps.y = ShadowSample( Map, Coord, Offset.zw  );
    taps.z = ShadowSample( Map, Coord, Offset.xy  );
    taps.w = ShadowSample( Map, Coord, Offset.zy  );

float shadow = dot(taps,0.25);
```

This approach can apply to arbitrary separable filters as we will see later, but for now we will keep things simple. To apply PQA, we replace the offset calculation with one that uses the quadrant vector, and then take one sample at each pixel, followed by a quad average:

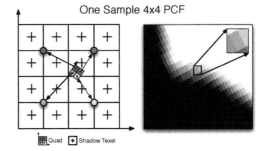

Figure 4.5. Half-resolution 4×4 PCF using quad LOD. The colored pixels correspond to the projection of one pixel quad into shadow space. Each pixel performs only one texture fetch, followed by a pixel quad average. The close-up illustrates half-resolution point sampling artifacts.

```
//Average coordinate for quad
Coord.xy = QuadAve2x2(Coord.xy);

//Fraction of a pixel
float2 a = frac(Coord.xy * SM_SIZE - 0.5 );

//Negative or positive offset to compute equal weights
float2 Offset = (-a + 0.5 + QuadVector.xy) * SM_TEXEL;
float tap = ShadowSample( Map, Coord, Offset );
float shadow = QuadAve2x2(tap);
```

We first compute the average texture coordinate for the quad. We then use the quadrant vector to select only the offset we need. Last, we take one sample in each pixel and then average the results. This is illustrated in Figure 4.5. Note that the offset calculation was also reduced from a `float4` to `float2` calculation.

At this point we are doing a lot of extra work to save only three samples, but once we extend this to larger kernels it starts to become quite effective. For example, if we use four samples per pixel we can now achieve 8×8 PCF (64 total texels) with only four bilinear samples, for a 16X improvement over the naive approach. The layout of these samples is illustrated in Figure 4.6 (right).

```
//Low and high offsets for this pixel
float4 l0h0 = (-a.xyxy + QuadVector.xyxy + 0.5 +
                          float4(-2,-2,2,2) ) * SM_TEXEL;

float4 t;
        t.x = ShadowSample( Map, Coord, l0h0.xy );
        t.y = ShadowSample( Map, Coord, l0h0.xw );
        t.z = ShadowSample( Map, Coord, l0h0.zy );
        t.w = ShadowSample( Map, Coord, l0h0.zw );

float shadow = PixelAve2x2(dot(t,0.25));
```

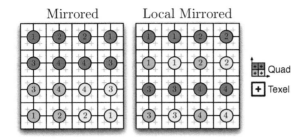

Figure 4.6. Different sample placements color coded by quad pixel. Simply mirroring samples is easier but results in samples that are very far apart, which can degrade cache performance (left). Local mirroring results in samples that are closer together but offsets can be more difficult to calculate symmetrically (right).

Although we can now sample very large kernels, we are outputting the same value for each pixel in the quad, resulting in quad-sized point sampling artifacts. Noncontinuous PCF is also quite undesirable, so it is important to add at least first-order continuity to our filter. We will now tackle both of these issues.

Higher-order filtering is more complicated since shadow texels are not located at fixed distances from the sampling location, thus weights need to be calculated dynamically. The most recent approach [Gruen 10] to achieving higher-order PCF filtering involves solving a small linear system for each sample to find the correct weights and offsets. The linear system is based on all the bilinear samples that would have touched the same texels.

We note that this can be largely simplified by using the work from [Sigg and Hadwiger 05]. Instead of replicating the weights produced by several bilinear samples and a grid of weights, we determine the weight for each texel using an analytic filter kernel. Because the kernel is separable, we can compute the sample offsets and weights separately for each axis. This is demonstrated using a full-sampled Gaussian kernel below.

```
{
    #define SIGMA (SM_TEXEL*2)
    #define ONE_OVER_TWO_SIGMA_SQ (1.0/(2.0*SIGMA*SIGMA))
    #define GAUSSIAN(v) (exp(-(v*v)*ONE_OVER_TWO_SIGMA_SQ))

    float4 GaussianFilterWeight(float4 offset)
    {
    return GAUSSIAN(offset) - GAUSSIAN(4*SM_TEXEL);
    }

    float4 linstep(float4 min, float4 max, float4 v)
    {
    return saturate((v-min)/(max-min));
    }
```

```
float4 LinearStepFilterWeight(float4 offset)
{
return linstep(SM_TEXEL*4.0,SM_TEXEL*2.0,abs(offset));
}

float4 SmoothStepFilterWeight(float4 offset)
{
return smoothstep (SM_TEXEL*4.0,SM_TEXEL*1.0,abs(offset));
}

float4 FilterWeight(float4 offset, const int filterType)
{
switch(filterType)
    {
    case 0:
    return LinearStepFilterWeight(offset,texelWidth);
    case 1:
    return SmoothStepFilterWeight(offset,texelWidth);
    case 2:
    return GaussianFilterWeight(offset,texelWidth);
    }
}

float Shadow8x8Hlaf(Texture2D Map, float4 Coord, const int
    filterType)
{
    //Compute average coord, and fraction of pixel
    Coord = QuadAve(Coord);
    float2 a = frac(Coord.xy*SM_SIZE - 0.5);

    //Low and high pixel center offsets (local mirrored)
    float4 offsets0 = (-a.xyxy + QuadVector.xyxy + float4
        (-2,-2,2,2))*SM_TEXEL;
    float4 offsets1 = offsets0 + SM_TEXEL;

    //Filter weights and offsets
    float4 g0 = FilterWeight(offsets0,filterType);
    float4 g1 = FilterWeight(offsets1,filterType);
    float4 g01 = g0 = g1;
    float4 bilinearOffsets = offsets0 + (g1/g01)*SM_TEXEL;

    //Gather 64 shadow map texels with 4 samples
    float4 taps;
    taps.x = ShadowSample(Map, Coord, bilinearOffsets.xy);
    taps.y = ShadowSample(Map, Coord, bilinearOffsets.zy);
    taps.z = ShadowSample(Map, Coord, bilinearOffsets.xw);
    taps.w = ShadowSample(Map, Coord, bilinearOffsets.zw);
    float4 weights = g01.xzxz*g01.yyww;

    //Sum weights and samples across the quad.
    float4 shadow_weight;
    shadow_weight.x = dot(taps,weights);
    shadow_weight.y = dot(1,weights);
```

```
            shadow_weight.xy = QuadAve(shadow_weight.xy);

            //Normalize our sample weight
            float shadow = shadow_weight.x/shadow_weight.y;
            return shadow;
        }
    }
```

We have shown a few Gaussian filters for both simplicity and readability; in practice, we prefer to use linear, quadratic, or cubic B-spline kernels. Note that we do not need to calculate weights for each texel, but rather for each row and column of texels. Bilinear offsets can then similarly be computed separately and weights simplified to the product between the sum of X and Y weights. The same approach can be applied for piecewise polynomial filters such as B-Splines, or using arbitrary filters with the offsets and weights stored in lookup textures as in [Sigg and Hadwiger 05].

At this point we now have very smooth shadows but still have the same value for all pixels in a quad. To smooth the point-sampled look, it would be optimal to bound all quad texels in shadow space and create a uniquely weighted kernel for each pixel, but without `Gather()` capability that would involve performing four

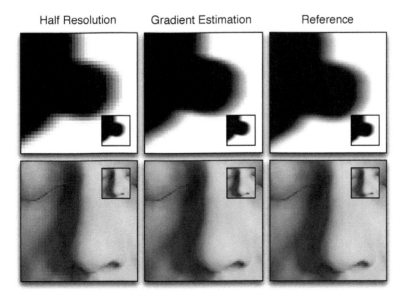

Figure 4.7. Gradient estimation for 8×8 bilinear PCF (four samples). These images are magnified to illustrate how even very naive gradient estimation can hide most quad artifacts. If using Shader Model 4 or 5, `Gather` samples can be used to avoid these artifacts altogether.

times the samples. We found that a good compromise when using bilinear PCF is to compute a simple gradient approximation along with the shadow value. Rather than using every texel to compute the gradient, we simply reuse the bilinear-filtered samples as if they had come from a lower-resolution shadow map. Although this is somewhat of a hack, thankfully it actually works quite well (see Figure 4.7). The weights for the derivative calculation will depend on the kernel itself (see Figure 4.8). The following code calculates a 4×4 Prewitt gradient which works well for low-order B-spline filters:

```
//Gradient estimation using Prewitt 4x4 gradient operator
float4 s_dxdy;
s_dxdy.xy = dot( taps, weights );
//Prewitt (x)
s_dxdy.z  = dot( taps, float4(3,3,1,1) * QuadVector.x );
//Prewitt (y
s_dxdy.w  = dot( taps, float4(3,1,3,1) * QuadVector.y );)
s_dxdy = QuadAve( s_dxdy ) * 4;
float shadow = s_dxdy.x;
```

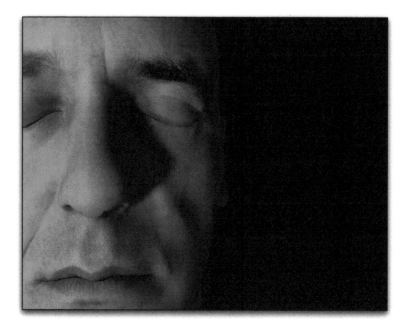

Figure 4.8. All of the images in Part II, Chapter 1 also make use of PQA for PCF shadows. This image uses 8×8 bilinear PCF filtering (four samples) and half the original ALU operations. Part of the shadow penumbra is used to mimic scattering fall-off, thus an inexpensive wide PCF kernel is crucial. Mesh and textures courtesy of XYZRGB.

```
shadow += dot((Coord.xy-realCoord), s_dxdy.zw );
return shadow;
```

The last issue that needs to be mentioned is handling anisotropy and mini-fication. Our gradient estimate works well on close-ups and will handle minifi-cation up to the size of the kernel used. However, under extreme minification the distance between the quad pixels in shadow space increases, and the linear gradient estimate breaks down. There are a number of ways we can deal with this. Firstly, if using a technique like cascading shadow maps (CSMs) we are unlikely to experience extreme minification since shadow resolution should be distributed somewhat equally in screen space. In other cases, one option is to generate mipmaps of the shadow map, allowing us to increase the kernel size to fit the footprint of the quad in shadow space. Alternatively, we can also forgo generating mipmaps and just sparsely sample a larger footprint in the shadow map. We have found that both of these solutions work adequately. Again, having `Gather()` support opens up several more options.

4.10   Discussion

We have demonstrated a new approach for optimizing shaders, by amortizing costly operations across pixel quads, that is natively supported by a large set of existing hardware. Our approach has the advantage of not requiring additional passes over the scene unlike other frame buffer LOD approaches. It also poten-tially allows for sharing redundant calculations and temporary registers between pixels, while still performing the final calculation at full resolution. We have also demonstrated how gradients can be used to generate smooth results within a quad while still supporting bilinear texture fetches. The primary drawback of our approach remains the lack of interpolation between neighboring quads that would be provided with something like bilateral upsampling. Interestingly, how-ever, our technique can help in either case, since our technique can also accelerate the bilateral upsampling operation itself.

Should PQA become a popular technique, hardware or software pipelines could make it much more efficient by exposing the registers of neighboring pixels directly in the pixel shader. Native API support for sharing registers between pixels would greatly simplify writing amortized shaders. The current cost of sharing results via derivative instructions makes it prohibitive in some cases.

We have found that our approach can also be applied to other rendering problems, such as shadow-contact hardening, ambient occlusion, and global illu-mination. Although we can not verify this at the time of writing, it also appears that all future hardware that supports Direct3D 11's fine derivatives will sup-port PQA.

4.11   Appendix A: Hardware Support

At the time of writing we have verified that PQA works on all recent NVIDIA hardware. We have tested several 8000 and 9000 series cards including mobile cards in laptops. Unfortunately all the ATI hardware we have tested so far, including the Xbox 360, do not support PQA as they use half-resolution derivatives. The PlayStation 3 console, on the other hand, does support PQA since it uses an NVIDIA GPU, making PQA feasible for current console games. Since Direct3D 11 specifies two types of derivatives, PQA will likely be supported by all hardware that supports Shader Model 5. At the time of writing we do not have access to any Intel graphics cards and thus we do not know which form of derivative Intel graphics cards use.

To detect if message passing works on an arbitrary card, we draw a small `rect` with a custom shader and look at (or read back) the results. The custom shader sets a variable to four in only one quad pixel and zero otherwise. The result of calling `QuadAve()` on that variable will be one for all pixels if message passing worked and something else otherwise. This test is repeated for all quad pixels.

Bibliography

[Gruen 10] Holger Gruen. "Fast Conventional Shadow Filtering." In *GPU Pro: Advanced Rendering Techniques*, pp. 415–445. Natick, MA: A K Peters, 2010.

[Montrym et al. 97] J.S. Montrym, D.R. Baum, D.L. Dignam, and C.J. Migdal. "InfiniteReality: A Real-Time Graphics System." In *Proceedings of the 24th Annual Conference on Computer Graphics and Interactive Techniques, SIGGRAPH '97*, pp. 293–302. New York: ACM Press/Addison-Wesley Publishing Co., 1997.

[Nehab et al. 07] Diego Nehab, Pedro V. Sander, Jason Lawrence, Natalya Tatarchuk, and John R. Isidoro. "Accelerating Real-Time Shading with Reverse Reprojection Caching." In *ACM Siggraph/Eurographics Symposium on Graphics Hardware*, pp. 25–35. Aire-la-Ville, Switzerland: Eurographics Association, 2007.

[Olano et al. 03] Marc Olano, Bob Kuehne, and Maryann Simmons. "Automatic shader level of detail." In *ACM Siggraph/Eurographics Conference on Graphics Hardware*, pp. 7–14. Aire-la-Ville, Switzerland: Eurographics Association, 2003.

[Ren et al. 06] Zhong Ren, Rui Wang, John Snyder, Kun Zhou, Xinguo Liu, Bo Sun, Peter-Pike Sloan, Hujun Bao, Qunsheng Peng, and Baining Guo. "Real-Time Soft Shadows in Dynamic Scenes using Spherical Harmonic Exponentiation." *ACM Siggraph Transactions on Graphics* 25:3 (2006), 977–986.

[Sigg and Hadwiger 05] Christian Sigg and Markus Hadwiger. "Fast Third-Order Filtering." In *GPU Gems 2*, Chapter 20. Reading, MA: Addison-Wesley Professional, 2005.

[Tomasi and Manduchi 98] C. Tomasi and R. Manduchi. "Bilateral Filtering for Gray and Color Images." In *Proceedings of the Sixth International Conference on Computer Vision, ICCV '98*, pp. 839–. Washington, DC: IEEE Computer Society, 1998.

[Yang et al. 08] Lei Yang, Pedro V. Sander, and Jason Lawrence. "Geometry-Aware Framebuffer Level of Detail." 27:4 (2008), 1183–188.

[Zhu et al. 05] T. Zhu, R. Wang, and D. Luebke. "A GPU Accelerated Render Cache." In *Pacific Graphics*, 2005.

5

A Rendering Pipeline for Real-Time Crowds

Benjamín Hernández and Isaac Rudomin

In motion pictures, large crowds of computer-generated characters are usually included to produce battle scenes of epic proportions. In real-time strategy games, it is common to find crowds as armies controlled by users (or AI), or crowds made up of non-player characters (e.g., groups of spectators in a stadium). In virtual environments, it is common to find crowd simulations that interact with other characters and with their surrounding environment.

In all cases, optimizations such as level of detail and culling should be performed to render the crowds. In this chapter, we propose a parallel approach (implemented on the GPU) for level of detail selection and view-frustum culling, allowing us to render crowds made up of thousands of characters.

5.1   System Overview

Our rendering pipeline is outlined in Figure 5.1. First, all necessary initializations are performed on the CPU. These include loading information stored on disk (e.g., animation frames and polygonal meshes) and information generated as a preprocess (e.g., character positions) or in runtime (e.g., camera parameter updates). This information is used on the GPU to calculate the characters' new positions, do view-frustum culling, assign a specific level of detail (LOD) for each character and for level of detail sorting and character rendering. A brief description of each stage is given here.

- Populating the virtual environment and behavior. In these stages we specify the initial positions of all the characters, how they will move through the virtual environment, and how they will interact with each other. The result is a set of updated character positions.

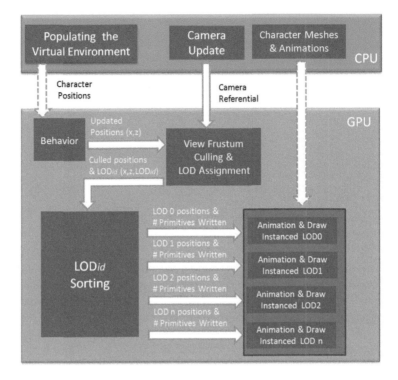

Figure 5.1. Rendering pipeline for crowd visualization. Dashed arrows correspond to data transferred from main memory to GPU memory only once at initialization.

- View-frustum culling and LOD Assignment. In this stage we use the characters' positions to identify those that will be culled. Additionally, we assign a proper LOD identifier to the characters' positions inside the view frustum according to their distance to the camera.

- LOD sorting. The output of the view-frustum culling and LOD assignment stage is a mixture of positions with different LODs. In the LOD sorting stage we sort each position, according to its LOD identifier, into appropriate buffers so that all the characters' positions in any one buffer have the same level of detail.

- Animation and draw instancing. In this stage we will use each sorted buffer to draw the appropriate LOD character mesh, using instancing. Instancing allows us to translate the characters across the virtual environment and add visual and geometrical variety to the individuals that form the crowd.

In the following sections, we will present a detailed description of how we implemented these stages.

5.2 Populating the Virtual Environment and Behavior

For simplicity, our virtual environment is a plane. It is parallel to the plane formed by the xz-axes. The initial positions of the characters are calculated randomly and stored into a texture.

For behavior, we implemented finite-state machines (FSMs) as fragment shaders. A FSM is used to update the characters' positions following [Rudomín et al. 05, Millán et al. 06], in which a character will consult the value of a labeled world map and follow a very simple FSM that causes it to move right until it reaches the right edge of the map, at which point the agent changes state and starts moving left until it gets to the left also ideal for this pipeline.[1]

Implementing FSM as fragment shaders needs three kinds of textures: a world-space texture, an agent texture, and an FSM-table texture. World-space textures encode values for each location in the virtual environment. This covers many types of maps: heightmaps, collision maps, interest area maps, or action maps. We consider these maps as maps labeled with some value on each pixel. Agent textures have a pixel for each character and encode the state s of the character and its position (x, z) in the world map. Finally, the finite state machine is represented as a texture where given a certain state of the character and a certain input, we can obtain a new state and position of the character following the basic algorithm shown in Listing 5.1.

```
given agent i
    state=agent[i].s; x=agent[i].x; z=agent[i].z;
    label=world[x,z];
    agent[i].s=fsm[state,label];
    agent[i].x += fsm[state,label].delta_x;
    agent[i].z += fsm[state,label].delta_z;
```

Listing 5.1. Basic algorithm to implement FSM as fragment shader.

5.3 View-Frustum Culling

View-frustum culling (VFC) consists of eliminating groups of objects outside the camera's view frustum. The common approach for VFC is to test the intersection between the objects and the six view-frustum planes using their plane equations to determine the visibility of each object. In our case, we implement a simpler

---

[1]The reason we recommend methods that use the GPU for behavior, in addition to the fact that these methods can simulate the behavior of tens of thousand characters efficiently, is that approaches using the GPU eliminate the overhead of transferring the new characters' positions between the CPU and and the GPU on every frame.

method called radar VFC [Puig Placeres 05]. Radar VFC is based on the camera's referential points. The method tests the objects for being in the view range or not, thus there is no need to calculate the six view-frustum plane equations.

On the other hand, objects tested against the view frustum are usually simplified using points or bounding volumes such as bounding boxes (oriented or axis-aligned) or spheres. In our case, we use points (the characters' positions) together with radar VFC to perform only three tests to determine the characters' visibility. In addition, to avoid the culling of characters that are partially inside the view frustum, we increase the view frustum size by Δ units[2] (Figure 5.2).

As mentioned earlier, radar VFC is based on camera referential points. In other words, the camera has a referential based on the three unit vectors $\hat{x}$, $\hat{y}$, and $\hat{z}$ as shown in Figure 5.3, where c is the position of the camera, n is the center of the near plane, and f is the center of the far plane.

The idea behind radar VFC is that once we have the character's position p to be tested against the view frustum, we find the coordinates of p in the referential and then use this information to find out if the point is inside or outside the view frustum.

The first step is to find the camera's referential. Let d be the camera's view direction, $\hat{u}$ the camera's up vector, then unit vectors $\hat{x}$, $\hat{y}$, and $\hat{z}$ that form the referential are calculated using Equations (5.1), (5.2), and (5.3).

$$\hat{z} = \frac{d}{\|d\|} = \frac{d}{\sqrt{d_x^2 + d_y^2 + d_z^2}} \tag{5.1}$$

$$\hat{x} = \frac{\hat{z} \otimes \hat{u}}{\|\hat{z} \otimes \hat{u}\|} \tag{5.2}$$

$$\hat{y} = \frac{\hat{x} \otimes \hat{z}}{\|\hat{x} \otimes \hat{z}\|} \tag{5.3}$$

Once we have calculated the referential, the next step is to compute the vector v that goes from the camera center c to the agent's position p using Equation (5.4):

$$v = p - c. \tag{5.4}$$

Next, the vector v is projected onto the camera referential, i.e., onto the $\hat{x}$, $\hat{y}$, and $\hat{z}$ unit vectors.

Radar VFC first tests vector v against $\hat{z}$; v is outside the view frustum if its projection $\text{proj}_{\hat{z}} v \notin (\text{ nearPlane, farPlane})$. Notice that the projection of a vector a into a unit vector $\hat{b}$ is given by the dot product of both vectors, i.e., $\text{proj}_{\hat{b}} a = a \cdot \hat{b}$.

If $\text{proj}_{\hat{z}} v \in [\text{nearPlane, farPlane}]$, then vector v is tested against $\hat{y}$; v will be outside the view frustum if its projection $\text{proj}_{\hat{y}} v \notin (-(h/2 + \Delta), h/2 + \Delta)$ interval,

---

[2]The value of Δ is obtained by visually adjusting the view frustum.

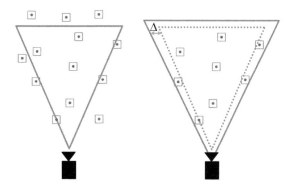

Figure 5.2. View-frustum culling.

where h is the height of the view frustum at position v and Δ is the value used to increase the view-frustum size as shown in Figure 5.2. The height h is calculated using Equation (5.5), where fov is the field-of-view angle:

$$h = \text{proj}_{\hat{z}} v \times 2 \times \tan \frac{\text{fov}}{2} : \text{fov} \in [0, 2\pi] \qquad (5.5)$$

If $\text{proj}_{\hat{y}} v \in (-(h/2 + \Delta), h/2 + \Delta)$, then vector v is tested against $\hat{x}$ (i.e., v is outside the view frustum if its projection $\text{proj}_{\hat{x}} v \notin (-(w/2 + \Delta), w/2 + \Delta)$ interval) where w is the width of the view frustum, given in Equation (5.6) and ratio is the aspect ratio value of the view frustum:

$$w = h \times \text{ratio} \qquad (5.6)$$

VFC and LOD assignment stages are performed using a geometry shader. This shader receives as input the agent texture that was updated in the behavior stage (Section 5.2), and it will emit the positions (x, z) which are inside the view

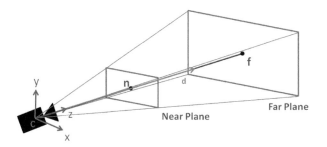

Figure 5.3. Camera's referential based on the three unit vectors x, y, and z.

frustum and a $\mathrm{LOD_{id}}$. The resultant triplets $(x, y, \mathrm{LOD_{id}})$ are stored in a vertex buffer object using the OpenGL transform feedback feature. Listing 5.2 shows the code that performs radar VFC in GLSL.

```
[vertex program]
void main(void)
{
    gl_TexCoord[0] = gl_MultitexCoord0;
    gl_Position = gl_Vertex;
}
[geometry program]
#define INSIDE   true
#define OUTSIDE false
uniform sampler2DRect position;
uniform float nearPlane, farPlane, tang, ratio, delta;
uniform vec3 camPos, X, Y, Z;

bool pointInFrustum(vec3 point)
{
    // calculating  v = p - c
    vec3 v = point - camPos;
    // calculating the projection of v into Z unit vector
    float pcz = dot(v,Z);


    // First test: test against Z unit vector
    if (pcz > farPlane || pcz < nearPlane)
        return OUTSIDE;

    // calculating the projection of v into Y unit vector
    float pcy = dot(v,Y);
    float h = pcz * tang;
    h = h + delta;

    // Second test: test against Y unit vector
    if (pcy > h || pcy < -h )
        return OUTSIDE;

    // calculating the projection of v into X unit vector
    float pcx = dot(v,X);
    float w = h * ratio;
    w = w + delta;

    // Third test: test against X unit vector
    if (pcx > w || pcx < - w )
        return OUTSIDE;

    return INSIDE;
}
```

```
void main(void)
{
    vec4 pos = texture2DRect(position,gl_TexCoordIn[0][0].st);
    if (pointInFrustum(pos.xyz))
    {
        gl_Position = pos;
        EmitVertex();
        EndPrimitive();
    }
}
```

Listing 5.2. Code for radar view frustum culling in GLSL.

5.3.1 Assigning Level of Detail

After determining which positions are inside the view frustum, the next step is to assign a LOD_{id} according to a given metric. In this case, we use discrete LOD^3 which consists of creating different LODs for each character as a preprocess. At runtime, the appropriate character's LOD is rendered using its LOD_{id}.

Metrics for assigning values to LOD_{id} can be based on distance to the camera, model size in screen space, eccentricity of the model with respect to the camera, or perceptual factors, among others. For performance and simplicity, we are using the distance to the camera as our metric; we also use visual perception to reduce the popping effect. The idea behind the distance to the camera metric is to select (or in our case, assign) the appropriate LOD based on the distance between the model and the viewpoint (i.e., coarser resolution for distant geometry). Nevertheless, instead of computing the Euclidean distance between the object and the viewpoint, we define the appropriate LOD as a function of the view range and the far plane. These values are obtained by the camera referential points.

The camera's view range is given by unit vector $\hat{z}$ and it is limited by the distance between the camera center, c, and the farPlane value. Thus, we test the projection of v onto $\hat{z}$ ($proj_{\hat{z}}v$), against different fixed intervals of the view range to assign a value to LOD_{id}.

A common approach for manually assigning values to LOD_{id} is using `if` statements as shown in Listing 5.3. Nevertheless, we can reduce GPU branching by eliminating the `if` statements and by using a sum of unit step functions instead (Equation (5.7)):

$$LOD_{id} = \sum_{i=0}^{n-1} U(proj_{\hat{z}}v - farPlane \times \tau_i) \tag{5.7}$$

---

[3]It has been shown in [Millán et al. 06] that 2D representations, such as impostors, make it possible to render tens of thousands of similar animated characters, but 2D-representation approaches need manual tuning and generate a huge amount of data if several animation sequences are present and/or geometrical variety is considered.

```
...
if projZv <= range0 then
    LODid = 0
else if projZv > range0 & projZv <= range1 then
    LODid = 1
else if projZv > range1 & projZv <= range2 then
    LODid = 2
...
```

Listing 5.3. Assigning $\mathrm{LOD_{id}}$ using **if** statements.

where n is the number of LOD meshes per character, $\tau_i \in (0,1)$, is a threshold that isotropically or anisotropically divides the view range visually calibrated to reduce popping effects and U is the unit step function given by:

$$U(t - t_0) = \left\{ \begin{array}{ll} 1 & \text{if } t \geq t_0, \\ 0 & \text{if } t < t_0. \end{array} \right.$$

Notice that if $n = 3$ (three LOD meshes per character), then $\mathrm{LOD_{id}}$ can receive three values, 0 when the characters are near the camera (full detail), 1 when the characters are at medium distances from the camera (medium detail) and 2 when the characters are at distances far from the camera (low detail).

Listing 5.4 shows the changes made in Listing 5.2 to add $\mathrm{LOD_{id}}$ calculation.

```
[geometry shader]
...
bool pointInFrustum(vec3 point, out float lod)
{
...
    // calculating the projection of v into Z unit vector
    float pcz = dot(v,Z);
...
    // For 3 LOD meshes:
    lod = step(farPlane*tao0, pcz) +
          step(farPlane*tao1, pcz) +
          step(farPlane*tao2, pcz);

    return INSIDE;
}

void main(void)
{
    float lod;
```

```
vec4 pos = texture2DRect(position,gl_TexCoordIn[0][0].st);
if (pointInFrustum(pos.xyz, lod))
{
    gl_Position = pos;
    gl_Position.w = lod;
    EmitVertex();
    EndPrimitive();
}
}
```

Listing 5.4. Assigning LOD_{id} using **step** functions.

5.4 Level of Detail Sorting

The result of the VFC and LOD assignment stage is that we have filled up a vertex buffer object (VBO) for all of the characters with positions inside the camera's view frustum. IBased on their distances to the camera, we have assigned a LOD_{id} for each position (Figure 5.4(a)). On the other hand, hardware instancing requires a single LOD mesh to draw several instances of the same mesh, thus we need to organize these positions according to their LOD_{id} in different VBOs.

Following [Park and Han 09], we will sort the output VBO from the VFC and LOD assignment stage into appropriate VBOs (that we will call $VBOs_{LOD}$) such that all of the characters' positions in a VBO have the same LOD_{id} (Figure 5.4(b)). Since we are using three LODs, we will use three VBOs.

In this case, we use transform feedback to populate each VBO_{LOD}. In total, we perform three transform feedback passes. In addition, transform feedback allows us to know how many primitives were written in each VBO_{LOD}. The number of primitives written will be used when calling the **Draw Instanced** routine.

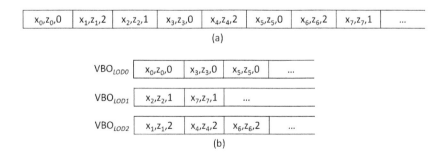

Figure 5.4. (a) Output VBO from VFC and LOD assignment stage. (b) Output of LOD sorting stage.

For each transform feedback pass, a geometry shader will emit only the vertices of the same LOD_{id}. This is shown in Listing 5.5. Notice that the uniform variable lod is updated each pass. In our case it will be set to 0 for a full-resolution mesh, 1 for a medium-resolution mesh, and 2 for a low-resolution mesh.

```
[geometry shader]
uniform float lod; // this variable is updated each pass
void main ()
{
    vec4 pos = gl_PositionIn[0];
    if ( lod == pos.w  )
    {
        gl_Position =  pos;
        EmitVertex();
        EndPrimitive();
    }
}
```

Listing 5.5. Geometry shader used to populate each VBO_{LOD}.

Figure 5.5 shows the output of this stage and the VFC and LOD assignment stage. The characters' positions are rendered as points. We have assigned a specific color for each VBO_{LOD}. In this case, red was assigned to VBO_{LOD0}, green to VBO_{LOD1}, and blue to VBO_{LOD2}.

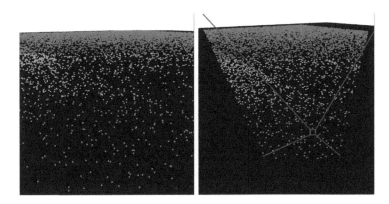

Figure 5.5. Output of LOD sorting stage, 4096 characters rendered as points. LOD0 is shown in red, LOD1 in green, and LOD2 in blue. Main camera view (left). Auxiliary camera view; notice that only positions inside the view frustum are visible (right).

5.5   Animation and Draw Instanced

As a preprocess, we load all of the character meshes and textures that will form
the crowd. We also define several character groups according to their geometrical
appearance. Animation is performed with a technique that reuses a character's
"rig" on the other characters of the group. With this method, the animation sequence is stored in a texture array in which each layer stores an animation frame.
Animation frames specify the rotation angles of the character's joints. These angles are used to pose a character, and by interpolating them, we perform character
animation totally on the GPU. However, approaches such as AniTextures [Bah-
nassi 06] and skinned instancing [Dudash 07] can be used as an alternative.

   At runtime, for each character group, we render the high-resolution instances
first using the positions stored in VBO_LOD0 to world-transform each instance;
then we render the medium-resolution instances using VBO_LOD1, and finally
the low-resolution instances using VBO_LOD2. In each call, we use the function glDrawElementsInstanced available in OpenGL. This function generates
a unique instance value called gl_InstanceId, which is accessible in a vertex
shader and t is used as an index to access the instance's specific position, animation frame, and its visual characteristics.

5.6   Results

We designed two tests to verify the performance of our pipeline. These tests were
performed on Windows Vista using an NVIDIA 9800GX2 card with SLI-disabled
and a viewport size of 900×900 pixels.

   The goal of the first test is to determine the execution time of the behavior, VFC and LOD assignments, and LOD sorting stages.[4] The goal of the
second test is to determine the execution time of the complete pipeline. The
first test consisted of incrementing the number of characters from 1K to 1M,
each character with three LODs. Timing information was obtained using timer
queries (GL_EXT_timer_query) which provides a mechanism used to determine
the amount of time (in nanoseconds) it takes to fully complete a set of OpenGL
commands without stalling the rendering pipeline.

   Results of this test are shown in the graph in Figure 5.6 (timing values are
in milliseconds). In addition, Figure 5.5 shows a rendering snapshot for 4096
characters rendered as points. Notice that the elapsed time for VFC and LOD
assignments and LOD sorting stages remains almost constant. When performing
transform feedback, we do not need any subsequent pipeline stages, thus rasterization is disabled.

   The second test consists of rendering a crowd of different characters. Each
character has three LODs, the character's LOD0 mesh is made of 2500 vertices,

---

[4]We do not provide the execution time of the animation and draw instanced stage, since
timing results are bigger by several orders of magnitude.

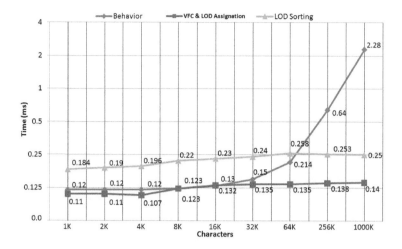

Figure 5.6. Test 1 results. Notice that timing results are in milliseconds.

the LOD1 mesh 1000 and LOD2 300. The goal of this test is to determine the execution time of all the stages of our pipeline using two different camera perspectives. In Perspective A (Figure 5.7), almost all characters are visible, while in Perspective B (Figure 5.8) almost all characters are culled.

Figure 5.7. Perspective A (8192 characters). Most of the characters are visible.

Figure 5.8. Perspective B (8192 characters). Most of the characters are culled.

Agents	t $\times 10^{-3}$	LOD0	LOD1	LOD2	Vertices $\times 10^{6}$	Visible %	Culled %
1024	47.62	274	644	54	1.35	95	5
2048	62.11	365	688	397	1.70	71	29
4096	95.60	450	1388	943	2.80	68	32
8192	159.24	483	1438	5085	4.17	86	14
12288	194.93	400	1905	7694	5.21	81	19
16384	261.78	476	2477	10388	6.78	81	19

Table 5.1. Results obtained in Perspective A.

Agents	t $\times 10^{-3}$	LOD0	LOD1	LOD2	Vertices $\times 10^{6}$	Visible %	Culled %
1024	19.49	161	0	0	0.40	16	84
2048	22.91	204	0	0	0.51	10	90
4096	49.33	412	314	0	1.34	18	82
8192	57.77	503	317	0	1.60	10	90
12288	72.99	471	995	0	2.20	12	88
16384	97.18	541	1546	0	2.90	13	87

Table 5.2. Results obtained in Perspective B.

These results are shown in Table 5.1 for Perspective A, and in Table 5.2 for Perspective B. The first column of both tables shows the number of rendered characters, the second one shows the time, in milliseconds, measured for each case. Columns three to five show how many characters per level of detail are rendered, and column six shows the total number of vertices, in millions, transformed by our animation shader. Finally, the last two columns show the percentage of characters that are visible or culled.

5.7 Conclusions and Future Work

We have shown that optimization techniques such as view-frustum culling and LOD selection in the GPU result in a very small time penalty. In our practical case, the stage that took more time to execute was animation and draw instanced, which was to be expected. Moreover, extra memory requirements do not exceed the amount needed to store a 32-bit floating texture of 512×512 pixels (i.e., for sixteen thousand characters we needed to allocate four floating-point vertex-buffer objects of 128×128, one auxiliary vertex-buffer object to store partial results obtained from the VFC and LOD assignment stage, and three vertex buffers to store the positions of each level of detail.)

However, performance results can be improved and memory requirements can be reduced by using the new OpenGL 4.0 characteristic called "multiple transform feedback," contained in the `ARB_transform_feedback3`, `ARB_gpu_shader5` and `NV_gpu_program5` extensions, which allows geometry shaders to direct each vertex arbitrarily to a specified vertex stream. Therefore, we will require only one transform feedback call for LOD_{id} sorting, and by combining the VFC and LOD assignment and LOD sorting stages we could dispense with the auxiliary vertex-buffer object used to store partial results obtained from the VFC and LOD assignment stage.

This pipeline can be extended by adding an occlusion-culling stage. Complex scenes such as those in which crowds are needed or those where landscapes are depicted with indigenous vegetation, human elements, buildings and structures can be enhanced. One approach is to perform occlusion culling via OpenGL occlusion queries. Nevertheless, the number of queries needed might not be enough for complex scenes made up of hundreds of thousands of elements. In addition, it requires synchronizing the CPU and the GPU, which might stall the pipeline. Another approach is to put extra cameras in the positions of big structures and perform radar view frustum culling (using the normalized version of the view frustum) and then take the complement of the visible set. This stage can be performed after the behavior stage and before the VFC and LOD assigment stage.

5.8   Acknowledgments

We wish to thank NVIDIA for its kind donation of the GPU used in the experiments.

Bibliography

[Bahnassi 06] Wessam Bahnassi. "AniTextures." In *ShaderX*[4]: *Advanced Rendering Techniques*. Hingham, MA: Charles River Media, 2006.

[Dudash 07] B. Dudash. *Skinned Instancing*. NVIDIA Technical Report, 2007.

[Millán et al. 06] Erik Millán, Benjamín Hernández, and Isaac Rudomín. "Large Crowds of Autonomous Animated Characters using Fragment Shaders and Level of Detail." In *ShaderX*[5]: *Advanced Rendering Techniques*. Higham, MA: Charles River Media, 2006.

[Park and Han 09] Hunki Park and Junghyun Han. "Fast Rendering of Large Crowds Using GPU." In *ICEC '08: Proceedings of the 7th International Conference on Entertainment Computing*, pp. 197–202. Berlin, Heidelberg: Springer-Verlag, 2009.

[Puig Placeres 05] Frank Puig Placeres. "Improved Frustum Culling." In *Game Programming Gems V*. Hingham, MA: Charles River Media, Inc., 2005.

[Rudomín et al. 05] Isaac Rudomín, Erik Millán, and Benjamín Hernández. "Fragment shaders for agent animation using Finite State Machines." *Simulation Modelling Practice and Theory* 13:8 (2005), 741–751.

6

Z^3 Culling
Pascal Gautron, Jean-Eudes Marvie, and Gaël Sourimant

6.1 Introduction

Virtual worlds feature increasing geometric and shading complexities, resulting in a constant need for effective solutions to avoid rendering objects invisible for the viewer. This observation is particularly true in the context of real-time rendering of highly occluded environments such as urban areas, landscapes, or indoor scenes.

Figure 6.1. In highly occluded scenes many fragments potentially cover a single pixel of the final image. Each of those fragments being shaded before getting eventually discarded by depth testing, this overlap results in a waste of computational power.

In those cases, even though many elements of the scene are occluded, the visibility tests are performed on the output of the shading stage. Complex shading is then evaluated for fragments that are eventually discarded by the depth tests (Figure 6.1).

This problem has been intensively researched in the past decades, resulting in numerous optimizations building upon the well-known Z-buffer technique. Among them, extensions of graphics hardware such as early-Z culling [Morein 00] efficiently avoid shading most of the invisible fragments. The only drawback of this technique is its reduced applicability range: early-Z culling is disabled if the fragment shader discards fragments or modifies their depth values, or if alpha testing is enabled [Nvidia 08]. While easily usable with simple shaders, more complex and costly shading techniques such as relief mapping [Policarpo and Oliveira 06] cannot benefit from such optimization. The principle of the programmable culling unit [Hasselgren and Akenine-Möller 07] solves this problem by introducing a specific programmable culling stage in the graphics pipeline. However, this stage is not yet embedded within current graphics hardware.

We introduce Z^3 culling for fast and programmable per-pixel visibility at the fragment-shading stage using alternate render buffers containing color and depth information. This method effectively avoids shading hidden fragments in a single pass, hence reducing the overall rendering costs while not introducing limitations

Figure 6.2. The overlapped fragments (shown in red) can be efficiently detected and discarded before shading, using Z^3 culling for increased performance. Unlike the early-Z culling approach, Z^3 culling is independent from shading operations, typically supporting programmable fragment discard and alteration of fragment depth, as well as alpha testing in this example.

on shader operations (Figure 6.2). Z^3 culling is also complementary with the existing culling stages of graphics hardware and could be easily integrated as an additional stage of the graphics pipeline.

6.2 Principle

Z^3 culling is a simple method for early detection of occluded fragments within the fragment shader. A first issue is the access to the occluder geometry: such detection requires the fragment shader to determine its own visibility compared to the rest of the scene. While the visibility is usually solved using the Z-buffer algorithm, most graphics APIs forbid binding the current depth buffer as a texture for use in the fragment shader.

We solve this problem using alternate render buffers: when rendering into a given buffer, depth information regarding previously rendered fragments is available in another buffer. The visibility of the fragments can then be evaluated efficiently using simple, cache-friendly texture fetches. We amortize the cost of swapping the render buffers by rendering object batches whose size can be adapted by real-time performance analysis.

Another key for the efficiency of the algorithm is the availability of relevant depth information: a reliable visibility information for a given fragment can be obtained only if all the potentially occluding geometry had been previously rendered. Based on this observation the object batches are ordered to optimize the occlusion detection.

6.3 Algorithm

The overall principle of Z^3 culling is illustrated in Figure 6.3. After allocating two RGBA buffers B_1 and B_2, B_2 is chosen as the current render target and B_1 is the source for existing color and depth. As shown in Algorithm 6.1, a batch of objects is rendered into B_2. For each fragment, the algorithm fetches the existing depth value stored in B_1 corresponding to the current location of the fragment. As B_1 is empty for this first batch, each fragment of the batch gets shaded: the resulting color and depth are stored into one RGBA value, in which the alpha channel encodes the depth of the fragment.

Then, B_1 becomes the current render target while B_2 holds the existing depth information. During the rendering of a second batch, the depths of the fragments are tested against the values stored in B_2: if the existing depth is smaller than the depth of the current fragment the fragment is not shaded, hence reducing the rendering time. The buffers are then swapped again for each object batch.

As buffers B_1 and B_2 only contain parts of the final image, the buffers are merged by selecting the pixels with the lowest depth value. Section 6.4 contains technical details for the implementation of Z^3 culling.

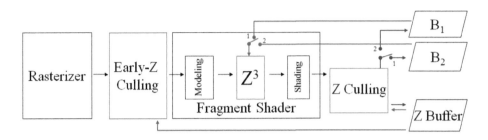

Figure 6.3. Z^3 culling is an additional, programmable depth-culling step at the fragment-shader stage. While rendering into B_2, the culling is performed using the partial depth information available in B_1 (Step 1). The buffers B_1 and B_2 are then swapped, hence maintaining information in both buffers (Step 2).

6.4 Implementation

Based on the high-level description of Z^3 culling presented in Algorithm 6.1, this section provides technical insights regarding buffer allocation and binding, splitting of the scene into batches, programmable culling, and buffer merging.

6.4.1 Framebuffer Setup and Binding

As current graphics APIs do not generally allow using the same memory area for both reading and writing, Z^3 culling considers two render buffers: a "read" buffer B_1 containing the closest previously rendered fragments, and a "write" buffer B_2 receiving the currently rendered fragments. Each of those buffers contain color information as well as depth values for each pixel: the combined color and depth information can be stored within a single floating-point RGBA buffer, where the alpha channel encodes the depth of the closest fragment.

Compared to a classical frame-buffer setup, this technique only introduces two additional render buffers, while keeping the classical color and Z-buffer untouched. Once the buffers are created, the read/write alternation can be performed by rendering the potentially visible objects as a set of batches: we first bind B_1 as the current render target and render a first object batch. Then, B_2 is bound as the render target while B_1 gets bound as a texture to serve as the source for previous fragment information. The second batch is then rendered, and the process is repeated for every batch of potentially visible objects.

At the end of the rendering of a frame, each render buffer contains a subset of the pixels of the final image. Each pixel contains both color and depth information. The final image is then obtained by combining B_1 and B_2, keeping only the closest pixels. To this end a screen-covering quad is rendered into the framebuffer, and a fragment shader outputs the pixels corresponding to the low-

Initialization:
Create render buffers $B1$ and $B2$

Main loop:
for each frame **do**
   readBuffer = $B1$
   writeBuffer = $B2$
   for all object batch b **do**
      Bind writeBuffer as the render target and readBuffer as a texture[1]
      for all object o ∈ b **do**
         for all fragment covered by o **do**
            // Compute fragment depth
            d_{cur} = fragmentDepth(...)
            // Fetch the depth of the closest existing fragment
            d_{ref} = readBuffer[fragmentCoord].a)
            // Compare current and reference depths
            if $d_{cur} < d_{ref}$ **then**
               // Shade current fragment and output its depth
               writeBuffer[fragmentCoord].rgb = shade(...)
               writeBuffer[fragmentCoord].a = d_{cur}
            else
               // Abort fragment shading
            end if
         end for
      end for
      swap(writeBuffer, readBuffer)
   end for
   finalImage = combine(writeBuffer, readBuffer)
end for

Algorithm 6.1. Z^3 culling.

est depth values (Listing 6.1[2]). Note that the fragment shader not only outputs the color of the pixels, but also their depth. This enforces the consistency of the depth buffer, hence allowing Z^3 culling to be used in conjunction with other rendering strategies. For example, opaque objects can be rendered using Z^3 culling, and transparent objects may be rendered with the classical back-to-front sorting, using the same depth buffer for visibility determination.

While the goal of the algorithm is the avoidance of overlapping fragments, objects within a given batch may overlap. In this case all the fragments of the

---

[1]The binding is typically performed using **glFramebufferTexture2D** and **glBindTexture** calls in OpenGL.
[2]The shader pseudocode follows the GLSL syntax.

```
uniform sampler2D B1, B2;

void main()
{
  // Fetch the color and depth information in each buffer
  vec4 colDepth1 = texture2D(colorDepth1, fragmentCoord);
  vec4 colDepth2 = texture2D(colorDepth2, fragmentCoord);

  // Compare the depths of each pixel of B1 and B2
  // and output depth and color of the closest pixel
  if ( colDepth1.a <= colDepth2.a)
  {
    gl_FragColor = vec4(colDepth1.rgb, 1.0);
    gl_FragDepth = colDepth1.a;
  }
  else
  {
    gl_FragColor = vec4(colDepth2.rgb, 1.0);
    gl_FragDepth = colDepth2.a;
  }
}
```

Listing 6.1. Combination of both render buffers to obtain the final image.

batch are rendered, relying on the classical depth test to determine the closest fragment after shading. The conservativeness of Z³ culling is then ensured at the cost of some unnecessary computations for intra-batch visibility.

6.4.2 Depth Batching

As for early-Z culling, the basis of Z³ culling is the knowledge of the depth of previously rendered fragments. Therefore, object ordering is as important as for early-Z culling. In a worst case scenario, the objects are rendered from back to front: in this case the current fragment is always closer to the viewpoint than the previously rendered fragments, hence preventing early culling.

In the spirit of early-Z culling, the object batches are roughly sorted from front to back to avoid this scenario. This is typically achieved by fast sorting of the bounding boxes of the objects. Besides the gain of culling efficiency, in many scenes objects with similar depths tend to be spread over image space (Figure 6.4). This observation subtends another performance increase: the more pixels are covered by a batch, the more information is available for culling the fragments of further batches.

Once the set of potentially visible objects has been divided into depth-sorted batches, the batches can be efficiently rendered into alternate render buffers using Z³-enabled fragment shaders (see Figure 6.5).

Original scene

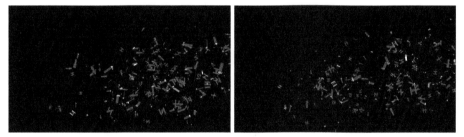

Batch 1   Batch 2

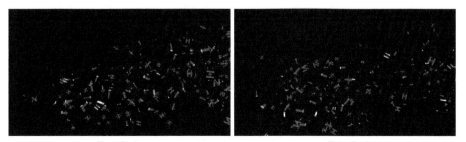

Batch 3   Batch 4

Figure 6.4. The use of depth batching groups the objects with similar depths, reducing the overall amount of overlaps while spreading the rendered objects over large parts of the image space.

Figure 6.5. Once the object batches have been rendered using buffer alternation, approximately half of the rendered pixels is contained in each buffer, while the Z-buffer contains the depth information for the entire scene (top). The final image is obtained by compositing B_1 and B_2, keeping only the closest pixels (bottom).

6.4.3 Programmable Culling

Culling information is obtained using a simple texture fetch within the source for previous fragment information. Listing 6.2 provides a trivial implementation of the classical early-Z culling using Z^3 culling.

```
uniform sampler2D readBuffer;

void main()
{
    // Fetch previous depth information
    float refDepth = texture2D(readBuffer, fragmentCoord).a;
    float fragDepth = gl_FragCoord.z;

    // Compare current and previous depths
    if (fragDepth > refDepth )
    {
        // If occluded, discard the fragment
        discard;
    }
    else
    {
        // Otherwise perform shading
        gl_FragColor.rgb = shade(...);
        // and output the fragment depth in the alpha channel
        gl_FragColor.a = fragDepth;
    }
}
```

Listing 6.2. Naïve implementation of early-Z using Z^3 culling.

This example raises an important observation: a fragment determined as occluded is discarded, thus not generating any data in the framebuffer. However, the main principle of Z^3 culling is to populate both render buffers to allow for efficient visibility culling. A discard operation thus corresponds to a missed opportunity to add relevant information into the current render buffer. More precisely, let us consider the example depicted in Figure 6.6: An object O_1 is rendered into B_1, and an object O_2 is rendered into B_2. A fragment of O_2 occluded by O_1 is then discarded, leaving the corresponding location in B_2 empty. Then,

```
// Compare current and previous depths
if (fragDepth > refDepth )
{
    // If occluded, replicate the reference
    gl_FragColor = refFragment;
    gl_FragDepth = refDepth;
}
else
{
    // Otherwise perform shading
    gl_FragColor.rgb = shade(...);
    // and output the fragment depth in the alpha channel
    gl_FragColor.a = fragDepth;
}
```

Listing 6.3. Optimized early-Z using Z^3 culling with fragment replication.

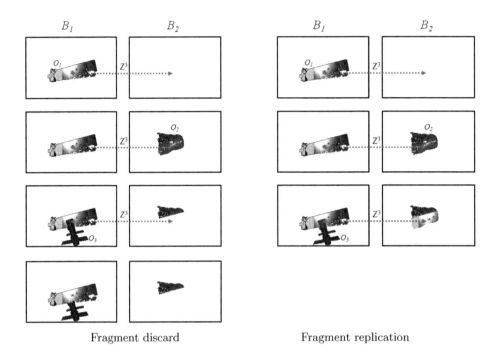

Fragment discard   Fragment replication

Figure 6.6. The information generated by rendering an object O_1 into a buffer B_1 (left, top row) is used to discard fragments of O_2 subsequently rendered into B_2 (left, second row, in red). When rendering O_3 into B_1, no information is available in B_2. The fragments of O_3 are then rendered (left, third row) and discarded after shading using the Z-buffer (left, bottom row). Replacing the fragments of the occludee O_2 by the fragments of the occluder O_1 propagates depth information across render buffers and avoids unnecessary shading of O_3 (right).

a fragment of an object O_3 rendered into B_1 is occluded by O_1. Due to the lack of information in B_2, Z^3 culling cannot detect the occlusion. The visibility test is then performed after shading using the classical Z-buffer.

To overcome this problem the discard operation can be advantageously replaced by a simple copy of the reference color and depth information. Relevant visibility is then propagated across buffers at virtually no cost, increasing the overall performance of the algorithm. In addition, the discard operation tends to introduce non-negligible costs into fragment shading, even on recent graphics hardware. Avoiding this call further reduces the execution time of the shader. Listing 6.3 provides the comparison and shading part of the implementation of early-Z culling.

Note that the culling and fragment replication can be performed at any stage of the shader to allow for fine performance tuning. For example, a shader con-

```
// Compare current and previous depths
if (fragDepth > refDepth )
{
    // If occluded, replicate the reference
    gl_FragColor = refFragment;
    gl_FragDepth = refDepth;
}
else
{
    // Otherwise compute alpha value
    float alpha = evalAlpha();
    // and perform Z3-friendly alpha test
    if (alpha < alphaThreshold)
    {
      gl_FragColor = refFragment;
      gl_FragDepth = refDepth;
    }
    else
    {
      // Evaluate costly shading if needed
      gl_FragColor.rgb = shade(...);
      // and output the fragment depth in the alpha channel
      gl_FragColor.a = fragDepth;
    }
}
```

Listing 6.4. Z^3 culling with optimized alpha test.

taining complex alpha evaluation for alpha testing as well as complex shading may contain several exit paths (Listing 6.4).

Note that in this case the built-in alpha test is disabled to take full advantage of Z^3 culling within the fragment shader: if the fragment does not pass the test, the shader propagates the fragment information from the reference buffer. In this regard Z^3 culling takes particular advantage of situations where early-Z culling cannot be applied, making those approaches complementary.

More complex shaders can make further use of this technique. For example, a shape-altering algorithm such as relief mapping can perform culling at several stages to avoid unnecessary computations.

6.5 Performance Analysis

Z^3 culling has been implemented within fragment shaders using an Nvidia GeForce GTX480. The presented scenes contains 15 K and 70 K objects featuring complex, early-Z unfriendly fragment shaders. The images are rendered into floating-point render buffers with a resolution of 1280×720. Compared to classical Z-buffering, Z^3 culling provides performance increases of 8 to 50% using batches of 50 objects (Table 6.1), while remaining applicable in any context.

Scene	# triangles	# objects	Z	Early-Z	Z³
Forest	70M	50K	90 ms	N/A ms	44.5 ms
Asteroids	35M	15K	215 ms	N/A ms	198 ms

Table 6.1. Render time comparisons between regular post-shading depth test and Z^3 culling (50 objects per batch). Due to the complexity of the shaders, early-Z culling is not applicable in this case.

The Z^3 culling technique provides significant speedups by introducing an alternation of render buffers as well as an early detection of occlusions within the fragment shader. In the remainder of this section, we analyze the costs of those operations and compare our technique with the built-in early-Z culling.

The alternation of render buffers described in our technique may generate pipeline stalls: rendering a batch into a buffer requires finishing all the previous operations on the reference buffer. In our test scenes the average cost of buffer swapping is around 25 μs per swap, typically representing an overhead of 5 ms (2.5%) per frame in the Asteroids scene with batches of 50 objects. We amortize the cost by adjusting the size of the object batches. This size can be adjusted either manually or automatically using a simple convergence based on the render time of the last frame. While the overhead does not completely vanish, the savings due to Z^3 culling remain significant, especially in scenes containing many objects. However, note that on certain platforms the use of a render target as a texture requires a "resolve" operation copying the contents of the render target into the texture. The cost of this operation must be taken into consideration while implementing our technique on such platforms.

Another overhead is the additional branching within the fragment shader: as shown in the above listings, the behavior of any shader using Z^3 culling depends on a depth test. This branching does introduce a cost, however this cost must be compared to the complexity of the shaders. In particular, Z^3 culling performs better on scenes containing very complex shaders, which typically also involve branching. This makes our approach complementary with early-Z culling: simple, nonbranching shaders without alpha testing or depth modification take full benefit of the built-in culling technique. Conversely, the rendering of objects featuring more complex shaders can be drastically optimized by Z^3 culling. In this regard, outputting the depth of the selected fragments at the end of rendering (Listing 6.1) proves particularly useful: simply-shaded objects can be rendered using classical techniques and combined with more complex shaders whose visibility is evaluated using Z^3 culling.

The analysis of the performance of Z^3 culling also requires a comparison with early-Z culling. However, as mentioned above, the test scenes shown in this chapter feature shaders containing instructions not compliant with early-Z culling.

Scene	# triangles	# objects	Z	Early-Z	Z^3
Forest	70M	50K	88 ms	18 ms	42 ms
Asteroids	35M	15K	214 ms	135 ms	195 ms

Table 6.2. Degrading the shaders by removing the instructions incompatible with early-Z culling makes the final image unusable, as this process alters the appearance of the objects. However, this table provides a comparison of the rendering times for classical depth testing, early-Z culling, and Z^3 culling. The values confirm the high efficiency of the hard-wired early-Z culling for simple shaders. Both culling methods are then complementary depending on the type of shaders used in the scene.

To provide a fair comparison we degraded the shaders to avoid such instructions. While the final image gets altered and non-usable, Table 6.2 provides an informative analysis of the performance of early-Z culling and Z^3 culling. As expected the built-in early-Z culling outperforms Z^3 culling when the shading remains simple, making those approaches complementary: simply-shaded objects can be rendered using early-Z culling, while more complex shaders can leverage Z^3 culling for higher efficiency.

Another aspect of this technique is the potential false negatives in the occlusion detection: for a given fragment, the expensive shading step is carried out only if the fragment is determined as visible. However, the available visibility information is inherently approximate as each of the additional buffers holds only a part of the rendered fragments. Consequently, some fragments may be erroneously considered as visible. As for the intra-batch occlusion, this results in some unnecessary computations but ensures the conservativeness of our visibility algorithm. Note that this solution does not introduce artifacts, as the occluded fragments eventually get discarded after shading by classical depth testing.

6.6 Conclusion

This chapter introduced Z^3 culling for simple and programmable elimination of occluded fragments before shading. Based on an alternation of render buffers, this technique provides significant performance increases especially in highly occluded scenes containing numerous objects with complex shading. We believe further performance could be achieved by implementing Z^3 culling in an additional stage in future graphics hardware for programmable fragment elimination, potentially taking advantage of the hierarchical representation of depth buffers.

Bibliography

[Hasselgren and Akenine-Möller 07] Jon Hasselgren and Tomas Akenine-Möller. "PCU: The Programmable Culling Unit." *SIGGRAPH '07, Transactions on Graphics* 26:3 (2007), 92.

[Morein 00] S. Morein. "ATI Radeon Hyper-Z Technology." Hot3D Proceedings (talk), ACM SIGGRAPH/Eurographics Workshop on Graphics Hardware, 2000.

[Nvidia 08] Nvidia. "GPU Programming Guide Version for GeForce 8 and Later GPUs." http://developer.download.nvidia.com/GPU_Programming_Guide/GPU_Programming_Guide_G80.pdf, 2008.

[Policarpo and Oliveira 06] Fabio Policarpo and Manuel M. Oliveira. "Relief Mapping of Non-Height-Field Surface Details." In *ACM SIGGRAPH Symposium on Interactive 3D Graphics and Games*, pp. 55–62. New York: ACM Press, 2006.

7

A Quaternion-Based Rendering Pipeline
Dzmitry Malyshau

7.1 Introduction

A matrix is the first thing every graphics developer faces when building an engine. It is a standard data object for representing 3D affine and projection transformations—covering most of the game developer's needs. Matrix operations have even been implemented in hardware used by a 3D graphics API like OpenGL. However, this is not the only way to represent transformations.

Quaternions were introduced by Sir William Rowan Hamilton in the middle of the nineteenth century, at a time when vector analysis did not exist. A quaternion is a hypercomplex 4D number of the form: $w + xi + yj + zk$. There are rules for quaternion multiplication, inversion, and normalization. Quaternions can effectively represent spatial rotations, by applying them to 3D vectors or when converted into 3×3 rotation matrices.

This chapter aims to explain pitfalls and advantages of the quaternion approach for graphics pipelines. There are many articles describing quaternion mathematics, such as [Void 03] and [Gruber 00], which we will not cover here, assuming that the reader is familiar with the basics. We will describe the KRI Engine (see [Malyshau 10a]) as a sample implementation of a complete quaternion-based rendering pipeline.

7.2 Spatial Data

Spatial transformation data combine *rotation*, *position*, and *scale*. Let's compare the most popular representation (i.e., a homogeneous matrix) with a new representation based on a quaternion (see Table 7.1).

We can conclude that quaternion representation is much more complex with regard to transformations in shaders, the manual perspective transform, and other

Type	Matrix	Quaternion (fixed handedness)
struct Spatial (*1)	mat3 rotation_scale; vec3 position;	quaternion rotation; vec3 position; float scale;
vectors to store (four-component)	three	two
understanding difficulty	easy	medium
interpolation flexibility (*2)	low	high
combining transforms cost	high	medium
applying transforms cost	low	medium
hardware support (*3)	high	medium
non-uniform scale support	yes	no
perspective transform	can be added easily, resulting in mat4	manual only

*1. Hereafter we use GLSL types (vec3,vec4,mat3,mat4,etc.).
*2. For the quaternion approach, you can use spherical linear interpolation (SLERP) or use dual-quaternion representation with little to no difficulty.
*3. Currently, there is no shading language with direct support of quaternions operations.
The only exception is the normalization operator, which uses a fast built-in function for vec4. However, other operations are easily written via traditional built-in cross and dot vector products (see quat_v.glsl).

Table 7.1. Comparison of homogeneous matrix versus quaternion transformation.

issues, but that it provides definite benefits like interpolation flexibility and more efficient storage, which are critical for dynamic graphics scenes.

7.3 Handedness Bit

One of the major differences between rotation matrices and quaternions is the handedness property. Matrices operate freely between right-handed and left-handed coordinate systems. Quaternions do not have this property (always preserving the given handedness upon transformation), so we need to define the corresponding matrix handedness globally and store the actual value together with the quaternion itself. For an orthonormal matrix M, handedness is equal to the determinant and computed as follows:

$$H = \text{Handedness}(M) = \det(M) = ((\text{Row}(0, M) \times \text{Row}(1, M)) \cdot \text{Row}(2, M)).$$
$$(7.1)$$

The handedness of an orthonormal matrix can be either $+1$, in which case it is right-handed, or -1, in which case it is left-handed. Assuming we defined quaternions to correspond to right-handed matrices with regard to the vector rotation, we can implement the matrix conversion routines as well as the direct point transformation by a quaternion. Rotation matrix handedness is usually fixed in 3D editors (this applies to Blender and 3DsMax), so our initial assumption is not an issue. However, when a matrix is constructed from arbitrary basis vectors (e.g., tangent space), its handedness can also be arbitrary—and that is a problem.

The issue can be resolved by adding a bit of information to the quaternion: the handedness bit. The algorithm for the matrix processing in the quaternion approach is given in Algorithm 7.1.

1. Given basis vectors, construct matrix M

2. Calculate handedness H, using Equation (7.1)

3. We have to make sure that M is right-handed before converting it to a quaternion. In order to achieve this we are going to multiply the first row of the matrix by the scalar H: Row(0,M) = Row(0,M) * H. This would not change the right-handed matrix (H == 1), but it would flip the handedness of a left-handed one (H == −1)

4. Transform to quaternion, Q = Quaternion(M)

5. Store (Q,H), instead of a matrix M

6. V'T(V) = Rotate(Q,V) * (H,1,1), negating x-coordinate of the transformation vertex V'

Algorithm 7.1. Calculating and applying the handedness bit.

We give here some example Blender API Python code that converts a tangent space into the quaternion:

```
bitangent = normal.cross(tangent.normalized())     # derive the bitangent from the mean
                                                   # tangent and a normal
bitangent *= vertex.face.handedness                # compensate for the opposite handedness
tangent = bitangent.cross(normal)                  # orthogonalize the tangent, defer
                                                   # handedness multiplication to the
                                                   # shader
tbn = mathutils.Matrix((tangent,bitangent,normal)) # composing ortho-normal right-handed
                                                   # tangent space matrix
vertex.quaternion = tbn.to_quaternion().normalized() # obtain the quaternion representing
                                                   # the vertex tangent space
```

7.4 Facts about Quaternions

Here we address some facts and myths about quaternions in an attempt to correct the common misunderstandings of their pros and cons and to provide needed information for using quaternions.

7.4.1 Gimbal Lock

According to Wikipedia, gimbal lock is the loss of one degree of freedom in a three-dimensional space that occurs when the axes of two of the three gimbals are driven into a parallel configuration, "locking" the system into rotation in a degenerate two-dimensional space. Gimbal lock is an attribute of the Euler angle representation of the rotation. Contrary to what some people believe, gimbal lock has nothing to do with either matrices or quaternions.

7.4.2 Unique State

There are always two quaternions (−Q, component-wise negative) that produce exactly the same rotation, thus representing the same state.

7.4.3 No Slerp in Hardware

Graphics hardware can linearly interpolate values passed from the vertex geometry into the fragment shader. One may conclude that quaternions should not be
interpolated this way, because spherical linear interpolation is the only correct
way to do that.

In fact, after normalizing the interpolated quaternion in the fragment shader
we get normalized Lerp (or Nlerp), which is very close to Slerp. According to
[Blow 04] it follows the same minimal curve; it just does not keep the constant
velocity. So for 3D meshes, it is perfectly fine to use hardware for interpolation
of quaternions.

It's important to note that Nlerp produces a larger error, the larger the angle
is between quaternions as four-component vectors. While this may seem to be a
problem, in fact the error is just four degrees for a 90-degree angle, according to
calculations by [Kavan et. al 06]. In practice, we need this HW interpolation for
vertex data, and your rendered mesh is not going to look smooth anyway if its
normals differ by more than 90 degrees on a single face.

7.4.4 Hypercomplex Four-Dimensional Number

You don't need to know the complete mathematical background of quaternions in
order to use them. Knowledge of the following operations is sufficient for graphics
developers: inversion, multiplication, interpolation, and applying rotation to a
vector.

The GLSL code for a sample rotation application is given below:

```
vec3 qrot(vec4 q, vec3 v) {
    return v + 2.0*cross(q.xyz, cross(q.xyz,v) + q.w*v);
}
```

7.5 Tangent Space

Tangent space is an orthonormal coordinate system of a surface point, constructed
from the tangent, bi-tangent, and normal. It is used for normal mapping as the
basis for normals stored in the texture. Object-space normal maps suffer from
reduced reusability across different meshes (and mesh parts—for texture tiling) in
comparison to tangent-space normal maps. The latter also support skinning and
morphing of the object that is normal-mapped; the only requirement is not to
miss the tangent space while processing the vertex position. Quaternions are very
effective for representing the tangent space. We will show this by comparing the
traditional pipeline (via a tangent-space matrix, also known as TBN—an acronym
for tangent, bi-tangent, normal) with a new pipeline based on quaternions.

7.5.1   TBN Pipeline

A 3D modeling program may provide both normal and tangent vectors, or just
a normal vector for exporting. In the latter case, your engine has to generate
tangents based on UV coordinates (exactly those used for normal mapping): in
this case, the tangent is calculated as a surface parametrization following the
orientation of the U-axis of the UV. Each vertex stores both normal and tangent
resulting in two vectors or six floats.

In the case of direct Phong lighting calculations, we just need to transform
a few vectors into the tangent space (namely the light vector and the view/half
vector). Then, the GPU pipeline interpolates them between vertices. We evaluate
the lighting using these two vectors and a surface normal fetched from a map.
The tangent space matrix is constructed by simply crossing the normal with the
tangent (their length and orthogonality can be ensured by the engine):

```
mat3 tbn = mat3(Tangent, cross(Normal,Tangent) ,Normal);
```

But there are scenarios where you need to interpolate the basis itself, for
example to store it in textures for particles or hair to be generated from it afterwards. First, if you need to store the basis, it will occupy two textures, seriously
affecting the storage requirements. Second, interpolated basis vectors are neither
orthogonal (in general) nor do they have unit lengths. The construction of the
TBN matrix is more costly in this case:

```
in vec3 Normal,Tangent;
vec3 n = normalize(Normal);
vec3 t = normalize(Tangent);
vec3 b = cross(n, t);
t = cross(b,n); //enforce orthogonality
mat3 tbn = mat3(t,b,n);
```

7.5.2   Quaternion Pipeline

The TBN matrix can be replaced by the pair: (quaternion, handedness). Each
vertex stores a single quaternion and a handedness bit: This requires 1+ vectors
or four floats and one bit. For example, the KRI engine stores handedness in the
`Position.w` component, supplying an additional quaternion as `vec4` for TBN.

Note that the normal is no longer needed—only the quaternion is provided by
the exporter and expected to be present for the renderer. This change introduces
a difficulty for the handling of objects with no UV coordinates, because we can't
compute either tangents or quaternions for them. Hence, it will be impossible to
compute even regular Phong lighting in contrast with the traditional approach
where the normal vector is always available. This limitation can be alleviated
by making all objects UV-mapped before exporting. Another solution is to have
a hybrid pipeline that switches between quaternion-rich and normal-only inputs,
but the implementation of such a dual pipeline is complex.

For direct Phong lighting calculations, we rotate vectors by our quaternion and apply the handedness bit as described in Algorithm 7.1. Computation-wise, it is not much more costly than the matrix pipeline, especially taking into account the general low cost of vertex shader computations (assuming that the number of fragments processed is significantly greater than the number of vertices, which should be the case for a properly designed engine).

In a more complex scenario, as in deferred lighting calculation, or baking the world-space surface basis into UV textures, the quaternion approach shows its full power. Storing the surface orientation requires only one texture (if you supply handedness in the position). Interpolation of the quaternion requires a special one-time condition to be met (an algorithm to accomplish this is presented below). At runtime an interpolated quaternion requires just a single normalization call:

```
in vec4 Orientation;
vec4 quat = normalize(Orientation);
```

Note that it is possible to not keep handedness as a vertex attribute (and pass it as a uniform instead) if one decides to split the mesh into two, each part containing all faces of the same handedness. In this case we would need to draw two meshes instead of one for each mesh consisting of faces with different handedness. This would save us a single floating-point operation in vertex attributes, but it would almost double the number of draw calls in a scene.

We can therefore conclude that quaternions require special handling: additional common routines in shaders, an additional preparation stage in the exporter (see Algorithm 7.2), and correct handedness application. But if they are handled properly, quaternions significantly reduce the bandwidth utilization and storage requirements. In advanced scenarios, they are extremely cheap computation-wise, compared to matrices.

7.6   Interpolation Problem with Quaternions

The interpolation problem originates from the fact that Q and −Q represent exactly the same orientation (Q is any quaternion). Hence, by interpolating between the same orientation represented with different signs, we produce a range of quaternions covering the hypersphere instead of just a constant value. In practice, this means that in a fragment shader the quaternion interpolated between vertex orientations will, in general, be incorrect.

The solution for this problem is a special preprocessing technique on the mesh, performed during the export stage. The technique ensures that dot(Q1,Q2)>=0 for each two orientations of vertices in the triangle, forcing all vertices of the triangle to be in the same four-dimensional hemisphere. The algorithm for processing each triangle is given in (Algorithm 7.2).

let Negative pair = a vertex pair, whose quaternions produce a negative dot product.
let N = number of negative pairs in the current triangle.
to Negate quaternion = multiply all its components by −1.
if N==0: OK, exit
if N==2: clone the common vertex (between two given negative pairs), negate the cloned quaternion; go to N==0 case
if N==3: clone any vertex, negating the quaternion; go to N==1 case
if N==1: divide the edge between a negative pair by inserting a vertex in the middle with attributes averaged from the pair (including quaternion); go to N==0 case.

Algorithm 7.2. Triangle preprocessing that guarantees correct quaternion interpolation.

As you can see, this procedure duplicates some vertices and even creates some faces. This doesn't look good at first, because we don't want to complicate meshes for drawing. However, the actual number of vertices added is quite small. For example, the test 10 K vertex mesh gains only 7.5% additional vertices and 0.14% additional faces.

While interpolation with quaternions is a complicated process, a solution is available preprocessing the data as described in Algorithm 7.2. Additionally, you may not need to interpolate the TBN of the vertices at all. For Phong lighting, for example, you can interpolate the light and camera vectors in tangent space. Interpolation of TBN quaternions (aside from being handy) is needed when lighting and normal extraction are separated (as for deferred techniques). When using this algorithm, the handedness becomes a property of a face as well as a property of a vertex, because each face now links vertices of the same handedness.

7.7 KRI Engine: An Example Application

The KRI engine's rendering pipeline works in the OpenGL 3 core context and does not contain matrices, but instead uses quaternions for both spatial transformations and tangent spaces.

7.7.1 Export

The exporter from Blender is written in Python. It computes a (normal, tangent) pair for each vertex, producing a (quaternion, handedness) pair. A special stage (Algorithm 7.2) duplicates a small number of vertices and faces in order to ensure the correct quaternion interpolation for the rendering. Transformation matrices for each spatial node are also converted into (quaternion, position, scale) form, ensuring uniform scale and uniform handedness across the scene.

7.7.2   Storage

Tangent space for vertices (as a quaternion) is stored as a `float vec4` attribute, and the handedness occupies the `Position.W` component. Spatial data uses the (quaternion, position, scale) form and is passed to the GL context as two vectors.

7.7.3   Skinning

Vertex data is skinned in a separate stage using transform feedback. Bone transformations are interpolated (on the CPU) and weighted (on the GPU) using a dual-quaternion representation (this is optional). Smaller spatial structure size allows the passing of 50% more bones in the shader uniform storage.

7.7.4   Render

A special GLSL object file (`quat_v.glsl`) is attached to each program before linking. It contains useful quaternion transformation functions that are missing from the GLSL specification. There are render components that use forward and deferred Phong lighting, as well as surface baking into UV textures (e.g., emitting particles/hair from the mesh surface, as used in [Malyshau 10b]).

An example of typical vertex transformation GLSL code (excluding projection) is given here:

```
uniform struct Spatial  {
    vec4 pos, rot;     // camera->world and model->world transforms
}s_cam, s_model;
// vertex attributes of position and quaternion
in vec4 at_vertex, at_quat;
// forward transform of a vertex (from quat_v.glsl)
vec3 trans_for(vec3,Spatial);
// inverse transform of a vertex (from quat_v.glsl)
vec3 trans_inv(vec3,Spatial);
. . .
vec3 v_world = trans_for(at_vertex.xyz, s_model); // world-space position
vec3 v_cam = trans_inv(v_world, s_cam);   // camera-space position
```

7.8   Conclusion

The OpenGL 3 core / ES 2.0 pipeline no longer pushes the programmer to use matrices. In this chapter, we showed some advantages of using quaternions and pointed out the complexities associated with them. We also used the KRI engine as a proof-of-concept for the idea of using quaternions as a full-scale matrix replacement in a real-world game engine scenario. We believe that quaternions will have a future much brighter than their past.

Bibliography

[Banks 94] Dadid C. Banks. "Illumination in Diverse Codimensions." In *Proceedings of SIGGRAPH '94, Computer Graphics Proceedings*. Annual Conference Series, edited by Andrew Glassner, pp. 327–334, New York: ACM Press, 1994.

[Blow 04] Jonathan Blow. "Understanding Slerp, Then Not Using It." *The Inner Product*. Available at http://number-none.com/product, Apr 2004.

[Gruber 00] Diana Gruber. "Do We Really Need Quaternions?" Game Dev.net. Available at http://www.gamedev.net/page/resources/_/do-we-really-need-quaternions-r1199, Sept 2000.

[Hast 05] Anders Hast. "Shading by Quaternion Interpolation." In WSCG (Short Papers), 53–56, 2005. Available at http://wscg.zcu.cz/wscg2005/Papers_2005/Short/B61-full.pdf.

[Kavan et. al 06] Ladislav Kavan, Steven Collins, Carol O'Sullivan, and Jiri Zara. "Dual Quaternions for Rigid Transformation Blending." Technical report TCD-CS-2006-46, Trinity College, Dublin, 2006.

[Malyshau 10a] Dzmitry Malyshau. "Quaternions." *KRI Engine*. Available at http://code.google.com/p/kri/wiki/Quaternions, 2010.

[Malyshau 10b] Dzmitry Malyshau. "Real-Time Dynamic Fur on the GPU." GameDev.net. Available at http://www.gamedev.net/page/resources/_//feature/fprogramming/real-time-dynamic-fur-on-the-gpu-r2774, Oct 2010.

[McMahon 03] Joe McMahon. "A (Mostly) Linear Algebraic Introduction to Quaternions." Program in Applied Mathematics, University of Arizona, Fall 2003.

[Svarovsky 00] J. Svarovsky. "Quaternions for Game Programming." In *Game Programming Gems*, edited by Mark DeLoura, pp. 195–299. Hingham, MA: Charles River Media, 2000.

[Void 03] Sobeit Void. "Quaternion Powers." GameDev.net. Available at http://www.gamedev.net/page/resources/_/reference/programming/math-and-physics/quaternions/quaternion-powers-r1095, Feb 2003.

8

Implementing a Directionally Adaptive Edge AA Filter Using DirectX 11
Matthew Johnson

8.1 Introduction

With the advent of DirectX 10 and beyond, more and more features are being offloaded from fixed-function hardware to programmable shaders. Until recently, the lack of flexible access to the sample information in antialiased (AA) buffers required developers to rely on fixed-function hardware filtering to convert these buffers to single-sample representations. Now, with access to sample information, developers seek even higher quality results with the same memory footprint. This allows the creation of new techniques to balance the performance and quality of the rendered images being generated.

This chapter describes a postprocessing AA technique, directionally adaptive edge antialiasing, based on the paper by [Iourcha et al. 09]. In this technique, the sample information is used to calculate a best-fit gradient line along the direction of candidate primitive edges to construct a filter that gives a better representation of edge information in the scene.

8.1.1 Standard Multisampling

Unlike supersampling, multisampling occurs at pixel (not sample) frequency for color samples, using the coverage information at discrete sample points to resolve[1] to a single sample texture. In the center of a triangle where the scan converter is rendering an interior pixel, there is no image quality advantage with multisampling aside from the texture filtering/interpolation. At primitive edges,

---

[1]The process of taking a buffer with multiple samples per pixel and generating a buffer with a single sample per pixel is defined as *resolving* the buffer.

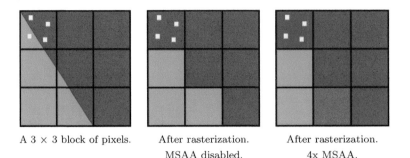

A 3 × 3 block of pixels.   After rasterization.   After rasterization.
                                   MSAA disabled.   4x MSAA.

Figure 8.1. A 3 × 3 region of pixels.

however, the hardware has access to the neighboring samples as well as coverage information. The standard resolve operation will blend the color value of every sample in a pixel using a simple box filter.

The performance win in multisampling is not necessarily in memory (a multisampled surface at 4x MSAA can be four times the size), but in performance. Ideally (unlike supersampling), there is no need to execute the pixel shader more than once per pixel.

When multisampling is disabled, any pixel center inside a triangle is drawn. This is shown in Figure 8.1. When multisampling is enabled, if one or more samples are covered by the triangle, then the pixel shader is executed once and the resultant color is replicated for all covered pixels. In Direct3D 10.1 and above, a pixel shader can also run at sample rate; however, this feature is orthogonal to adaptive edge AA.

As shown in Figure 8.1, the 4x MSAA sample pattern in the upper left pixel shows three out of four samples that are covered (e.g., an edge pixel). A simple box filter resolve will calculate the final pixel color as

$$\frac{3 \times \text{red} + 1 \times \text{blue}}{4}. \tag{8.1}$$

Although the box filter is sufficient in many cases, it is not a panacea: the box filter resolve utilizes no information about neighboring samples to determine an even closer estimate of the actual slope of the primitive edge being rendered. With additional information, an even better antialiasing filter can be constructed.

8.1.2 Directionally Adaptive Edge Multisampling

As demonstrated in Equation (8.1), a simple box filter only averages the samples available to it in each individual pixel. This limitation is especially noticeable at steep edges or low-frequency data, in which the gradual changes in gradient between adjacent pixels can be lost. In the example of one red and one blue tri-

Red	Blue
0%	100%
25%	75%
50%	50%
75%	25%
100%	0%

Table 8.1. Color permutations in Figure 8.1 (4x MSAA).

angle being rendered, Table 8.1 shows that the number of unique color gradations along the edge is limited by the total sample count.

An alternative AA filter is called *directionally adaptive edge antialiasing*. The key difference is that instead of evaluating a simple box filter, it evaluates an edge filter by finding a best-fit "gradient" vector perpendicular to the triangle edge.

Figure 8.2 visualizes a close-up of a triangle edge rasterized with no AA, with 4x MSAA, and with adaptive edge AA. The quality improvement with directionally adaptive AA is more pronounced on longer, straighter edges. Along the triangle edge, the color value is the average of red and blue. Perpendicular to the edge, the color value varies smoothly between solid red and solid blue.

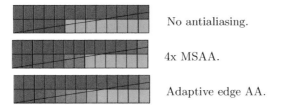

No antialiasing.

4x MSAA.

Adaptive edge AA.

Figure 8.2. Close-up of triangle edge rasterization.

8.1.3 Adaptive Edge Equation

Iourcha, Yang, and Pomianowski constructed an approximation equation for the estimated color value $f(v)$ of any sample position by taking into account the slope of the triangle edge and a "gradient" perpendicular to the triangle edge [Iourcha et al. 09]:

$$f(v) \approx \tilde{f}(\vec{g} \cdot v) = C_1(\vec{g} \cdot v) + C_0, \tag{8.2}$$

where $v, \vec{g} = [x, y] \in \mathbb{R}_2$, constants $C_0, C_1 = [\text{red}, \text{green}, \text{blue}] \in \mathbb{R}_3$, and $\tilde{f}$ is an approximation function that inputs a scalar and returns a color. The gradient $\vec{g}$ is a 2D vector and is perpendicular to the rasterized triangle edge. Although not a true gradient, this vector points in the direction of the color gradation. Position v is any arbitrary 2D pixel or sample coordinate on the Cartesian grid.

This approximation equation allows us to estimate the color of any sample position in a given pixel, instead of the set of sample colors bounded by the MSAA sample count.

To solve for $\tilde{f}$ in this equation, it is necessary to find the gradient vector. For easier calculation, Equation (8.2) is centered by substituting $v_i = v_i - \bar{v}$ and $f(v_i) = f(v_i) - \overline{f(v)}$ such that

$$\sum_{i=0}^{n} v_i = 0 \quad \text{and} \quad \sum_{i=0}^{n} f(v_i) = 0,$$

where n is the number of color samples, v_i is the raster sample position (x, y), $\bar{v}$ is the mean of all sample positions, and $\overline{f(v)}$ is the mean of all color samples. Then $C_0 = 0$ and C_1 is a constant relative to the original C_0. Because the gradient is a vector and vectors are directionally invariant to translation, this is a valid substitution. Now, Equation (8.2) can be solved by finding the least squares fit,

$$F = \sum_{i=0}^{n} ||C_1(\vec{g} \cdot v_i) - f(v_i)||^2. \tag{8.3}$$

To solve this least squares fit, treat it like a vector minimization problem in calculus by solving for the derivative of F and setting each component equal to 0. Because this is a vector-valued function, that gives us $[\text{red}, \text{green}, \text{blue}]^{T}$ color values, the partial derivative of each color component is set to 0. Because $f(v_i)$ and v_i are centered, $C_0 = 0$ and Equation (8.2) becomes

$$f(v) \approx \tilde{f}(\vec{g} \cdot v) = C_1(\vec{g} \cdot v).$$

Let F be the sum of the least square difference between color value $f(v_i)$ and $f(\vec{g} \cdot v)$:

$$F = \sum_{i=0}^{n} ||\tilde{f}(\vec{g} \cdot v_i) - f(v_i)||^2. \tag{8.4}$$

The easiest way to evaluate this equation is to examine each component separately. Focus on the red component (subscript r):

$$f(v)_r \approx \tilde{f}(\vec{g} \cdot v)_r = \text{red}(\vec{g} \cdot v),$$

because the red component of C_1 is scalar r. Equation (8.4) becomes

$$F(r) = \sum_{i=0}^{n} (\tilde{f}(\vec{g} \cdot v_i)_r - f(v_i)_r)^2$$

$$= \sum_{i=o}^{n} (r(\vec{g} \cdot v_i) - f(v_i)_r)^2,$$

and

$$\frac{dF(r)}{dr} = \sum_{i=0}^{n} 2(\text{red}(\vec{g} \cdot v_i) - f(v_i)_{\text{r}})(\vec{g} \cdot v_i)$$

$$= 2 \text{ red} \sum_{i=0}^{n} (\vec{g} \cdot v_i)^2 - 2 \sum_{i=0}^{n} f(v_i)_{\text{r}}(\vec{g} \cdot v_i).$$

Solving for the minimum by setting $dF(r)/dr = 0$ and then solving for the red component gives

$$\text{red} = \frac{\sum\limits_{i=0}^{n} f(v_i)_{\text{r}}(\vec{g} \cdot v_i)}{\sum\limits_{i=0}^{n} (\vec{g} \cdot v_i)^2}.$$

This is also done for the other two color components. Solving for C_1 yields

$$C_1 = \begin{bmatrix} \text{red} \\ \text{green} \\ \text{blue} \end{bmatrix} = \frac{1}{\sum\limits_{i=0}^{n} (\vec{g} \cdot v_i)^2} \begin{bmatrix} \sum\limits_{i=0}^{n} f(v_i)_{\text{r}}(\vec{g} \cdot v_i) \\ \sum\limits_{i=0}^{n} f(v_i)_{\text{g}}(\vec{g} \cdot v_i) \\ \sum\limits_{i=0}^{n} f(v_i)_{\text{b}}(\vec{g} \cdot v_i) \end{bmatrix}$$

$$= \frac{\sum\limits_{i=0}^{n} f(v_i)(\vec{g} \cdot v_i)}{\sum\limits_{i=0}^{n} (\vec{g} \cdot v_i)^2}. \tag{8.5}$$

Substituting Equation (8.5) into Equation (8.3) gives us the function to minimize. Expanding Equation (8.3) by using the vector form of the law of cosines and simplifying gives[2]

$$\sum_{i=0}^{n} \|f(v_i)\|^2 = \frac{\left\| \sum\limits_{i=0}^{n} f(v_i)(\vec{g} \cdot v_i) \right\|^2}{\sum\limits_{i=0}^{n} (\vec{g} \cdot v_i)^2}. \tag{8.6}$$

Because the first sum is constant, only the second term should be maximized (giving us the minimum value because this term is negative):

$$\frac{\sum\limits_{i=0}^{n} \|f(v_i)\|^2 (\vec{g} \cdot v_i)^2}{\sum\limits_{i=0}^{n} (\vec{g} \cdot v_i)^2}. \tag{8.7}$$

---

[2]The derivation for this substitution is given in the appendix (Section 8.4).

The expression in Equation (8.7) is the ratio of two positive quadratic forms of $\vec{g}$,

$$\frac{\mathbf{A}\vec{g} \cdot \vec{g}}{\mathbf{B}\vec{g} \cdot \vec{g}},$$

where

$$\mathbf{A} = \mathbf{C}^{\mathrm{T}}\mathbf{C},$$

$$\mathbf{C} = \sum_{i=0}^{n} f(v_i){v_i}^{\mathrm{T}} = \sum_{i=0}^{n} \begin{bmatrix} R_i \\ G_i \\ B_i \end{bmatrix} \begin{bmatrix} x_i & y_i \end{bmatrix},$$

$$\mathbf{B} = \sum_{i=0}^{n} v_i {v_i}^{\mathrm{T}} = \sum_{i=0}^{n} \begin{bmatrix} x_i \\ y_i \end{bmatrix} \begin{bmatrix} x_i & y_i \end{bmatrix}. \tag{8.8}$$

The vectors are column vectors.

Because each sample position in the set is centered, matrix $\mathbf{B}$ is a 2×2 matrix with a similar construct as a covariance matrix. If the sample positions in the sample pattern are constant relative to every pixel, it can be precalculated. If they are taken at integer pixel locations only, e.g.,

$$\begin{bmatrix} 0 \\ 0 \end{bmatrix}, \begin{bmatrix} \pm 1 \\ 0 \end{bmatrix}, \begin{bmatrix} 0 \\ \pm 1 \end{bmatrix}, \begin{bmatrix} \pm 1 \\ \pm 1 \end{bmatrix},$$

then $\mathbf{B}$ is $s\mathbf{I}$, where s is the distance in pixels from the center pixel. In the case of a 3×3 block of pixels, $s = 14$; hence,

$$\mathbf{B} = \mathbf{I} = \begin{bmatrix} 1 & 0 \\ 0 & 1 \end{bmatrix}.$$

Using a 3×3 pixel region is sufficient to calculate the gradient with reasonable speed and accuracy. Thus, it is only necessary to solve for $\mathbf{A}$. Because each sample position and color value is centered, matrix $\mathbf{A}$ is a 2×2 matrix with a similar construct as a covariance matrix. The value $\mathbf{A}\vec{g} \cdot \vec{g}$ is maximized when the resultant vector is parallel to $\vec{g}$. This occurs when $\mathbf{A}\vec{g} = \lambda\vec{g}$, where λ is an arbitrary scalar factor, turning it into an eigenproblem.

Let

$$\mathbf{A} = \begin{bmatrix} a & b \\ c & d \end{bmatrix};$$

then, solving for the characteristic equation, we have

$$\det \begin{bmatrix} a - \lambda & b \\ c & d - \lambda \end{bmatrix} = (a - \lambda)(d - \lambda) - bc$$

$$= \lambda^2 - (a + d)\lambda + (ad + bc). \tag{8.9}$$

Thus there are two solutions for the eigenvalues:

$$\lambda = \frac{a+d}{2} \pm \frac{\sqrt{4bc + (a-d)^2}}{2}.$$

With this matrix, we are interested only in the largest eigenvalue (the positive term), because its corresponding eigenvector is in the direction of the gradient. Solve for the eigenvector:

$$(\mathbf{A} - \lambda\mathbf{I})\vec{g} = 0, \quad \vec{g} \neq [0,0,0]^{\mathrm{T}}.$$

So $(\mathbf{A} - \lambda\mathbf{I})$ is singular. Within some application-defined epsilon, if $c \neq 0$, then

$$\vec{g} = \begin{bmatrix} \lambda - d \\ c \end{bmatrix};$$

else if $b \neq 0$, then

$$\vec{g} = \begin{bmatrix} b \\ \lambda - a \end{bmatrix}.$$

If both $b = c = 0$, the matrix is already diagonalized and $\vec{g}$ is any arbitrary 2D vector and should therefore be masked out. This occurs when the discriminate in Equation (8.9) is close to or equals 0.

8.1.4   Edge Pixels

Identifying edge pixels using an MSAA buffer is relatively simple. In DirectX 10 and beyond, you can iterate through all the samples and see if any of the sample color values differ; if they do, it is an edge pixel. This works pretty well, but because of texture coordinate extrapolation or precision issues the rasterizer may calculate a slightly different sample color on the same pixel for each triangle rendered that shares the same primitive edge. One way to filter out these small differences is to use an epsilon as shown in Listing 8.1.

```
bool compareSample(float3 c0, float3 c1)
{
    static const float eps = 0.001f;

    float3 d = abs(c0 - c1);

    return (d.r > eps) || (d.g > eps) || (d.b > eps);
}

float4 PS_EDGE_DETECT(VS_OUTPUT In) : SV_Target
{
    float width;
    float height;
    float sampleCount;
```

```
tMs.GetDimensions(width, height, sampleCount);

uint2 e;
e.x = In.TexCoord.x * width;
e.y = In.TexCoord.y * height;

bool edgePixel = false;

float3 c[4];
c[0] = tMs.Load(e, 0);
c[1] = tMs.Load(e, 1);
c[2] = tMs.Load(e, 2);
c[3] = tMs.Load(e, 3);

if (compareSample(c[0], c[1]) ||
    compareSample(c[1], c[2]) ||
    compareSample(c[2], c[3]))
{
    edgePixel = true;
}

if (edgePixel == false)
{
    discard;
}

return float4(1.0f, 1.0f, 1.0f, 1.0f);
}
```

Listing 8.1. Detecting edge pixels with 4x MSAA.

Another way to check is to use centroid sampling and check SV_Position in the pixel shader (which is in screen space). If the position has shifted from the center, it is an edge pixel. In DirectX 11 you can also check SV_Coverage as input to the PS and verify that the mask is unequal to (1 << sampleCount) - 1. In the case of 4x MSAA, a pixel is an edge pixel if the coverage is not equal to 0xF. Unfortunately, while both of these techniques are valid, they will also pick up interior triangle edges as well (though the threshold pass may be able to filter these out).

8.1.5 Masking

Knowing the edge pixels from the previous pass, further pixels can be eliminated from processing by comparing every pixel in the scene by a set of masking patterns.

As shown in Figure 8.3, every center pixel can be validated against a set of 3×3 sample pattern masks to ensure that the pixel lies across a flat or diagonal edge that can be processed by this filter. If it does not match any of these patterns, then filtering is skipped and a standard resolve is used instead; for example, if the center pixel is the only edge pixel, the algorithm skips this pixel because it does not belong to a "dominate" edge [Iourcha et al. 09]. With DirectCompute,

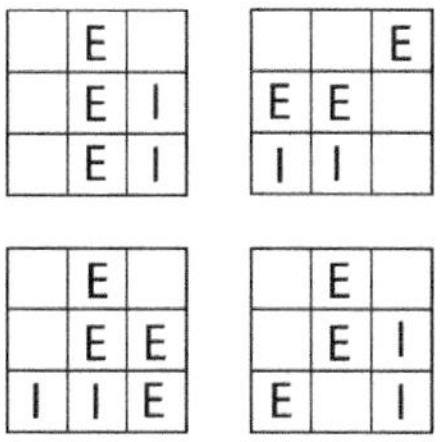

	E					E
	E	I		E	E	
	E	I		I	I	

	E				E	
	E	E			E	I
I	I	E		E		I

Figure 8.3. Sample masking patterns: E = edge pixel, I = interior pixel.

many of these passes can be combined. This will be discussed in the DirectX 11 implementation in Section 8.2.

8.1.6 Thresholding

Isolines are paths on a graph along which a particular value is constant. In this paper, the term is overloaded to include paths along edges of the image identified by the edge detect pass. Because this is a linear approximation filter, the best results are obtained when the isoline is flat and not curved.

To detect this scenario and eliminate further pixels, it is necessary to implement thresholding. The benefits of thresholding include that it

- speeds up postprocessing by focusing only on edges that will see quality improvements using the adaptive edge filter,

- avoids excessive blurring of corner features in the image,

- tweaks the amount that can be tweaked on a per-app basis.

For thresholding, we need to exclude pixels in which the curvature is too high. For the target pixel grids that benefit from this filter, simply use the standard MSAA resolve. Assuming v_i and $f(v_i)$ are centered, the difference between the actual color value and the estimated color value at a sample position (relative to our edge equation) is

$$\delta(v_i) = f(v_i) - C_1(\vec{g} \cdot v_i).$$

Because $\delta(v_i)$ is a vector, we want to calculate the total threshold as a magnitude of all these differences:

$$\sum_{i=0}^{n} ||\delta(v_i)|| = \sum_{i=0}^{n} ||f(v_i) - C_1(\vec{g} \cdot v_i)||. \tag{8.10}$$

Equation (8.10) can be solved by a simpler approximation. For example, it is easier to experimentally derive a threshold value across all pixels that look good for a particular application [Iourcha et al. 09]:

$$\frac{\sum\limits_{i=0}^{n} ||\delta(v_i)||^2}{\sum\limits_{i=0}^{n} ||f(v_i)||^2} \leq \text{threshold}^2, \tag{8.11}$$

where a pixel is rejected if Equation (8.11) is greater than the squared threshold.

8.1.7 Final Pixel Color

When you are calculating the final color, it is not necessary to actually solve for C_0 or C_1. Instead, for every pixel color, several samples are weighted among a 3×3 pixel grid, as shown in Figure 8.4.

To find this weight value for every sample position v_i, the procedure in Figure 8.4 constructs a line along the orthogonal of the gradient (the isoline) that intersects each sample position in the dashed rectangle in Figure 8.4. This rectangle is inscribed in the pixel region, aligns with the slope of the line, and bounds a set of sample positions that we are interested in weighting. Note that along this line, the color value does not change (because $(\vec{g} \cdot v_i) = 0$ and only C_0 remains), so the sample weight is influenced only by the slope of the line, not the distance between the sample position and the center pixel.

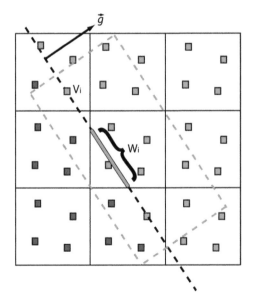

Figure 8.4. Sample weights along each isoline.

Finally, clip this line along the pixel boundaries. The length of this clipped line is the weight value. For every sample i, the weight is calculated as

$$w_i = ||(v_i + t_i \vec{g}_\perp||,$$

where n is the total number of color samples used for the approximation, v_i is the sample position in the inscribed rectangle, and $t_i = [t_{\min}, t_{\max}]$ are the floating-point minimum and maximum intersection values after the isoline is clipped to the center pixel boundary. These weight values are not normalized and may be greater than 1, so it is necessary to normalize the final color by the sum of all the weights:

$$\text{color} = \frac{\sum_{i=0}^{n} w_i f(v_i)}{\sum_{i=0}^{n} w_i}.$$

Every color sample k yields a unique clipped isoline, so $t_{\min}$ and $t_{\max}$ vary per sample. Weighting each color sample by the length of each clipped isoline acts as an integration model to yield the final pixel color [Iourcha et al. 09].

8.2 Implementation

8.2.1 DirectX 10 Implementation

The original paper by Iourcha, Yang, and Pomianowski describes a multipass approach that is useful for a DirectX 10 implementation [Iourcha et al. 09]. The following full-scene passes are described:

1. Identify edge pixels using MSAA buffer. Seed framebuffer by performing standard resolve.

2. Mask out candidate pixels using edge patterns.

3. Compute edge gradients for all masked pixels. Perform thresholding to further eliminate pixels.

4. Calculate the final framebuffer color as described in Section 8.1.7. Reading from the original MSAA surface, weight every sample color value in a 3×3 pixel grid for each candidate pixel.

8.2.2 DirectX 11 Implementation

According to [Thibieroz and Cebenoyan 10], compute shaders should target pixel shaders with a heavy texture or ALU bottlenecks. Because this algorithm is heavy on both, this is a potential candidate for compute shader optimizations.

As always, experimentation is needed to determine which path has the highest performance depending on the target platform. Dividing the full screen into 8×8 pixel blocks allows for the execution of 64 threads in parallel; this is the maximum number of threads per wavefront on current ATI hardware:

```
pDevice11->Dispatch(backBufferWidth/8, backBufferHeight/8, 1);
```

The following Compute Shader 5.0 pass is proposed:

1. Ensure the swap chain was created with DXGI_USAGE_UNORDERED_ACCESS bind flags. Seed by performing a standard resolve.

2. In the compute shader, create group shared memory to cache an 8×8 block of pixels, including room for border pixels outside the immediate block as shown in Listing 8.2.

```
struct Pixel
{
    float3  color[MsaaCount];
    bool    isEdgePixel;
};

groupshared Pixel pixelBlock[8+w][8+h];

[numthreads(8, 8, 1)]

void CSMain(uint2 blockIndex  : SV_GroupThreadID,
            uint2 pixelIndex  : SV_DispatchThreadId)
{

...

}
```

Listing 8.2. Shared memory for caching pixel blocks.

3. For a 3×3 pixel block, we only need a border of one pixel on each boundary side, so $w = h = 2$. To reduce thread-group shared memory (TGSM) in Shader Model 5.0, you can also pack colors in uint instead of float4 and pack edge pixel bitmasks (1 bit per pixel) in uint instead of bool, at the expense of more ALU operations. For example, you would need to use InterlockedAnd to clear the correct bitmask and InterlockedOr to set only the packed part; however, this could cause contention if multiple threads are operating atomically on the same shared memory location.

4. For each compute thread,

    (a) populate the color array with all the colors from the MSAA texture color,

    (b) compute whether the pixel is an edge pixel and store it in `isEdgePixel`.

5. Issue a `GroupMemoryBarrierWithGroupSync` to ensure all prior thread work has completed.

6. Mask out the candidate pixel using edge patterns, and continue if it passes the test. Masking is achieved by looking at the `isEdgePixel` of each pixel in the 3 ×3 neighborhood of the candidate pixel and comparing it to the edge mask pattern.

7. Compute the edge gradient for each pixel.

    (a) As an optimization, the number of samples n in Equation (8.8) can be reduced to nine: one pixel in each 3×3 pixel grid. Edge pixels that have different sample colors can be averaged out. In practice, this does not affect the accuracy of the calculated gradient [Iourcha et al. 09].

    (b) Perform thresholding to see if the pixel should be eliminated.

8. If the target pixel is not eliminated, calculate the final framebuffer color as described in Section 8.1.7.

    (a) Weight every sample color value in a 3×3 pixel grid for each candidate pixel.

    (b) Output the color to the framebuffer (bound as a UAV).

There are a few advantages to using a compute shader. Texture fetches are reduced because compute shader fetches are cached and stored in TGSM for a 10×10 pixel block $(8 + w, 8 + h)$. For every compute thread (each pixel), the 3×3 neighborhood of pixels can be cached in temporary registers to avoid fetching from TGSM more than once. This could reduce fetch overhead because the edge detect, edge gradient, and final color calculations require access to the same 3×3 neighborhood of color samples. On some architectures, flow control can save time by early exit of a complete 8×8 thread block. If an 8×8 thread block does not have any candidate pixels after thresholding, the final pass (Step 8) is skipped. Finally, API and driver overhead are eliminated by collapsing all passes into a single compute shader postprocess pass.

8.2.3   DirectX 11 Implementation on Downlevel Hardware

On some 10.x hardware platforms (such as the ATI Radeon 48xx series), a restricted form of Compute Shader is supported. Compute Shader 4.0 and 4.1 have the following restrictions:

- Only a single raw or structured UAV may be bound.

- Group shared memory is limited to 16 Kb.

- Group shared memory can be written only to an area indexed by SV_Group-Index.

- Only one group-shared variable may be declared.

- No access to atomic instructions, append/consume, double-precision, etc.

The difference between Compute Shader 4.0 and 4.1 is that the latter has access to Vertex Shader 4.1 model instructions.

The algorithm for downlevel hardware works similarly to the Compute Shader 5.0 model; however, there is no way to output to a Texture2D directly from a UAV. To work around this limitation, output to a buffer resource and then render a full-screen pass using a pixel shader to read from the buffer resource.

Another restriction (as already mentioned) is that group shared memory needs to be indexed by SV_GroupID when writing to it. Sixty-four compute threads are not enough to cover the whole 8×8 block with border pixels (in the case of a 3×3 region, this is a 10×10 pixel block). Therefore the numthreads will need to be increased (in the 10×10 case, 100 threads per thread group). Only compute threads that are in the 8×8 pixel block and that will write to the structured resource (e.g., the border pixel threads are only used to populate group shared memory). This restriction might necessitate adjusting the block size to have better performance for the target hardware; for example, one could divide the scene into 6×6 blocks, leaving 8×8 pixel blocks including the border pixels. To check support for Compute Shader 4.0, call CheckFeatureSupport with D3D10_X hardware options. If ComputeShaders_Plus_RawAndStructuredBuffers_Via_Shader_4_x is true, then downlevel computing is supported.

8.3 Conclusion

This paper describes a directionally adaptive edge antialiasing reference implementation for improving image quality with the same memory footprint of multisampling. It offers a clear and thorough mathematical derivation to fully explain the approach, so that any necessary adaptations can be made for quality or performance trade-offs. This work also gives an overview of DirectX 10 and DirectX 11 paths. AA research is a constantly moving field; newer and newer techniques are being developed continuously that have various performance and quality trade-offs. Understanding of different approaches paves the way for developing an algorithm that is the best fit for your game or application. Consult the bibliography and appendix for additional implementation or theoretical details.

8.4 Appendix

Substituting Equation (8.5) into Equation (8.3) gives us the function to minimize:

$$||A - B||^2 = ||A||^2 - 2A \cdot B + ||B||^2,$$

where

$$||A||^2 = ||C_1||^2 \sum_{i=0}^{n} (\vec{g} \cdot v_i)^2,$$

$$-2A \cdot B = -2C_1 \cdot \sum_{i=0}^{n} f(v_i)(\vec{g} \cdot v_i),$$

$$||B||^2 = \sum_{i=0}^{n} ||f(v_i)||^2.$$

The expression $2A \cdot B$ is simplified by moving the C_1-term outside the summation because

$$(s \cdot \vec{a}_0) + (s \cdot \vec{a}_1) + \ldots + (s \cdot \vec{a}_n) = s \cdot (\vec{a_0} + \vec{a}_1 + \ldots + \vec{a}_n)$$

and $(\vec{a}s \cdot \vec{b}) = (\vec{a} \cdot s\vec{b})$. Next, substitute the value of C_1 from Equation (8.5) and simplify:

$$||A||^2 = \left|\left| \frac{\sum_{i=0}^{n} f(v_i)(\vec{g} \cdot v_i)}{\sum_{i=0}^{n} (\vec{g} \cdot v_i)^2} \right|\right|^2 \sum_{j=0}^{n} (g \cdot v_j)^2,$$

$$-2A \cdot B = -2 \left(\frac{\sum_{i=0}^{n} f(v_i)(\vec{g} \cdot v_i)}{\sum_{i=0}^{n} (\vec{g} \cdot v_i)^2} \right) \cdot \sum_{j=0}^{n} f(v_j)(\vec{g} \cdot v_j),$$

$$||B||^2 = \sum_{j=0}^{n} ||f(v_j)||^2.$$

To simplify the $||A||^2$ term, in general,

$$\frac{\sum_{j=0}^{n} a_j^2}{\left|\left| \sum_{i=0}^{n} a_i^2 \right|\right|^2} = \frac{1}{\sum_{i=0}^{n} a_i^2},$$

because $i = j$ and n is the same. To simplify the $2A \cdot B$ term, note that

$$\sum_{i=0}^{n} \vec{a}_i \cdot \sum_{j=0}^{n} \vec{a}_j = \sum_{i=0}^{n} \vec{a}_i^2$$

because $i = j$, n is the same, and $(\vec{a} \cdot \vec{a}) = ||\vec{a}||^2$.

Moving $||B||$ to the left, simplifying, and combining like terms, we get Equation (8.6).

Bibliography

[Iourcha et al. 09] Konstantine Iourcha, Jason C. Yang, and Andrew Pomianowski. "A Directionally Adaptive Edge Anti-Aliasing Filter." In *Proceedings of the Conference on High Performance Graphics*, pp. 127–133. Edited by Stephen N. Spencer, David McAllister, Matt Pharr, and Ingo Wald. New York: ACM, 2009.

[Larson et al. 98] Ron Larson, Robert P. Hostetler, and Bruce H. Edwards. *Calculus with Analytic Geometry*, Sixth Edition. Boston: Houghton Mifflin, 1998.

[Lengyel 03] Eric Lengyel. *Mathematics for 3D Game Programming & Computer Graphics*, Second edition. Hingham, MA: Charles River Media, 2003.

[Thibieroz 09] Nicolas Thibieroz. "Shader Model 5.0 and Compute Shader." Game Developers Conference 2009. Available online (http://developer.amd.com/documentation/presentations/Pages/default.aspx).

[Thibieroz and Cebenoyan 10] Nicolas Thibieroz and Cem Cebenoyan. "DirectCompute Performance on DX11 Hardware." Game Developers Conference 2010. Available online (http://developer.amd.com/documentation/presentations/Pages/default.aspx).

9

Designing a Data-Driven Renderer
Donald Revie

9.1 Introduction

Since the advent of hardware acceleration, rendering 3D graphics has been almost entirely achieved through the use of a handful of APIs. It is thus accepted that almost all engines that feature real-time 3D visuals will make use of one or more of these. In fact, as computing complexity and power increase, it becomes inconceivable that a single development studio could create proprietary code to access the abilities of hardware or implement all the newest techniques in fields such as physics and AI. Thus, engine development focuses more and more on integrating functionality exposed by APIs, be that hardware, OS features, or middleware solutions [Bell 10].

Each API is built using its own model and paradigms best suited to a specific problem domain, expressing in higher-level terms the structures and concepts of that domain. Graphics APIs are no different in this respect, typically exposing the hardware as a virtual device that must send relatively large amounts of information to the hardware when rendering each frame.

The engine itself can also be thought of as an interface, exposing a superset of the functionality found in all its components in a consistent manner. This interface forms the environment within which the core logic of the game or simulation is implemented. Thus, the engine must adapt the concepts and functionality of its constituent APIs to its own internal model, making them available to the game logic.

This chapter explores designing a renderer to bridge the gap between the logical simulation at the core of most game engines and the strictly ordered stream of commands required to render a frame through a graphics API. While this is a problem solved by any program used to visualize a simulated scene, the solution presented here focuses on providing a flexible data-driven foundation on which to build a rendering pipeline, making minimal assumptions about the exact rendering style used.

The aim is to provide a solution that will decouple the design of the renderer from the engine architecture. Such a solution will allow the rendering technology on individual projects to evolve over their lifetime and make it possible to evaluate or develop new techniques with minimal impact on the code base or asset pipeline.

9.2 Problem Analysis

So far we have defined our goal as exposing the functionality of a graphics API in a way consistent with our engine, placing emphasis on flexibility of rendering style. As a top-level objective this is sufficient but provides very little information from which to derive a solution. As already stated, every API is designed to its own model requiring its own patterns of use coinciding to a greater or lesser extent with that of the engine. To determine this extent and thus the task of any renderer module, both the API and the intended engine interface must be explored in detail. Discussion of these matters will be kept at a design or conceptual level, focusing on the broader patterns being observed rather than on the specifics of implementation in code. In this way the problem domain can be described in a concise manner and the solution can be applicable to the widest possible range of graphics API and engine, regardless of language or other implementation details.

9.2.1 Graphics API Model

Most graphics APIs belong to one of two groups, those based on the OpenGL standards [Shreiner et al. 06] and those belonging to Microsoft's Direct3D family of libraries [Microsoft 09]. At an implementation level, these two groups are structured very differently: OpenGL is built on the procedural model informed by its roots in the C language, and Direct3D has an object-oriented structure using the COM (Component Object Model) programming model. Despite this, the underlying structure and patterns of use are common to both groups [Sterna 10] (and most likely all other APIs as well). Above this implementation level we can work with the structures and patterns common to all graphics APIs and define a single model applicable to all.

No doubt many of these concepts will be very familiar to most graphics programmers, however in programming how a thing is thought about is often more important than what that thing is. Therefore, this section is intended to achieve a consensus of view that will form the foundation for the rest of the chapter. For instance, this section is not concerned with what the graphics API does, only the patterns of interaction between it and the application.

Graphics device. The graphics API is designed to wrap the functionality of hardware that is distant from the main system architecture, be it an expansion card with self-contained processor and memory or a completely separate computer accessed via a network connection; communication between the main system and the graphics hardware has historically been a bottleneck. This distance is addressed by the concept of a virtual device; the exact term varies between APIs. Differing hardware devices, and even software in some cases, are exposed as a uniform set of functionality that can be roughly divided into three groups:

1. Resource management. This controls the allocation and deallocation of device-owned memory, typically memory local to the hardware device, and controls direct access to this memory from the main system to avoid doing so concurrently from both the main system and the graphics hardware.

2. State management. Operation of the graphics hardware is too complicated to pass all pertinent information as parameters to the draw function. Instead, execution of the draw command is separated from the configuration of the device. Calling such functions does not modify the device resources in any way and their effects can be completely reversed.

3. Execution. This executes a draw or other command (such as clearing a framebuffer) on the current device configuration. The results may permanently modify resources owned by the device.

Graphics pipeline. The main function of the graphics device is to execute draw commands, thus much of the device is dedicated to this task. The core of the device is structured as a series of stream processing units (Figure 9.1), each with

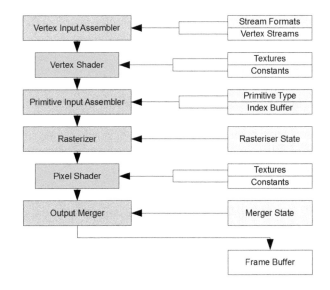

Figure 9.1. Pipeline (DX9).

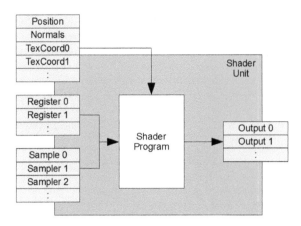

Figure 9.2. Shader unit.

its own specific function in transforming streams of vertex information into pixels
in the framebuffer. For the purposes of this chapter two distinct types of unit
comprise the stages of the pipeline.

Fixed function units such as the raster, merge, and triangle assembler stages
are characterized by having a set of specific state values used to configure operations during that stage of the pipeline. For instance, the raster stage supports
various culling conditions that may determine the face winding during rasterization or may mask off a subsection of the framebuffer for rendering. The various
different states and their descriptions fall outside the scope of this chapter—it is
enough to simply define them as a group of hard-coded device states.

In contrast, the programmable shader units (Figure 9.2) have various generic
resources associated with them. The nature of each unit remains fixed by its place
in the pipeline, but the exact function is defined by the shader program loaded
into the unit at the time a draw call is made. To accommodate this flexibility,
the resources associated with shader units are not fixed to a specific meaning like
the state values of other stages; instead, they are general-purpose resources that
are made visible to both the shader program and application. These resources
include the following:

- Input streams. Multiple streams of equal length may be attached to the
  shader, and the program is executed once for each element. These are the
  only values that can change across all iterations of the shader in a single
  draw call.

- Output streams. Each execution of the shader program will output a value
  into one or more output streams.

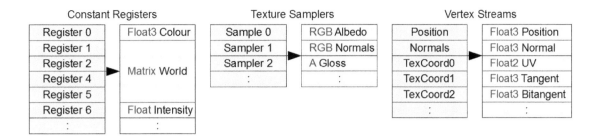

Figure 9.3. Parameter naming.

- Constant registers. Each shader unit has a number of constant registers that may be set before a draw call is made; the values stored will remain constant for all iterations of the shader.

- Texture samplers. Textures allow the shader access to multidimensional arrays of data. This data can be randomly indexed into, using various filtering options.

While increasing flexibility, these generic resources pose a problem. Without imposing a standardized mapping of resources between the shader and the engine, there is little indication telling the engine which values to associate with a given register, sampler, or stream index. Enforcing such a standard would conflict with the stated goal of maximizing flexibility and thus is not acceptable.

Fortunately high-level shading languages such as HLSL, Cg, and GLSL provide a simple and elegant solution (Figure 9.3). They expose these resources as named parameters that can be defined within the shader program, either on a global scope or as arguments. Each parameter must be identified with a type and name and, in some cases, can be given an optional semantic, too. This information is also exposed to the engine, providing the same amount of detail as the fixed function state with the flexibility of being defined in data (shader code). Thus, emphasis moves from interfacing with a finite set of standardized state values to an unlimited set of values defined by a combination of type and name and/or semantic, creating a very different challenge for engine design.

It should also be noted that the structure of the pipeline is not fixed across all APIs. With each generation of hardware, new features are exposed, extending and altering the layout of the pipeline (Figure 9.4). Over the last four generations of the Direct3D API, there has been a substantial movement from fixed function to programmable stages. It can be assumed that this trend will continue in the future, and any solution should acknowledge this.

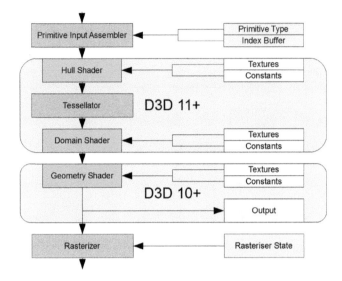

Figure 9.4. Pipeline expansions.

Command buffer. As the device is merely sending commands to the graphics hardware, these are not carried out immediately but are instead queued in a command buffer to be sent to the graphics hardware for execution. By examining the command buffer, we can clearly discern a pattern of use across the whole frame (Figure 9.5). Several state-setting commands are followed by the execution of a draw (or clear) command. Each recurrence of this pattern involves the configuration of the pipeline for a single draw call followed by its execution.

For the purposes of this chapter, this recurring pattern is defined as a *batch*. A batch describes a single unit of execution on the device, that contains all the state setting commands required to configure the pipeline and the draw command itself. Therefore, the rendering of a frame can be described as a series of batches being executed in order (Figure 9.6).

Summary. In summary, it can be said that the modern graphics API does not recognize higher-level concepts that might be associated with rendering such as

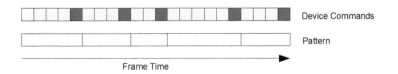

Figure 9.5. Command buffer.

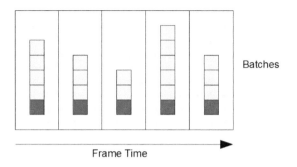

Figure 9.6. Batches.

lights, characters, sprites, or postprocesses. Instead, it focusses on providing a homogenizing interface exposing a uniform set of features on a range of hardware. A typical pattern of use involves

- over the course of a session, managing resources in device memory to ensure they are available during rendering;

- over the course of a frame, constructing batches by assigning appropriate shaders to the programmable units and then gathering both fixed function state information and shader parameters from the application. These batches must then be executed in the correct order to generate a command buffer for the frame.

9.2.2 Engine Model: Intended Pattern of Use

Every engine follows a design model dictated by the personal requirements and tastes of its authors; thus, in contrast to the graphics API, it is very difficult to define a general model that will fit all engines. It is, however, possible to select common examples of rendering during a typical game or simulation and from these derive patterns that could be expected to exist in most engines. By combining and refining these patterns, a general model for all rendering can be derived. These examples of rendering may often be considered the domain of separate modules within the engine, each using a model of rendering that best suits that domain. They may even be the responsibility of different authors, each with their own style of system design. By providing a single interface for rendering at a level above that of the API, it is much simpler to create rendering effects that cross the boundaries between these systems or to build new systems entirely.

3D scene rendering. Rendering 2D images of increasingly complex 3D scenes has been the driving force behind graphics development for many years now. Graphics

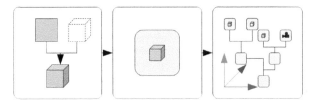

Figure 9.7. 3D scene creation.

APIs like OpenGL and Direct3D were originally designed with 3D rendering in mind. The older versions of the pipeline were entirely fixed function, consisting of stages like the *transformation* and *lighting* of vertices, focusing on processing 3D geometric data. This rigidity has been largely superseded by the flexibility of the programmable pipeline, but the focus on processing 3D geometry is still prevalent. Typically in real-time 3D applications, a complete visual representation of the scene never actually exists. Instead, the simulation at the core of the engine approximates the scene as a collection of objects with a visual representation being composited only upon rendering.

The visual representations of objects within the scene are usually constructed in isolation as part of the asset-creation process and imported into the simulation as data (Figure 9.7). Many simulated objects—entities—of a single type may reference the same visual representation but apply their own individual attributes, such as position and orientation, when rendering. The visual scene itself is constructed around the concept of nested local spaces defined relative to one another. Meshes are described as vertex positions relative to the local space of the whole mesh, visible entities are described as a group of meshes relative to the entity's local origin, and that entity may be described relative to a containing space, all such spaces ultimately being relative to a single root origin. This system has the great advantage of allowing many entities to share the same mesh resources at different locations within the scene. By collapsing the intervening spaces, the vertex positions can then be brought into the correct world-space positions.

Rendering involves the further step of bringing these world-space vertices into the 2D image space of the framebuffer (Figure 9.8). To do this we need to define

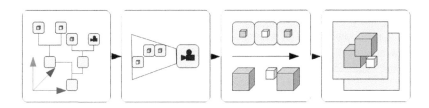

Figure 9.8. 3D scene rendering.

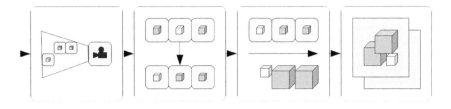

Figure 9.9. Order-dependent rendering.

a point of view within the scene and a space representing the visible volume of the scene to be projected. These additional transforms are encapsulated within the camera or view frustum entity. Similarly, output information needs to be specified regarding to which framebuffer and, if necessary, to which subsection of that framebuffer the scene is to be rendered. This information could be added to the camera object or embodied in further objects. Most importantly, it illustrates a key disjoint between the representational information stored within or referenced by the individual entities and the output information responsible for compositing the scene as an image.

In some cases, such as the rendering of transparent geometry within the scene, there are further constraints placed on the order in which entities may be rendered (Figure 9.9). This is due to the use of linear interpolation when compositing such entities into the existing scene. To achieve correct composition of the final image, two additional criteria must be met. Transparent entities must be rendered after all opaque parts of the scene, and they must be ordered such that the transparent entities furthest from the camera render first and those closest render last.

There are occasions, such as rendering real-time reflections, where rendering the scene from the main viewpoint will be reliant on output from a previous rendering of the scene, typically from another viewpoint. This creates a scenario where the entire pipeline for rendering is instantiated multiple times in a chain. This could even occur dynamically based on the contents of the scene itself, with later instances of the pipeline being dependent on the results of those prior (Figure 9.10).

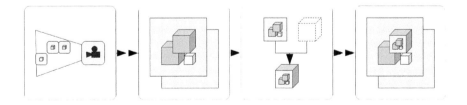

Figure 9.10. Result-dependent rendering.

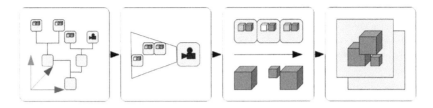

Figure 9.11. Differing representations.

In some cases it is possible that the required output will not be identical to that of the main viewpoint. For instance, rendering a shadow map from the perspective of a light should result in only depth information. To use the same resources, such as shaders and textures, needed to produce a fully colored and lit image would be highly inefficient. Therefore, multiple potential representations need to be referenced by any given entity and selected between based on the required output (Figure 9.11).

Postprocessing. The previous section focused on projecting geometric shapes from 3D space into a 2D framebuffer. The postprocessing stage is instead mostly concerned with operations in image space. Modifying the contents of previous render targets, postprocessing systems often reference the high-level concept of image filtering [Shodhan and Willmott 10].

However, the graphics hardware is unable to both read from and write to a single framebuffer, with the exception of specific blending operations. This necessitates a pattern of use whereby the postprocessing system accesses the results of previous framebuffers as textures and writes the modified information into a new framebuffer (Figure 9.12). Each stage within postprocessing typically requires rendering as little as a single batch to the framebuffer. This batch will likely not represent an object within the simulation; it will merely consist of a screen-aligned quad that will ensure that every pixel of the source image is processed and output to the framebuffer. More complex postprocesses may require a number of stages to create the desired effect. This will result in a chain of dependent batches each using the output of one or more previous framebuffers. Upon examination it can

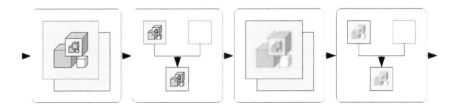

Figure 9.12. Postprocessing.

then be said that the required functionality for postprocessing is not dissimilar to that required for reflection or shadow map creation as described in the 3D scene rendering section. In fact, with regard to effects such as heat haze, there is some overlap between the two areas of rendering.

GUI rendering. In contrast to 3D scene rendering, the GUI system typically is not interested in projecting 3D entities but operates in a much more confined volume of space encapsulating the screen. This space is populated with various objects each of which might represent a single element of the interface. There may be a wide range of elements, from active elements such as text or status bars to interactive elements such as buttons, all of which represent elements of the logical if not physical simulation, or static decorative elements.

While these elements and the space within which they exist are often assumed to be inherently 2D in nature, in composing a working interface it is often necessary to layer multiple elements one atop the other in a single area of the screen. For instance, a text element may appear in front of a decorative sprite, thus adding a strict order of rendering that must be observed. This ordering can be represented by adding depth to the space and the position of elements (Figure 9.13). In practice it might be more effective to construct the GUI as any other 3D scene containing transparencies, treating GUI elements as normal entities, thus making effective use of the structures already implemented for such scenes. This approach has the added benefit of addressing the difficulties of constructing interfaces that work well when rendering in stereographic 3D.

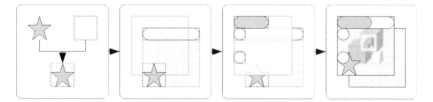

Figure 9.13. GUI rendering.

Summary. In summary, it can be said that by broadening the definitions of entity, scene, space, and camera, the same structures required for rendering 3D scenes can be extended for use in postprocessing and GUI rendering. Any object that needs to be rendered should be defined as an entity within a scene regardless of whether it is a character, terrain section, postprocessing stage, or GUI element. Similarly, all scenes must be rendered through the use of a pipeline of objects that provide

- contextual information for shaders (such as view and projection matrices),

- culling information about the volume being rendered,

- a correct rendering order of entities,

- output information on the render area and framebuffer to be used.

This investigation of potential rendering patterns is by no means exhaustive. It is therefore important that any solution be extensible in nature, allowing for additional patterns to be readily integrated.

9.2.3 Renderer Model

The graphics API and a potential engine-level interface for rendering have been examined, and simplified models have been constructed to describe typical patterns of activity in both. By combining the two models it is possible to accurately describe the desired behavior of the renderer. At various points in the execution of the application, the renderer will be required to perform certain functions.

Session. All visible elements of the game should be represented by entities that provide a single interface for rendering regardless of whether they are 3D, 2D, or a postprocessing stage. Each visible entity will need to reference resources in the form of shaders, meshes, textures, and any other information that describe its visual representation in terms of batch state (Figure 9.14).

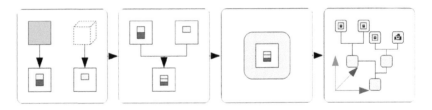

Figure 9.14. Session setup.

Frame. Over the course of each frame, various targets must be rendered to in a specific order creating multiple stages of rendering. Each stage requires rendering for the previous stage to be complete, perhaps to allow for a change to a new framebuffer or viewport or for constrictions on the composition of the current one such as transitioning from opaque to transparent entities.

Stage. Each stage forms a pipeline consisting initially of a camera object that filters entities from the scene it is observing, culling based on its own criteria. The resulting group of entities can then be sorted using the operation specified in this particular stage. Once correctly ordered, the entities are queried for any representative data relevant to this stage (Figure 9.15).

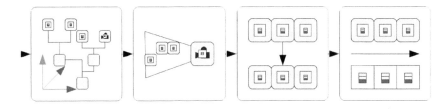

Figure 9.15. Stage rendering.

Batch. Representative data from an entity is used to form the basis for a single batch. The other elements of the rendering stage then provide the remainder of the batch's state, such as the correct viewport dimensions and framebuffer. This batch can now be executed before moving onto the next (Figure 9.16).

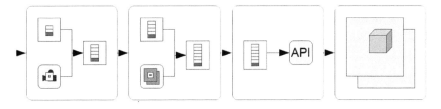

Figure 9.16. Batch rendering.

9.2.4   Further Considerations

Having defined the basic operations of the renderer, there are a number of additional requirements to consider during its development.

Exposing diverse API features. Though APIs employ the same general model, some useful features will be unique to certain APIs and new features will become available as hardware advances. It is important to allow the renderer to be quickly extended to expose these.

Supporting multiple rendering techniques. An entity with specific visual properties may exist in multiple projects with different rendering styles (e.g., forward/deferred shading) or in the same project across multiple platforms with differing hardware features. It is important to be able to choose between different implementations of a single visual effect, preferably from a single data set.

Extensible architecture. New graphics techniques are constantly being developed, and it is important that any new patterns of rendering be easily integrated into the renderer with minimal impact to code or data formats.

Resource management. Device resources are finite and any solution should attempt to minimize duplication of resources wherever possible. A comprehensive resource management scheme, however, is beyond the scope of this chapter.

9.3   Solution Development

Before outlining an exact design for the renderer, it is a good idea to determine a general approach to the implementation, which can further inform decisions.

9.3.1   Object-Based Pipeline

The design of the renderer and additional constraints lend themselves well to a highly modular implementation. By examining the model derived in Section 9.2.3, we can see a pattern emerging where the functions of the renderer are independent operations performed in series to construct a single batch. This design pattern is often defined as a *pipeline* or *pipes and filters* pattern [Buschmann et al. 96]. Rather than encapsulating functionality in a monolithic object or function, a system is constructed as a series of autonomous components sharing a single interface where the output of one object becomes the input for the next. The same pattern can also be observed in many asset pipelines used by developers to process assets before loading them into an engine and in the graphics pipeline described in the API section. In some ways the renderer pipeline can be thought of as a continuation of these two pipelines, bridging the gap between the assets and the device state. Such fine-grained modularity allows for the decoupling of the composition of the pipeline as data and the function of its components as code with numerous benefits.

Accessibility. With a little explanation, artists and other asset creators should be able to understand and modify the data set used to configure the renderer without programmer intervention. This process can be further improved by providing tools that will allow users to author a renderer configuration via a visual interface.

Flexibility. It should be possible to change the structure of the renderer quickly by modifying the data set from which it is created, even while the engine is running. This allows for quick testing of various configurations without affecting the project's work flow and also for opportunities to optimize rendering as requirements may vary over a session.

Extensibility. Objects allow the architecture to be extended by adding new object types that match the same interface but bring new behaviors, thus providing a degree of future proofing with regards to new rendering patterns or to exposing new API features.

9.3.2   Device Object

It has already been posited that all graphics APIs have a central device object, whether explicitly, as in the case of the Direct3D libraries, or implicitly. To improve the portability of the renderer code, it makes sense to write its components to use a single interface regardless of the underlying API. Equally, it makes sense for this interface to formalize the concept of the device object, even if such a concept already exists in the API.

To properly abstract all possible APIs, the device object must expose a superset of all the functionality provided. If a feature is not supported on a given API, then it would need to be emulated or, because the renderer is configured through data, it could warn that the current data set is not fully supported. As new features become available, the device interface would need to be extended before additional renderer components could be written to expose them.

9.3.3   Deriving State from Objects

As described previously, when rendering each batch, the renderer will iterate over the list of objects forming the entity and the pipeline, deriving from each a portion of the state required to render that batch. It is important to differentiate between the various types of states found in the graphics pipeline (Section 9.2.1) and also between the objects representing entities within the simulation and those representing the pipeline (Section 9.2.3). Iteration will ensure that objects get access to the device for state setting.

Fixed function state. Objects that contain fixed function state are simple to manage. When iteration reaches such a node in the pipeline or entity, the node will be able to access the device and make the correct calls.

Shader parameters. Correctly setting the values of shader parameters is a considerably more difficult challenge. Each parameter is identified by a type and a name and an optional semantic (where semantics are supported by the shading language); there is a certain amount of redundancy between the name and semantic values. While the semantic quite literally represents the meaning of the parameter, a good name should be equally expressive; in practice, the name is quite often a shorthand version of the semantic (for instance, a world-view matrix might have the semantic `WORLDVIEW` but have the abbreviated name `WVm`).

It is usually enough to match either the name or semantic rather than both; each has its own benefits and drawbacks. Names are a requirement of any parameter and thus are guaranteed to be available in all shader code; however, naming conventions cannot be guaranteed and would have to be enforced across a whole project. There exists a Standard Annotations and Semantics (SAS) initiative that looks to solve this problem by standardizing the use of semantics between applications.

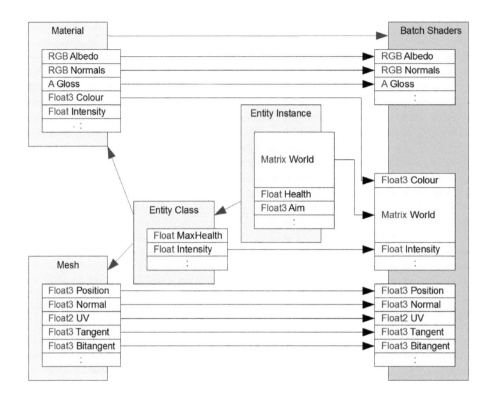

Figure 9.17. Parameter setting.

To correctly set the parameter, an equivalent variable must be found within the logic of the program. Unfortunately, compilation usually strips the context from variables, preventing us from simply performing a search of each object's member variables by type and name (Figure 9.17). Two possible solutions might be considered:

- Build a search function into any object that provides such variables; it will return a pointer to the member variable that best matches the parameter (or a NULL pointer if none can be found) [Cafrelli 01]. This approach may be best suited to existing engines that use an inheritance hierarchy of entity types. It has the drawback of enforcing a fixed naming or semantic vocabulary in code.

- Define entity types using data aggregation instead of classes; each object can store its variables as a structure of nodes that can actually be searched based on type and name or semantic. This may not be realistic in many engine architectures, but it has the added benefit of flexibility, allowing new data to be inserted into an entity and to be automatically picked up by the assigned shaders.

Due to the cost of searching for data, these links between shader parameters and variables should be formed once per session when initializing the entity and its shaders rather than per frame. These links can be divided into two groups, those involving data that represent the entity and those involving the current context or configuration of the pipeline at the time of rendering.

Representational objects. Every visible object is represented by a single unique entity within the scene; however, that entity can reference resource objects that may be shared by any number of other entities. Collectively, these objects provide information required to represent the entity as one or more batches under various different conditions. This information is limited to values that remain static across the period of a frame (such as the entities' absolute positions in the world space). It is taken in isolation and further information is required to dictate how the entity will appear at the exact moment of rendering (such as the position of the particular camera in use). For each of its potential batches, the entity stores links between all the shader parameters and variables used to set them. Where the relevant data is available within the entity or one of its referenced resources, this is used.

Contextual/pipeline objects. Where data is not available directly to the entity, it can be referenced from a global context entity. This entity is unique and contains all the variables needed to describe the current state of the pipeline from within a shader. As the pipeline changes over the course of a frame, its components modify the variables stored in the context entity, thus ensuring any batches rendered will gain the correct inputs.

9.4 Representational Objects

As stated, the visual representation of a single entity is built up from multiple objects. Each object references a more general resource and adds an extra layer of specificity, progressing from generic shared resources to a unique instance of an entity. In effect, this creates a hierarchy with resources becoming more specific as they near the root (Figure 9.18).

The exact nature of these resources is somewhat arbitrary, and the structures used could easily vary between engines. The criteria for their selection is to group states roughly by the frequency with which they change between batches; a shader might be used multiple times with different parameters, thus it will change with a lower frequency. As the specificity of an object increases so does the frequency with which it will change.

As each successive layer of the hierarchy is more specific, any values provided by it will take precedence over those from more general resources.

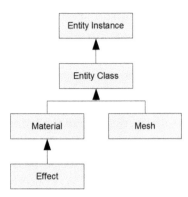

Figure 9.18. Hierarchy of resources.

9.4.1   Effect

The concept of the effect makes aspects of the programmable graphics pipeline accessible in a way that does not require deep knowledge of graphics or API programming. It does this by encapsulating these elements in a structure based not on their purpose within the pipeline but on the end result, a unique visual quality (Figure 9.19).

While the structure of the effect is fairly well standardized, interpretation of the components involved is quite open. In this chapter, the interpretation is informed by the meaning of component names, documentation provided by APIs in which effects are a feature, and existing sources on the subject [St-Laurent 05].

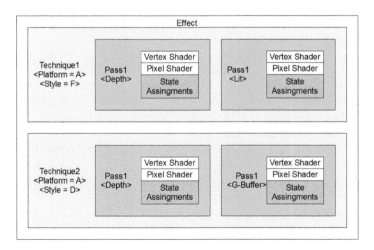

Figure 9.19. Effect structure.

Techniques. The visual quality embodied by any particular effect can often be achieved in a number of ways, each with various trade-offs and requirements. Each technique within the effect is a different method for achieving comparable results. By applying annotations to the individual techniques, it is possible to group them by various criteria, such as features required or relative cost, allowing the renderer to algorithmically select the appropriate technique depending on the circumstances.

Passes. It may not always be possible to achieve an effect with a single batch, instead requiring multiple successive batches that may render at various points throughout the frame. Each technique is constructed from one or more passes; these passes can be annotated to direct the renderer to execute them at the correct point within the frame.

Passes contain states with a similar frequency of change, such as shaders or state assignments, which are rarely useful taken individually due to their interdependence on one another to create an overall pipeline configuration. Therefore, each pass within the technique combines shaders and state assignments but omits many of the shader parameter values, effectively creating an interface to the graphics pipeline allowing the effect as a whole to be parameterized.

Default values. Having the effect provide default values for all its parameters reduces the time required to implement new techniques. It minimizes the number of values that need to be overridden by more specific resources to just those that are strictly necessary, many of which may be automatically provided.

9.4.2 Assets

Assets further specialize a particular effect by providing inputs to some of the parameters. They are typically authored, at least in part, using tools external to the engine. The end result is a visual representation of an object in isolation.

Although the terms *material* and *mesh* are typically used in 3D asset creation, these are equally applicable to GUI or postprocess rendering.

Material. Typically, the material consists of constant and texture information that specializes the effect to emulate the qualities of a certain substance. More generally, to extend the concept to postprocessing, it can be considered an authored configuration or tuning of the effect with static values.

Mesh. A mesh is the set of all vertex data streams and indexes and thus encapsulates all the varying input for an effect. There are many cases in which this information is not used directly as provided by asset creation tools. Instead, systems within the engine will generate or modify vertex streams before transferring them to the graphics device—this could include animation of meshes, particle effects, or generating meshes for GUI text.

A more complete resource management system would likely support instancing of these resources to improve efficiency. However, such details are beyond the scope of this chapter.

9.4.3 Simulation

Where resources in the assets section were largely concerned with the visual attributes of batches, this section is concerned with objects representing the logical attributes.

Entity class. As part of the game design process, archetypal entities will be described in terms of visual and logical attributes shared by many individual entities. These attributes do not vary between individual entities and do not vary over the course of a game session, so they can be safely shared.

Entity instance. Individual entities are instances of a specific class; they represent the actual simulated object. As such they contain all the values that make each instance unique, those which will vary over the course of a game session and between individual instances.

9.5   Pipeline Objects

The pipeline is made up of a series of interchangeable objects, each of which observes the same interface. This pipeline controls the rendering of a group of entities during one stage of the frame (Figure 9.20).

9.5.1 Contextual Objects

Contextual objects provide values to the effect in a similar way to representative ones. However, there is a level of indirection involved; the effect parameters are linked to values defined within a global context object, and these values are manipulated over the course of the frame to reflect the current context in which batches are being rendered.

   The values are specific to each object only; they cannot provide concatenations of these with any belonging to the entity currently being rendered, although this functionality could be added as an additional stage in rendering.

Camera. The camera object will also likely be an entity within the scene, though perhaps not a visible one. It is responsible for the transforms used to project entities from their current space into that of the framebuffer. The camera may also provide other information for use in effects, such as its position within world space. The exact details are at the discretion of those implementing the system.

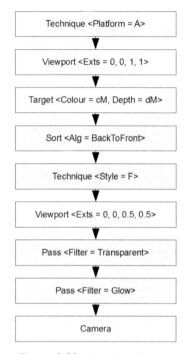

Figure 9.20. Pipeline objects.

Viewport. The viewport defines a rectangular area of the framebuffer in which to render, the output image being scaled rather than cropped to fit. The viewport could be extended to work using relative values as well as absolute ones, decoupling the need to know the resolution of any particular target when authoring the pipeline. This could be further extended to permit nesting of viewports, with each child deriving its dimensions relative to those of its immediate parent.

Target. The render target defines the contents of the framebuffer to be used, referencing either a client area provided by the platform or textures that may be used in further stages of rendering.

9.5.2 Control Objects

In contrast, control objects do not set the states of effect parameters. Instead, they control the order and selection of the batches being rendered.

Camera. In addition to providing contextual data during rendering, the camera object may also perform culling of entities before they are queried for representational data.

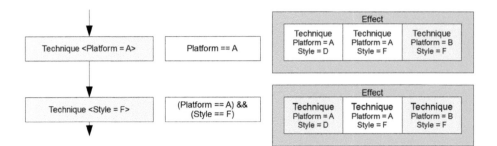

Figure 9.21. Technique filters.

Layer. Layers can be used for course-grained control of rendering across a single render target. This forces one set of batches to be rendered only after the previous set has completed. As the name suggests, they are analogous with layers in art packages like Photoshop or GIMP.

Sorting algorithm. Defining a sorting algorithm for the pipeline will force entities to be sorted by arbitrary criteria before any rendering is performed. This is a requirement for compositing semitransparent batches onto a single layer of rendering, but it can also be used to gain additional performance by sorting batches based on material or approximate screen coverage.

Technique filter. Technique filters can be applied to provide additional information for choosing the correct technique from an effect. Each filter can provide values in one or more domains, such as platform, required features, or rendering style. Each domain can only have a single value at any point in the frame, and these are matched to the domain values specified by the effect techniques available to select the best suited (Figure 9.21).

The domains and values are not defined anywhere in the code and only appear in the pipeline configuration and effect files, allowing each project to define their selection. Technique filters are largely optional, being most useful for larger projects and those using extensive effect libraries.

Pass filter. Pass filters are a requirement for the pipeline to operate correctly. These work differently from the technique filters in that each filter just has an identifying value and any number of pass filters can be active at a single point in the frame. When rendering an entity, all passes within the current technique that match an active filter will be rendered. The order in which they are presented in the technique will be observed regardless of any sorting algorithm in use (Figure 9.22). If no passes match the active filters, then nothing will be rendered.

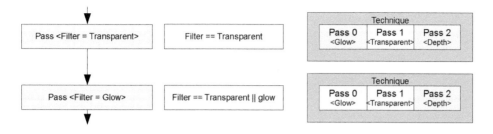

Figure 9.22. Pass filters.

9.6 Frame Graph

The configuration of the pipeline varies from stage to stage over the course of each frame. As with the representative resources, the components of the pipeline vary with different frequencies. It is therefore possible to describe the pipeline over the course of a whole frame as a graph of the various components (Figure 9.23).

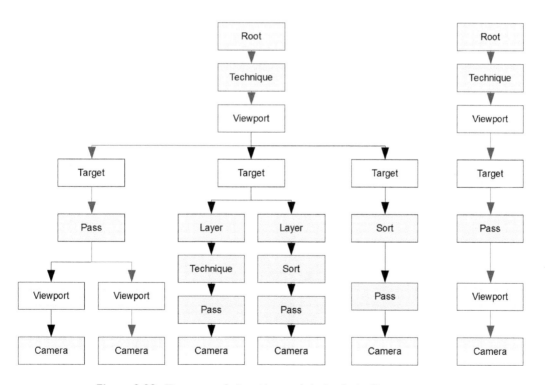

Figure 9.23. Frame graph iteration and derived pipeline.

This graph effectively partitions the frame based on the current stage of rendering, with the nodes being active pipeline components. The components touched by iterating through the graph from root to leaf form the pipeline at that stage of the frame. Each leaf node represents a complete pipeline configuration for which rendering must occur. By traversing the graph depth first, it is possible to iterate through each of the pipeline configurations in sequence, thus rendering the entire frame.

As each node in the graph is iterated over, it is activated and modifies the context object or the control state of the pipeline. Once the leaf node is reached, the camera object begins the rendering of that stage, iterating over the scene graph and processing the visible entities based on the pipeline state. Upon completion of the stage, iteration returns back through the graph undoing the changes made by the various nodes in the graph.

While the concept of the pipeline remains valid, this behavior of modifying global states makes the implementation of the system more akin to a stack. Changes are pushed onto the stack as each node is visited and then popped from the stack upon returning. This reduces the frequency of certain state changes immensely, making it considerably more efficient than having each batch iterate along the full pipeline as it is being rendered.

9.7   Case Study: Praetorian Tech

Praetorian is Cohort Studio's proprietary engine technology. It was developed to provide the studio with a solid platform on which to build full titles and prototypes across multiple platforms (Figure 9.24).

Figure 9.24. Prototypes developed by Cohort Studios: *Wildlife* (left) and *Pioneer* (right).

Figure 9.25. Various rendering styles tested on the *Me Monstar* motion prototype: custom toon shading defined by Andreas Firnigl (left), soft ambient lighting (center), and deferred shaded fur (right).

9.7.1 Motivation

Praetorian was developed with the intention of maximizing code reuse across multiple simultaneous projects. With this in mind, it made sense to define those features unique to each project through data and scripts instead of engine code, allowing artists, designers, and gameplay programmers to control the look and feel of their project in great detail (Figure 9.25). As described earlier, effect files were a natural solution to exposing programmable graphics via data. Being compatible with a large range of art packages meant that many artists were already familiar with their use and in some cases with authoring them. However, it was soon discovered that more advanced visual effects required multiple passes throughout the course of a frame, something which effect files alone could not define. A data structure was needed that could map out the frame so as to give points of reference and control over the order of rendering at various levels of granularity.

9.7.2 Implementation Details

Praetorian's design was based on the concepts described in the introduction to this chapter. At its core lies a highly flexible architecture that split the functionality of objects, as provided by the engine's subsystems, from the raw data stored in the central scene graph. As such all entities within the scene were represented in code by a single class that stored a list of data objects, with distinctions. An entity containing references to a mesh and material could be drawn; one with a physics object would be updated by the physics simulation; and so on. Thus, a single conceptual entity such as a character or light could be represented as a single entity in the scene or by a subgraph of entities grouped under a single root node. Such details were largely informed by the assets produced by artists and designers rather than led by code.

This approach made it simple to add subgraphs to the scene that could embody many of the renderer concepts discussed in this chapter. The design described throughout this chapter is a refinement of the resulting architecture.

9.7.3 Analysis

The purpose of the renderer design was to separate graphics development from that of the engine, exposing through data the functionality of the graphics API beyond that already provided by effect files. In this it proved highly successful, initially in moving from forward to deferred shading on our main project and then in experimenting with a number of styles and variations including deferred and inferred lighting, various forms of cell shading, and other nonphotorealistic rendering methods. All this could occur in parallel to the main development of the projects with the roll-out of new styles being performed gradually to ensure that builds were unharmed by the introduction of potential bugs.

Another area where the design proved successful was in the definition of postprocessing techniques; these benefited from the same development environment as other effects but also from being fully configurable across multiple levels within the same project.

As with any design decisions, there were trade-offs made when developing the renderer, some of which have been addressed to various degrees in the revised design. To a certain extent, the data-driven nature of the renderer became a limitation in its initial and continuing development. In the case of some simple tasks, it took considerably longer to design and implement an elegant way to expose functionality through data than it would to do so through code. Once such structures are in place, however, the savings in time can quickly make up for the initial investment. Praetorian's initial structure was significantly more rigid than that described in this chapter—this made adding special-case behaviors, such as shadow frustum calculations or stereographic cameras, more difficult to implement.

As the renderer configurations became more complex so too did the XML files used to describe them. This had the undesired effect of reducing the system's accessibility and increasing the likelihood of errors occurring. One solution would have been to create a visual editor to interpret the files, something that is highly recommended to anyone implementing a similar renderer design.

The generalized nature of the architecture also had the effect of making optimization more difficult. By making minimal assumptions about the batches being rendered, it can be difficult to maximize efficiency. The greatest gains were made in performing as much processing as possible during loading or as part of the asset pipeline, moving the workload away from the time of rendering. This had an impact on the runtime flexibility of the system, forcing entities to be reinitialized if data was added or removed, but overall it was necessary to maintain realistic frame rates.

9.8 Further Work and Considerations

9.8.1 Optimization: Multithreaded Rendering Using Thread-Local Devices

Some APIs support the creation of multiple command buffers on separate threads. Where this is available, it would be possible to have multiple threads process the frame graph simultaneously. Each thread would iterate until it reached a leaf node. It would then lock the node before processing the resultant pipeline as normal. Should a thread reach an already locked node, it would simply skip that node and continue iteration until it discovered an unlocked leaf node or the end of the frame graph.

To make this approach safe from concurrency errors, each thread would have a local device with a subset of the functionality of the main device. This would also require thread-local context entities to store the state of the current pipeline; as no other objects are modified during rendering, the scene and pipeline objects can be accessed concurrently.

9.8.2 Extension: Complex Contextual Data

Some shaders will require data that does not exist within a single entity, such as a concatenated world-view-projection matrix. This data can be created in the shader from its constituent parts but at a considerably higher performance cost than generating it once per batch. Thus, a system could be added to perform operations on values in the context entity and the entity being rendered to combine them prior to rendering. In its most advanced state, this could take the form of executable scripts embedded in an extended effect file, a kind of *batch shader*.

9.8.3 Debugging: Real-Time Toggling of Elements in Pipeline

Shaders for displaying debug information can be added to entities by inserting additional techniques into their effects. These techniques can then be activated by adding the correct filters to the frame graph, and these sections can then be toggled to render various entities under different conditions, showing information such as normals, overdraw, or lighting. As the renderer automatically binds shader parameters to entity data it is possible to visualize a wide range of information by modifying only the shader code. This debugging information is strictly controlled by data, and as such it is simple to introduce and remove, allowing individual developers to tailor the output to their specific needs and then remove all references before shipping.

9.9 Conclusion

The renderer described in this chapter successfully decouples the details of graphics rendering from engine architecture. In doing so it tries to provide an interface that better fits the needs of graphics programmers and asset creators than those currently available—one that takes its lead from the incredibly useful effect structure, attempting to expand the same data-driven approach to the entire rendering pipeline.

The principles discussed have been used in several commercial game titles and various prototypes, being instrumental in the rapid exploration of various graphical styles and techniques that could be freely shared across projects. In the future it might even be possible to expand on these concepts to create a truly standardized notation for describing graphics techniques in their entirety, regardless of the application used to display them.

9.10 Acknowledgments

Thanks to everyone who worked at Cohort Studios over the years for making my first real job such a great experience. I learned a lot in that time. All the best wherever the future finds you. Special thanks go to Andrew Collinson who also worked on Praetorian from the very beginning, to Bruce McNeish for showing a lot of faith in letting two graduate programmers design and build the beginnings of an engine, and to Alex Perkins for demanding that artists should be able to define render targets without programmer assistance, even if they never did.

Bibliography

[Bell 10] G. Bell. "How to Build Your Own Engine and Why You Should." *Develop* 107 (July 2010), 54–55.

[Buschmann et al. 96] F. Buschmann, R. Meunier, H. Rohnert, P. Sommerland, and M. Stal. *Pattern-Oriented Software Architecture*. Chichester, West Sussex, UK: John Wiley & Sons, 1996.

[Cafrelli 01] C. Cafrelli. "A Property Class for Generic C++ Member Access." In *Game Programming Gems 2*, edited by Mark DeLoura, pp. 46–50. Hingham, MA: Charles River Media, 2001.

[Microsoft 09] Microsoft Corporation. "DirectX SDK." Available at http://msdn.microsoft.com/en-us/directx/default.aspx, 2009.

[Shodhan and Willmott 10] S. Shodhan and A. Willmott. "Stylized Rendering in Spore." In *GPU Pro*, edited by Wolfgang Engel, pp. 549–560. Natick, MA: A K Peters, 2010.

[Shreiner et al. 06] D. Shreiner, M. Woo, J. Neider, and T. Davis. *OpenGL Programming Guide*, Fifth edition. Upper Saddle River, NJ: Addison Wesley, 2006.

[St-Laurent 05] S. St-Laurent. *The COMPLETE Effect and HLSL Guide.* Redmond, WA: Paradoxal Press, 2005.

[Sterna 10] W. Sterna. "Porting Code between Direct3D9 and OpenGL 2.0." In *GPU Pro*, edited by Wolfgang Engel, pp. 529–540. Natick, MA: A K Peters, 2010.

10

An Aspect-Based Engine Architecture
Donald Revie

10.1 Introduction

The definition of what constitutes an engine varies across the industry. At its most basic, the term describes a code base that provides common functionality across multiple projects. The aim is to share the cost in resources required to develop this functionality. More advanced engines provide a platform and tools that can have a substantial impact on the game development process. The architecture of an engine determines how flexible, functional, reliable, and extensible that engine is and thus how successfully it can be used across multiple projects.

With an emphasis on modularity and encapsulation to divide large systems into more manageable components, the principles of object-oriented programming (OOP) embody many of these attributes. As games tend to center on a simulation made up of objects, most engines apply these principles on an object level, creating various classes of object, often in an inheritance hierarchy, with progressively complex functionality.

Aspect-based engines instead apply these principles on an engine level. Using aggregation the engine is constructed of modules, called *aspects*, each of which supplies a strict subset of the required functionality such as rendering, audio, or physics simulation. These aspects share a common interface allowing them to communicate with the core of the engine and access shared data describing the current game state. In theory each aspect is a separate engine with a very specific task, interpreting the shared data in the core via a narrow viewpoint that best fits the functionality it provides.

10.2 Rationale

Engine design and development is not just a problem of programming, it is also one of management. For developers who have limited resources in both staff and time, the approach taken to developing their engine will have a vast impact on everyone involved in developing and using it. This means that any such engine is unlikely to be developed by a dedicated team with months of time to plan and execute; instead, it will have to be written rapidly with the immediate needs of projects in mind.

An aspect-based engine architecture reduces this burden of management by creating a simple interface and set of rules to which all aspects must be written. Once the core and its interface to the aspects are defined, work on the aspects themselves can be carried out by individuals or teams with a considerable amount of autonomy. Interactions between the aspects and thus their authors remain informal, being implemented entirely through manipulating the core of the engine via the aspect interface.

As such, this architecture is well suited to small or distributed teams who cannot afford to establish a dedicated structure to design and manage all the elements of their engine but would still like to take advantage of the benefits that developing their own technology provides. The highly modular nature also allows for changes in development direction or the accommodation of multiple projects with widely varying requirements.

Next, we describe details of the architecture of the engine that can be summarized by the engine's core, the aspects, and their interactions.

10.3 Engine Core

The core is the most important element of the engine; all the aspects can be replaced or altered at any time but each one is highly dependent on the interface and functionality provided by the core, making it vital that the core remains stable throughout development. The function of the engine core is to store the structure and state of the game or simulation upon which the aspects will act. As the name suggests, the core is the very center and foundation upon which the rest of the engine is constructed (Figure 10.1).

10.3.1 Scene Graph

One component at the core of the engine design is a representation of the game's simulated environment, the actual logical representation of objects and concepts that interact to create everything within the game. This representation is stored as a scene graph of sorts, a tree structure where each node represents a point of interest within the simulation. However, its function is not as strictly defined as the term *scene graph* might suggest. This tree does not necessarily represent a single physical space; one branch, or subgraph, might store the information for a 3D scene while another might store a 2D GUI and another purely abstract data (Figure 10.2).

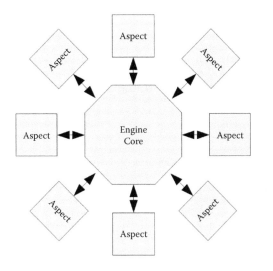

Figure 10.1. The core of the engine is the common link between its many aspects.

10.3.2 Scene Nodes

Because the scene graph does not impose specific meanings upon its subgraphs, the structure of the simulation is defined purely via data. This information is stored within the nodes of the scene graph and must be interpreted by the aspects. To facilitate this level of flexibility, the nodes of the scene graph are not defined using an inheritance hierarchy, as might usually be the case, but are instead constructed using aggregation at runtime.

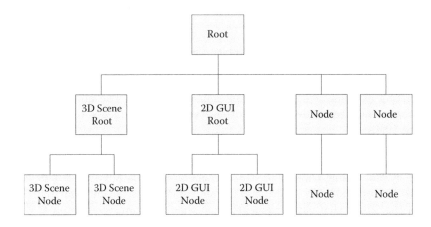

Figure 10.2. Scene graph layout.

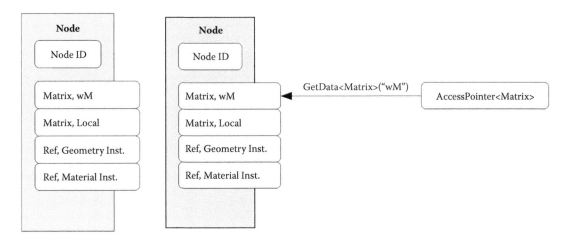

Figure 10.3. Node composition.   **Figure 10.4.** Data access request.

Each node within the scene graph stores a list of data attributes, identified by name and type (Figure 10.3). The meaning of a node and the makeup of its attributes are not restricted or defined by the engine design, allowing for any number of meanings to be expressed as required.

A node might describe a physical object, such as a light or camera from a 3D scene. Likewise it might describe a bone from a character's animation rig or a mouse cursor. It may even represent an abstract concept, such as a victory condition, within the rules of the game. The meaning of each node is determined by its relative position in the graph, its attributes, and how those things are interpreted by the aspects that make up the rest of the engine.

10.3.3 Data Access

One consequence of implementing nodes using aggregation is that there is no interface providing a direct means of accessing the data contained within a node. Instead access must be requested, the calling code querying the node to see if it contains an attribute with the desired name and type. The node then returns an access pointer templated to the correct type and increments a reference count (Figure 10.4).

In a multithreaded environment, safe access through these pointers, and to the rest of the core elements, requires a mutual exclusion (mutex) to be acquired by the calling thread. In this circumstance it is often more efficient for aspects to duplicate any relevant data and operate on an internal representation of the object that can be synchronized with the core scene graph at defined points.

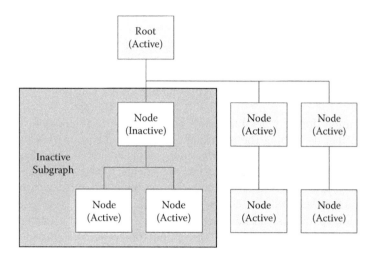

Figure 10.5. Deactivation being propagated from the root node of a subgraph.

10.3.4   Subgraph State

Nodes within the scene graph can be in one of several states that impact all the child nodes in the subgraph rooted at that node (Figure 10.5):

- Active. When a node is active it means that all interested aspects are able to process it and update any data or internal resources associated with it.

- Inactive. Subgraphs can be deactivated at any time. Once inactive the nodes should be treated by the aspects as if they don't exist but can retain any resources. Subgraphs are appended to the scene in an inactive state to allow aspects to initialize any associated resources before updating begins.

- Pending deletion. All nodes within the subgraph are inactive and will shortly be deleted. Aspects should prepare for this by cleaning up any associated resources.

As with all node attributes, the exact definition of subgraph states can be defined by the users of the engine. However, additional care should be taken due to the wide impact of such states and how various aspects might interpret them.

10.3.5   Event Queue

The scene graph and its constituent nodes describe the current structure and state of the simulation. This simulation, however, will not remain static. It will be characterized by changes to the structure of the scene and the contents of the nodes as the logic of the simulation is played out.

The engine aspects must be aware of and react to such changes in the simulation state. While this could be performed by aspects continuously inspecting elements of the scene for change, it would be prohibitively slow. A more efficient solution is to maintain a queue of events describing such changes that each aspect can review during its update, ignoring any events that are not relevant to its function.

Events use a similarly flexible definition to the rest of the engine. Each event has an identifier describing the nature of the event and can provide two pointers to either nodes or data within specific nodes. This is sufficient to describe most events within the simulation, flagging either a change in the status of a node, and thus the subgraph rooted in it, a change in a specific attribute within the node, or an interaction between two nodes.

More complex events can be described using additional attributes within the referenced node or by creating a node within the scene to represent the event itself. Thus a collision between two nodes that results in a sound and particle effect could spawn a new subgraph containing these elements, rather than an event describing them.

10.4   Aspects

The engine core stores the current state of the simulation and any changes that have occurred recently. It is not concerned with the contents of the simulation or how it might work. Instead, all operations carried out by the engine occur within the aspects.

An aspect is an engine module that exists to provide a limited subset of engine functionality. This might include rendering, animation, physics, audio, and even the logic of the game. As such, aspects are often used to wrap the functionality of individual APIs for tasks such as physics, synchronizing the API's internal simulation with the corresponding objects within the engine core. The scope of each aspect is completely arbitrary, a single aspect could be used to encapsulate all the functionality provided by an existing third-party engine, framework, or group of related APIs. Similarly a single API may have its functionality subdivided between multiple aspects if that best fits their purpose.

One restriction of this architecture is that aspects should adhere to strict dependency rules: they can share knowledge of base engine libraries, the engine core, and shared libraries but should not know about one another (Figure 10.6). This means that all access to shared resources should be performed through the interfaces supplied by the engine core, thus preventing any coupling or interdependencies forming between aspects. Thus if two aspects share a base library with specific classes, this data can be embedded into entities like data of any other type. As it is only relevant to the interested aspects, it remains opaque to the rest of the engine.

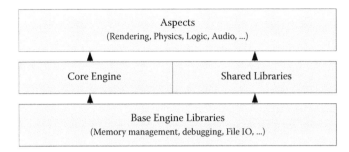

Figure 10.6. Dependency layers.

Aspects should be designed to keep this kind of sharing to a minimum. Static resources like the current graphics device/context or window handle should not be shared between aspects, though where sharing is unavoidable, these should provide a mutex to control access.

By maintaining these rules, aspects will operate independently and be much easier to maintain and replace. An audio aspect using one API will be interchangeable with an aspect using another API. Each aspect can therefore be developed and tested independently, interacting with each other by manipulating the engine core.

The engine manages all aspects through a single interface, initializing, updating, and shutting down aspects in an order specified by the user of the engine. This could in theory be performed through data, allowing the engine to construct itself from dynamically linked libraries at runtime.

10.4.1 Scene Interpretation

Each aspect should maintain an internal structure of references to nodes in which it is interested. Interest is determined by querying the node's attributes looking for specific patterns. For instance, a node with an identifier matching a rigid body would be of interest to the physics aspect, whereas one that referenced a geometry and material instance would be of interest to the render aspect. The nature of this structure and the way it references the nodes can be tailored to the aspect, allowing the most efficient solution for the functionality it provides. This could be a spatial tree for operations based on the relative position of nodes, such as frustum culling visible nodes against a camera node, or a simple linked list of nodes that can be iterated over once per frame (Figure 10.7).

When an aspect is registered with the engine core, it parses the whole of the existing scene graph and registers interest in any nodes. From then on it will receive events regarding changes to nodes and to the structure of the scene graph, allowing it to synchronize its own internal structures.

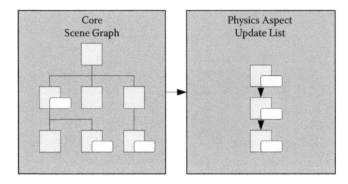

Figure 10.7. Aspects reinterpret the scene structure as required.

10.4.2 Node Interfaces

When presented with a new subgraph, an aspect inspects the nodes within, querying for patterns of data that would indicate that the node represents a concept that the aspect recognizes. This pattern of attributes can be thought of as an interface that the node exports via a subset of its attributes (Figure 10.8).

In most cases these interfaces will be predefined by the aspect, mapping directly to objects within their functional domain. An audio aspect might interpret nodes as potential sound emitters, receivers, or environmental modifiers. While an animation aspect will be interested in nodes representing bones or skinned mesh segments.

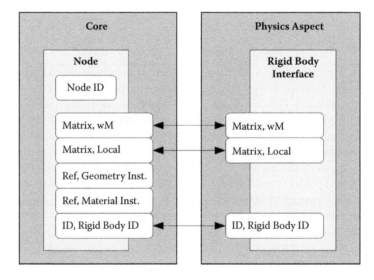

Figure 10.8. Aspects reinterpret nodes based on the attributes they exhibit.

In some cases interfaces will be defined via data loaded into the aspect. In
this way the engine can request access to arbitrary attributes, usually after ascer-
taining that the node represents the desired object using a separate predefined
interface. This allows the engine to map attributes of a node to the inputs of
a script or shader automatically without needing to understand the contents of
either the node or the intended target.

It is usually preferable for the aspect to use the interface to synchronize its
own internal objects with the scene graph rather than perform operations directly
on the shared data. In the case of aspects that wrap APIs, these objects will likely
already be provided and indeed be required to use the desired functionality. This
allows aspects to perform operations in parallel; they are only required to lock
the core of the engine at set points to synchronize their internal data with the
central simulation.

10.5 Common Aspects

10.5.1 Render Aspect

The chapter "Designing a Data-Driven Renderer" in *GPU Pro 3* [Revie 12] describes in detail the key elements of a render aspect. The design illustrates the
flexibility of the core scene representation in defining objects with a wide range of
concepts, from concrete entities such as cameras or lights to the abstract elements
of the frame graph, used to control the order of rendering. It also describes the
process of interrogating objects to retrieve arbitrary input for shaders.

10.5.2 Logic Aspect

The logic aspect is where any game-specific functionality should be added. This
is the aspect that will interpret objects in the scene graph as the entities they
represent in the game, such as players, enemies, weapons, and power-ups. It will
update the scene using the rules of the game provided.

The way in which the logic aspect is implemented can vary greatly and should
be subject to the needs of the project and the makeup of the team. A program-
mercentric team might want to handle a lot of the logic through code, hiding the
interface to the engine core behind their own entity classes and structures. Alternatively the logic aspect can be completely data-driven, executing script files
attached to the individual nodes and exposing the contents of the attached nodes
as parameters or objects within the script language.

10.5.3 Data Instrumentation Aspect

By implementing an aspect that simply exposes the components of the core
through a simple GUI, users of the engine can directly observe the internal state
of the engine and even edit the values of individual node attributes. Depending

on the level to which such an aspect is developed, it could vary in functionality from a simple debugging tool displaying attribute values as formatted strings to an in-game editor capable of manipulating the structure of the scene graph and rendering complex widgets for editing node attributes.

10.5.4 File Aspect

Notable by its absence from the engine core is any ability to load data from files into the engine. That is because this functionality also is supplied by an aspect. The loading of the scene data into the core is controlled by the file aspect, an aspect that looks for nodes with attributes that reference filenames. Once found these names are submitted to a factory system.

Factories. This factory system itself follows a modular structure. Each file type is associated with a factory module that processes the file, constructing a subgraph from its contents. This subgraph is then passed back to the factory aspect, which can then replace the file-referencing node with the subgraph that it represented. Once inserted into the scene, the new subgraph will be parsed by all the aspects, including the file aspect, ensuring that any file references contained within the subgraph will also be processed.

As such factory modules exist above the aspects in the dependency rules, it is possible for them to have knowledge of individual aspects. If a file contains resources only pertinent to a single aspect, then the factory can communicate directly with the aspect or even be a part of the aspect itself, bypassing the need to insert this data into the scene graph.

Scene conditioners. When a scene is constructed from a variety of file types and by recursively dereferencing nodes, in this fashion it can result in a structure with many redundant nodes and various other inefficiencies. To counteract this, a further system of modules is used to iterate over sections of the scene graph, analyzing and optimizing its structure. These conditioning modules can also be used to add further attributes to entities required by an aspect, thus acting as a preprocessing stage for the aspects.

When a subgraph is constructed by the factory system, it is processed by preinsertion conditioners. Then, once it has been inserted into the scene graph, it can be processed by a set of post-insertion conditioners to perform further operations based on the context of its position within the graph. The tasks carried out by these conditioners are specific to the engine, the design of the aspects, and the types of files being loaded. Their modular nature makes it simple to construct a small, highly specialized conditioner for each task.

Pre-insertion conditioners are often used to optimize scene data that may be needed during the authoring of the assets but not required in the specific game. Doing so in the conditioning stages reduces the complexity of the factories, allowing for a finer grained control. These might include tasks such as

- the removal of collision geometry that has been exported to matching API-specific files earlier in the asset pipeline but still exists in the source file;

- the removal of editor-specific nodes representing cameras and other UI elements that exist within the scene.

Post-insertion conditioners, on the other hand, perform tasks that require knowledge of the context into which a file's contents is dereferenced. Such tasks might include

- generating unique IDs with which to reference each node;

- propagating transforms to the dereferenced subgraph so that the nodes are positioned and oriented relative to the subgraph's immediate parent in the scene;

- collapsing long columns of redundant nodes that contain no data beyond transforms and only a single child. These are often created during the dereferencing process and artificially increase the depth of the scene.

Offline processing. The flexibility of the architecture allows it to be used in constructing not just various engine configurations but also tools that work upon the same data set. Such tools can be used to process or analyze scene data offline using a very different set of aspects and conditioners from those involved in the game itself.

These can be built into the asset pipeline to automatically process data exported from authoring programs and create files optimized for loading directly into the game on a range of target platforms.

10.6   Implementation

One of the key principles of this engine design is the construction of scene nodes through data aggregation rather than explicit classes within the engine's code. Much of the interaction between the aspects and the core scene will be informed by the implementation of this principle. It is therefore worthy of more in-depth discussion.

Nodes are in essence containers that associate a description of each attribute, a name and a type identifier, with a pointer to the relevant data. The Standard Template Library (STL) provides a variety of containers with different properties and a shared interface (see Listing 10.1), making it relatively simple to choose one to fit any given situation [SGI 11]. In this instance an associative container like a map or set (or multimap/multiset if you want to allow duplicate attribute names) would be an obvious choice because it features easy searching of content and does not require elements to be stored in contiguous memory, which can cause excessive fragmentation when inserting/deleting contents.

```
std::map<std::pair<attribute name, attribute type>, attribute data>
```

Listing 10.1. Using a map to store attributes.

In reality, all searching, insertion, and removal of data should ideally be restricted to the initialization and shutdown of objects, making the choice of container less vital. Custom allocators can be written to further reduce the impact of memory reallocation from containers, although their implementation is beyond the scope of this chapter.

The attribute data can be of any type. However, a container may only hold objects of a single type. Therefore, a layer of indirection must be introduced by storing a set of uniform pointers to the nonuniform set of attribute data. Data could be constructed on the heap and then the pointer returned cast to void. This has the notable drawback of discarding any type information regarding the data and the possibility of calling its destructor without being able to cast it back to the original type.

Another solution is to construct an attribute interface class from which a templated class can be automatically derived for each attribute type. This will allow information about the type to be accessible via the interface class as well as provide the appropriate virtual destructor to clean up the attribute data. Through the use of compile time features, generally provided as part of runtime type information (RTTI), it is possible to retrieve a simple type information object that represents the type of data being stored, allowing it to be identified and compared against other types. (See Listing 10.2.) Such an implementation will allow the attribute objects to not only store correctly typed pointers to their respective data, but also to store the identifying name of the attribute and provide access to a type info object. As such, a separate key is not required to identify the attribute when searching, and the contents of the node can be stored using a set constructed with a custom sorting algorithm that interrogates the interface pointer for the name and type of the attribute.

10.7 Aspect Interactions

Aspects are deliberately independent of one another, and the core of the engine interacts with them all through a generic interface. The only code that knows about the composition of the engine will be the project-specific code used to assemble all the relevant modules, aspects, factories, and conditioners, though even this could theoretically be performed through data.

During the course of a session, the core of the engine will be initialized, then each aspect will be initialized in turn before being registered with the core to receive events and be provided with access to the scene representation. Once

```
class iAttribute
{
public:
    virtual                          ~iAttribute()=0;

    virtual type_info                GetTypeID()        const=0;
    virtual const std::string&       GetName()          const=0;
};

template<typename _tAttribute>
class cAttribute : public iAttribute
{
public:
    cAttribute(): m_name(), m_pData(NULL) {}
    ~cAttribute()                            { if(m_pData) delete m_pData; }

    type_info          GetTypeID() const { return typeid(_tAttribute); }
    const std::string& GetName()   const { return m_name; }

    _tAttribute*       GetPointer()       { return m_pData; }

private:
    std::string    m_name;
    _tAttribute*   m_pData;
};
```

Listing 10.2. Attribute classes.

this occurs the engine can start one or more threads and from these execute any update loops that the aspects may require. It is here that any aspect precedence should be resolved; correct functioning of the engine may be dependent on the order of updates, and there will usually be an optimal order and frequency with which aspects should be updated.

10.7.1 Aspect Update

As each aspect is autonomous, being in effect a *vertical slice* of engine functionality, each has its own update loop performing all the operations needed to manage both the core scene and its own internal resources in respect to its subset of functionality (Figure 10.9).

When it is time for the aspect to update, it must acquire a lock on the core of the engine, then process any new events that have occurred since the last update, parsing subgraphs that have been added to the scene or removing aspects for nodes that will soon be deleted. It will also need to synchronize the values in its own internal objects with those of the corresponding scene nodes before releasing the lock. At this point the aspect is potentially updating in parallel with the rest of the engine, performing any internal logic. Once its internal state is fully updated, the aspect reacquires the lock upon the core of the engine, synchronizes the core entities with any relevant data, and generates new events before again

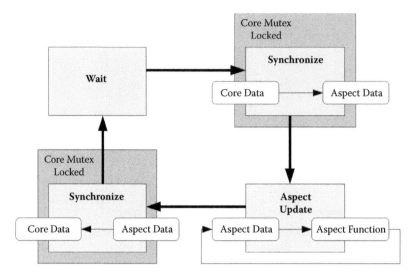

Figure 10.9. Aspect update loop.

releasing the lock. It must now wait for a period of time until the next update step can be performed.

10.7.2 Example: Entity Changing Color Upon Taking Damage

This simple example describes a possible set of operations that might occur in an aspect-driven engine when a bullet strikes a character in the game causing the target's material values to change.

1. During the update of the physics aspect, a bullet object intersects the collision hull of a character. This generates an internal event in the physics API. Upon synchronizing with the core at the end of its update, the physics aspect pushes a collision event referencing the bullet and the character onto the event queue.

2. When the logic aspect next updates, it retrieves the collision event from the queue. It recognizes the event type "Collision" and is observing both of the referenced nodes. It calls the collision handler script functions for both the bullet and the character. The collision handler for the bullet requests that the subgraph representing the bullet be removed from the scene. That of the character changes the character's internal state to "damaged," subtracts the bullet's damage attribute from the character's health attribute, and modifies the character's color attribute from white to red.

3. Once the logic aspect releases its lock on the core, the render aspect is able to start updating. It notices the pending removal state change on the

bullet subgraph and cleans up the internal entity that it uses to represent the bullet. It then proceeds to synchronize the shader inputs for all the currently visible entities with the attributes of their respective nodes. In doing so it pulls the new color value from the character's attribute, and when the relevant batch is rendered, the character is now tinted red.

10.8   Praetorian: The Brief History of Aspects

Praetorian, Cohort Studios' proprietary engine, was developed using the aspect-based architecture described. The engine's purpose was to enable the company to quickly develop prototypes of games within a wide range of genres and then to rapidly bring the most promising projects to full production.

Initially it was planned to develop these games using middleware to save development time; however, while evaluating third-party engines, it became clear that they were often better suited to one genre or another or they placed restrictions on the features that could be added. Therefore it was decided to allow a small group with limited resources to begin work on an internally developed engine that could be used across the wide range of projects envisaged.

An alternative agile-themed approach might have been to develop engine functionality directly within projects, refactoring the code as the project developed until any common functionality fell out into modules that could be shared. However, such an approach might take far longer to produce an engine that could be used as the foundation for a wide range of games with several projects needing to reach completion.

The first goal of the new engine was to reduce the amount of new code that needed to be written, reusing existing technology or incorporating third-party APIs wherever possible. In that light, it made sense to create a core scene representation onto which these disparate modules could be attached.

The term *aspect* was originally encountered in research regardingmultithreaded access to a single scene graph in OpenSG [Voss et al. 02], indicating that each thread or remote client would maintain a specific viewpoint on the contents of the scene graph. This diverged from simple multithreaded access into the idea of such viewpoints differing based on the task required and then into the concept of aspects as described in this chapter.

Further research suggested that adopting an aggregation-based approach to entities over inheritance would further increase the flexibility of the system [Cafrelli 01]. This would neatly sidestep the issue of developing a hierarchy of entities that could meet the needs of all the aspects without creating dependencies between them.

The last component of the core to be implemented was the event system. Although it was in the initial design, it had been dropped to help speed up the development of the aspects that depended on the core interface being complete.

Event management was later implemented though not as a central part of the core. Events were used within the transform aspect to correctly propagate updates of node positions to their children, then used in relation to collision events between physics objects, and finally were implemented within the scene graph to facilitate asynchronous operations on the structure of the scene graph, processing insertions and removals. In hindsight it would have been more efficient to implement event handling from the outset even if it meant proceeding with a less efficient design.

Development of the aspects progressively added functionality to this core. The first usable build of the engine simply consisted of the render aspect and a simple file loading module that could parse Collada data and push it into the core (later formalized as the Collada factory used by the file aspect). This allowed assets to be exported from model-editing software and imported directly into the engine. Shortly after this the first pass of the physics aspect allowed the objects exported with additional data to be updated by a physics simulation. This was followed by a scripting aspect that updated objects with associated Lua scripts to perform game logic.

Within a relatively short period of time, project teams were able to start building games on a simple but functional data-driven engine that grew in functionality as it was required.

10.9 Analysis

As with all designs, there are benefits and limitations to building an engine based upon aspects. The characteristics of the aspect-based architecture predominantly benefit the development process through modularity and flexibility of data, but the rigid structure and indirection create limits on efficiency.

Benefits. The benefits of building an engine based upon aspects include the following:

- Promoting a data-driven development philosophy helps to engage asset creators and designers.

- The highly modular drop in/drop out architecture allows quick changes to the engine.

- The modular nature allows quicker tracking and debugging of errors.

- Encapsulation accelerates the integration of third-party APIs.

- The direct connection of shader and script inputs makes developing new graphics techniques and prototype game features easier and quicker.

- Decentralizing the knowledge and management of functionality increases the autonomy of the programmers of different aspects.

Limitations. The following are some of the limitations:

- The creation of duplicate or redundant data within the aspects and the aggregate structure used to store data in the core can significantly reduce memory efficiency.

- The asynchronous nature of aspects can be difficult for programmers to work with as cause and effect are rarely directly adjacent in the code.

- Trying to maintain complete autonomy between aspects across multiple threads of execution requires additional mechanisms to coordinate the order of updates.

10.10   Conclusion

There are as many ways to write an engine as there are programmers. The aspect-based architecture is as much a concession to the individuality of developers and the needs of their projects as it is an engine design in itself. At the same time, while the strict rules regarding encapsulation of aspects and accessing shared data inevitably limit optimization, they help to structure and inform the design of functionality, making it quicker to implement what is required.

The intention is to provide developers with a simple, easy-to-follow framework that helps accelerate engine development but leaves them with the freedom to explore structures and techniques where desired.

The use of this engine architecture has been observed across a wide range of projects, and it appears, on the whole, to meet these goals. There will always be situations that stretch the abilities of an engine, but none so far have proved insurmountable within the limits of this design.

10.11   Acknowledgments

Thanks to everyone who worked at Cohort Studios and in particular those whose work had an impact on Praetorian and its design. Thanks to Andrew Collinson who worked on Praetorian from the very beginning and Bruce McNeish for having the foresight to let us start building it, despite being straight out of university. Also, thanks to Gordon Bell for showing a lot of faith when I told him things "should just work" and to Peter Walsh for lending his many years of experience and a truly comprehensive range of anecdotes. Thanks to Shaun Simpson for helping to push the engine design so much further in so many ways and to Dave Sowerby for the scripting aspect and his tireless work in actually making a game, which is after all the reason behind all this.

Bibliography

[Cafrelli 01] C. Cafrelli. "A Property Class for Generic C++ Member Access." In *Game Programming Gems 2*, edited by Mark DeLoura, pp. 46–50. Hingham, MA: Charles River Media, 2001.

[Revie 12] D. Revie, "Designing a Data-Driven Renderer." In *GPU Pro 3*, edited by Wolfgang Engel, pp. 291–319. Boca Raton, FL: CRC Press, 2012.

[SGI 11] Silicon Graphics International. *Standard Template Library.* http://www.sgi.com/tech/stl/, 2011.

[Voss et al. 02] G. Voss, J. Behr, D. Reiners, and M. Roth. "A Multi-Thread Safe Foundation for Scene Graphs and Its Extension to Clusters." In *Proceedings of the Fourth Eurographics Workshop on Parallel Graphics and Visualization*, pp. 33–37. Aire-la-Ville, Switzerland: Eurographics Association, 2002.

11

Kinect Programming
with Direct3D 11
Jason Zink

11.1 Introduction

The Microsoft Kinect is a sensor peripheral originally released for use with the Xbox 360 and later on the PC. The sensor includes a variety of different inputs, including a microphone array, color image acquisition, and a special depth image-acquisition system. With these diverse inputs, Microsoft has developed a number of algorithms that can be used to sense and track the position, pose, and voice status of one or more users—which can subsequently be used by a game or application as input. This allows for a number of new ways for a user to interact with their computers—instead of using a gamepad, the user interacts with the application in a very natural way.

Applications that wish to utilize the Kinect and the data streams that it produces can do so with the Kinect for Windows software development kit (SDK) [Microsoft 12]. To properly obtain and interpret these data streams, a developer must understand the mechanics of how the device operates and also have a clear understanding of what can and can't be done with it. This chapter seeks to provide the theoretical underpinnings needed to use the visual and skeletal data streams of the Kinect, and it also provides practical methods for processing and using this data with the Direct3D 11 API. In addition, we will explore how this data can be used in real-time rendering scenarios to provide novel interaction systems.

11.2 Meet the Kinect

We will begin our investigation of the Kinect by examining how its camera systems function. The camera system is essentially composed of a color (RGB) camera, an infrared (IR) projector, and an IR camera. These three elements are shown

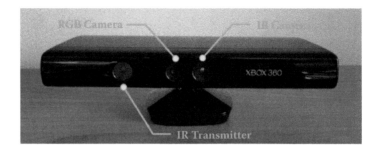

Figure 11.1. The Kinect sensor and its individual camera system components.

in Figure 11.1. These sensors, when used together, provide a form of a vision system that can be used to track and inspect the scene in front of them. We will investigate each of these devices in more detail in the following sections.

11.2.1 Color Camera

We begin with the color camera, as this is probably the most familiar device for most developers (and consumers in general for that matter). This camera functions more or less the same as a traditional web cam does. Visible light from the scene enters into the camera lens and eventually strikes a sensing element inside of the camera. With a large array of sensing elements arranged in a rectangular grid, the camera can determine the amount of visible light in the scene over a predefined area at a particular moment in time. This general concept is used to synthesize a camera image at regular time intervals, which ultimately produces a video stream. The geometry involved in this process is depicted in Figure 11.2.

With this in mind, we can consider the geometric interpretations of the scene

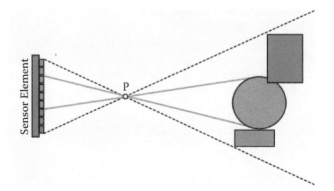

Figure 11.2. The geometry of the Kinect color camera.

that are used in such an imaging system. It is quite common to utilize a pin-hole camera model, in which we make the assumption that all light that enters the camera and strikes the sensing element does so through a single point, the pinhole. This point is referred to as the center of projection, and it is essentially the same concept as the camera location when rendering a scene. We will examine the mathematical properties of this camera configuration in Section 11.3, "Mathematics of the Kinect," but for now we can simply accept that we are able to capture the projected 2D image of the 3D world being viewed by the camera.

The color images obtained by the Kinect are made available to the developer at a variety of frame rates and data formats. At the time of writing this chapter, the available resolutions span from 1,280 × 960 all the way down to 80 × 60. This selectable resolution allows the developer to only receive the size of data that is most relevant for them, reducing bandwidth if a full size image isn't needed. The available data formats include an sRGB and a YUV format, which again allow the data to be provided to the program in the most suitable format for a given application. Not all resolutions are valid for all formats, so please consult the Kinect for Windows SDK documentation [Microsoft 12] for more details about which combinations can be used.

11.2.2 Depth Camera

The Kinect's depth-sensing system is much more unique than its color-based brother. As mentioned above, the depth-sensing system actually uses two devices in conjunction with one another: an infrared projector and an infrared camera. The IR projector applies a pattern to the scene being viewed, producing an effect similar to that shown in Figure 11.3. The infrared camera then produces an image that captures the pattern as it interacts with the current scene around the Kinect. By analyzing the pattern distortions that are present in the image, the distance from the Kinect to the point in the scene at each pixel of the infrared image can be inferred. This is the basic mechanism used to generate a secondary image that represents the depth of the objects in the scene.

Figure 11.3. Sample infrared and depth images produced by the Kinect depth-sensing system.

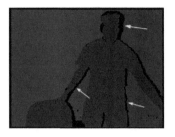

Figure 11.4. Blind spots in the depth image caused by the offset of the IR transmitter and receiver.

It is worth noting the location of the IR transmitter and receiver with respect to one another, as well as the color camera. The IR transmitter is located at the far side of the Kinect, with the color and IR cameras located in the center of the device. The relative locations of these components on the Kinect have a significant effect on their respective operations. For example, since the IR transmitter is offset from the IR camera, the portions of the scene that can be "viewed" by each of them are slightly different. This effect is depicted in Figure 11.4, where it can be seen that there are portions of the scene where no depth information is available.

In a real-time rendering context, you could imagine a very similar configuration with a camera and a spotlight light source that are oriented in a similar fashion as the IR transmitter and receiver are. The blind spot corresponds to the "shadow" produced by the spot light, and the camera is still able to "see" a portion of the shadow. This same effect applies to the relationship between the depth camera and the color camera as well. There will be portions of the scene that are visible in the color image that aren't visible in the depth image and vice versa. In addition, this also means that a scene point within one image may or may not be at the same pixel location within the other image. Since the two cameras are close together these discrepancies are usually minimal, but they still exist and must be taken into consideration. We will consider how to handle these effects in Section 11.3, "Mathematics of the Kinect."

Similar to the color-image stream, the depth data is made available to the application in a variety of resolutions and data formats. The depth data itself provides a 13-bit value representing the camera space Z-coordinate of the object being sensed at each pixel. This value provides a millimeter precision value, with a valid data range of either 800 mm to 4,000 mm or 400 mm to 3,000 mm depending on the operational mode selected. In addition, the remaining 3 bits per pixel can be used to provide a player ID produced by the Kinect skeletal system. The available resolutions are 640 × 480, 320 × 240, or 80 × 60. Once again, please check the SDK documentation for full details about the possible combinations of these options.

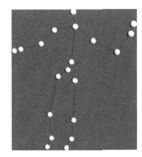

Figure 11.5. A visualization of the skeletal information available from the Kinect.

11.2.3 Skeletal Tracking

As discussed earlier in the chapter, one of the biggest advances that the Kinect provides is the ability to view a user with the sensing systems we have just described and to discern where they are within the scene and what pose they are holding. This is made possible by the Kinect by analyzing each pixel of the depth frame and applying a decision tree algorithm to determine to which part of a human body that pixel is most likely to belong [Shotton et al. 11]. All of this work is largely hidden from the developer—we simply receive the benefit that we know what the user's pose is in any give frame.

In general, the skeletal information that is available is quite similar to the skeletal information that one would expect when rendering a skinned model [Fernando and Kilgard 03]. (See Figure 11.5.) Each joint is represented by an absolute position and optionally an orientation that describes that portion of the model. In recent releases of the Kinect for Windows SDK, there is even support for different types of skeletons. For example, when a user is standing, it is possible to obtain a full 20 joint skeleton. However, when a user is sitting it is also possible to obtain a smaller skeleton that only includes a reduced subset of 10 joints corresponding to the upper body. This allows for a wide variety of usage scenarios and gives the developer freedom to choose how to interact with the user.

11.3 Mathematics of the Kinect

In this section we will look at the mathematics required to interpret the various camera spaces in the Kinect and to develop the needed concepts for matching objects in each space together. As we have just seen, the Kinect has two different camera systems, producing color and depth images. Both of these cameras can be handled in the same manner, using the pinhole camera model. Understanding this model will provide the necessary background to take an object found in one of the camera images and then determine to what that object correlates in the other image.

As a brief aside, conceptually the acquisition of an image with a camera uses the same geometric concepts as rendering an image, except that the two operations are effectively inverses of one another. In rendering we have a geometric model of the objects in the scene, and then we project them to an image plane. With a camera, the 2D image is generated for us by the real world, and we are trying to convert back to a 3D geometric representation of the objects in the scene. Keeping this in mind during the following discussion should provide some familiarity to the concepts being discussed.

11.3.1 Pinhole Camera Model

The simplest camera model is typically referred to as a *pinhole camera*. This name comes from the fact that we assume that all light that enters the camera to create the image enters through only a single point and is then striking an image sensor inside the camera. An example of this type of camera configuration is depicted in Figure 11.6, which only considers the y- and z-axes for the sake of simplicity.

Using this image as a reference, we can develop the equations that govern the projection of 3D objects to 2D representations of those objects in an image. On the right side of the diagram, we can see an example point P that we want to project onto our image plane. The light that is reflected off of point P travels toward the camera, and only some small amount of the light is able to enter the camera through the pinhole. That light then strikes the image sensor, which we will simply refer to as the image plane.

The path along which this light travels defines two triangles: one outside of the camera and one inside of the camera. Since the interior angles of both of the

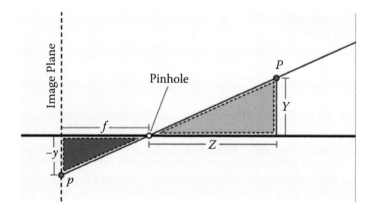

Figure 11.6. The pinhole camera model.

triangles are the same, we can use similar triangles to determine where the point P will project to:

$$\frac{y}{f} = \frac{Y}{Z},$$

$$y = \frac{yY}{Z}.$$

Here we denote world coordinates in 3D space as capital letters, while the image space coordinates are denoted with lowercase letters. The same relationship can be used to show the mapping of P in the x-direction as well:

$$x = \frac{fX}{Z}.$$

With these two simple relationships, it is possible to project a point in the scene to a point in the image. However, to go the other direction and take an image point and unproject it back into the world, we can only determine a ray along which the point must lay. This is because a traditional camera only produces an intensity value at each pixel—you no longer have any information about how deep into the scene the point was when the image was taken. Fortunately for us, the Kinect has two different camera systems—one of which produces a depth value at each pixel. The next section discusses how to take advantage of this fact and find a mapping between the 2D depth and color images we are given and the 3D objects that appear in them.

11.3.2 Kinect Coordinate Systems

When we are given a depth image from the Kinect, we are essentially given three pieces of data for each pixel. The first two are the x and y image coordinates where that particular pixel is located. In addition, the value stored at that pixel provides the world-space distance from the depth camera. This is precisely the Z distance that we used from Figure 11.6 when projecting a point onto the image. Given this additional piece of data, we can easily determine the world-space point that every pixel in the depth image represents by changing around our previous equations:

$$X = \frac{xZ}{f},$$

$$Y = \frac{yZ}{f}.$$

This allows us to utilize the Kinect to produce 3D representations of the scene that it is viewing. That is already an interesting capability, but we also want to be able to map the color-image stream to this 3D representation so that we can produce a colored surface and take full advantage of the Kinect's abilities. The process for doing this requires us to know how to take a depth pixel, convert it to world space, and then determine where that point would project to in the color image. This is more or less converting from the depth camera's coordinate system to the color camera's coordinate system.

We have already discussed most of the required concepts to do this. The conversion from depth-image pixel to world space is already described above. We also know the final step in the process, which is to project from world coordinates to the color-image coordinates. However, we need to know what is different about how the world space is perceived by each of the cameras. In Figure 11.1 we can see that the depth and color cameras are offset from one another. This means that an object that appears in the center of the depth-image stream will appear off-center in the color-image stream. Our mapping process requires us to know how to compensate for this offset—we want to know where in the color image our depth pixels will end up!

This process is actually quite common in computer vision, and it is typically referred to as *stereo calibration* [Bradski and Kaehler 08] and is used to find corresponding points in two cameras. The process itself can be somewhat complex, although there are fairly good examples available in open-source libraries. However, the hard work of performing this calibration is already performed for us by the Kinect SDK. A set of functions are provided to map between depth-image coordinates and color-image coordinates that uses the factory calibration of the Kinect. This is a very useful set of tools that can handle most of the heavy lifting for us. We will use these functions in our example application later in this chapter.

11.4 Programming with the Kinect SDK

At this point, we are now ready to see in more detail how we can acquire the Kinect data streams and use them in an example application. This section will cover how to initialize the runtime and start acquiring data. Next we will discuss how to map that data into a Direct3D 11 resource and finally how to use and interpret those resources for a visualization of the Kinect data. The example program has been written with the Hieroglyph 3 [Hieroglyph 3 12] open-source Direct3D 11 framework. The framework, along with the example program and utility code, is available for download from its Codeplex project page. The general interfacing to the Kinect is available in the GlyphKinect project, while the example application is available in the KinectPlayground project.

To enable your application to receive information from the Kinect, you must first install the Kinect for Windows SDK. This SDK is freely available from Microsoft [Microsoft 12] and is provided with an installer that takes care of setting up the drivers and the build environment for the Kinect (there are good installation instructions available with the SDK, so we won't repeat them here).

```
hr = NuiInitialize(
    NUI_INITIALIZE_FLAG_USES_DEPTH_AND_PLAYER_INDEX |
    NUI_INITIALIZE_FLAG_USES_SKELETON |
    NUI_INITIALIZE_FLAG_USES_COLOR );
```

Listing 11.1. Initializing the Kinect runtime.

Once the SDK is installed, we must build the connection between the Kinect API and our target application. This is actually a fairly painless process, but it requires some thought to be put into how the Kinect data is received and stored for later use. There are two options provided by the runtime for getting access to the data. The user can either poll the runtime to find out if new data is available, or an event system can be used in which the runtime signals to the application when new data is ready for processing. We will discuss the event-based model since it is more efficient, and we will describe its implementation here.

11.4.1 Initialization and Acquisition

The first step in getting access to the Kinect data is to initialize the runtime. This is done with a single function, NuiInitialize, whose arguments allow you to specify which data streams you are interested in receiving. In Listing 11.1 we request the three data streams that have been discussed earlier in this chapter: the color-image stream, the depth-image stream with player index, and also the skeletal player data stream.

After we tell the runtime what data we want, then we simply need to provide a mechanism for the runtime to signal that the data is available for reading. This is performed with a set of events, each of which is used to indicate that data is available from one of the data streams. The application creates an event and then passes it to the runtime when opening each data stream. In return we receive a handle with which to identify the data stream. The resolution and format of the data stream is configured during the opening of the stream. This process is shown in Listing 11.2 for the depth-image stream.

```
m_hNextDepthFrameEvent = CreateEvent( NULL, TRUE, FALSE, NULL );

hr = NuiImageStreamOpen(
    NUI_IMAGE_TYPE_DEPTH_AND_PLAYER_INDEX ,
    NUI_IMAGE_RESOLUTION_320x240 ,
    0,
    2,
    m_hNextDepthFrameEvent ,
    &m_pDepthStreamHandle );
```

Listing 11.2. Opening a data stream.

```
HRESULT hr = NuiImageStreamGetNextFrame(
    m_pDepthStreamHandle,
    0,
    &pImageFrame );

INuiFrameTexture * pTexture = pImageFrame->pFrameTexture;
NUI_LOCKED_RECT LockedRect;
pTexture->LockRect( 0, &LockedRect, NULL, 0 );

if( LockedRect.Pitch != 0 ) {

    BYTE * pBuffer = (BYTE*) LockedRect.pBits;

    if ( m_pSysMemDepthBuffer != NULL ) {

        USHORT * pBufferRun = (USHORT*) pBuffer;

        for( int y = 0 ; y < 240 ; y++ ) {
            for( int x = 0 ; x < 320 ; x++ ) {

                USHORT s = * pBufferRun;
                USHORT RealDepth = (s & 0xfff8) >> 3;
                USHORT Player = s & 7;


                pBufferRun++;
                USHORT * pDestBuff =
                 (USHORT*)(&(m_pSysMemDepthBuffer[(x+320*y)*2]));
                *pDestBuff = RealDepth;
            }
        }

        m_DepthFrameTimer.Update();
        m_pSysMemDepthBuffer = NULL;
    }
}

NuiImageStreamReleaseFrame( m_pDepthStreamHandle, pImageFrame );
```

Listing 11.3. Acquiring a depth frame from the Kinect runtime.

What we have set up here is the mechanism for the runtime to let us know when the next depth image frame is ready. The passed-in event will be triggered when the frame is ready, and the handle is used to refer to the depth frame later on. Once the runtime signals that a frame is ready for reading, the application must acquire access to it using runtime methods. To complete this event-based system, we utilize a separate processing thread that simply waits for the event to be signaled and then copies the frame data as necessary. This process is depicted in Listing 11.3, once again for the depth data stream.

Getting the data from the runtime consists of four general steps. First, we acquire the frame using the NuiImageStreamGetNextFrame function. This returns a structure that contains an INuiFrameTexture pointer, which holds the actual frame data. Next we lock this texture interface, read the raw frame data out, and finally release the frame after we are finished with it. The actual bit format for each image or data stream will vary based on the data formats that you have configured during initialization, but this general process allows the developer to easily access all of the stream-based data that the Kinect runtime makes available. For example, instead of receiving an `INuiFrameTexture` pointer, when working with the skeletal information the application will access an `NUI_SKELETON_FRAME` structure. Further examples of reading out each type of data can be found in the example program.

11.4.2 Direct3D 11 Resource Selection

Once the data streams of the Kinect are accessible to our application, we have to do something with the data that they carry. In order to use this data with Direct3D 11, we must first select an appropriate Direct3D 11 resource to house the data streams for us. In general, Direct3D 11 requires us to follow a particular sequence when updating a resource with data from the CPU. Resources must be created with the specification of their intended "usage." This usage indicates how the resource will be read from and/or written to by the application. Since the resources will be written to by the CPU and read by the GPU, this means that we need to perform a two-step update process. First the CPU will update a staging resource, which is then followed by copying the contents of the staging resource to an additional default usage resource. (See Figure 11.7.) This second resource is then accessible for reading within the programmable pipeline stages of the GPU.

In addition to choosing the usage options of our resources, we also need to decide what type of resource would make the most sense for holding the desired data. In general, the type of resource will be dictated by the way that an application will be using the Kinect data. For our two image-based data streams, a natural first choice for holding each frame would be a texture resource. These textures would be created with their own appropriate formats for the data that they are holding, but accessing their contents would be fairly intuitive.

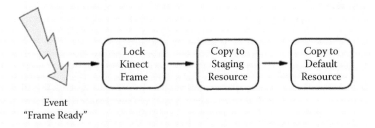

Figure 11.7. The process of acquiring data from the Kinect runtime and using it in the GPU.

However, we should also consider which programmable pipeline stage will be using these resources before finally deciding on a resource type. If the resources will be used within the compute-shader stage, then there is a choice of using either a buffer or a texture resource—whichever fits better with the threading model to be used in the compute shader. If the resources will be used directly to perform some rendering in the graphics pipeline, then the choice is based more upon which pipeline stage will be used to read the data. When the pixel shader will be consuming the data, then a texture resource probably makes the most sense due to the similarity of pixel to texel orientation. However, if the data will be read elsewhere in the pipeline, then either a buffer or a texture may make more sense. In each of these examples, the key factor ends up being the availability of addressing mechanisms to access the resources.

With these considerations in mind, we have chosen to utilize the `Texture2D` resource type for the color, depth, and depth-to-color offset data in the sample application since we are performing the manipulation of the frame-based data streams in the graphics pipeline. You may have noticed the mention of the depth-to-color offset data, which hasn't been described up to this point. This is a resource used to map from a depth pixel to the corresponding coordinates in the color pixel, using the Kinect API functions to fill in the data with each depth frame that is acquired. This essentially gives a direct mapping for each pixel that can be used to find the correspondence points between the depth and color frames.

We have also chosen to acquire the color data stream at a resolution of 640 × 480, with the sRGB format. The depth data stream will use a resolution of 320 × 240 and will contain both the depth data and the player index data. Finally, the skeletal data is only used on the CPU in this application, so we simply keep a system memory copy of the data for use later on.

11.4.3 Rendering with the Kinect

After selecting our resource types, and after configuring the methods for filling those resources with data, we are now ready to perform some rendering operations with them. For our sample application, we will be rendering a 3D reconstruction of the depth data that is colored according to the color camera frame that is acquired with it. In addition, a visualization of the skeletal joint information is also rendered on top of this 3D reconstruction to allow the comparison of the actual scene with the pose information generated by the Kinect.

The first step in the rendering process is to determine what we will use as our input geometry to the graphics pipeline. Since we are rendering a 3D representation of the depth frame, we would like to utilize a single vertex to represent each texel of the depth texture. This will allow us to displace the vertices according to the depth data and effectively recreate the desired surface. Thus we create a grid of indexed vertices that will be passed into the pipeline. Each vertex is

```
VS_OUTPUT VSMAIN( in VS_INPUT v)
{
    VS_OUTPUT o;

    // Multiplying the retrieved depth by 0.001 is done
    // to convert to meters.
    float fDepth =
        ((float)KinectDepthBuffer[
            int2( v.coords.x, 240-v.coords.y ) ]) * 0.001f;

    uint2 uiOffsets =
        KinectOffsetBuffer[ int2( v.coords.x, 240-v.coords.y ) ];

    o.colorOffset =
        float2 ( (float)uiOffsets.x / 640.0f,
                 (float)uiOffsets.y / 480.0f );

    float3 normal =
        ComputeNormal( int2( v.coords.x, 240-v.coords.y ) );

    float diffuse =
        max( dot( normal, normalize( float3( 1.0f, 0.0f, 1.0f )) ),
             0.0f );

    // x_meters = ( x_pixelcoord - 160) * z_meters *
    // NUI_CAMERA_DEPTH_IMAGE_TO_SKELETON_MULTIPLIER_320x240

    // y_meters = ( y_pixelcoord - 120) * z_meters *
    // NUI_CAMERA_DEPTH_IMAGE_TO_SKELETON_MULTIPLIER_320x240

    float x_meters = (v.coords.x-160) * 0.003501f * fDepth;
    float y_meters = (v.coords.y-120) * 0.003501f * fDepth;
    float4 DepthCamViewSpace =
        float4( x_meters, y_meters, fDepth, 1.0f );

    o.position = mul( DepthCamViewSpace, WorldViewProjMatrix );
    o.height = fDepth;

    return o;
}
```

Listing 11.4. The vertex shader for rendering a 3D reconstruction of a depth frame.

given its integer coordinates of the pixel in the depth texture that it should be representing.

Next we will consider the pipeline configuration that we will use to render the geometry. In total, we will use the vertex shader, the geometry shader, and the pixel shader stages. We will consider the vertex shader first, which is shown in Listing 11.4. It starts out by reading the depth data and the offset for the depth-to-color mapping frame texture. This offset is supplied in pixels, so we scale it accordingly to produce texture coordinate offsets out of them. Next we calculate a normal vector from the depth texture by using a Sobel filter. The normal vector is not strictly needed, but it can be used to perform lighting operations on the reconstructed surface if desired.

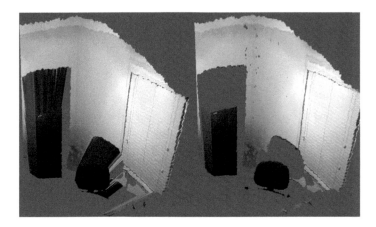

Figure 11.8. Removal of unwanted triangles from our surface reconstruction.

Now we take the depth pixel data and convert it to a 3D position in the depth camera's view space. This is performed using the relationships we provided earlier, where the focal length and camera parameters are baked into constants (the values of the constants are taken from the Kinect for Windows SDK header files). After this we project the depth-camera view-space coordinates to clip space for rasterization and also keep a copy of the original depth value for use later on.

Each of these vertices is then assembled into a triangle by the graphics pipeline and passed to the geometry shader. The main reason for using the geometry shader is to detect and remove triangles that have excessively long edges. If there is a long edge on a triangle, it would typically mean that the triangle spans a discontinuity in the depth frame and it doesn't represent a real surface. In that case we can skip the passing of the triangle into the output stream. Figure 11.8 demonstrates the removal of these unwanted features, and the geometry shader to perform this operation is shown in Listing 11.5.

After the geometry passes the geometry shader, it is rasterized and passed to the pixel shader. In the pixel shader we can simply sample the color frame texture with our offset coordinates. This performs the mapping from depth space to color space for us and allows us to minimize the amount of work needed to be performed at the pixel level. The pixel shader code is provided in Listing 11.6.

The end result of this rendering is a reconstructed 3D representation of what is visible in front of the Kinect. The final step in our sample application is to visualize the skeletal data and how it corresponds to the reconstructed surface. We receive the complete skeletal data from the Kinect runtime and simply create a sphere at each joint to show where it lies. Since the joint positions are provided in the depth-camera view space, there is no need for further manipulations of the data. The overall results of our sample application can be seen in Figure 11.9.

```
[maxvertexcount(3)]
void GSMAIN( triangle VS_OUTPUT input[3],

            inout TriangleStream<VS_OUTPUT> OutputStream )
{
    float minHeight = min( input[0].height, input[1].height );
    minHeight = min( minHeight, input[2].height );

    float maxLength =
        max( length( abs(input[0].height - input[1].height) ),
             length( abs(input[1].height - input[2].height) ) );

    maxLength =
        max( maxLenth,
             length( abs(input[2].height - input[0].height) ) );

    if (( minHeight > 0.1f ) && ( maxLength < 0.075f )) {
        for ( int i = 0; i < 3; i++ ) {
            OutputStream.Append(input[i]);
        }
    }
    OutputStream.RestartStrip();
}
```

Listing 11.5. The geometry shader for expelling elongated triangles.

```
float4 PSMAIN( in VS_OUTPUT input ) : SV_Target
{
    float4 vValues = KinectColorBuffer.Sample(
        LinearSampler, input.colorOffset );
    return ( vValues );
}
```

Listing 11.6. The pixel shader for sampling the color frame data.

Figure 11.9. The final output from the sample application.

11.5   Applications of the Kinect

Now that we have seen the Kinect data streams used in a live application, we should have a feel for what types of data are available to us for use in an application. We can now take a moment and consider several potential types of applications that can be built around it. As described in the introduction, this data is very unique and allows the developer to interact with their users in very new and novel ways. This section will briefly describe several uses for the Kinect to get the reader thinking about the possibilities—and hopefully lead to more ideas for uses of this intriguing device.

11.5.1   3D Scanning

At first thought, it is very common to see the Kinect as a very inexpensive 3D scanner. Certainly, having the ability to generate a 3D model of a real-world object would have many potential practical uses. However, in practice this isn't quite as straightforward as initially thought. The depth data that is received in each depth frame is not a complete surface mapping due to the blind spots that we discussed earlier. In addition, the depth data that is available within the frame is typically somewhat noisy over time. These restrictions introduce complications to the implementation of such a scanner system.

However, even with these limitations in mind, it is indeed possible to perform a 3D scanning function with a fairly high fidelity. The Kinect Fusion algorithm [Izadi et al. 11] utilizes computer vision algorithms that track the location and orientation of a handheld Kinect device. By knowing its own position relative to the object being scanned, multiple depth frames can be taken over time to build a volumetric model of that object. Using multiple frames allows the blind spots from one frame to be filled in by the data introduced in a subsequent frame. This process is repeatedly performed, and over time a complete model can be built. The final generated volumetric model can then be either converted to a renderable mesh or stored in whatever desired output format for later use. Thus for the cost of a computer and a Kinect, you can produce a 3D scanner!

11.5.2   Interactive Augmented Reality

If we have the ability to generate models of a particular object, then by extension it should also be possible to generate a model of the complete environment that is surrounding the Kinect as well. With a fairly accurate model of the surroundings around a user, it becomes possible to use this information within a rendered scene that combines the physically acquired Kinect data with simulation-based data. For example, after acquiring a model of the area surrounding your desk, you could then produce a particle system simulation that interacts with the model. Each particle can interact with objects in the scene, such as bouncing off of your desk.

The resulting combined scene can then be rendered and presented to the user in real time from the perspective of the Kinect. Since the volumetric model of the environment really is actually volumetric, the rendering of the particle system will properly occlude rendered objects if a physical object obstructs the view of it from the Kinect. This provides a very powerful mechanism for incorporating game elements into a realistic scene.

11.5.3 User Pose and Gesture Tracking

The production of the user pose information is perhaps the most widely known application of the Kinect data streams. This is essentially provided to the developer for free, with a stream of skeletal frames being provided by the Kinect runtime. With skeletal information available for the user in the scene, it becomes quite easy to render an avatar that appears in the pose in which the user is currently. For example, the user could move around their living room and see a rendered representation of their favorite character onscreen that is moving in the same manner. This effect is not only a novelty. This mechanism can be used as the input method for a game or simulation. In such a scenario, the avatar could interact with a game environment and replicate the user's actions in the game, letting them interact with a virtual scene around them.

However, since the virtual scene is likely not going to match exactly the physical scene surrounding the user, this method will quickly become limited in what interactions can be modeled. Instead, the user's movements can be translated into the detection of gestures as they move over time. These gestures can then be used as the input mechanism for the game or simulation. This breaks the direct dependency between the virtual and physical scenes and allows the developer to both interact with their users directly and also provide them with a large scene to interact with as well. This is the typical method employed by games that currently use the Kinect.

11.5.4 Rendering Scenes Based on User Pose

Another interesting area that the Kinect can be used for is to manipulate rendering parameters by monitoring the user. A prime example of this is to modify the view and projection matrices of a rendered scene based on the location and proximity of a user's head to the output display. For example, when a user is standing directly in front of a monitor, the typical view and projection matrices are more or less physically correct. However, when the user moves to stand to the right of the display, the view and projection matrices used to project the scene onto the monitor are no longer correct.

The Kinect can be used to detect the user's head location and gaze and modify these matrix parameters accordingly to make the rendered scene change correctly as the user moves. The effect of this is that a display serves as a type of window into a virtual scene, which is only visible by looking "through" the display. This introduces many new potential uses and interactions that can be integrated into an application. For example, in an adventure game the user can move around and gain a better view of the scene around them, potentially finding new items that aren't visible by standing directly in front of the display.

11.6   Conclusion

We have taken a brief tour of the Kinect device and studied what it can do, how we as developers connect to and use its data streams, and also some of the interesting and novel applications that could arise from its use. There is a vibrant development community building around the Kinect, with significant support from Microsoft for this popular device. It remains to be seen what the next fantastic application of the Kinect will be, but I hope that this chapter has helped put the reader into the position that they can start building it!

Bibliography

[Bradski and Kaehler 08] Gary Bradski and Adrian Kaehler. *Learning OpenCV: Computer Vision with the OpenCV Library.* Sebastopol, CA: O'Reilly Media, 2009.

[Fernando and Kilgard 03] Randima Fernando and Mark Kilgard. *The Cg Tutorial: The Definitive Guide to Programmable Real-Time Graphics.* Boston: Addison-Wesley Professional, 2003.

[Hieroglyph 3 12] Hieroglyph 3 Rendering Library. http://hieroglyph3.codeplex.com, last accessed August 27, 2012.

[Izadi et al. 11] Shahram Izadi, David Kim, Otmar Hilliges, David Molyneaux, Richard Newcombe, Pushmeet Kohli, Jamie Shotton, Steve Hodges, Dustin Freeman, Andrew Davison, and Andrew Fitzgibbon. "KinectFusion: Real-Time 3D Reconstruction and Interaction Using a Moving Depth Camera." In *Proceedings of the 24th Annual ACM Symposium on User Interface Software and Technology*, pp. 559–568. New York: ACM, 2011.

[Microsoft 12] Microsoft Corporation. Kinect for Windows homepage. http://www.microsoft.com/en-us/kinectforwindows/, last accessed August 27, 2012.

[Shotton et al. 11] Jamie Shotton, Andrew Fitzgibbon, Mat Cook, Toby Sharp, Mark Finocchio, Richard Moore, Alex Kipman, and Andrew Blake. "Real-Time Human Pose Recognition in Parts from Single Depth Images." In *Proccedings og the 2011 IEEE conference on Computer Vision and Pattern Recognition*, pp. 1297–1304. Los Alamitos, CA: IEEE Press, 2011.

12

A Pipeline for
Authored Structural Damage
Homam Bahnassi and Wessam Bahnassi

12.1 Introduction

There are scenarios in which a game needs to show damage and injuries to characters and buildings. Severe damage cannot be conveyed acceptably by classic decal approaches, as the structure of the object itself changes. For example, a character might have holes in its body, or severed limbs, or a building façade might take rocket damage in various locations causing holes in the structure.

In this chapter, we present a description of a full pipeline for implementing structural damage to characters and other environmental objects that is comparable to previous work in the field. We cover details for a full pipeline from mesh authoring to displaying pixels on the screen, with qualities including artist-friendliness, efficiency, and flexibility.

12.2 The Addressed Problem

True structural damage often requires change in shape. The modeling of the 3D object may differ in the damaged parts. There are tools and methods that automatically calculate fracture and damage on objects, but these methods generally work in cases where damage detail is not important and the structure of the object is generally uniform (e.g., concrete columns or wood planks). The other possibility is to add damage detail manually according to an artistic vision. We call this *authored damage*, and it has the capability of revealing any details the artist finds interesting (e.g., rebars in concrete walls or internals of a space alien). It is true that authored damage can lack in variety when compared to an automatic method due to the latter being able to generate virtually unlimited possibilities of fracture and damage, but even nowadays the automatic methods tend to "bake" their fracture calculations to avoid performance issues at runtime, thus reducing variety in a similar way as authored damage does. In this chapter, we concentrate on authored damage techniques.

We aim in this chapter to find a solution to the problem that fulfills the following goals as much as possible:

- Artist-friendliness. The technique should not add complexities to the authoring process or requirements that interfere with common authoring techniques.

- Flexibility. It should be able to support an unrestricted number of damage areas on a single object in unrestricted locations.

- Rendering efficiency. It should have a predictable rational cost and avoid taxing the original object rendering with expensive shader costs or reducing overall efficiency.

In the next few sections we review previous work and compare it against the goals above, then we describe our own technique and compare it also to the same set of goals.

12.3 Challenges and Previous Work

Previous work addressing the issue exists with varying capabilities and features [Vlachos 10, Reis 10, Kihl 10]. In all of these works, it is clear that the main difficulty is in hiding the original undamaged mesh geometry in order to make a clean location for the damage geometry to replace it. This step is necessary because, in most cases, the damage shape "eats away" from the original structure, thus some parts of the original 3D object need to be removed.

There are a number of existing techniques for hiding geometry from a 3D object in real time. The list below shows a selection of these techniques. It also includes some of the shortcomings of each of them.

- Modeling the original object in separate pieces that can be shown/hidden selectively at runtime: Although this is simple, it suffers from a few issues. First, it can be inconvenient for artists to build objects in separate pieces (particularly animated characters). Second, rendering of such an object might require several draw calls, which can cause performance issues in some cases.

- Collapsing bones to hide geometry by forcing triangles to become degenerate around a certain point [Reis 10]: This is effective and easy to implement; however, it is limited to skinned meshes only and cannot handle arbitrary geometry-hiding locations (i.e., only terminal limbs can be hidden).

- Using alpha-testing to kill pixels of the geometry to be hidden [Vlachos 10]: This technique offers flexible per-pixel geometry hiding. However, it has the following disadvantages (most are already listed in [Vlachos 10]):

  ○ It is not very efficient as the hidden pixels will execute their pixel shader even though alpha-testing might kill them, and pixel processing cost is not saved for hidden pixels.

  ○ The use of alpha-testing may interfere with early-Z optimization on some GPU architectures (e.g., Playstation 3 RSX) and thus results in reduced depth-testing efficiency for the entire rendered object.

  ○ The technique evaluates a parametric ellipsoid for each damage area in the shader. This puts a practical limitation on the number of evaluated ellipsoids, which in turn limits the number of damaged areas that may appear on a single object at once (only two were allowed in [Vlachos 10]).

  ○ Killing pixels in the shape of an ellipsoid results in curved cuts that are difficult to fill accurately with replacement damage geometry. The workaround (which our artists found inconvenient) is to add a thick edge or "lip" around the actual damage geometry to cover the empty areas between the ellipsoid and the damage geometry.

The second part of the problem is the rendering of damage geometry in an optimal manner. Although this part of the problem is not as challenging as the first part, it can still benefit from some optimizations that we will cover in this chapter.

12.4 Implementation Description and Details

From the previous section one can conclude that finding an optimal solution for the problem is not a straightforward task, but there are a few lessons that can be learned to reach better results:

- It is more efficient to hide geometry by triangle culling than per-pixel culling.

- Per-pixel culling makes it difficult for artists to fill the gaps.

- If support for an unrestricted number of damage areas is needed, then the calculations must be independent of the number of damage areas; otherwise, performance will increasingly suffer the more damage areas are supported.

On a high level, the approach we propose can be summarized by the following steps:

1. Authoring step. An artist paints groups of polygons on the mesh with vertex colors to mark them as "hide-able."

2. Pipeline step. The content pipeline processes each colored polygon group and assigns it an ID.

3. Runtime step. At runtime, the programmer decides to hide all polygons belonging to a certain ID, so he passes the ID in a bit field to the vertex shader. The vertex shader collapses the marked polygons, effectively preventing them from rasterizing any pixels. The programmer then renders fill geometry in place of the hidden polygons.

Next, we delve into the details of each of the above mentioned steps. Then we will analyze the technique and see if it achieves the goals mentioned in Section 12.2.

12.4.1 Authoring Step

The first step is to decide what damage will appear on the 3D object. For each enumerated damage area, we assign it a unique color code. This color will be used to mark polygons of the 3D object to be hidden when the respective damage is to appear at runtime. Table 12.1 shows an example for a hypothetical character object.

Once the table is set, the artists use the color-coding scheme to paint *polygons* of the 3D object belonging to each supported damage area using per-vertex coloring techniques (see Figure 12.1). This is necessary to later allow the programmer to hide the polygons at runtime before he renders the replacement damage geometry.

It is important to note that even though we are using per-vertex colors, the artist should restrict the painting to entire polygons, not individual vertices. This is key to allow proper polygon hiding, otherwise rendering artifacts will appear (see Figure 12.2).

In Maya, this can be achieved by selecting the polygons that belong to a particular damage area and applying the corresponding color code value using the "Apply Color" command. In Maya 2012, this command can be accessed from the "Polygons" module under the "Color" menu. In the command options, the

Damage	Color Value	Color Sample	Color Name	Color ID
Head	255/0/0		Red	1
Left shoulder	0/0/255		Blue	2
Left arm	0/255/0		Green	3
Left palm	255/255/0		Yellow	4
Chest	255/0/255		Pink	5
Stomach	0/255/255		Cyan	6
...	...	...	...	...

Table 12.1. Damage-area color-code table for a hypothetical character object.

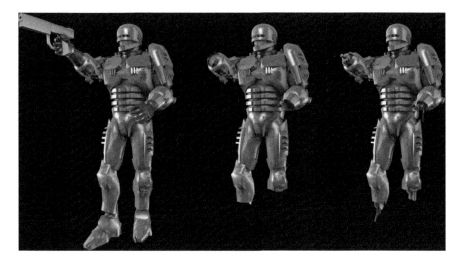

Figure 12.1. Painting polygons to mark them as "hide-able" at runtime (left). The model with marked polygons hidden, leaving gaps to be filled by damage geometry (center). Filling the gaps with damage geometry (right).

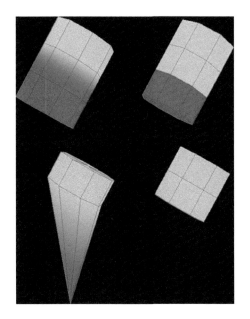

Figure 12.2. Incorrect painting (top left) results in stretching polygons when applying the technique at runtime (bottom left). Proper painting is applied to whole polygons (top right), resulting in proper hiding at runtime (bottom right).

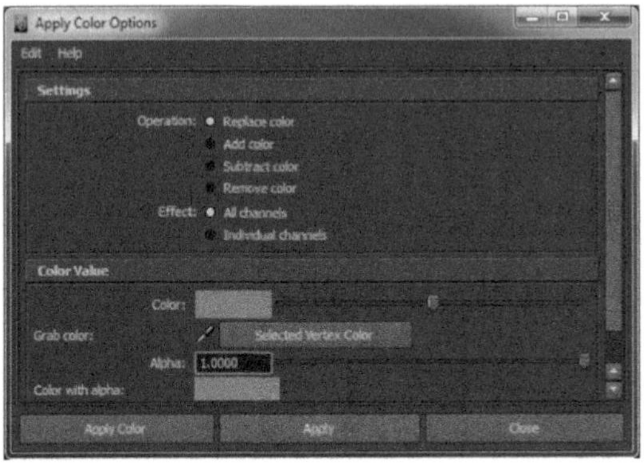

Figure 12.3. Recommended settings for the "Apply Color" command in Maya.

"Operation" should be set to "Replace color" or else the applied color may not be the same as the one selected in the option box (see Figure 12.3).

In Softimage, the same result can be achieved by using the "Paint Vertex Color Tool" under "Property\Map Paint Tools." Color and other painting options can be set through the "Brush Properties" under the same menu (see Figure 12.4). The following recommended options can be set under the "Vertex Color" tab in the brush property page:

- Color Paint Method to Raycast.

- Bleeding to Polygon.

These values allow the artist to paint colors on polygons quickly without being afraid of bleeding on vertices of adjacent polygons.

Finally, in 3dsMax, one can add the "VertexPaint" modifier to the object. This will open a floating window where the artist can control brush options. The "Opacity" value should be set to 100 to get the exact selected color. Then the

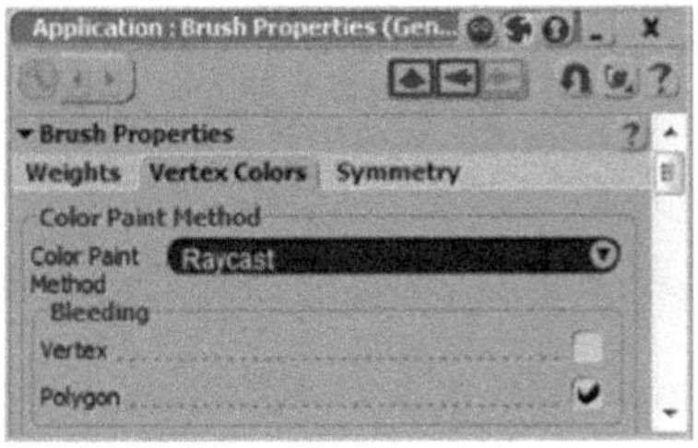

Figure 12.4. Recommended settings for "Brush Properties" in Softimage.

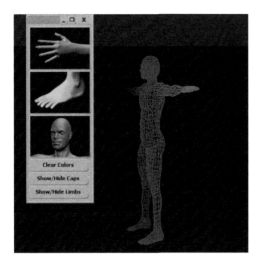

Figure 12.5. A custom toolbar in Softimage with three commands for applying vertex colors for each damage area, in addition to other commands for visualizing the damage effects.

artist can either apply the color using the "Paint All" button on the selected polygons, or he can use the brush tool to paint the colors on vertices directly.

To avoid applying incorrect colors and to minimize painting time, a custom tool can be developed to store the color codes for each damage area. The artist can use this tool to apply the correct colors without needing to memorize their values or mappings. (See Figure 12.5.)

Once the polygons are marked, the artist can then hide them in the 3D authoring tool and build the replacement damage geometry to fit their place accurately.

The main 3D object is then exported along with its per-vertex color channel and the accompanying damage meshes for processing in the pipeline step.

12.4.2 Pipeline Step

The goal of the pipeline step is to transform the marked damage areas into data that can be easily and effectively used at runtime. Table 12.1 shows the color coding scheme used for an object. The last column assigns a single integer value (*color ID*) to each color code entry. This is the value that will be used at runtime to identify each damage area. We use the data-processing pipeline to detect the color coding of each polygon and assign it its matching ID instead. Later, we will see how this ID is used in the runtime step.

The data-processing pipeline usually performs tasks such as reading mesh data from source files, cleaning the mesh and optimizing it, compressing its data, and checking it for validity. We add one more step that does the following:

1. Validate the presence of vertex color information in meshes that support damage, otherwise consider this an export error (missing required information).

2. For each vertex, compare its color with the colors in the damage areas table. If the color was not found, then return an error (unknown color code used for marking a damage area).

3. Obtain the ID of the color found from the table, and store the ID in the final mesh vertex information. If the vertex does not belong to any damage area, set the ID to zero.

   It is possible to store this number in its own vertex attribute or to try to compress it. For example, we can store the ID in the vertex normal by adding 1 to the ID value then multiply it by the vertex normal value. To extract the value in the shader, simply take the vertex normal length and subtract 1 from it. The original vertex normal can be reclaimed by standard normalization. This trick requires no additional space of per-vertex data, but it might not work if the vertex normal is already compressed by some form.

This color ID is all that is needed to support hiding the polygons at runtime. The damage geometry exported with the main object can be processed using the standard mesh-processing pipeline.

12.4.3 Runtime Step

The final step of the process is to actually use the data to control the visibility of damage on the object at runtime. For each object supporting damage, we prepare a bit field that holds flags representing the visibility of each damage area on the object, where the first bit represents the damage area with ID 1 from the damage table, and so on. To hide the polygons of the object associated with a particular color code, we raise the bit matching the ID to 1. Notice that multiple bits may be set to 1 simultaneously, resulting in the ability to show/hide different damage area polygons freely. Damage areas that are not "damaged" yet should set their respective bits in the bit field to 0.

When the time comes to render the object, the damage bit field is set as a vertex-shader constant. The vertex shader then checks if the damage ID value of the vertex has its respective bit set to 1 in the bit field. If so, the position of the vertex is set to (0, 0, 0); otherwise it is left untouched.

Note that this bit-check operation is an integer computation that is not supported by all shader models and current-generation console GPUs. Thus, we will describe a way to achieve the same result with floating-point mathematics only for such cases.

```
// Return 1 if bit at zero-based index is 1 in the bit field;
// otherwise return 0.
float checkBit(float bitField, float bitIndex)
{
    float bitValue = pow(2,bitIndex);
    bitField = fmod(bitField,bitValue*2);
    return (bitField - bitValue) >= 0.0f ? 1.0f : 0.0f;
}
```

Listing 12.1. Code for the checkBit() function.

Bit-field check using floating-point mathematics. The damage bit-field value is stored on the CPU as an integer variable. However, current-generation shader models do not support useful integer operations, so we have to do the work with floating-point mathematics. First, store the bit-field value in a vertex shader constant. We store the value "logically." That is, if our bit-field is 010110, then this translates to 22 in decimal, so we set the constant value to 22.0f for the vertex shader. Then, in the vertex shade,r we can pass this value to the function checkBit() in Listing 12.1.

Listing 12.2 shows an example of how to use the checkBit() function to detect whether the vertex belongs to a damaged area or not.

It is important to note that using floating-point mathematics to do the bit check cannot benefit from all bits available in the floating-point variable. If we were doing integer mathematics, then a standard 32-bit integer can represent 32

```
extern float damageBitField;

VS_OUTPUT VS_Main(VS_INPUT In)
{
    .
    .
    .
    // Check whether this vertex belongs to a "damaged" area.
    // Damage ID is compressed with vertex normal.
    float damageID = round(length(In.normal))-1;
    if (damageID > 0)
    {
        float damaged = checkBit(damageBitField, damageID-1);
        In.position *= 1.0f-damaged; // Collapse vertex if damaged
    }
    .
    .
    .
}
```

Listing 12.2. Sample code of a vertex shader that supports damage.

damaged areas, but due to how floating-point numbers work, we are limited to 24 damaged areas per single-precision floating-point variable.[1]

One might note that this effectively limits us to 32 or 24 damaged areas at most (depending on whether we use integer or floating-point mathematics). But, in fact, it is still possible to support more bits at a fixed cost by utilizing more than one variable to store the bit field. The only reason we have limited ourselves to a single variable for the bit field so far is for ease of explanation and that it is expected that not many objects exceed that number of damage areas. Thus, the code given in Listings 12.1 and 12.2 is a simpler and faster version than the more general case we are going to show next.

Expanding the bit field into a bit array. To support an unrestricted number of damage areas, we have to modify the above method slightly. First, the bit field is now turned into a bit array on the CPU side. At render time, the bit array must be converted into an array of floating-point vectors of enough size to hold all bits in the array in the same way we did in the single variable case. Next, in the shader, based on the damage ID, we calculate the array index of the floating-point variable that holds the bit value. That variable is then passed to `checkBit()` and everything else remains unchanged. Listing 12.3 adds this operation to the same sample code in Listing 12.2.

Rendering replacement damage geometry. Now that we have managed to hide polygons of a damaged area in an effective manner, all that remains is to fill the gaps with replacement geometry that depicts the damage shapes. There are a few ways to do this, each having its pros and cons:

1. Rendering damage geometry in the same draw call as the main object: The benefit of this way is that no additional draw calls are ever needed for the damaged object. The disadvantage is that if the damage geometry is dense then rendering power may be wasted on processing vertices that remain hidden for quite some time (depending on gameplay circumstances). On some platforms this might be OK, as vertex processing power is often underused. However, this is not always the case (e.g., the Playstation 3 RSX is relatively slow in vertex processing).

   To implement this method, the damage-geometry vertices must be identified uniquely from the main-object vertices. This can be represented by one single bit in the vertex attributes (e.g., the sign of UV coordinate x). Then, depending on whether the vertex belongs to the main object or not, the condition for collapsing the vertex based on its damage ID is reversed.

---

[1]You can safely represent integer numbers in a 32-bit floating-point variable to a value up to 16,777,215 (0xFFFFFF) that is 24-bits wide. Higher numbers can still be represented, but discontinuities occur (e.g., 16,777,217 cannot be represented), thus going to such limits is not reliable.

```
extern float damageBitArray[16]; // Set to maximum size needed.

VS_OUTPUT VS_Main(VS_INPUT In)
{
    .
    .
    .
    // Check whether this vertex belongs to a "damaged " area.
    // Damage ID is compressed with vertex normal.
    float damageID = round(length(In.normal))-1;
    if (damageID > 0)
    {
        // Assume a single-precision floating-point number
        // can represent an integer number of about 24 bits.
        float bitArrayIndex;
        damageID = modf((damageID-1)/24, bitArrayIndex) * 24;
        float damageBitField = damageBitArray[bitArrayIndex];
        float damaged = checkBit(damageBitField, damageID);
        In.position *= 1.0f-damaged; // Collapse vertex if damaged
    }
    .
    .
    .
}
```

Listing 12.3. Sample code of the more complex case of supporting an unrestricted number of damage areas in the vertex shader.

2. Rendering each damage geometry in a separate draw call: This is the direct method, but it suffers from increased draw-call count per damaged object. For certain platforms, this can be more efficient than wasting time processing hidden damage-geometry vertices all the time.

12.5 Level of Detail

One important aspect to 3D objects is that they might be authored in multiple levels of detail (LODs), which are used to increase rendering efficiency at runtime by reducing the geometric detail of a 3D object as it covers smaller area of the screen. Since our technique is tightly bound to the topology of the 3D object, any change in this topology requires adjusting the marked damage polygons and their replacement damage geometry. This requires that when the artist builds additional LODs for a certain 3D object, he must remember to mark the damage polygons in those additional LODs in a similar way to the main LOD. The replacement geometry could also benefit from having LODs of their own, but in some cases authoring LODs for those pieces of geometry is not necessary, and the main LOD version can be reused as is with lower main-object LODs. It really depends on the type of 3D object and how it was modeled.

12.6   Discussion

If we compare our proposed technique with the goals we set in Section 12.2, we can find that it manages to largely achieve all of the three aspects together:

1. Artist-friendliness. Artists can easily mark hidden polygons and can accurately model replacement damage geometry. Supporting LODs requires a little bit of rework, but unfortunately that is how LODs are done.

2. Flexibility. The technique supports an unrestricted number of damage areas on a single object in unrestricted locations. The only limitation is that damage areas cannot overlap (a vertex may belong to only one damage area at a time).

3. Rendering efficiency. The only cost added is a few conditional vertex-shader instructions. The cost is irrespective of the number of damage areas on the object. Additionally, we do not require any changes to the object's pixel shader nor its rendering states. There is no need for alpha-testing nor other tricks that might hinder hardware optimizations.

There are many damage effects that can benefit from this technique. However, some games might have different requirements that are not compatible with this technique. In that case, we hope at least that we have succeeded in giving some ideas to build upon when developing new techniques for damage effects.

12.7   Conclusion

In this chapter, we have studied the possible approaches of rendering authored structural damage on 3D objects. A review of previous work is made with a description of the advantages and drawbacks of each technique mentioned. A high-level description of a new artist-friendly, efficient, and flexible technique for rendering authored damage is presented, followed by detailed implementation steps covering the entire pipeline from content authoring to rendering at runtime, including a few tricks for simulating bit-testing with floating-point mathematics on shader profiles that do not support native integer operations. The matter of supporting LODs is highlighted, followed finally by a discussion that compares the new technique to the ideal-case goals.

There is potential for further expansion of the technique so that it supports the complex case of overlapping damage areas.

12.8   Acknowledgments

We would like to thank Abdulrahman Al-lahham for his help and time reviewing this chapter.

Bibliography

[Kihl 10] Robert Kihl. "Destruction Masking in Frostbite 2 Using Volume Distance Fields." SIGGRAPH Course: Advances in Real-Time Rendering in 3D Graphics and Games, Los Angeles, CA, July 2010. (Available at http://advances.realtimerendering.com/s2010/Kihl-Destruction% 20in%20Frostbite(SIGGRAPH%202010%20Advanced%20RealTime% 20Rendering%20Course).pdf.)

[Reis 10] Aurelio Reis. "Real-Time Character Dismemberment." In *Game Engine Gems 1*, edited by Eric Lengyel, Chapter 19. Burlington, MA: Jones and Bartlett Publishers, 2010.

[Vlachos 10] Alex Vlachos. "Rendering Wounds in Left 4 Dead 2." Presentation, Game Developers Conference 2010, San Francisco, CA, March 9, 2010. (Available at http://www.valvesoftware.com/publications/ 2010/gdc2010_vlachos_l4d2wounds.pdf.)

13

Quaternions Revisited
Peter Sikachev, Vladimir Egorov, and Sergey Makeev

13.1 Introduction

Quaternions have been extensively used in computer graphics in the last few years. One defines a quaternion as a hypercomplex number, $w + xi + yj + kz$, but in practice it is convenient to consider it to be a 4D vector (x, y, z, w) with a special operation of multiplication defined for it. In 3D computer graphics, quaternions can be used to encode rotations and coordinate systems.

In this chapter we describe the experience of using quaternions in the MMO-RPG engine. In comparison with [Malyshau 12], we propose a quaternion interpolation solution that does not increase vertex count. Besides, we go deeper in detail regarding precision and performance issues. Finally, we strive to cover a broader range of problems, including normal mapping, skinning, instancing, morph targets, and nonuniform scale.

13.2 Quaternion Properties Overview

While strict wording may be found in the excellent book [Lengyel 11], we will summarize some key quaternion properties below. The quaternion $\mathbf{q}$ is called *normalized* if $\|\mathbf{q}\| = \sqrt{x^2 + y^2 + z^2 + w^2} = 1$. The geometric meaning of a normalized quaternion (x, y, z, w) can be easily perceived if we re-write it as

$$(x, y, z, w) = \left(x' \sin\left(\frac{\alpha}{2}\right), y' \sin\left(\frac{\alpha}{2}\right), z' \sin\left(\frac{\alpha}{2}\right), \cos\left(\frac{\alpha}{2}\right) \right).$$

This quaternion encodes an α radians rotation around the axis (normalized vector) (x', y', z'). This notation immediately provides us with the following properties for quaternions:

- The quaternion $\mathbf{q}$ is equivalent to the quaternion $k\mathbf{q}$ where $k \in \mathbb{R}$.

- The normalized quaternions (x, y, z, w) and $(-x, -y, -z, -w)$ are equivalent.

- The inverse rotation for the quaternion (x, y, z, w) is denoted by the quaternion $(x, y, z, -w)$.

The angle between two normalized quaternions $\mathbf{q_1}$, $\mathbf{q_2}$ can be found as $\theta = 2\arccos(q_1, q_2)$, where (q_1, q_2) is a per-component dot product of q_1 and q_2. In this chapter all quaternions are implied to be normalized if not noted otherwise.

13.3   Quaternion Use Cases

In our engine we used quaternions for multiple purposes. Our goal was to replace bulky 3×3 rotation and tangent-space matrices throughout the entire engine. This affected the following engine components:

- normal mapping,

- generic transforms,

- instancing,

- skinning,

- morph targets.

For each of these cases we discuss the implications in the following individual sections.

13.4   Normal Mapping

Normal mapping was an initial reason to use quaternions engine-wide. Normal mapping requires one to define a so-called tangent space at each surface location: a coordinate system, which is defined by tangent, bi-tangent (often erroneously called bi-normal), and normal (TBN).

Usually, these basis vectors are defined per model vertex and then interpolated inside triangles, and this is where the problems arise. First, TBN occupies at least six interpolator channels (provided we reconstruct the third vector using a `cross` instruction and pack a handedness bit without wasting an extra interpolator channel). This may be alleviated by packing TBN, but it comes at a pixel shader additional cost.

Second, TBN might need orthonormalization multiple times throughout the pipeline. In the case of a model-view matrix containing a nonuniform scale, we need to use inverse-transpose of the model-view matrix to transform TBN (tangents and bi-tangents use the same transform as normals). It is very expensive to invert a matrix in a shader, and in the case of a model-view inverse-transpose matrix pre-computation, we would need to pass this matrix through vertex attributes per instance in case of instancing. One possible hack is to re-use the original model-view matrix to transform TBN, but in this case we need to orthonormalize TBN afterwards to avoid lighting artifacts.

Moreover, TBN becomes unnormalized and loses orthogonality during interpolation. Hence, orthogonalization and normalization also need to be performed in a pixel shader. In our experience, this takes a significant amount of ALUs in vertex and pixel shaders.

We tried several methods enabling normal mapping without TBN in our engine. [Mikkelsen 10] needs so-called derivative maps as an input, which can be obtained from normal maps. However, on our assets this method was capable of conveying much less detail than regular normal mapping, which was unacceptable for artistic reasons.

We also tried the method in [Schüler 06]. It implies additional ALU cost for differential chain rule application. However, the greatest limitation appeared to be pipeline issues: the TBN basis generated by Autodesk Maya did not coincide with one derived from the texture-coordinate gradient. This resulted in different parameterizations, making it impossible to reuse already existing normal maps.

Encoding TBN with quaternions allows us to overcome these problems. However, there are several problems with this approach. One is TBN matrix *handedness*, which we will not discuss here as it is covered in detail in [Malyshau 12].

The other problem is quaternion interpolation. Quaternion *spherical linear interpolation* (SLERP) produces correct results without a prior alignment. However, since vertex attribute interpolation is not programmable, we interpolate quaternions linearly, which causes issues. [Malyshau 12] proposes a solution that increases the original vertex count by 7.5% and polygon count by 0.14%. Below, we propose a solution, which works for any correctly UV-mapped model, that does not change vertex and polygon count at all. Let us first explain the ground for this problem.

Let us consider quaternions $\mathbf{q}_1 = (x_1, y_1, z_1, w_1)$ and $\mathbf{q}_2 = (x_2, y_2, z_2, w_2)$. If their dot product $(\mathbf{q}_1, \mathbf{q}_2)$ is positive, the quaternions will interpolate along the shortest arc; otherwise they interpolate along the longest. That being said, if we take a $-\mathbf{q}_1$ quaternion (instead of an equivalent $\mathbf{q}_1$), the interpolation arc will be reversed. For vertex normals inside the triangles, we will expect to interpolate along the shortest arc. Yet, for a closed model, that might not always be the case. A natural solution to this will be to *align* all quaternions at the model's neighboring vertices by multiplying one of them by -1 so that their dot product becomes positive. However, this will not solve the problem in most cases.

Let us consider a cylinder model as in Figure 13.1. We will take a quaternion $\mathbf{q} = (0, 0, 0, 1)$ at the point A as a reference and start aligning all the quaternions

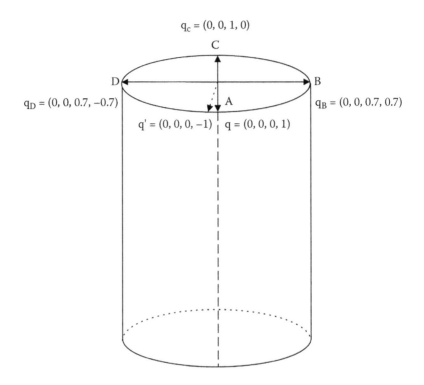

Figure 13.1. Aligning quaternions for the cylinder object.

on the cylinder surface one after another in the counterclockwise direction. As one can observe, when we return to point A after a turn around, the respective quaternion at this point will be $\mathbf{q'} = (0, 0, 0, -1)$. This means that neighboring vertices at point A will be *misaligned*, resulting in the long-arc quaternion interpolation as shown in Figure 13.2.

The geometrical justification for this effect lies in the quaternion nature. If we recall that a quaternion $\mathbf{q} = (x\sin(\frac{\alpha}{2}), y\sin(\frac{\alpha}{2}), z\sin(\frac{\alpha}{2}), \cos(\frac{\alpha}{2}))$, it becomes clear that while our turn around the angle α (and respective normal) made a complete $360°$, which corresponds to the full period of the function, it only made a half-period (since we have $\frac{\alpha}{2}$ as an argument) for the quaternion.

In the general case, this problem is unsolvable without a topology alteration. However, for a real in-game UV-mapped asset, we will never have a situation when we can find a closed chain of adjacent vertices on the surface of a model so that a normal makes a $360°$ rotation when we traverse this chain. This is true because a closed mesh cannot be correctly UV-mapped so that a texture, unique at each point, can be applied to this mesh. If we get back to the cylinder sample and try to map a 2D texture to the cylindrical surface (Figure 13.3),

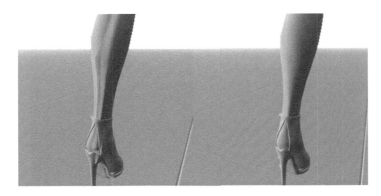

Figure 13.2. Normal rendering. Incorrectly interpolated quaternions (left) and correctly interpolated quaternions after alignment (right). [Image courtesy of Mail.Ru Group.]

this would mean that, at some point, a u-coordinate will change from 0 to 1 at the neighboring vertices, resulting in the whole texture u-range being mapped to the single triangle. To avoid this, artists duplicate the vertices of the model, having as a result vertices $\mathbf{v}$ and $\mathbf{v}'$ with the same position but different texture coordinates. This fact allows us to align quaternions at neighboring vertices without any further vertex duplication, which is described in Algorithm 13.1.

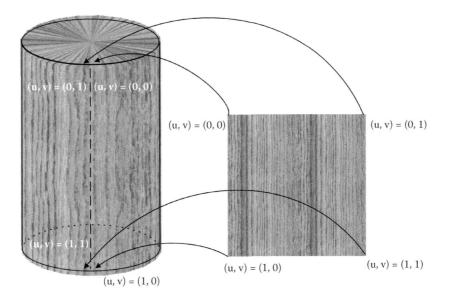

Figure 13.3. Textured cylinder object.

Require: Initialize all vertex flags as *non-traversed*
1: **while** *non-traversed* vertex exists **do**
2:     select any *non-traversed* vertex as **q**
3:     set **q** flag as *traversed*
4:     **for** every *non-traversed* vertex **q′** sharing edge with **q do**
5:         set **q′** flag as *traversed*
6:         align **q′** to **q**
7:         repeat recursively from step 4 for **q**:=**q′**
8:     **end for**
9: **end while**

Algorithm 13.1. Quaternion alignment algorithm for UV-mapped meshes.

13.5   Generic Transforms and Instancing

If we compare encoding transformations with quaternions and with matrices, quaternions will have several advantages. First, a transformation matrix needs 4×3 values to encode position, rotation and scale, while with *SQTs* (scale-quaternion-translation) we need only eight values provided we assume the scale to be uniform. Second, reverse rotation comes virtually for free in the case of quaternions, while for matrices this is a quite costly operation. Finally, multiplying two 3×3 rotation matrices will result in 45 scalar operations (additions and multiplications), while quaternions can be multiplied using a total of 28 scalar operations.

Therefore, we used quaternions in our engine as widely as possible. However, we have experienced several caveats with them.

The first one comes from the fact that a normalized quaternion **q** being multiplied by itself several times (i.e., $\mathbf{q}^n$) becomes significantly unnormalized. For example, an incremental rotation of an object at a same angle may lead to this. A straightforward solution to this is normalizing a quaternion multiplication product, but this significantly reduces efficiency, as normalization is usually a relatively slow operation. An alternative solution will be keeping a normalization assertion check for a debug version of an application and eliminating cases of all possible multiplications of a quaternion on itself.

Another limitation for quaternions is nonuniform scale. In *Skyforge* we needed a nonuniform scale for a family of effects classified as "channeling." Figure 13.4 shows an example of a channeling effect. The particular feature of this family of effects is that an effect is stretched between two arbitrary points in space. Hence, a nonuniform scale is needed to be applied to them.

While a nonuniform scale may co-exist with quaternions, we have faced several limitations, which should be taken into consideration at early production stages. They come from the fact that we effectively decouple scale from rotation (in contrast to conventional 3×3 scale-rotation matrices).

Figure 13.4. Channeling spell being cast. [Image courtesy of Mail.Ru Group.]

First, only *axis-aligned nonuniform* scale may be encoded. Figure 13.5 shows the difference between encoding the same transform with an SQT and a scale-rotation matrix. While a single scale-rotation transform performed by a scale-rotation matrix can also encode only an axis-aligned nonuniform scale, a superposition of these transforms can encode a non-axis-aligned scale, while a superposition of SQTs will always keep all scales axis-aligned. This means, for instance, that a box will always remain a box after any SQT transformations (keeping straight angles around its corners), but this is not a case for an arbitrary scale-rotation matrices superposition. In our experience, we did not have a strong need for such transformations. However, this can slightly increase the mesh count, as, for instance, different rhombi can no longer be encoded with a single mesh with different transformations applied.

Second, with SQTs all scale transformations are done in the *object space*. For instance, if you rotate an object at a $90°$ angle in the xy-plane and then scale along the x-axis, it will be scaled along the y-axis instead, as shown in Figure 13.6. In terms of channeling effects, this imposed a restriction on the content. All objects that a channeling effect consists of should be aligned along the major axis of the effect; otherwise, they will be stretched orthogonally to the effect direction.

For instanced objects, encoding rotation with quaternions worked straightforwardly. We provide more details on this in Section 13.8.

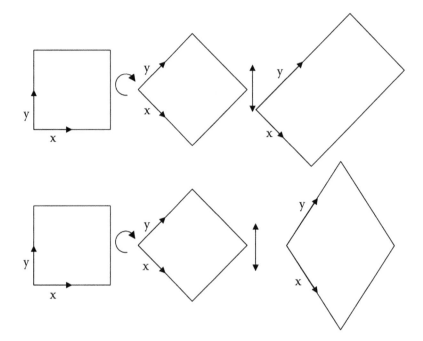

Figure 13.5. A box being rotated and scaled using SQT (top) and scale-rotation matrix (bottom). Object xy-axis is shown.

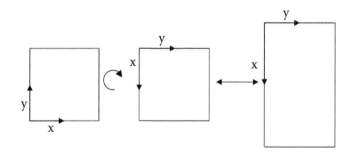

Figure 13.6. 90° rotation and scaling with SQT.

13.6   Skinning

In our engine we pack bone data for skinning into a texture. There are several reasons for this. First, as the game is supposed to run on a DirectX 9 compatible hardware, only 256 constants are available in the general case. Second, we wanted to enable character instancing: in the case of storing skinning data in a single texture, we need to store only a texture offset per instance. Thus, we

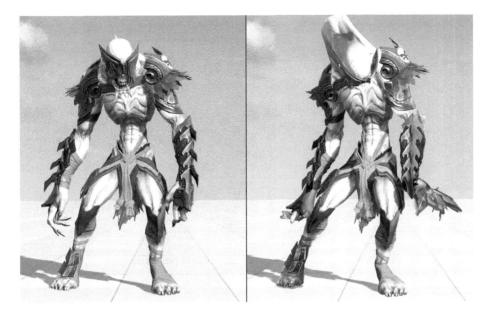

Figure 13.7. Matrix palette skinning (left) and direct quaternion blending (right). [Image courtesy of Mail.Ru Group.]

pack all bones of all characters in a single 2D texture, the format of which is discussed below. In fact, we use this texture as a "large constant buffer" which we dynamically address using an instance ID, in order to make skinning work for many characters on DirectX 9 compatible hardware.

A straightforward solution for using quaternions in skinning would be to interpolate quaternions, corresponding to different bones, *before* applying rotation; in the same way as matrices are interpolated in the *matrix palette skinning* approach, as proposed in [Hejl 04]. However, our experience shows that this method produces incorrect results when a vertex is skinned to several bones, which have significant rotation from a bind pose, as shown in Figure 13.7.

The mathematical reason for this lies in the fact that quaternions *cannot be correctly blended*. Provided quaternions can be very effectively *interpolated*, this sounds a bit controversial; therefore we provide a proof below.

Let us consider Figure 13.8. A quaternion $\mathbf{q}_2$ defines a $180 - \epsilon°$ rotation in an xy-plane and $\mathbf{q}_3$ corresponds to a $180 + \epsilon°$ rotation. If we blend quaternions $\mathbf{q}_1$, $\mathbf{q}_2$ and $\mathbf{q}_1$, $\mathbf{q}_3$ with weights $\lambda_1 = \lambda_2 = \lambda_3 = 0.5$, resulting quaternions $\mathbf{q}_4$ and $\mathbf{q}_5$ will point in significantly different directions if we use shortest-arc interpolation for blending. Taking ϵ infinitely small proves that the blending result of $\mathbf{q}_1$ and $\mathbf{q}_2$ ($\mathbf{q}_3$) is not *continuous*.

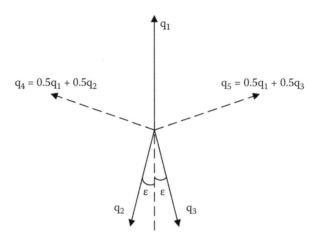

Figure 13.8. Discontinuity of blending two quaternions.

Furthermore, blending three or more quaternions is not *commutative*. Let us consider Figure 13.9. Quaternions $\mathbf{q}_1$, $\mathbf{q}_2$, and $\mathbf{q}_3$ specify $0°$, $140°$, and $220°$ rotations in the xy-plane, respectively. Let us set quaternion weights to $\lambda_1 = \lambda_2 = \lambda_3 = \frac{1}{3}$. The case where we blend quaternions in order $\mathbf{q}_4 = (\lambda_1\mathbf{q}_1 + \lambda_2\mathbf{q}_2) + \lambda_3\mathbf{q}_3$ will differ from the result when we blend them in order $\mathbf{q}_5 = (\lambda_1\mathbf{q}_1 + \lambda_3\mathbf{q}_3) + \lambda_2\mathbf{q}_2$.

Having said that, we do not blend quaternions directly. Instead, we blend final transformed vertex positions. This, obviously, slightly increases ALU count in the shader code, but we benefit from a reduced skinning texture size and fewer vertex texture fetches, as shown in Section 13.8.

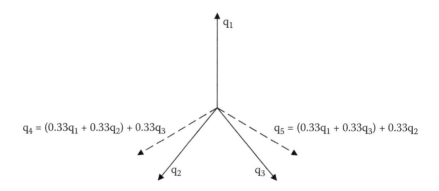

Figure 13.9. Ambiguity of blending three quaternions.

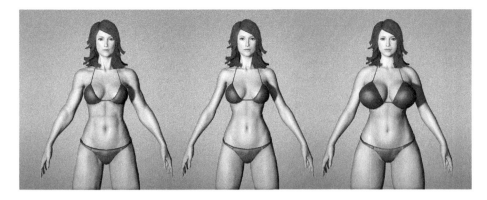

Figure 13.10. Original character (left) and two extreme morph targets (center, right). [Image courtesy of Mail.Ru Group.]

13.7 Morph Targets

As *Skyforge* is an MMORPG game, we want to give players as many opportunites to customize characters as possible. One of the most interesting customizations enables a player to change body proportions of his or her character in a continuous fashion. This is implemented via interpolation of each vertex between two so called *morph targets*, i.e., separate vertex streams. An example of such an interpolation is shown in Figure 13.10.

Regarding quaternions, only a few considerations should be kept in mind for morph targets. First, meshes, corresponding to different targets between which we are interpolating, should have the same topology and *uv*-mapping. This obviously includes handedness of initial TBN in vertices. Second, after we convert TBNs to quaternions, we should align quaternions, corresponding to the same vertex in different targets. This can be obtained naturally, if we start Algorithm 13.1 for both targets at the same vertex, as meshes share the same topology.

13.8 Quaternion Format

In this section we discuss how we store quaternions in memory and how we pack them when sending to GPU. Table 13.1 shows layouts we use for quaternions in our engine.

The most interesting case is a vertex quaternion. Our experiments have shown that 8-bit precision is enough for per-vertex quaternions. However, since TBNs can have different handedness, we also need to store a handedness bit. We did not want to spend another channel on it, so we came up with two solutions.

Case	Channels				
Vertex Quaternion	x (int8)	y (int8)	z (int8)	h (1b)	w (7b)
Model Transform	x (float32)	y (float32)	z (float32)	w (float32)	
Instance Data	x (int16)	y (int16)	z (int16)	w (0, calculated)	
Bone Transform	x (float16)	y (float16)	z (float16)	w (float16)	

Table 13.1. Quaternion packing for different scenarios. h stands for quaternion handedness.

First, we could store in the same byte a handedness bit and a sign bit for w and then reconstruct w in the shader as we operate onto normalized quaternions. We abandoned this approach, as unpacking w would lead to the sqrt instruction, which is costly and should be avoided in the shader.

Instead, we packed a handedness into the first bit and packed w into the remaining seven last bits (as an unsigned integer). It turned out that even seven bits is enough in the case of vertex quaternion. Furthermore, this approach resulted in a very fast unpacking, as shown in Listing 13.1. A nice property of this packing is that it interpolates correctly in all cases of vertex quaternions and morph targets. We implicitly use the fact that it is never a case in practice to interpolate quaternions with different handedness. In this case, the first bit of quaternions to be interpolated would always be the same, resulting in correct interpolation of low seven bits.

For model transforms, as we operate them on the CPU side, we store the quaternion values in float32 format. To pack a quaternion of instance rotation, we opted for int16 for several reasons. First, we wanted to keep instance vertex layout as small as possible, and 32-bit formats are definitely an overkill for a quaternion in terms of precision. Quaternion's values are limited to the $[-1, 1]$ domain, so we need only fixed-point precision. Unfortunately, 8-bit formats were not enough as they provide around 1–2° angle steps. While this was enough for a vertex quaternion, in the case of encoding an instance's position, such a

```
float UnpackFirstBitFromByte( float argument )
{
   return saturate((argument * 255.0f - 127.5f) * 100.0f);
}

float UnpackLow7BitsFromByte( float firstBit, float argument )
{
   return (argument * 255.0f - 128.0f * firstBit) / 127.0f;
}
```

Listing 13.1. Vertex quaternion unpacking.

```
inline uint16 Float2fp16( float x )
{
 uint32 dwFloat = *((uint32 *)&x);
 uint32 dwMantissa = dwFloat & 0x7fffff;
 int32 iExp = (int)((dwFloat>>23) & 0xff) - (int)0x70;
 uint32 dwSign = dwFloat>>31;


 int result = ( (dwSign<<15)
  | (((uint32)(max(iExp, 0)))<<10)
  | (dwMantissa>>13) );
 result = result & 0xFFFF;
 return (uint16)result;
}
```

Listing 13.2. `float32` to `float16` fast conversion.

large angle step resulted in non-smooth rotation and difficulties in aligning static instanced geometry for map designers.

Finally, we experimented with quaternion packing for skinning. Initially, we stored a skinning bone 3×3 scale-rotation matrix and position (12 values in total) in a `float32` RGBA texture. Therefore, we needed three vertex texture fetches per bone and we wasted 25% of the skinning texture for better alignment, resulting in four `float32` RGBA texels per bone. After switching to quaternions, we used SQT encoding with a uniform scale: this resulted in eight values in total. That allowed us to store a single bone information only in two texels, thus making two vertex texture fetches per bone. As we packed skinning values in a texture, the format of different SQT components had to stay the same. Scale and transform needed a floating-point format; this is why we picked `float16` (a.k.a. `half`). The only issue we tackled in packing was a low speed of a standard DirectX fp16 packing function, which resulted in significant CPU stalls. To address this, we used a fast packing method similar to [Mittring 08]. However, we enhanced this method, making it work for all domain values, unlike the original one. The resulting code is shown in Listing 13.2.

13.9 Comparison

After the transition to quaternions had been done, we made a comparison, shown in Table 13.2. As could be observed, using quaternions significantly reduces memory footprint. In the case of normal mapping, the number of `nrm`, `rsq`, and `rcp` instructions is also decreased, which provides better performance increase than one could be expected from the raw ALUs figures. In the case of skinning and instancing, instruction count increases, but in our experience, ALUs have not been a bottleneck in vertex shaders.

Case	Matrix/TBN				Quaternion			
Measured Value	ALUs		Memory		ALUs		Memory	
Pipeline Stage	VS	PS	VS	VS→PS	VS	PS	VS	VS→PS
Normal Mapping	15	12	7	7	13	12	4	5
Instancing (Scale+Rot)	15	-	20	-	21	-	12	-
Skinning	33	-	64	-	71	-	16	-

Table 13.2. Comparison of 3×3 rotation matrices/TBN and quaternions performance (in ALUs) and memory footprint (vertex attributes (TBN, instance data)/vertex texture fetch (skinning) size in bytes (VS)/interpolator channels count (VS→PS)).

13.10 Conclusion

In this chapter we tried to fully cover our experience with quaternions. We have used quaternions throughout the whole engine, significantly reducing memory and bandwidth costs. There are, however, certain pitfalls, which we described, that we hope will not prevent quaternions from replacing matrices in modern engines.

13.11 Acknowledgments

The authors would like to thank Victor Surkov for helping with the illustrations for this chapter.

Bibliography

[Hejl 04]   Jim Hejl. "Hardware Skinning with Quaternions." In *Game Programming Gems 4*, edited by Andrew Kirmse, pp. 487–495. Boston: Cengage Learning, 2004.

[Lengyel 11]   Eric Lengyel. *Mathematics for 3D Game Programming and Computer Graphics*, Third edition. Boston: Cengage Learning PTR, 2011.

[Malyshau 12]   Dzmitry Malyshau. "A Quaternion-Based Rendering Pipeline." In *GPU Pro 3*, edited by Wolfgang Engel, pp. 265–273. Boca Raton, FL: A K Peters/CRC Press, 2012.

[Mikkelsen 10]   Morten S. Mikkelsen. "Bump Mapping Unparametrized Surfaces on the GPU." *Journal of Graphics, GPU, and Game Tools* 1 (2010), 49–61.

[Mittring 08]   Martin Mittring. "Advanced Virtual Texture Topics." In *ACM SIGGRAPH 2008 Games*, pp. 23–51. New York: ACM, 2008.

[Schüler 06]   Christian Schüler. "Normal Mapping without Precomputed Tangents." In *ShaderX5: Advanced Rendering Techniques*, edited by Wolfgang Engel, pp. 131–140. Boston: Cengage Learning, 2006.

14

glTF: Designing
an Open-Standard
Runtime Asset Format
Fabrice Robinet, Rémi Arnaud,
Tony Parisi, and Patrick Cozzi

14.1   Introduction

This chapter presents work by the COLLADA Working Group in the Khronos
Group to provide a bridge between interchange asset formats and the runtime
graphics APIs. We present the design of glTF, an open-standard transmission-
format that bridges the gap between COLLADA and engines based on WebGL,
OpenGL, and OpenGL ES. glTF strives to provide a common foundation for
developers to efficiently load assets into their engine. We discuss the format
itself, the open-source content pipeline tool that converts COLLADA to glTF,
and REST-based cloud services.

14.2   Motivation

Art assets account for a significant amount of the development costs of modern games and graphics applications. In 2003, the effort to provide a common
asset description format for content pipeline tools started at Sony Computer
Entertainment, and led to the COLLADA spec a few years later. Although the
compatibility of assets among modeling packages is now largely solved, engine developers still need to build their own content pipelines and transmission format
to produce optimized assets for their engines.

   While work on COLLADA continued, the Khronos Group released new specifications for runtime APIs to provide hardware accelerated graphics. This includes
WebGL, OpenGL, and OpenGL ES. Even though the asset format and GL APIs

emanate from the same group, there is no easy way for a developer to take assets and use them in their engine. Two major issues create a gap. The content has to be processed to fit within the data format that is required by the GL APIs, and the content has to be formatted for transmission and parsing performance.

The idea of creating a new spec focusing on the runtime use rather than content-creation needs was raised a few years ago in the working group, and it finally resulted in the work done by the authors of this chapter to introduce glTF—the GL Transmission Format. By analogy, this format is in the same category as the audio and video formats, such as MP3 and MPEG, that have been key in supporting the consumption of media content and dramatically impacted the ecosystem and consumers. We hope that glTF will help 3D content be easily deployed and consumed.

Although significant work has been done, at the time this book goes to press, glTF is still a work in progress; it is not an official Khronos-ratified specification yet.

14.3   Goals

14.3.1   Easy and Efficient to Render

A glTF asset is composed of a .json file for the structure, .bin files for numerical data, .glsl (text) files for shaders, and image files. The .json file references the other files. The .bin files store data as little endian since this covers the vast majority of the market.

glTF uses JSON to define the node hierarchy, materials, lights, and cameras and the binary blobs to store geometry and textures. (See Figure 14.1.) JSON is cross-platform, compact, and readable, allows validation, and minifies and compresses well. Binary blobs, unlike JSON data, allow efficient creation of GL buffers and textures since they require no additional parsing, except perhaps decompression. glTF specifically targets the GL APIs, so the runtime engine can efficiently load and render the asset because most of the data processing is done by the content pipeline.

14.3.2   Balanced Feature Set and Extensible

Only allowing features directly supported by the GL APIs would make glTF too limited. Likewise, including all features in interchange formats would make glTF too complex for runtime use. We carefully selected features, such as the node hierarchy, materials, animation, and skinning, to balance the trade-offs between simplicity and completeness.

Unlike interchange formats, which need to preserve data used for authoring, glTF only preserves data used for rendering. For example, COLLADA allows

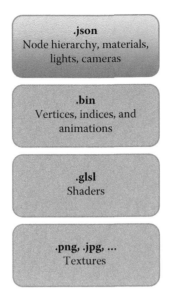

Figure 14.1. Set of files defining a glTF asset.

several transforms and transform representations per node; glTF only has one transform per node and fewer representations.

We recognize that many engines will need features beyond what glTF defines. For this, glTF is extensible to support engine-specific features by allowing metadata on all JSON object properties.

14.3.3 Code, Not Just Spec

A spec alone is not sufficient to make glTF successful. We believe that an open-source content pipeline that converts COLLADA to glTF is important for adoption. We developed such a tool, COLLADA2GLTF, as open-source on GitHub [Khronos 14a]. COLLADA2GLTF provides developers an accessible on-ramp for getting content into their engine and serves as a reference implementation for converters for other model formats. We selected COLLADA because of our familiarity with it, its open-standard, and its widely available exporters.

To ensure that a glTF renderer is easy to implement, we developed several glTF renderers while working on the spec, including JavaScript open-source implementations in Three.js [Mrdoob 14], Cesium [Analytical Graphics 14], rest3d viewer [AMD 14], and Montage with straight WebGL [Fabrobinet 14]. (See Figure 14.2.) In many cases, we implemented a renderer multiple times as spec work progressed.

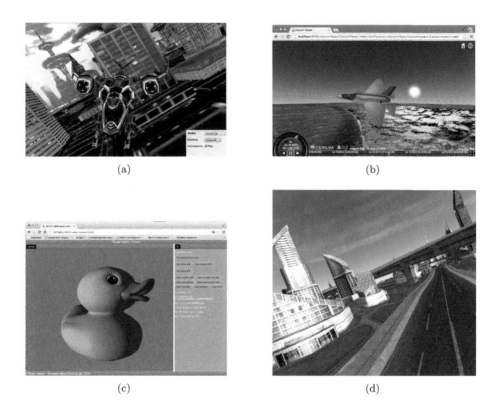

(a)   (b)

(c)   (d)

Figure 14.2. (a) glTF asset in Three.js. [Model from 3drt.com.] (b) glTF asset in Cesium being driven by Cesium's animation engine. (c) glTF and COLLADA assets can be loaded and displayed in the rest3d viewer. (d) glTF asset in the MontageJS viewer. [Model from 3drt.com.]

14.3.4 Community

To enable early community involvement, we also used the public GitHub repo for spec work [Khronos 14a]. We used GitHub issues to discuss spec details and wrote the draft spec in a markdown file in the repo. As expected, the working group still did the majority of the work, but community feedback is valuable and also gives developers more buy-in since their voices are heard. In addition, the public archives are a useful resource for why design decisions were made.

14.3.5 WebGL, OpenGL, and OpenGL ES

glTF is a runtime format for WebGL, OpenGL, and OpenGL ES. However, we are pragmatic about where we expect initial adoption—by the WebGL community.

WebGL engines are still young, and most either use an ad-hoc custom asset format or support a subset of COLLADA. WebGL engines will benefit from a carefully crafted runtime format and a supporting open-source content pipeline.

We spoke with game developers with established OpenGL and OpenGL ES engines, and their feedback on glTF is pretty consistent: it is a good idea but they usually have their own format and content pipeline already in place. However, for new engines and independent developers, whose growth has been phenomenal recently, glTF lowers the barriers to integrate 3D content without requiring heavier solutions.

14.4   Birds-Eye View

A glTF asset is made up of components familiar to most graphics developers such as nodes, meshes, and materials. Figure 14.3 shows the organization of the top-level glTF properties, i.e., properties whose parent is the glTF asset's root. A design goal is to provide the required structure without unnecessary indirection and overhead.

At the highest level, a scene is composed of one or more root nodes. Nodes have a transform, e.g., a 4×4 matrix, and an array of child nodes, forming a node hierarchy that positions each node in the scene. A node can contain either a camera, a light, or an array of meshes, which is the most common case.

A mesh contains an array of primitives (not shown in Figure 14.3 because they are not a top-level glTF property), each of which references attributes and indices defining the mesh's geometry, and a material defining its shading.

An attribute defines the section of a `bufferView` that contains data for one attribute in the mesh, including a stride, so multiple attributes can be interleaved in the same `bufferView`, and a bounding box, so the runtime engine doesn't need to recompute a bounding volume. Similarly, indices define a section of a `bufferView` containing index data for a mesh. Of course, different meshes may point to the same attributes or indices just like different nodes may point to the same mesh.

`bufferViews` point to a subset of a buffer, which can reference an external .bin file or have the binary data encoded in the JSON. There can be one or more buffers, and a single buffer can contain heterogeneous data, e.g., vertex attributes and indices.

In addition to referencing attributes and indices, a primitive in a mesh also references a material, which is an instance of a technique, i.e., a technique plus its parameter inputs, which correspond to GL uniforms, including textures and their sampler state. A technique defines the parameter inputs and a pass that defines the attribute inputs, the shader program containing vertex and fragment shaders, and the render states. Like buffers, shader source and image files may be stored in external files or embedded in the JSON.

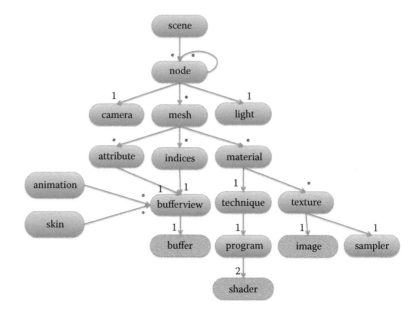

Figure 14.3. Structure of top-level glTF JSON properties. Properties in gray may reference external files or have embedded data.

Animations and skins reference `bufferView`s in a similar fashion to attributes and indices. They also reference nodes and other properties to change their values over time.

A glTF asset may use most or all of these top-level properties to define a scene, or it could contain just meshes or techniques, for example. Next, we'll look at buffers, materials, and animations in more detail.

14.5   Integration of Buffer and Buffer View

Buffers and their associated buffer views are fundamental building blocks of glTF assets. A glTF JSON file relies on binary data for heavy payloads such as vertices and indices. Consequently, glTF needs to describe these data. The typed array specification [Vukicevic 11] is a natural choice because

- it was created by capturing the requirements of a GL-based API, namely WebGL,

- it provides a relevant API to describe arrays whether glTF is implemented using JavaScript or C++,

- when possible, glTF relies on proven APIs from widely adopted specs.

To implement buffers, glTF borrowed two fundamental types from typed arrays:

- `ArrayBuffer` for entries in buffers property, and

- `ArrayBufferView` for entries in the `bufferViews` property.

Both `buffers` and `bufferViews` implement the same interface of their respective typed-array counterpart. However, types are not named exactly the same because glTF `buffers` and `bufferViews` contain additional properties. In the JSON snippets in Figure 14.4, properties in blue come directly from typed arrays. Properties in red are not part of typed arrays and were added to provide

- external storage via a path property,

- a hint about the kind of data stored via a target property, which is optional but a useful optimization for binding the corresponding VBO once and just updating the offset for subsequent draw calls.

```
"buffers":
{
  "office": {
    "byteLength": 829958,
    "path": "office.bin"
  }
},

"bufferViews": {
 "bufferView_7958": {
   "buffer": "office",
   "byteLength": 686264,
   "byteOffset": 0,
   "target": "ARRAY_BUFFER"
 },
 "bufferView_7959": {
   "buffer": "office",
   "byteLength": 143694,
   "byteOffset": 686264,
   "target": "ELEMENT_ARRAY_BUFFER"
 }
}
```

While buffers and `bufferViews` provide access to data, other concepts are needed:

- Types: In order to map directly to GL APIs, glTF reuses existing GL types.

- Interleaving: Typed arrays deal with contiguous buffers, but to interleave vertex attributes, other properties like stride are needed. Also, semantically, count fits better than length.

For these reasons, and in order to get the best of typed arrays and GL worlds, vertex attributes and indices wrap buffer views as follows:

```
{
  "bufferView": "bufferView_29",
  "byteOffset": 0,
  "byteStride": 12,
  "count": 2399,
  "type": "FLOAT_VEC3"
}
```

Finally, it's up to the runtime engine to define how buffers are loaded, e.g., using multiple accesses to files at different offset for progressive loading or by loading all data at once. The number of external files storing buffers is up to the content pipeline.

The same flexibility applies to the way GL resources are created. It's up to the engine to create a vertex buffer that contains all the attributes of the scene or to create multiple buffers. `bufferViews` and their wrappers allow adapting any resource management scheme.

14.6 Code Flow for Rendering Meshes

In glTF, a mesh is simply an array of primitives to be rendered. A primitive specifies its type, matching the GLenum type used by `drawElements`; indices; a material; and vertex attributes, which are shared for a given mesh. This design for meshes is due to modeling tools grouping primitives that share vertex attributes into a single mesh.

Special care is made to make sure that the "flow" of glTF maps well with the "code flow" when implementing using a GL API. For meshes, Figure 14.4 shows how glTF properties map to actual GL APIs concepts.

For clarity, Figure 14.4 omits reordering primitives to render opaque primitives before primitives requiring blending. Next we look at materials, techniques, and passes. By implementing them, rendering order comes naturally.

14.7 From Materials to Shaders

Modern GL APIs require binding a program and setting up shaders. Here, we walk through the layers between materials at the highest level and programs at the lowest levels.

Most shaders take uniform inputs. At the highest level, these values come from parameters within materials. To specify which implementation of shaders these parameters should use, a material refers to a technique. This design allows multiple materials to share the same technique. Thus, multiple materials are

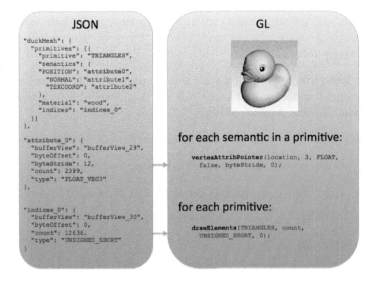

Figure 14.4. Mapping glTF to GL APIs.

naturally ordered by techniques, shaders, and even GL states since they are also specified within techniques under passes.

Figure 14.5 is a possible workflow. Advanced engines may differ, but this schema shows that even the most naive renderer following glTF flow of properties would de-facto apply fundamental GL principles for efficient rendering, such as minimizing the number of states changes.

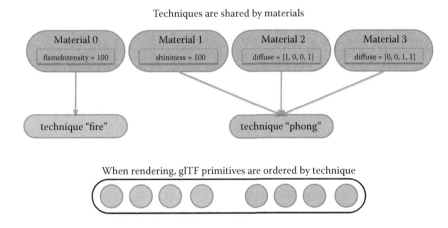

Figure 14.5. Materials share techniques.

Techniques and passes are key concepts for understanding lower-level rendering concepts.

A technique's role is

- to declare parameters along with their types and optional default values (technique parameters are located at the root level of a technique so that they can be shared by all passes),

- to refer to the first pass that acts as an entry point for the rendering.

A pass contains all the implementation details:

- which program to bind, which in turns specifies vertex and fragment shaders,

- list of attributes and uniforms both pointing to parameters,

- list of GL render states to be set.

To fully set up rendering, passes allow atomically binding a program and enabling GL states along with their associated functions. Properties such as double-sided or transparency from higher-level properties emphasize that generating shaders from high-level material definitions cannot be dissociated from generating states on their side.

Not all engines will want to import shaders and states, especially for lighting shaders relying on deferred rendering. For such engines, within passes, a `details` property can be generated by COLLADA2GLTF to specify every relevant aspect to be able to regenerate the shaders and states on the fly.

Both the specification and COLLADA2GLTF currently only support a single pass using forward rendering. However, considering further evolutions and multiple passes, it was critical to provide an extensible way to declare passes.

14.8 Animation

glTF supports a variety of industry-standard animation techniques, including key frames, skinning, and morphs. While it is up to the runtime engine to implement the animation algorithms, glTF faithfully represents the data generated by content-creation tools in support of these capabilities.

An animation is composed of a set of channels, samplers, and parameters. A *channel* connects a sampled data stream to a property of a target object. The sampled data stream is defined via a *sampler,* which takes input data, output data, and an interpolation type. Sampler input is typically a buffer of `FLOAT` values representing time, but it could be a stream of any type of scalar values. Sampler output is a buffer of values of any valid glTF type, such as `FLOAT_VEC3`. Currently, only the `LINEAR` interpolation type is supported; other types of interpolation will be possible via future extensions.

The channel's *target* object contains the ID of a node in the glTF node hierarchy. The property to be animated is represented via a *path*, a string that contains a value such as `translation`, `rotation`, or `scale`. It is up to the runtime engine to map these standardized names to its own properties. For example, the Three.js viewer maps `translation` to `position`, the internal name for translation of a 3D object in the Three.js scene graph.

The sampler's input and output data are supplied by referencing *parameters*. Parameters are named objects defined in the animation's `parameters` property. The scope for parameter names is local to the containing animation. Each parameter references a named `bufferView` from the `bufferViews` section of the glTF file, specifying an offset, data type, and size.

Listing 14.1 shows the JSON for animating the translation of node `node-cam01 -box` using key frames. The animation defines one channel that connects the sampler `animation_0_translation_sampler` to the `translation` property of the node. The sampler uses the parameter `TIME` as its input to linearly interpolate one of the properties. Note that the `TIME` parameter can be shared among other samplers, such as for animation rotation and scale; this is a typical usage scenario that keeps all properties synchronized and represents the data compactly.

Channels are also used to drive skinned animations. With skinning, channels define animations of nodes representing joints in a skeleton. Skins, joints, and vertex weights are defined to be friendly for hardware-accelerated skinning. For example, glTF defines a `WEIGHT` semantic type for use with hardware techniques:

```
"weight": {
  "semantic": "WEIGHT",
  "type": "FLOAT_VEC4"
}
```

14.9 Content Pipeline

The content pipeline, as shown in Figure 14.6, is the process by which the content is optimized and formatted for a specific runtime. Typically, processing involves creating objects that are directly consumable by the runtime engine, such as creating triangles out of surfaces and other primitives, and then splitting and formatting in bundles that are efficient for loading and parsing.

Figure 14.6. A typical content pipeline.

```
"animation_0": {
 "channels": [{
   "sampler": "animation_0_translation_sampler",
   "target": {
   "id": "node-cam01-box",
   "path": "translation"
}],
 "count": 901,
 "parameters": {
   "TIME": {
     "bufferView": "bufferView_4509",
     "byteOffset": 0,
     "count": 901,
     "type": "FLOAT"
   },
   "translation": {
     "bufferView": "bufferView_4509",
     "byteOffset": 3604,
     "count": 901,
     "type": "FLOAT_VEC3"
   }
 },
 "samplers": {
   "animation_0_translation_sampler": {
     "input": "TIME",
     "interpolation": "LINEAR",
     "output": "translation"
   }
 }
}
```

Listing 14.1. Animation listing.

glTF targets GL APIs by creating structures that can be sent directly to a runtime engine built with WebGL, OpenGL ES, or OpenGL. glTF consists of a set of files that are directly compatible with web technology—a JSON file, binary files, GLSL shaders, and images. COLLADA2GLTF is the open-source converter from COLLADA to glTF. As shown in Figure 14.7, it can be used as-is, be incorporated into a content pipeline, or serve as a reference implementation for other converters.

14.9.1   COLLADA2GLTF

COLLADA2GLTF content processing incorporates several stages that progressively transform the content into the data structure accepted by GL APIs:

- Triangulate: Geometry is transformed into primitives accepted by GL. The most common one is TRIANGLES.

- Single index: Only one index per vertex attribute can reference all the attributes associated. Modelers often use one index per attribute, which

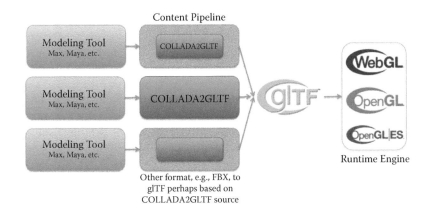

Figure 14.7. glTF content pipeline examples.

avoids vertex data duplication. This step reorganizes the data and duplicates vertices when necessary so that only one index per vertex is used.

- Split: Without extensions, WebGL and OpenGL ES 2.0 have indices range limitations, so meshes need to be split when they exceed the UNSIGNED_SHORT type.

- Skinning optimizations: In a modeler, skinned meshes may have any number of influences per bone. In GL, the limitation is given by the vertex shader, where the number of influences has to be fixed to fit inside a vertex attribute. Typically, this step creates four influences per bone, providing good performance and matching what is usually found in interactive applications. In order to host all the referred "bone matrices," the mesh may also be split to comply with the maximum number of vector uniforms that a destination GL API supports.

- Shaders: Taking into account all parameters impacting rendering (e.g., lights, lighting model, skinning, etc.), this step generates shaders that match the material description, which is typically the "common profile" for COLLADA. Along with shaders, this step also generates GL states. Shaders are provided with no further formatting, they are saved as the ASCII .glsl file that can be passed directly to the GLSL compiler.

- JSON formatting: The data structure created by the converter is finally serialized into a JSON file. The JSON file is relatively small as the bulk of the content will be stored in the binary file.

- Image conversion: As of now, the converter only performs alpha channel checks to know whether blending should be enabled.

- Binary formatting: Numerical data is serialized into a binary file or files that exactly match the GL buffer format, so that it can be easily loaded and sent to the API without any parsing or further processing by runtime, except perhaps decompression.

- Additional steps: Additional content processing of formatting can be added to this pipeline. For instance, when the content is provided via a web server, servers generally (zlib) compress files on the fly before sending them to the client. This is an example of the integration of glTF in an existing runtime environment.

COLLADA2GLTF is written in C++ using OpenCOLLADA [Khronos 14b] for reading COLLADA files and Rapidjson [Kennytm 11] for writing the glTF .json files. The conversion and optimization stages are written from scratch.

14.9.2 rest3d

glTF closes the gap between content creation and content deployment and provides core technology to enable moving the content pipeline in the cloud. More and more workflows are moving to the cloud. There are many benefits including the following:

- Safety: Data is not stored locally, so it is safe no matter what happens to your computer.

- Security: Data access can easily be restricted to those with access rights.

- No install: Software is always up to date and there is no need to install it.

- Sharing: All data are available to all users. This makes global collaboration easier.

- Content management: Data is cheap in the cloud, so there is no problem keeping a copy of everything and enabling users to go back in time.

- Cloud processing: Once the content is in the cloud, processing can happen in the cloud, so complex operations are possible using any device.

- Deployment: Deploying content and web applications is as easy as sending a URL out.

- SaaS: The Software as a Service (SaaS) business model makes it possible for customers to pay for only what they need and enables service providers to tailor to individual needs.

Figure 14.8. Managing content in the cloud.

There are also disadvantages such as trusting the cloud provider to keep our data secure and initially moving our data to the cloud. But those are manageable; for instance, data can be encrypted.

Moving workflows into the cloud requires new technologies and trade-offs. Not having direct access to data on the local disk, asynchronous processing, and latency are issues that need to be addressed. Before being practical and effective, a majority of the ecosystem has to be available and interoperable in the cloud.

Cloud service providers have been very successful at providing an interface to their data and services through an API designed to follow the REST protocol [Fielding 00]. rest3d's goal is to research how such a cloud API can be designed to enable a 3D content ecosystem to be moved to the cloud [AMD 14].

The first step is to enable tools to dialog with the cloud as shown in Figure 14.8. COLLADA works well for transmitting data between various modeling tools and the cloud. Existing content-management systems can handle XML documents, as well as provide queries and search, i.e., `XQUERY`, inside the document. Additional metadata can be attached to the content and provide specific services, for example geo-specific information added to COLLADA for 3D content placed on Google Earth. Modeling tools as a cloud service are already available, such as http://clara.io/, https://tinkercad.com/, and http://home.lagoa.com/.

Once the content is available in the cloud, we can move the content pipeline, and more specifically, glTF conversion, into the cloud. Content can be processed on-demand for a particular device's needs. This solves the fragmentation of devices issue that is inherent in cloud computing and the explosion of devices that consumers expect to be able to use to access the same content. This is mostly solved for video and audio, where the size and quality of content streamed is based on the capacity of the target device and the available bandwidth. rest3d and glTF work together to enable this for 3D content. (See Figure 14.9.)

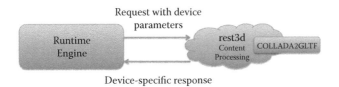

Figure 14.9. Moving the content pipeline into the cloud.

The rest3d open-source project is an experiment to provide client and server code to study the issues openly and converge toward a practical specification. Currently, it includes an XML database system, a nodejs http server, and client code for a basic UI, WebGL viewer, and model loaders. The system is able to fetch, parse, and display 3D content for both COLLADA and glTF. Parsing data and preparing it for WebGL visualization is an order of magnitude ($10\times$–$20\times$) faster with glTF than COLLADA. glTF becomes significantly better for models that need a lot of content processing.

A sample application was created to demonstrate using a web browser and server as a glTF conversion service. This shows that using these technologies, it is straightforward to create an easy-to-use tool that would always be up to date with the latest runtime format, and that can keep the content uploaded to be automatically converted when needed. The URL of the converted content can be used to be incorporated in the assets. Since it is a cloud service, a model converted a long time ago can keep the same URL, and it will automatically be reprocessed if needed so that it is always up to date.

Balancing the number of http requests, the size of each unit of content, and caching behavior is dependent on the type of application and content. rest3d aims to provide control over those parameters when running the converter and additional packaging on the server. One area of work, already available in the rest3d repo, is a geometry compression technique that can be applied to the geometry at the end of the COLLADA2GLTF processing pipeline. The client has the option to ask the server to compress the geometry, which will optimize the bandwidth and transfer time, at the cost of decompression on the client side.

14.10 Future Work

As we prepare the glTF spec for ratification, we are still finalizing the format itself and continuing to build open-source tools.

Compression is a promising area to expand on. At the time of writing this chapter, two early integrations of compression libraries have been tested with COLLADA2GLTF:

- Open3DGC—an efficient TFAN compression [Mammou et al. 09],

- webgl-loader—a fast and compact mesh compression for WebGL [Wonchun 14].

Figure 14.10 shows early results using Open3DGC. These numbers are promising, and typically for very dense meshes, the ratio between uncompressed and compressed data is even better. Our next integration step is to investigate memory footprint and processing impact while decoding compressed meshes.

Model	COLLADA		glTF		glTF+Open3DGC ascii		glTF+Open3DGC binary	
	XML	gzip	raw	gzip	raw	gzip	raw	raw bin gzip JSON
			bin:102k JSON:11k	bin:81k JSON:2kb	ascii:29k JSON:11k	ascii:19k JSON:2k	bin:18k JSON:11k	bin:18k JSON:2k
	336k	106k	113k	83k	40k	21k	29k	20k

Figure 14.10. Compression test with Open3DGC.

Similar to the GL APIs, glTF will support profiles and extensions to allow use of functionality not available everywhere. For example, a profile for modern OpenGL or OpenGL ES would allow using binary shaders to improve load times.

The current content pipeline in COLLADA2GLTF is a good start, but more stages are planned to fully support COLLADA and better optimize the output glTF. These stages include tessellating splines, flattening meshes and nodes, optimizing and minifying GLSL, and minifying JSON. There is also a lot of parallelism within and across stages that can be exploited to improve the latency of asset conversion. Finally, improving the architecture so the optimization stages can be done independent of converting to glTF will make the content pipeline useful beyond glTF. A high-quality open-source content pipeline for glTF is key for its adoption and success.

14.11 Acknowledgments

Khronos, WebGL, COLLADA, and glTF are trademarks of the Khronos Group Inc. OpenGL is a registered trademark and the OpenGL ES logo is a trademark of Silicon Graphics International used under license by Khronos.

Bibliography

[AMD 14] AMD. *rest3d GitHub Repo*. http://github.com/amd/rest3d, 2014.

[Analytical Graphics 14] Analytical Graphics, Inc. *Cesium GitHub Repo*. https://github.com/AnalyticalGraphicsInc/cesium, 2014.

[Fabrobinet 14] Fabrobinet. *MontageJS Viewer GitHub Repo*. https://github.com/fabrobinet/glTF-webgl-viewer, 2014.

[Fielding 00] Roy Thomas Fielding. "Architectural Styles and the Design of Network-based Software Architectures." PhD thesis, University of California, Irvine, CA, 2000.

[Kennytm 11] Kennytm. *Rapidjson GitHub Repo*. https://github.com/kennytm/rapidjson, 2011.

[Khronos 14a] Khronos Group. *glTF GitHub Repo.* https://github.com/KhronosGroup/glTF, 2014.

[Khronos 14b] Khronos Group. *OpenCOLLADA GitHub Repo.* https://github.com/KhronosGroup/OpenCOLLADA, 2014.

[Mammou et al. 09] K. Mammou, T. Zaharia, and F. Prêteux, "TFAN: A Low Complexity 3D Mesh Compression Algorithm." *Computer Animation and Virtual Worlds* 20:2–3 (2009), 343–354.

[Mrdoob 14] Mrdoob. *Three.js GitHub Repo.* https://github.com/mrdoob/three.js, 2014.

[Vukicevic 11] Vladimir Vukicevic and Kenneth Russell, editors. *Typed Array Specification.* https://www.khronos.org/registry/typedarray/specs/1.0/, 2011.

[Wonchun 14] Wonchun. *webgl-loader*, Google Code project. https://code.google.com/p/webgl-loader/, 2014.

15

Managing Transformations in Hierarchy

Bartosz Chodorowski and Wojciech Sterna

15.1 Introduction

One of the most fundamental aspects of 3D engine design is management of spatial relationship between objects. The most intuitive way of handling this issue is to organize objects in a tree structure (hierarchy), where each node stores its local transformation, relative to its parent.

The most common way to define the local transformation is to use a so-called TRS system (present in most modeling packages or game engines like in [Technologies 05]), where the transformation is composed of translation, rotation, and scale.[1] This system is very easy to use for both programmers using the engine as well as non-technical users like level designers. In this chapter we describe the theory behind such a system.

To render an object described with TRS, we need to determine the final world matrix to pass it to the render system. We thus merge translation, rotation, and scale into one local transformation matrix and combine it with local transformations of the node's ancestors to obtain the node's final world matrix.

One problem with the system (and any other that merges rotation and scale components into a single matrix) is decomposition of a matrix back to TRS. It turns out that this problem is often ill-defined and no robust solution exists. We present an approximate solution that works reasonably well in the majority of cases.

Finally, tightly related to decomposition is switching a node's parent. Usually, after that operation has been performed, we would most likely want to retain the global transformation of the node. This problem can be alleviated using the presented decomposition algorithm.

---

[1]As you will see later in this chapter's formulas, the term SRT would be more appropriate (because we are using row-major notation). However, we decided to stick to TRS to be consistent with [Technologies 05].

15.2   Theory

In this section of the chapter all mathematical machinery will be presented. First, the hierarchy concept will be described. This will be followed by some basic theoretical formulations.

15.2.1   Hierarchy Concept

Keeping objects in hierarchy is a well-known concept. Every object (a hierarchy node) can have a number of *children* and only one *parent*. Technically, we want every object to store a pointer to its parent (or NULL value when we have no parent, i.e., the object is at the top of the hierarchy). It can also be convenient to store and manage a list of pointers to the children so that we have fast access to them. The aforementioned structure is in fact a *tree*.

We assume that a node stores its translation, rotation, and scale (*TRS*) that are relative to its parent. Therefore, we say these properties are *local*. When we move an object, we drag all its children with it. If we increase scale of the object, then all of its children will become larger too.

Let us consider an example of three unit cubes (of width, height, and length equal to 1). Figure 15.1 shows the objects and enlists their TRS values.

One interesting thing to note here is the location of object C. It is two units away on the X axis from object A despite the fact that its local translation is $x = -1$. That is because object A has the scale component $x = 2$.

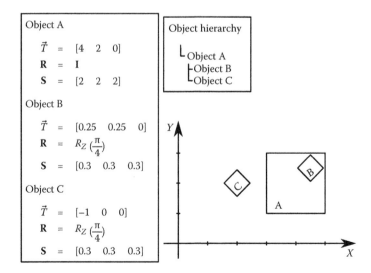

Figure 15.1. First example.

15.2.2 Transformations Composition

Local TRS uniquely defines a local transformation matrix $\mathbf{M}$. We transform vector $\vec{v}$ in the following way:

$$\vec{v'} = \vec{v}\mathbf{SR} + \vec{T} = \vec{v}\mathbf{SRT} = \vec{v}\mathbf{M}, \qquad (15.1)$$

where $\mathbf{S}$ is an arbitrary scale matrix, $\mathbf{R}$ is an arbitrary rotation matrix, $\mathbf{T}$ is a translation matrix, and $\vec{T}$ is the vector matrix $\mathbf{T}$ is made of.[2]

To render an object, we need to obtain its *global* (world) transformation by composing local transformations of all the object's ancestors up in the hierarchy.

The composition is achieved by simply multiplying local matrices. Given a vector v_0, its local matrix $\mathbf{M_0}$, and the local matrix $\mathbf{M_1}$ of v_0's parent, we can find the global position v_2:

$$\vec{v}_2 = \vec{v}_1 \mathbf{M}_1 = \vec{v}_0 \mathbf{M}_0 \mathbf{M}_1.$$

Using vector notation for translation, we get

$$\vec{v}_2 = \vec{v}_1 \mathbf{S}_1 \mathbf{R}_1 + \vec{T}_1 = (\vec{v}_0 \mathbf{S}_0 \mathbf{R}_0 + \vec{T}_0)\mathbf{S}_1 \mathbf{R}_1 + \vec{T}_1 \qquad (15.2)$$
$$= \vec{v}_0(\mathbf{S}_0 \mathbf{R}_0 \mathbf{S}_1 \mathbf{R}_1) + (\vec{T}_0 \mathbf{S}_1 \mathbf{R}_1 + \vec{T}_1)$$

Given that we store local transformations in TRS, it would be useful if we could decompose the global $\mathbf{M}_0 \mathbf{M}_1$ matrix into TRS. We can easily extract the translation vector $\vec{T}_0 \mathbf{S}_1 \mathbf{R}_1 + \vec{T}_1$ but scale and rotation $\mathbf{S}_0 \mathbf{R}_0 \mathbf{S}_1 \mathbf{R}_1$ is somehow combined. It turns out that in the general case we cannot extract the $\mathbf{S}$ and $\mathbf{R}$ matrices out of the $\mathbf{S}_0 \mathbf{R}_0 \mathbf{S}_1 \mathbf{R}_1$ matrix. It stems from the following theorem.

Theorem 15.1. *There exist a rotation matrix $\mathbf{R}$ and a scale matrix $\mathbf{S}$ such that $\mathbf{RS}$ cannot be expressed in the form of $\mathbf{S'R'}$, where $\mathbf{S'}$ is a scale matrix and $\mathbf{R'}$ is a rotation matrix.*

Proof: Consider

$$\mathbf{S} = \begin{bmatrix} 1 & 0 & 0 \\ 0 & 2 & 0 \\ 0 & 0 & 1 \end{bmatrix}, \qquad \mathbf{R} = \begin{bmatrix} 1 & 0 & 0 \\ 0 & \frac{\sqrt{2}}{2} & -\frac{\sqrt{2}}{2} \\ 0 & \frac{\sqrt{2}}{2} & \frac{\sqrt{2}}{2} \end{bmatrix}.$$

Let us suppose by contradiction that there exist a scale matrix $\mathbf{S'}$ and a rotation matrix $\mathbf{R'}$ such that $\mathbf{RS}=\mathbf{S'R'}$. Moreover,

$$\mathbf{S'} = \begin{bmatrix} s'_1 & 0 & 0 \\ 0 & s'_2 & 0 \\ 0 & 0 & s'_3 \end{bmatrix}, \qquad \mathbf{R'} = \begin{bmatrix} r'_{11} & r'_{12} & r'_{13} \\ r'_{21} & r'_{22} & r'_{23} \\ r'_{31} & r'_{32} & r'_{33} \end{bmatrix}.$$

---

[2]In expression $\vec{v}\mathbf{SR} + \vec{T}$ terms $\mathbf{S}$ and $\mathbf{R}$ are 3×3 matrices and $\vec{T}$ is a 3-component vector. In $\vec{v}\mathbf{SRT}$ all $\mathbf{S}$, $\mathbf{R}$ and $\mathbf{T}$ terms are 4×4 matrices.

We evaluate the left side of the equation

$$\mathbf{RS} = \begin{bmatrix} 1 & 0 & 0 \\ 0 & \sqrt{2} & -\frac{\sqrt{2}}{2} \\ 0 & \sqrt{2} & \frac{\sqrt{2}}{2} \end{bmatrix}$$

and the right side

$$\mathbf{S'R'} = \begin{bmatrix} s'_1 r'_{11} & s'_1 r'_{12} & s'_1 r'_{13} \\ s'_2 r'_{21} & s'_2 r'_{22} & s'_2 r'_{23} \\ s'_3 r'_{31} & s'_3 r'_{32} & s'_3 r'_{33} \end{bmatrix}.$$

We compare entries from the first row and use the fact that $\mathbf{R'}$ is orthonormal. We get a system of equations

$$\begin{cases} 1 = s'_1 r'_{11}, \\ 0 = s'_1 r'_{12}, \\ 0 = s'_1 r'_{13}, \\ {r'_{11}}^2 + {r'_{12}}^2 + {r'_{13}}^2 = 1, \end{cases}$$

which we solve for s'_1, thus yielding $s'_1 = \pm 1$.

Considering the second and the third rows in a similar way, we get $s'_2 = \pm \frac{\sqrt{2}\sqrt{5}}{2}$ and $s'_3 = \pm \frac{\sqrt{2}\sqrt{5}}{2}$.

Since $\det(\mathbf{AB}) = \det(\mathbf{A}) \det(\mathbf{B})$ and $\mathbf{RS} = \mathbf{S'R'}$ and $\det(\mathbf{S'}) = s'_1 s'_2 s'_3$,

$$\det(\mathbf{R'}) = \frac{\det(\mathbf{R}) \det(\mathbf{S})}{\det(\mathbf{S'})} = \frac{1 \cdot (1 \cdot 2 \cdot 1)}{\pm 1 \cdot \frac{\sqrt{2}\sqrt{5}}{2} \cdot \frac{\sqrt{2}\sqrt{5}}{2}} = \pm \frac{4}{5} \neq 1,$$

which contradicts the assumption of $\mathbf{R'}$ being an orthonormal rotation matrix and finishes the proof.   □

15.2.3 Skew Problem

Let us go back for a minute to the example shown in Figure 15.1. If we change the x component of scale of object A, we will get a situation that is depicted by Figure 15.2.

Applying a *nonuniform scale* (coming from object A) that follows a local rotation (objects B and C) will cause objects (B and C) to be *skewed*. Skew can appear during matrices composition but it becomes a problem during the decomposition, as it cannot be expressed within a single TRS node. We give an approximate solution to this issue in Section 15.2.4.

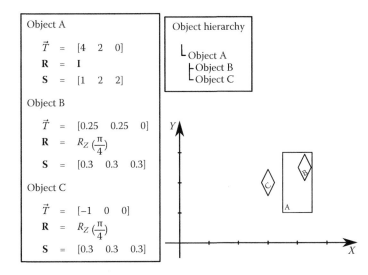

Figure 15.2. Modified example.

15.2.4 Decomposition of Global Transform to TRS

While we already know that in the standard TRS system, due to skew, we cannot always decompose a global transformation into global TRS values, we aim to find an algorithm that gives us at least an approximate solution.

Let an object have n ancestors in the hierarchy tree. Let $\mathbf{M}_1, \mathbf{M}_2, \cdots, \mathbf{M}_n$ be their local transformation matrices, $\mathbf{M}_0$ be a local transformation matrix of the considered object, and $\mathbf{M}_i = \mathbf{S}_i \mathbf{R}_i \mathbf{T}_i$.

Let us denote $\mathbf{M}_{TRS\Sigma} = \mathbf{M}_0 \mathbf{M}_1 \cdots \mathbf{M}_n$ ($TRS\Sigma$ means here that the matrix holds pretty much everything including translation, rotation, scale, and skew). We also define $\mathbf{M}_{TR} = \mathbf{R}_0 \mathbf{T}_0 \mathbf{R}_1 \mathbf{T}_1 \cdots \mathbf{R}_n \mathbf{T}_n$ (TR indicates that the matrix holds information about translation and rotation).

Global translation is easily extractible from $\mathbf{M}_{TRS\Sigma}$; we just look at the fourth row of the matrix.

Global rotation is determined simply by taking $\mathbf{M}_{TR}$ stripped of the translation vector, giving us $\mathbf{M}_R$ matrix. This matrix will usually have to be converted to a quaternion or to Euler angles. [Dunn and Parberry 02] provides extensive coverage on how to do this.

Global scale is the trickiest part. To get reasonable values for it, we determine $\mathbf{M}_{RS\Sigma}$ matrix (which is $\mathbf{M}_{TRS\Sigma}$ matrix with zeroed translation part). Then, we compute $\mathbf{M}_{S\Sigma} = \mathbf{M}_{RS\Sigma} \mathbf{M}_R^{-1}$. Voilà—here we have the skew and the scale combined. We use diagonal elements of $\mathbf{M}_{S\Sigma}$ to get the scale, and we choose to ignore the rest that is responsible for the skew.

15.2.5 Parent Switch in Hierarchy

In a 3D engine we often need to modify objects' parent-children relationship. One condition that most engines try to enforce is that after changing the parent of an object, the object's *global* transformation remains unchanged. In other words, we want to change the *local* transformation such that the *global* transformation is still the same. Obviously, that forces us to recompute local TRS values of the object whose parent we're changing. Note that if the previous parent's scale is nonuniform and it's different from the nonuniform scale of the new parent, the skew of the object will change and as such the geometrical appearance of the object will be different.

Having our condition from the previous paragraph in mind, we can see that the TRS decomposition problem is a special case of the parent switching problem— when we move an object to the top of the hierarchy so that it has no parent, its new local TRS becomes also its global TRS. Obviously, we want our parent switching algorithm to work in the general case, but given the algorithm from Section 15.2.4, that is a short way to go.

To get from the current local space to a new local space (parent changes, global transform stays the same), we first need to find the global transform of the object by going up in the hierarchy to the root node. Having done this we need to go down the hierarchy to which our new parent belongs.

Let $\mathbf{M}'_0$ be the new parent's local transformation matrix. Let that new parent have n' ancestors in the hierarchy tree with local transformations $\mathbf{M}'_1, \mathbf{M}'_2, \cdots,$ $\mathbf{M}'_{n'}$, where $\mathbf{M}'_i = \mathbf{S}'_i \mathbf{R}'_i \mathbf{T}'_i$. The new local transformation matrix can thus be found using the following formula:

$$
\begin{aligned}
\mathbf{M}_{TRS\Sigma} &= \mathbf{M}_0 \mathbf{M}_1 \cdots \mathbf{M}_n (\mathbf{M}'_0 \mathbf{M}'_1 \cdots \mathbf{M}'_{n'})^{-1} \\
&= \mathbf{M}_0 \mathbf{M}_1 \cdots \mathbf{M}_n \mathbf{M}'_{n'}{}^{-1} \mathbf{M}'_{n'-1}{}^{-1} \cdots \mathbf{M}'_0{}^{-1}.
\end{aligned}
$$

Similarly,

$$
\begin{aligned}
\mathbf{M}_{TR} &= \mathbf{R}_0 \mathbf{T}_0 \mathbf{R}_1 \mathbf{T}_1 \cdots \mathbf{R}_n \mathbf{T}_n (\mathbf{R}'_0 \mathbf{T}'_0 \mathbf{R}'_1 \mathbf{T}'_1 \cdots \mathbf{R}'_{n'} \mathbf{T}'_{n'})^{-1} \\
&= \mathbf{R}_0 \mathbf{T}_0 \mathbf{R}_1 \mathbf{T}_1 \cdots \mathbf{R}_n \mathbf{T}_n (\mathbf{R}'_{n'} \mathbf{T}'_{n'})^{-1} (\mathbf{R}'_{n'-1} \mathbf{T}'_{n'-1})^{-1} \cdots (\mathbf{R}'_0 \mathbf{T}'_0)^{-1}.
\end{aligned}
$$

Now we simply use the algorithm from Section 15.2.4 to get the new local TRS values.

15.2.6 Alternative Systems

Here we present some alternatives to the standard TRS system.

Uniform scale. This is probably the simplest solution proposed in [Eberly 07]. Instead of allowing the system to handle nonuniform scale, we might decide that we can get away with just using uniform scale. This can be a limiting constraint though. The good thing about it is that the skew problem is completely gone.

Let us reformulate equation (15.1) with uniform scale factor s:

$$\vec{v'} = \vec{v}s\mathbf{R} + \vec{T} = \vec{v}s\mathbf{R}\mathbf{T} = \vec{v}\mathbf{M}.$$

Equation (15.2) now becomes

$$\vec{v}_2 = \vec{v}_1 s_1 \mathbf{R}_1 + \vec{T}_1 = (\vec{v}_0 s_0 \mathbf{R}_0 + \vec{T}_0)s_1 \mathbf{R}_1 + \vec{T}_1$$
$$= \vec{v}_0(s_0 \mathbf{R}_0 s_1 \mathbf{R}_1) + (\vec{T}_0 s_1 \mathbf{R}_1 + \vec{T}_1).$$

Since matrix-scalar multiplication is commutative, we can thus write

$$\vec{v}_2 = \vec{v}_0(s_0 s_1 \mathbf{R}_0 \mathbf{R}_1) + (\vec{T}_0 s_1 \mathbf{R}_1 + \vec{T}_1).$$

Term $\mathbf{R}_0\mathbf{R}_1$ is an orthonormal rotation matrix. Scaling such a matrix by a scalar geometrically does nothing more but simply scales the basis vectors encoded in this matrix. This means that we can extract the scale factor from the $s_0 s_1 \mathbf{R}_0 \mathbf{R}_1$ matrix by just calculating length of one of its basis vectors.

Nonuniform scale in last node. This solution is an extension of the previous one and was also proposed in [Eberly 07]. The idea is to give the TRS system the ability to store nonuniform scale but only in the last nodes of the hierarchy. This solution still avoids the skew problem (because there is no parent that could store a nonuniform scale) but at the same time offers a little bit more flexibility.

The aforementioned alternatives just scratch the surface and in specific applications more complex systems might be needed.

15.3   Implementation

Here we shall discuss selected parts of the source code of a demo that accompanies this book. The demo contains a full implementation of the `Node` class, which is equipped with a rich set of functions for transform (node) manipulation. We will discuss the most interesting excerpts from that implementation, leaving the rest for self-study.

15.3.1   Class Fields

Listing 15.1 depicts the `Node` class's fields.

Fields `localTranslation`, `localRotation`, and `localScale` define the TRS system that we have discussed throughout this chapter. We choose to store all components in the local space but that does not have to be the case. We could equally well store just global components, or even both. All these fields are

```
public:
    string name;

private:
    Node* parent;
    vector<Node*> children;

    Vector3 localTranslation;
    Quaternion localRotation;
    Vector3 localScale;

    Matrix localMatrix;
```

Listing 15.1. Node class fields.

private so the class's users don't need to know what is actually stored inside the class; the implementation is up to us. Note, however, that the interface (discussed in the next section) exhibits functionality to set/get both local and global transforms. Choosing rotation representation in the form of a quaternion is also our implementation choice. Nothing prevents us from using here a 3×3 rotation matrix, but that would obviously be a waste of memory (four floats against nine). We could actually save one more float by storing Euler angles instead of a quaternion. However, quaternions are much neater to work with (in terms of composition and interpolation). More on this can be found in a thorough case study in [Dunn and Parberry 02].

The last field, localMatrix, is here to act as a sort of cache. It is expensive in terms of memory to store such a big matrix, but given how often we need to find the local matrix in code, we decided to have it here and recompute only when needed. Obviously, if memory is more precious to us than computations, we can remove this field and always compute the local matrix on the fly.

15.3.2 Class Interface

Listing 15.2 presents a list of public methods Node class exposes. Some have been skipped (marked with [...] comment) so that we can focus on functions that are of greatest interest to us as well as for compactness reasons.

There are two functions for altering the local translation vector. The difference is that SetLocalTranslation resets the old translation vector to completely new values while LocalTranslate just adds a new vector to the current localTranslation. The same scheme goes for local rotation functions.

There is also a SetLocalScale function, which does exactly what we can expect from it. However, there is no SetGlobalScale function. That is because when using the TRS system with nonuniform scale, there is just no single global scale value. Global scale is a combination of both local scales and local rotations of all nodes in the hierarchy. We can, however, get the global scale (function GetGlobalLossyScale) just as we did in Section 15.2.4.

```
void SetParent(Node* newParent);
void SetChild(Node* newChild) { newChild->SetParent(this); }

// local translation sets
void SetLocalTranslation(float x, float y, float z,
    bool useLocalRotation = false);
void LocalTranslate(float x, float y, float z,
    bool useLocalRotation = false);

// global translation sets [...]

// local rotation sets
void SetLocalRotation(const Quaternion& rotation);
void LocalRotate(const Quaternion& rotation);
void SetLocalEulerAngles(float x, float y, float z);

// global rotation sets [...]

// local scale sets
void SetLocalScale(float x, float y, float z);

// local gets [...]

// global gets

Vector3 GetGlobalTranslation() const;
Quaternion GetGlobalRotation() const;
Vector3 GetGlobalEulerAngles() const;
Vector3 GetGlobalLossyScale() const;

Vector3 GetGlobalRight();
Vector3 GetGlobalUp();
Vector3 GetGlobalBackward();
Vector3 GetGlobalForward();

Matrix GetGlobalMatrix() const;
Matrix GetGlobalMatrix_TranslationAndRotation() const;
Matrix GetGlobalMatrixWithoutLocalMatrix() const;
```

Listing 15.2. Node class interface.

All of the set functions that alter a node's local TRS call the UpdateLocalMatrix function, which updates the localMatrix cache matrix. That means that after calling functions that set local translation, rotation, and scale, UpdateLocalMatrix gets called more than once without actually being used anywhere. There are two optimizations available here. One is to use a dirty flag that would defer the call to UpdateLocalMatrix until any function that needs it is called. Another idea is to expose a function that sets all parameters (translation, rotation, and scale) one by one and then calls the update function. However, none of these are present in the demo application for the sake of simplicity.

Function GetGlobalMatrix returns the global transformation matrix. GetGlobal Matrix_TranslationAndRotation does this as well but does not involve scale. This is, in fact, matrix $\mathbf{M}_{TR}$ from Section 15.2.4. The last function, GetGlobalMatrix

```
inline void Node::SetGlobalTranslation(float x, float y, float z)
{
    localTranslation =
        Vector3(Vector4(x, y, z, 1.0f) *
        GetGlobalMatrixWithoutLocalMatrix().GetInversed());

    UpdateLocalMatrix();
}
```

Listing 15.3. Node::SetGlobalTranslation.

WithoutLocalMatrix, deserves a little bit more attention and will be discussed in the context of the SetGlobalTranslation function, whose implementation is in Listing 15.3. This method finds the node's local-to-global transform matrix but does not take the node's local transform into account (only its ancestors). Taking the inverse of this matrix creates a transform that goes from the global space to the node's parent space. Now, if we had some global coordinates and multiplied them by this matrix, we would find out what these coordinates are in the node parent's local space. This is exactly what we understand as setting global translation and this function implements that.

15.3.3 Demo Application

The demo application accompanying this chapter makes extensive use of the Node class that has just been described. The application can render up to four unit cubes whose local components we can change (through standard input; select each cube with keys 1, 2, 3, or 4). We can also change parent-child relationships.

The aforementioned four cubes can be reset to one of four initial coordinate configurations. The first configuration (F1 key) depicts the skew problem. When the green object's parent is set to 0 (no parent), the skew is gone. The remaining three configurations (keys F2, F3, and F4) all set local components to the same values but differ in the moment when the parent-child relationships are determined. Have a look at the code to examine those cases and see how they affect the global transforms of the objects.

One more interesting thing in the demo is the way the free camera movement is implemented. It uses Node class and needs very few easy-to-understand code lines to achieve the desired effect.

15.4 Conclusions

Managing transformations in hierarchy is one of the most fundamental aspects of every 3D engine. In this chapter we have thoroughly described a TRS system that is quite easy to both understand and implement and offers a lot of flexibility, while at the same time minimizing drawbacks related to using nonuniform scale.

Bibliography

[Dunn and Parberry 02] Fletcher Dunn and Ian Parberry. *3D Math Primer for Graphics and Game Development*, First edition. Plano, TX: Wordware Publishing, 2002.

[Eberly 07] David H. Eberly. *3D Game Engine Design*, Second edition. San Francisco, CA: Morgan Kaufmann Publishers, 2007.

[Technologies 05] Unity Technologies. "Unity 3D." http://unity3d.com/, 2005.

16

Block-Wise Linear Binary Grids
for Fast Ray-Casting Operations
Holger Gruen

16.1   Introduction

Binary grids only contain one bit of information per cell. Even reasonably high grid resolutions (e.g., $4096 \times 4096 \times 256$ amount to 512 MB of memory) still fit into GPU memory and are thus practical in real-time situations.

This chapter examines the benefits of a block-wise linear memory layout for binary 3D grids. This memory layout allows mapping a number of volumetric intersection algorithms to binary AND operations. Bulk-testing a subportion of the voxel grid against a volumetric stencil becomes possible. The number of arithmetic operations and the amount of memory words to be accessed is lower than for regular sampling schemes.

Below, techniques for rendering binary grids are discussed. The text then describes how to use block-wise linear grids to cast rays through the grid to detect occluded light sources in the context of an indirect illumination rendering technique as a real-world use case. Finally, various other use cases for using block-wise linear grids are discussed.

16.2   Overview

There is a wealth of work regarding the use of binary voxel grids in 3D graphics: [Eisemann and Décoret 06] lists various applications, specifically some from the area of shadowing; [Penmatsa et al. 10] describes a volumetric ambient occlusion algorithm; and [Kasik et al. 08] presents the use for precomputed visibility applications, to name a few.

The rendering of binary voxel grids (BVGs) is often realized by mapping the third axis (e.g., the z-axis) of the grid to the bits of the pixels of a multiple render target (MRT) setup. During rendering, voxels/bits along the z-axis are set using

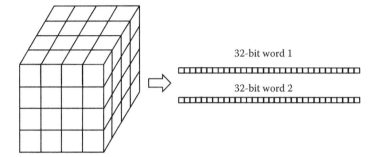

Figure 16.1. A $4 \times 4 \times 4$ voxel grid fits into two consecutive 32-bit words.

blending operations of the graphics hardware. A pixel/fragment shader computes which bit to set and computes the outputs accordingly.

Specifically, on more modern hardware and with modern graphics APIs, binary blend operations can be used to switch on specific bits in render targets using unsigned integer pixel formats.

The downside of this approach is that voxelization is only possible along one view direction per rendering pass.

With the use of scattering pixel/fragment shaders, this changes as one can now render along three view directions and scatter to the same binary grid using interlocked binary `OR` operations.

How to make use of the geometry shader stage to only render one geometry pass to voxelize a scene is described in [Crassin and Green 12].

16.3 Block-Wise Linear Memory Layout

Block-wise memory layouts are used in GPU architectures to improve cache coherency during texturing operations. The idea is to store a small 2D block of texels into a contiguous block of memory instead of using a scanline after scanline memory layout.

This idea extends into 3D textures and can also be applied to binary voxel grids.

Trivially, any portion of the binary voxel grid of size $2^N \times 2^N \times 2^N$ fits into $\frac{2^N \times 2^N \times 2^N}{32}$ 32-bit integer words.

Figure 16.1 depicts a simple example and shows the simple case of a $4 \times 4 \times 4$ subgrid being mapped to two 32-bit integer words.

Please note that the case of $2 \times 2 \times 2$ voxels is not considered here as the benefits of packing such a small part of the grid can be ignored in the context of this chapter.

Subgrids of size $4 \times 4 \times 4$ may seem small, but they can be used as the building blocks for compositing the storage pattern for bigger blocks.

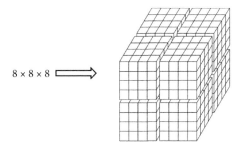

Figure 16.2. Here, $8 \times 8 \times 8$ voxels fit into eight $4 \times 4 \times 4$ blocks.

These bigger blocks store each of the $4 \times 4 \times 4$ subblocks—of which they are comprised—in two consecutive 32-bit integer locations. Figure 16.2 depicts this idea for a $8 \times 8 \times 8$ block that maps to sixteen 32-bit integer words.

In order for readers to start using the described memory layout, Listing 16.1 provides an implementation of a function that can be used to compute the buffer address and bit-value for a given grid size and block size.

Please note that the number of bits that are set in each $4 \times 4 \times 4$ portion of the grid can be used to compute a value for volumetric coverage. Modern GPUs have operations that can count the nonzero bits in integer values—thus mapping bits to coverage is efficient.

Another way to efficiently implement storing $4 \times 4 \times 4$ bits in a memory coherent way instead of using a 1D buffer of unsigned integer under Direct3D 11 can be the use of a `RWTexture3D<uint2>`. In this case, each texel can be used to encode a $4 \times 4 \times 4$ of the grid.

16.4 Rendering Block-Wise Linear Binary Voxel Grids

Assuming Direct3D 11 class hardware, a simplified version of voxelization can be implemented very similar to what is described in [Crassin and Green 12].

In the following description, a geometry shader is used during rendering in order to allow sending the voxelized geometry only once. The geometry shader projects each triangle in a way that maximizes its rasterized surface area or the number of pixels is covers. This is achieved by setting a per-triangle view matrix that looks along the normal of the triangle.

In this chapter, a geometry shader is used for convenience only. It is also possible to use a vertex shader (using ideas from [Gruen 12]) to get all the data for a triangle directly from the vertex buffer. Alternatively, all data necessary to set up the per-triangle view matrix can be stored per vertex, which also allows skipping the use of the geometry shader stage.

Please note that the following code doesn't implement a solid voxelization strategy. Only the voxels that intersect the plane of the triangle are set.

```
// Return the offset into the buffer in bytes in .x and the
// value to OR to the 32-bit integer to set the grid pos in .y
uint2 computeOffsetAndVal(float3 pos, // 3D pos in the grid
                          float GridSize, // size of the grid
                          float BlockRes) // block-size,
                                          // e.g., 8 to pack 8x8x8
{
    // Compute which of the BlockRes x BlockRes x BlockRes blocks
    // 'pos' is in
    float3 block_pos = floor( floor( pos ) * (1.0f/BlockRes) );

    // Compute 3D position within subblock
    float3 sub_pos = floor( floor( pos ) % BlockRes );

    // Compute the size of a grid with grid cells each BlockRes wide
    float RGS = GridSize/BlockRes;

    // block size in bytes
    uint block_size = uint( BlockRes * BlockRes * BlockRes ) / 8;

    // byte offset to the BlockRes x BlockRes x BlockRes 'pos' is in
    uint block_off = block_size * uint( block_pos.x +
                                        block_pos.y * RGS +
                                        block_pos.z * RGS * RGS );
    // Compute which of the final 4x4x4 blocks the voxel resides in
    float3 sub_block_pos = floor( sub_pos * 0.25f );

    // Compute the bit position inside the final 4x4x4 blocks
    float3 bit_pos = sub_pos % 4.0f;

    // Compute the size of a block in 4x4x4 units
    Float FBS = BlockRes * 0.25f;

    // Compute byte offset for final 4x4x4 subblock in the current
    // BlockRes x BlockRes x BlockRes block
    uint off = 8.0f * ( sub_block_pos.x +
                        sub_block_pos.y * FBS +
                        sub_block_pos.z * FBS * FBS );
    return uint2(
                // Add memory offsets and add final offset base on z
                block_off + off + ( bit_pos.z > 1.0f ? 0x4 : 0x0 ),

                // Compute bit position in 32-bit word
                0x1 << uint ( bit_pos.x + bit_pos.y * 4.0f +
                            ( bit_pos.z % 2.0f ) * 4.0f * 4.0f )
                );
}
```

Listing 16.1. Compute the offset and bit position for a position in a block-linearly stored binary grid.

Listing 16.2 shows shader fragments of such an implementation. Here, the assumption is that tessellation isn't enabled, as otherwise the domain shader needs to take the role of the vertex shader fragment given below.

Assuming a viewport with a resolution sufficient to deliver a reasonable number of pixels to the pixels shader is set, Algorithm 16.1 is used. Listing 16.2 provides the implementation details.

1. Set up a viewport with sufficient resolution to grant a dense enough rasterization of the triangles.

   - Experiments have shown that a resolution of two times the dimension of the grid is a good resolution.

   - The application passes the dimension as a constant in 'g_ViewportResolution' to the shaders.

2. Disable back-face culling and depth testing.

3. Set up the UAV for the 'RWByteAddressBuffer BinaryGrid' in the pixel shader (see Listing 16.2).

4. The vertex shader (see Listing 16.2), on-top of what it does for vertex processing, passes on the world-space position of each vertex.

5. The geometry shader sets up a viewing matrix that looks along the world-space normal of the triangle, maximizing its projected area, and passes grid-space positions to the pixel shader.

6. The pixel shader computes the offset into the grid buffer using the function from Listing 16.1. It then uses an interlocked operation to set the bit for the current grid position.

Algorithm 16.1. One-pass voxelization.

```
struct GS_RenderGridInput
{
    float3 f3WorldSpacePos : WSPos;
    ...
};
GS_RenderGridInput VS_BinaryGrid( VS_RenderSceneInput I )
{
    GS_RenderGridInput O;
    // Pass on world-space position---assuming WS is passed in
    O.f3WorldSpacePos = I.f3Position;
    // Compute/pass on additional stuff
    ...
    return O;
}
struct PS_RenderGridInput
{
    float4 f4Position : SV_POSITION;
    float3 f3GridPosition : GRIDPOS;
};
[maxvertexcount(3)]
void GS_BinaryGrid( triangle GS_RenderGridInput input[3],
                inout TriangleStream<PS_RenderGridInput> Triangles )
{
    PS_RenderGridInput output;
    // g_WorldSpaceGridSize contains the world-space size of the
    // grid
    float3 f3CellSize = g_WorldSpaceGridSize.xyz *
                            ( 1.0f / float(BINARY_GRID_RES).xxx );
```

```
float3 gv[3], v[3];

// Compute grid-space positions from world-space positions;
// g_SceneLBFbox contains the left, bottom, and front points
// of world-space bounding box of the grid
gv[0] = ( input[0].f3WorldSpacePos - g_SceneLBFbox.xyz ) /
          f3CellSize;

gv[1] = ( input[1].f3WorldSpacePos - g_SceneLBFbox.xyz ) /
          f3CellSize;

gv[2] = ( input[2].f3WorldSpacePos - g_SceneLBFbox.xyz ) /
          f3CellSize;

// Compute triangle edges
float3 d0 = gv[1] - gv[0];
float3 d1 = gv[2] - gv[0];

// Compute triangle normal
float3 N = normalize( cross( d0, d1 ) );
float3 C = ( 1.0f/3.0f ) * ( gv[0] + gv[1] + gv[2] );

// Move eye position to 1 unit away from the triangles center
float3 Eye = C - N;

// Set up view axis for looking along the triangle normal
float3 xaxis = normalize( d1 );
float3 yaxis = cross( N, xaxis );

// Set up view matrix for looking along the triangle normal
float4x4 ViewMatrix = {
                xaxis.x, xaxis.y, xaxis.z, -dot( xaxis, Eye ),
                yaxis.x, yaxis.y, yaxis.z, -dot( yaxis, Eye ),
                N.x, N.y, N.z, -dot( N, Eye ),
                0.0f , 0.0f , 0.0f , 1.0f
                };

// Compute view-space positions
v[0] = mul( ViewMatrix, float4( gv[0], 1.0f ) ).xyz;
v[1] = mul( ViewMatrix, float4( gv[1], 1.0f ) ).xyz;
v[2] = mul( ViewMatrix, float4( gv[2], 1.0f ) ).xyz;

// Set up a projection matrix using a constant;
// g_ViewportResolution is a constant set by the application
float4x4 ProjMatrix =
{

    2.0f / g_ViewportResolution, 0.0f, 0.0f, 0.0f,
    0.0f, 2.0f / g_ViewportResolution, 0.0f, 0.0f,
    0.0f, 0.0f, 1.0f, -0.5f,
    0.0f, 0.0f, 0.0f, 1.0f
}

// Project vertices and pass on grid-space position
[unroll]for( int i = 0; i < 3; ++i )
{
    output.f4Position = mul( ProjMatrix, float4( v[i], 1.0f ) );
    output.f3GridPosition = gv[i];
    Triangles.Append( output );
}
    Triangles.RestartStrip();
}

RWByteAddressBuffer BinaryGrid :               register( u0 );
```

```
void PS_BinaryGrid( PS_RenderGridInput I )
{
    uint old;
    // BINARY_GRID_RES holds the resolution/size of the binary grid
    float3 f3GridCoord = max( (0.0f).xxx,
                              min( ( BINARY_GRID_RES -1 ).xxx,
                                   floor( I.f3GridPosition ) ) );
    // Compute the offset and the values of the bit to manipulate
    uint2 off_val = computeOffsetAndVal( f3GridCoord );

    // Turn on the bit for the current grid position
    BinaryGrid.InterlockedOr( off_val.x, off_val.y, old );
}
```

Listing 16.2. Vertex and geometry shader fragments for one-pass voxelization under Direct3D 11.

16.5   Casting Rays through a Block-Wise Linear Grid

Algorithm 16.2 details one way to cast rays through the grid. It does it in a way that benefits from the memory layout of block-wise linear grids. It tests for intersections by building small ray segments in local registers holding grid-aligned $4 \times 4 \times 4$ test blocks. The actual intersection test only amounts to doing two binary AND operations. The memory cost for this ray intersection test is lower than performing four isolated load operations into a grid that has a "normal" memory layout.

16.6   Detecting Occlusions during Indirect Light Gathering

The article [Gruen 11] describes the implementation of a reflective shadow map (RSM)–based one-bounce indirect illumination algorithm (see [Dachsbacher and Stamminger 05]). An RSM, in a nutshell, is a G-buffer as seen from the point of the light and usually consists of the combination of a depth buffer, a buffer that contains surface normals, and a buffer that contains the colors of the lit scene.

In order to detect occluded RSM pixels, a grid of singly linked lists of triangles is build. A set of rays is cast through this grid trying to find blocked RSM pixels and to compute the color of the blocked indirect light. In a final pass, the blocked indirect light is subtracted from the indirect light that is the result of running a filter kernel over the RSM treating its pixels as virtual point lights (VPLs).

Replacing the grid of lists of triangles by a binary block-wise linear grid is straightforward. Instead of using a compute shader for rasterizing blocker triangles into the grid, the voxelization algorithm described in Algorithm 16.1 is used to create a binary 3D grid.

Using the freely available assets and shaders from [Gruen 11], the scenario was recreated using a block-wise linear binary grid for detecting occluded VPLs to estimate blocked indirect light.

For all voxels along the ray, start an iterator $V(I)$ at the start point of the ray.

1. Determine which $2^N \times 2^N \times 2^N$ block B that $V(I)$ sits in.

2. Determine which $4 \times 4 \times 4$ subblock S of B that $V(I)$ sits in.

3. Reserve two 32-bit integer registers $R[2]$ to hold a ray subsection.

4. Build a ray segment in R.

   (a) For all voxels v along the ray starting at $V(I)$ that are still inside S,

      i. set the bit in R to which v maps,

      ii. advance I by 1.

5. Load two 32-bit integer words $T[2]$ from the buffer holding G that contain S.

6. Perform the following bitwise AND operations:

   (a) $R[0]$ & $T[0]$,

   (b) $R[1]$ & $T[1]$.

7. If any of the tests in Steps 6(a) or 6(b) return a nonzero result, the ray has hit something.

Algorithm 16.2. Casting a ray in small segments.

Listing 16.3 provides the implementation details. In order to hide the fact that a discrete binary grid is used, the edges cast through the grid are randomized using pseudorandom numbers. Also, instead of computing unblocked and blocked indirect light separately, the shaders in Listing 16.3 cast a ray segment toward each VPL that is considered.

```
// Compute a long word sized offset into the grid for a grid
// position 'pos'
uint compute4x4x4BlockLWOffset( float3 pos, float GridRes, float
  BlockRes )
{
  float3 block_pos = floor( floor( pos ) * (1.0f/BlockRes) );
  //local address in block
  float3 sub_pos = floor( floor( pos ) % BlockRes );

  uint block_off = ( BINARY_BOCK_SIZE / 4 ) *
                uint( block_pos.x + block_pos.y * (GridRes/BlockRes)
                     + block_pos.z * (GridRes/BlockRes ) *
                     (GridRes/BlockRes));

  float3 sub_block_pos = floor( sub_pos * float(1.0f/4.0f) );

  uint off = 2.0f * ( sub_block_pos.x +
```

```
                           sub_block_pos.y * ( BlockRes * 0.25f ) +
                           sub_block_pos.z * ( BlockRes * 0.25f ) *
                                                ( BlockRes * 0.25f ) );
   return block_off + off;
}

// Trace an edge through the binary grid in 4x4x4 blocks
float traceEdgeBinaryGrid( float3 f3CPos, // start pos of ray

                           float3 f3CN, // normal at start pos of ray
                           float3 f3D, // normalized direction of ray
                           float3 f3Pos, // end pos of ray/egde
                           float3 f3N ) // normal at end pos
{
   float fCount = 0.0f;

   // g_SceneBoxSize is the world-space size of the scene
   float3 f3CellSize = g_SceneBoxSize.xyz *
                       ( 1.0f / float(BINARY_GRID_RES).xxx );

   // Step along normal to get out of current cell
   // to prevent self-occlusion;
   // g_SceneLBFbox is the left, bottom, and front pos of the world box
   float3 f3GridPos = ( f3CPos + ( f3CN * f3CellSize ) --
                                   g_SceneLBFbox.xyz ) / f3CellSize;
   float3 f3DstGridPos = ( f3Pos + ( f3N * f3CellSize ) --
                                   g_SceneLBFbox.xyz ) / f3CellSize;

   // Clamp to the grid;
   // BINARY_GRID_RES holds the resolution/size of the binary grid
   float3 f3GridCoord = max( (0.0f).xxx, min(( BINARY_GRID_RES-1 ).
                        xxx, floor( f3GridPos ) ) );

   float3 f3DstGridCoord = max( (0.0f).xxx, min((BINARY_GRID_RES-1).
                        xxx, floor( f3DstGridPos ) ) );

   // Compute position in a grid of 4x4x4 blocks
   float3 f3SubPos = f3GridCoord%4.0f;
   float3 f3Dg = f3DstGridCoord - f3GridCoord;
   float3 f3AbsD = abs( f3Dg );
   float fMaxD = max( max( f3AbsD.x, f3AbsD.y ), f3AbsD.z );

   // Scale step to step 1 pixel ahead
   f3Dg *= rcp(fMaxD);

   // Where do we step out of the local 4x4x4 grid?
   float3 f3LocalDest = ( f3Dg < 0.0f ? -1.0f : 4.0f );
   float fLoopCount = 0.0f;

   // Only step along two 4x4x4 segments
   while( fMaxD >= 0.0f && fLoopCount <= 2.0f )
   {
        float3 f3Steps = abs( ( f3LocalDest - f3SubPos ) / f3Dg );
        float fSteps     = floor( min( min( f3Steps.x, f3Steps.y ),
                             f3Steps.z ) );
        uint offset      = compute4x4x4BlockLWOffset( f3GridCoord,
                             BINARY_GRID_RES, BINARY_BLOCK_RES );
        uint2 lineseg    = uint2( 0,0 );
        uint2 grid;

        fLoopCount += 1.0f;

        // Load the local 4x4x4 grid
        grid.x = g_bufBinaryGrid[ offset++ ];
```

```
              grid.y = g_bufBinaryGrid[ offset ];

              // Build line mask for current 4x4x4 grid
              [unroll]for( int ss = 0; ss < 4; ++ss )
        {
              [flatten]if( fSteps > 0.5f )
              {
                  uint bitpos = uint( f3SubPos.x + ( f3SubPos.y * 4.0f ) +
                                       ( ( f3SubPos.z % 2.0f ) * 16.0f ) );

                  lineseg.x |= f3SubPos.z > 1.0f ? 0x0 : ( 0x1 << bitpos );
                  lineseg.y |= f3SubPos.z < 2.0f ? 0x0 : ( 0x1 << bitpos );

                  f3SubPos += f3Dg;
                  f3GridCoord += f3Dg;
                  fMaxD -= 1.0f;
                  fSteps -= 1.0f;
                }
          }

          if( ( ( lineseg.x & grid.x ) | ( lineseg.y & grid.y)) != 0x0 )
          {
              fCount += 1.0f;
              break;
          }

          // Recompute sub pos
          f3SubPos = f3GridCoord%4.0f;

      }
      return fCount;
}

// publicly available pseudorandom number algorithm
uint rand_xorshift( uint uSeed )
{
  uint rng_state = uSeed;

  rng_state \ = (rng_state << 13);
  rng_state \ = (rng_state >> 17);
  rng_state \ = (rng_state << 5);

  return rng_state;
}

float computeFakeNoise( uint uSeed )
{
  uint uRand = rand_xorshift( uSeed );
  uRand = rand_xorshift( uRand );
  uRand = rand_xorshift( uRand );
  return float( uRand ) / 4294967295.0f;
}

// Compute the indirect light at f3CPosOrg casting rays to test
// for blocked VPLs
float3 computeIndirectLight(float2 tc, // RSM texture coord
                            float2 fc, // fractional texture coord
                            int2 i2Off,// offset for dithering
                            float3 f3CPosOrg, // current pos
                            float3 f3CN ) // normal at current pos
{
  float2 tmp;
  float3 f3IL = (0.0f).xxx;
  int3 adr;
```

```
    float3 f3CPos = f3CPosOrg;

  adr.z = 0;
  adr.y = int( tc.y * g_vRSMDimensions.y + (-LFS) + i20ff.y );

  // Loop over sparse VPL kernel
  for( float row = -LFS; row <= LFS; row += 6.0f, adr.y += 6 )
{
    adr.x = int( tc.x * g_vRSMDimensions.x + (-LFS) + i20ff.x );

    for( float col = -LFS; col <= LFS; col += 6.0f, adr.x += 6 )
    {
            float3 f3Pos, f3Col, f3N;

            // Unpack G-buffer data
            float3 f3Col, f3Pos, f3N;
            GetGBufferData( f3Col, f3Pos, f3N );

            // Compute indirect light contribution
            float3 f3D = f3Pos.xyz - f3CPosOrg.xyz;
            float fLen = length( f3D );
            float fInvLen = rcp( fLen );
            float fDot1 = dot( f3CN, f3D );
            float fDot2 = dot( f3N, -f3D );
            float fDistAtt = saturate( fInvLen * fInvLen );

            // Form factor like term
            fDistAtt *= saturate( fDot1 * fInvLen ) *
                        saturate( fDot2 * fInvLen );

            // Compute noise for casting a noisy ray
            float fNoise1 = 0.15f * computeFakeNoise( uint(adr.x
                                              + fc.x *  100));
            float fNoise2 = 0.15f * computeFakeNoise( uint(adr.y
                                              + fc.y *  100));

            f3Pos -= f3D * fInvLen * fNoise1;
            f3CPos += f3D * fInvLen * fNoise2;

            if( fDistAtt > 0.0f )
            {
                f3IL += f3Col * fDistAtt * traceRayBinaryGrid
                  ( f3CPos.xyz, f3CN, f3D * fInvLen, f3Pos, f3N );
            }
        }
    }
    return f3IL;
}
```

Listing 16.3. Compute indirect light tracing rays through a binary grid for each VPL.

Please note that the noisy indirect light is computed at a reduced resolution, as described in [Gruen 11]. The resulting indirect light gets blurred bilaterally and is then up-sampled to the full resolution.

The screenshots in Figures 16.3, 16.4, and 16.5 have been generated with and without the detection of occluded VPLs.

Figure 16.3. Screenshot 1: the scene without indirect light.

16.7   Results

One goal of this chapter is to show that using block-wise binary grids does help
to speed up ray casting through a binary voxel grid.

In order to prove this, a standard implementation of traversing the grid has
been implemented as well.

Table 16.1 shows the performance of both methods on a $64 \times 64 \times 64$ grid on an
NVIDIA GTX680 at 1024×768. In the final test, the standard implementation
is also allowed to operate on a packed grid in order to show that just the ability
to perform block-wise tests is already enough to generate a speedup.

In the test scene and the test application, block-wise tests allow for a speedup
of around 20%.

16.8   Future Work

The following describes future work that has not been implemented yet. The algorithms are therefore not necessarily detailed enough to be directly implemented
but are an outlook to what would be interesting to implement next.

16.8.1   Casting Cone Stencils

The algorithm for casting a cone through a block-linear BVG G is detailed in
Algorithm 16.3. It performs intersections by intersecting small ray segments

Figure 16.4. Screenshot 2: the scene with indirect light but without detecting occluded VPLs.

Figure 16.5. Screenshot 3: the scene with indirect light from only unoccluded VPLs.

Packed Grid + standard ray marching	~ 180 fps
Packed Grid + block-wise tests	~ 150 fps

Table 16.1. Performance comparison.

1. Determine which $4 \times 4 \times 4$ subblock S of G contains the position of the current pixel.

2. Take the world-space tangent at the current pixel and divide it by the world-space size of a $4 \times 4 \times 4$ subblock of $G \Rightarrow T$.

3. Take the world-space bi-tangent at the current pixel and divide it by the world-space size of a $4 \times 4 \times 4$ subblock of $G \Rightarrow BT$.

4. Iterate along points P on a ray segment starting at S (stepping from one $4 \times 4 \times 4$ block to the next).

   (a) Compute cone radius $r(P)$.

   (b) Divide r by the world-space size of a $4 \times 4 \times 4$ subblock.

   (c) Iterate points hp from $P + r \times (-T - BT)$ to $P + r \times (T - BT)$.

       i. Iterate points vp from hp to $hp + r \times BT$.

          A. Zero an array of two integer registers R.

          B. Set all bits in R (representing a $4 \times 4 \times 4$ block of G) for positions that intersect the original cone.

          C. Load the $4 \times 4 \times 4$ block at vp from G into registers $T[2]$.

          D. If $(R[0]$ AND $T[0])$ or $(R[1]$ AND $T[1])$, then the cone hits the grid; Exit the test.

Algorithm 16.3. Casting a cone through a block-linear BVG.

with the voxel grid. If this is not intended, it is possible to change the code to test step by step. Please note that the coherency of memory accesses for this is still higher than performing texture lookups for each step along the ray.

16.8.2   Arbitrary Other Stencils

If possible, one should try to construct any stencil in $4 \times 4 \times 4$ subblocks in order to perform the intersection test in block-wise way for efficiency.

   If dynamic construction is not feasible, a number of stencils can be precomputed and stored in a buffer that is available to the GPU. This works especially well if the stencils can be defined in grid space and don't depend on data from the test origin—e.g., they don't depend on the per-pixel normal or other per pixel attributes.

16.8.3   Using Grid Mipmaps

It is possible to build mipmaps of a block-wise–linear binary grid. The most obvious way is to down-sample an $8 \times 8 \times 8$ block into a $4 \times 4 \times 4$ block. The strategies on how to down-sample each $2 \times 2 \times 2$ block into just one bit do vary depending on the application.

Similar in spirit to [Crassin et al. 11] one could switch to testing a lower mip for intersections after a certain distance when, e.g., testing ray segments. This would speed up the testing of longer rays.

16.9 External References

The assets and shaders used in [Gruen 11] are available in the "Downloads" section of the CRC Press webpage for *GPU Pro 2* at http://www.crcpress.com/ product/isbn/9781568817187.

Bibliography

[Crassin and Green 12] Cyril Crassin and Simon Green. "Octree-Based Sparse Voxelization Using the GPU Hardware Rasterizer." In *OpenGL Insights*, edited by P. Cozzi and C. Riccio, pp. 259–278. Boca Raton, FL: CRC Press, 2012.

[Crassin et al. 11] Cyril Crassin, Fabrice Neyret, Miguel Sainz, Simon Green, and Elmar Eisemann. "Interactive Indirect Illumination Using Voxel Cone Tracing." In *Symposium on Interactive 3D Graphics and Games*, p. 207. New York: ACM, 2011.

[Dachsbacher and Stamminger 05] Carsten Dachsbacher and Marc Stamminger. "Reflective Shadow Maps." In *Proceedings of the 2005 Symposium on Interactive 3D Graphics and Games*, pp. 203–231. New York, ACM Press, 2005.

[Eisemann and Décoret 06] Elmar Eisemann and Xavier Décoret. "Fast Scene Voxelization and Applications." In *Proceedings of the 2006 Symposium on Interactive 3D Graphics and Games*, pp. 71–78. New York, ACM, 2006.

[Gruen 11] Holger Gruen. "Real-Time One-Bounce Indirect Illumination and Shadows using Ray Tracing." In *GPU Pro 2: Advanced Rendering Techniques*, edited by Wolfgang Engel, pp. 159–172. Natick, MA: A K Peters, 2011.

[Gruen 12] Holger Gruen. "Vertex Shader Tessellation." In *GPU Pro 3: Advanced Rendering Techniques*, edited by Wolfgang Engel, pp. 1–12. Boca Raton, FL: A K Peters/CRC Press, 2012.

[Kasik et al. 08] David Kasik, Andreas Dietrich, Enrico Gobbetti, Fabio Marton, Dinesh Manocha, Philipp Slusallek, Abe Stephens, and Sung-Eui Yoon. "Massive Model Visualization Techniques." SIGGRAPH course, Los Angeles, CA, August 12–14, 2008.

[Penmatsa et al. 10] Rajeev Penmatsa, Greg Nichols, and Chris Wyman. "Voxel-Space Ambient Occlusion." In *Proceedings of the 2010 ACM SIGGRAPH Symposium on Interactive 3D Graphics and Games*, Article No. 17. New York: ACM, 2010.

17

Semantic-Based Shader Generation Using Shader Shaker

Michael Delva, Julien Hamaide, and Ramses Ladlani

17.1   Introduction

Maintaining shaders in a production environment is hard, as programmers have to manage an always increasing number of rendering techniques and features, making the amount of shader permutations grow exponentially. As an example, allowing six basic features, such as vertex skinning, normal mapping, multitexturing, lighting, and color multiplying, already requires 64 shader permutations.

Supporting multiple platforms (e.g., HLSL, GLSL) does not help either. Keeping track of the changes made for a platform and manually applying them to the others is tedious and error prone.

This chapter describes our solution for developing and efficiently maintaining shader permutations across multiple target platforms. The proposed technique produces shaders automatically from a set of handwritten code fragments, each responsible for a single feature. This divide-and-conquer methodology was already proposed and used with success in the past, but our approach differs from the existing ones in the way the fragments are being *linked* together. From a list of fragments to use and thanks to user-defined semantics that are used to tag their inputs and outputs, we are using a pathfinding algorithm to compute the complete data flow from the initial vertex attributes to the final pixel shader output.

Our implementation of this algorithm is called Shader Shaker. It is used in production at Fishing Cactus on titles such as *Creatures Online* and is open source for you to enjoy.

17.2   Previous Work

As mentioned earlier, there are two main categories of issues graphic programmers may have to deal with at some point when it comes to shader maintenance: the (possibly high) number of feature permutations and the multiple backends to support (e.g., HLSL, GLSL).

17.2.1   The Permutation Hell Problem

The *permutation hell* problem is almost as old as the introduction of programmable shaders in the early 2000s. [Kime 08] categorizes the solutions to this problem into three main families (code reuse through includes, subtractive approaches, and additive approaches). To these categories, we added a fourth one that we will call *template-based approaches*.

Code reuse.   This should be the solution that is the most familiar to programmers. It consists of implementing a library of utility functions that will be made available to the shaders thanks to an inclusion mechanism (e.g., include preprocessor directive) allowing code to be reused easily. The main function of the shader can then be written using calls to these functions and manually feeding the arguments. This is a natural way of editing shaders for programmers, but it gets difficult for the less tech savvy to author new permutations and still requires maintaining all permutations by hand.

A related solution is the one described in [Väänänen 13], where the Python-based Mako templating engine is used to generate GLSL shaders.

Subtractive solutions.   Über-shader solutions rely on one (or a few) mammoth shader(s) containing all the code for all features. The different permutations are generated using a preprocessor to select the relevant portions of code. This technique has proved to be a valid solution for a long time and has been used in countless productions. Nevertheless, its major drawback is that über-shaders are usually hard to maintain (because of their length and the lack of readability caused by the preprocessor directives), especially in a multilanguage environment. Another problem with this approach is that shader semantics can also be tricky to work with (their number is limited and they sometimes need to be sequentially numbered, making it hard to use them with a simple preprocessor).

Additive solutions.   These work the other way around by defining a series of elementary *nodes* (or functions) to be aggregated later (either online or offline) to produce the shader. The aggregation is performed by wiring nodes' inputs and outputs together, either visually using a node-based graph editor or programmatically. This approach has seen lots of implementations [Epic Games Inc. 15, Holmér 15] largely because of its user friendliness, allowing artists to produce visually pleasing effects without touching a single line of code. Its main drawback remains the difficulty to control the efficiency of the generated shaders [Ericson 08, Engel 08b].

A complete system for generating shaders from HLSL fragments is described in [Hargreaves 04] in which each shader fragment is a text file containing shader code and an interface block describing its usage context. In this framework, fragments are combined without actually parsing the HLSL code itself. The system was flexible enough to support adaptive fragments, which could change their behavior depending on the context in which they were used, but lacked the support of a graph structure (i.e., the system was restricted to linear chain of operations). Tim Jones implemented this algorithm for XNA 4.0 in [Jones 10].

Trapp and Döllner have developed a system based on code fragments, typed by predefined semantics that can be combined at runtime to produce an über-shader [Trapp and Döllner 07].

In [Engel 08a], Wolfgang Engel proposes a shader workflow based on maintaining a library of files, each responsible for a single functionality (e.g., lighting.fxh, utility.fxh, normals.fxh, skinning.fxh), and a separate list of files responsible for stitching functions calls together (e.g., metal.fx, skin.fx, stone.fx, eyelashes.fx, eyes.fx). This is similar to the node-based approach, but it is targeted more at programmers. As will be shown later, our approach is based on the same idea but differs from it (and the other node-based solutions) by the fact that the wiring is done automatically based on user-defined semantics.

Template-based solutions. The last category finds its roots in the famous template method pattern [Wikipedia 15b], where the general structure of an algorithm (the program skeleton) is well defined but one is still allowed to redefine certain steps.

This is one of the higher-level techniques adopted by Unity (alongside the regular vertex and fragment shaders), which is itself borrowed from Renderman: the surface shader [Pranckevičius 14b]. By defining a clear interface (predefined function names, input and output structures), the surface shader approach allows the end user to concentrate on the surface properties alone, while all the more complex lighting computations (which are much more constant across a game title) remain the responsibility of the über-shader into which it will be injected. It should be noted that it would be possible to combine this with any of the previous three methods for handling permutations at the surface level only.

Taking the idea a bit further, [Yeung 12] describes his solution where he extends the system with interfaces to edit also the vertex data and the lighting formula. Unnecessary code is stripped by generating an abstract syntax tree and traversing it to obtain the variables' dependencies.

17.2.2 The Language Problem

Extensive reviews about the different techniques and tools available to maintain shaders across different languages are available in [Pranckevičius 10a, Pranckevičius 12, Pranckevičius 14a]. We refer the reader to these articles for more information, but we summarize the approaches to handling this problem into the following four families.

The manual way. This could eventually be performed with the help of macros where the languages do differ, but it does not scale well. It is still tricky because of subtle language differences and is hard to maintain.

Use another language. Use a language (eventually a graphical one) that will compile into the target shader language as output.

Cross-compile from one language to another. Lots of tools are available to translate from one language to the other at source code level. The problem can be considered as solved for DirectX 9–level shaders, but there is still work to do for supporting the new features that have appeared since then (e.g., compute, geometry, etc.).

Compile HLSL to bytecode and convert it to GLSL. This is easier to do than the previous technique but suffers from a partly closed tool chain that will run on Windows only.

17.3   Definitions

Our technique is based around the concepts of *fragments* and *user-defined semantics* (not to be confused with the computer graphics fragment used to generate a single pixel data).

- Fragment: In this context, a fragment is a single file written in HLSL that is responsible of implementing a single feature and that contains all the information required for its execution, including uniforms and samplers declarations, as well as code logic. A fragment example is provided in Listing 17.1.

- User-defined semantic: A user-defined semantic is a string literal used to tag a fragment input or output (e.g., `MeshSpacePosition`, `ProjectedPosition`). This tag will be used during shader generation to match a fragment's output to another one's input. User-defined semantics use the existing HLSL semantic feature, used for mapping input and output of shaders.

17.4   Overview

Shader Shaker, our shader generator, uses a new idea to generate the shader. User-defined semantics are added to intermediate variables, as shown in Listing 17.1. The generation algorithm uses those intermediate semantics to generate the list of call functions. The algorithm starts from expected output, e.g.,

```
float4x4 WvpXf;

void GetPosition(
    in float3 position : VertexPosition ,
    out float4 projected_position : ProjectedPosition
    )
{
    projected_position = mul( float4( position , 1 ), WvpXf );
}
```

Listing 17.1. GetPosition fragment.

LitColor, and creates a graph of the function required to generate the semantic up to the vertex attributes.

To generate a shader, one has to provide the system with a list of fragments to use (vertex_skinning + projected_world_space_position + diffuse_texturing + normal_mapping + blinn_lighting, for example). Thanks to the semantics, it is possible to link the desired fragments together to produce the final output semantic required by the system (e.g., LitColor) and generate the corresponding complete shader.

Fragments are completely uncoupled; code can be written without consideration of where the data comes from. For example, for a fragment that declares a function that needs an input argument with a semantic of type ViewSpaceNormal, the tool will search another fragment with a function that has an output argument of the very same semantic to link to this one. In deferred rendering, the fragment that provides this output argument with the semantic ViewSpaceNormal would read the geometry buffer to fetch that value, whereas in forward rendering, a function could, for example, just return the value of the view-space normal coming from the vertex shader. In any case, the fragment in the pixel shader that uses this ViewSpaceNormal is agnostic to where the data it needs comes from.

To achieve this, the code generator adopts a compiler architecture, going through separate phases:

- HLSL fragments are processed by Shader Shaker to generate for each of them an abstract syntax tree (AST).

- The ASTs are processed to create a final AST, which contains all the needed code (functions/uniforms/samplers). The algorithm (explained in detail in the following section) generates this final AST from the required output semantics (the output of the pixel shader), then goes upward to the input semantics, calling successively all functions whose output semantic match the input semantic of the previous function.

- Eventually, this final AST is converted to the expected output language (e.g., HLSL, GLSL, etc.).

As the concept has been introduced, let's dig into the algorithm.

```
struct FunctionDefinition
{
    set<string> InSemantic;
    set<string> OutSemantic;
    set<string> InOutSemantic;
};
```

Listing 17.2. `FunctionDefinition` structure.

17.5   Algorithm Explanation

The algorithm used to generate the shader is inspired by the A* path-finding algorithm [Wikipedia 15a]. The idea is to find a path from the required output semantic to the existing input semantics, i.e., the vertex attributes. The path is searched using open and closed semantic sets, in the same way as the open and closed node lists of the original algorithm. To successfully generate the code, the compiler must be provided the following information:

- the list of fragments to use, i.e., the feature list;

- the list of required output semantics (each of them will be mapped to a system semantic such as `COLOR0`; multiple render target code can be generated by defining multiple final output semantics);

- the list of available input semantics (this can change from mesh to mesh, creating tailored shaders for a given vertex format).

After the parsing of all fragments, the AST is inspected to extract the signature of functions. Each function that declares one or more semantics for its arguments is processed, others being considered as helper functions. A `FunctionDef inition` structure describing the function is filled up with these semantics information (see Listing 17.2). A fragment is then defined by a map of definitions addressed by function names. It's important to notice that `inout` function arguments are supported. It's useful when a fragment wants to contribute to a variable, like summing different lighting into a final lit color or when transforming a vertex position through several fragments. When processing an `inout` semantic, the semantic is kept in the open set. As each function can only be used once, another function outputting the semantic is required.

The code generation is done in two steps. The first step consists of the creation of the call graph. The algorithm is described in Listing 17.3. This algorithm generates a directed acyclic graph of all function calls from the output to the input. The second step consists of code generation from the call graph. As the graph represent the calls from the output, it must be traveled depth first. To

```
open = {required semantic}
closed = {}

repeat until open is empty
    for each fragment from last to first
        for each semantic in open
            if unused function with semantic
                          in OutSemantic exists
                add_function( function )
                restart
            end
        end
    end

    report error, semantics in open set do not resolve
end

add_function( f )
    node = { f, f.InSemantic, f.InOutSemantic}
    open -= f.InSemantic
    open += f.OutSemantic
    //Add inout semantic back in the open set
    open += f.InOutSemantic
    closed += f.InSemantic
    //Link node that required the semantic
    for each semantic in { f.OutSemantic, f.InOutSemantic }
        node[ semantic ].children.add( node )
    end

    //Report as requiring those semantics
    for each semantic in { f.InSemantic, f.InOutSemantic }
        node[ semantic ] = node
    end
    //Remove semantic provided by vertex
    open -= Vertex.AttributeSemantics;
end
```

Listing 17.3. Code generation.

simplify code generation and debugging, the semantic is used as the variable name. The code generation algorithm is described in Listing 17.4. Finally, a map of user semantics to system semantics is generated, information to be used in the engine to bind vertex attributes accordingly.

To illustrate this algorithm, a toy example will be executed step by step. The fragments are defined as shown in Listing 17.5, Listing 17.6, and Listing 17.7. The function definitions are created as shown in Listing 17.8. The required semantic is LitColor. The algorithm generates a graph as shown in Figure 17.1. One can see the open and closed set populated as the algorithm creates the graph. Finally, the graph is processed to create the code shown in Listing 17.9. It is important to notice that the code just uses functions declared in fragments. The final code aggregates all the fragments codes, only with semantic information removed. It's not the purpose of this module to prune unused code. This step can be left to further modules.

```
write function definition with required attributes/varyings
for each node in depth first order
    for each output variable
        if variable has not been encountered yet
            write variable declaration
        end
    end

    write function call

end
```

Listing 17.4. Code generation.

```
Texture DiffuseTexture;

sampler2D DiffuseTextureSampler
{
    Texture = <DiffuseTexture>;
};

void GetDiffuseColor( out float4 color : DiffuseColor,
    in float2 texcoord : DiffuseTexCoord
    )
{
    color = tex2D( DiffuseTextureSampler, texcoord );
}
```

Listing 17.5. Diffuse color from texture fragment.

```
void ComputeNormal( in float3 vertex_normal : VertexNormal,
    out float3 pixel_normal : PixelNormal )
{
    pixel_normal = normalize( vertex_normal );
}
```

Listing 17.6. Simple normal fragment.

```
float4 SomeLighting( in float4 color : DiffuseColor,
    in float3 normal : PixelNormal ) : LitColor
{
    return ( AmbientLight
        + ComputeLight( normal ) )* color;
}
```

Listing 17.7. Some lighting fragment.

```
GetDiffuseColor :
{
    InSemantic : { "DiffuseTexCoord" }
    OutSemantic : { "DiffuseColor" }
}

ComputeNormal :
{
    InSemantic : { "VertexNormal" }
    OutSemantic : { "PixelNormal" }
}

SomeLighting :
{
    InSemantic : { "DiffuseColor", "PixelNormal" }
    OutSemantic : { "LitColor" }
}
```

Listing 17.8. Function definition examples.

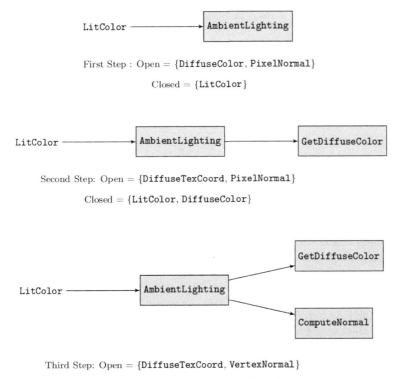

Figure 17.1. Graph generation process.

```
float4 main( in float3 VertexNormal : NORMAL,
    in float2 DiffuseTexCoord : TEXCOORD0 )
{
    float4 DiffuseColor;
    GetDiffuseColor(DiffuseColor, DiffuseTexCoord);
    float3 PixelNormal;
    ComputeNormal(VertexNormal,PixelNormal);
    float4 LitColor
        = SomeLighting(DiffuseColor, PixelNormal);
    return LitColor;
}
```

Listing 17.9. Generated code.

17.6   Error Reporting

17.6.1   Syntax Errors

Syntactic errors existing in fragments are reported as a shader compiler would. Each fragment should be a valid compilation-wise shader. This is detected when parsing the fragments.

17.6.2   Fragment Compliance

A fragment must comply to a list of rules:

- It must only output a given semantic once.

- It must define all constants and sampler it uses.

If either of these rules is broken, the generator reports the error and how to fix it.

17.6.3   Missing Semantics

If any semantic is not found while generating the call graph, the user is informed and the generation is stopped.

17.6.4   Graph Cycles

When a node is inserted in the graph, the graph is checked for cycles. If any are found, the semantics found in the cycle are output.

17.6.5   Mismatching Types for a Semantic

After graph generation, a sanity check is run to ensure all occurrences of a semantic are of the same type. No automatic casting is allowed (e.g., from `float3` to `float2`).

17.6.6   Target Code Restrictions

When targeting a specific platform, additional conditions are checked (e.g., sampler count, vertex attribute count, unsupported texture fetch in vertex shader, etc.)

17.7   Usage Discussions

On top of solving the permutation and the multiplatform problems mentioned earlier, this technique offers the ability to support some noteworthy tricks and features. This discussion lists how they can be leveraged to improve both programmers' and artists' experiences.

17.7.1   Fragments Variants

By using a system similar to [Frykholm 11], it becomes easy to allow your engine file system to choose among multiple variants of a given fragment (e.g., `lighting.fx`, `lighting.low.fx`). We exploit this feature for various purposes:

Platform-specific code. When dealing with multiple graphic platforms, it may happen that the default implementation of a fragment cannot be used natively because the resulting shader is not compatible with the rendering API, or the hardware (e.g., vertex texture fetch). This mechanism allows us to provide a platform-specific version of a given fragment.

Graphic quality. The same principle can be used to manage graphic quality settings. Depending on user settings or based on device capabilities, appropriate fragments can be selected to balance quality against performance.

17.7.2   Fragment Metadata

Each fragment can be associated with a metadata file to ease its integration into the tools. In our case, we chose to export this metadata automatically from the fragments themselves and in JSON format. The available information includes the list of uniforms, the list of textures, a description of what the fragment does, etc.

Thanks to this information, it is easy to populate a combo box from which the artists can select the fragment they want to add to the current material and then tweak the settings the newly added fragment offers.

Furthermore, this metadata also allows us to match the required attributes against the mesh vertex format. A missing component in the vertex format triggers an error, whereas unused data can be stripped safely.

17.7.3 Data-Driven Features

Adding a new rendering feature to the engine and the editor is as easy as adding a new fragment file to the fragment library. As the editor is data-driven, no intervention of a programmer is needed: reloading it is enough. Still, creating a new fragment requires an understanding of the underlying concept. It also requires knowledge of the set-defined semantic, as it could be project specific.

17.7.4 Programming

Accessing the metadata of generated shaders can be leveraged as a data-driven feature, e.g., binding the vertex attributes and the uniforms without using the rendering API to enumerate them. This is even more useful when the graphics API doesn't allow us to do so at all.

17.7.5 Debugging

Programmers can easily debug shaders that are generated by Shader Shaker. Indeed, the output semantics are provided as arguments to the generation process. If an issue is suspected at any level, the shader can be regenerated with an intermediate semantic as the output semantic. For example, if we want to display the view-space normal, the `ViewSpaceNormal` semantic is provided as the output semantic. If the semantic variable type is too small to output (e.g., `float2` while ouputs should be `float4`), a conversion code is inserted.

17.7.6 Choice of Semantics

Semantics are just considered links by the algorithm. Nevertheless, the choice of semantics is really important. If the set is not chosen correctly, new features might require redesigning it, which would require existing fragments' refactoring. The set should be documented precisely to remove any ambiguity on the usage.

17.8 What's Next

While Shader Shaker in its current form is already used with success in our games and tools, there is still room for improvements.

- Use custom semantics for uniforms and samplers. For now, the semantic resolution is only applied to functions and input/output arguments. Applying it to uniforms can be convenient, allowing some values to be passed either at the vertex level or as uniforms.

- The concept of semantic could be augmented. Semantics could have additional properties, such as default values, ranges, normalization, etc. On top of function calls, extra code would be emitted to answer extra specifications.

- Some improvements can be made to the error reporting. In case of an error when generating a shader, the exact position of the error in fragments could be provided with the line number. Also, currently the tool is not yet able to detect cycles in dependency between fragments. It will be of a great help to be able to detect those. Another improvement related to error reporting is a finer detection of grammar errors in the fragments.

- As said before, Shader Shaker does not do any optimizations over the generated shader. Converting Shader Shaker as a frontend to already existing modules, which could take care of those optimizations, would be an interesting improvement. In our toolchain at Fishing Cactus, we already execute the GLSL optimizer [Pranckevičius 10b, Pranckevičius 15] over the generated GLSL files produced by Shader Shaker. We could, for example, integrate LLVM [LLVM 15] at different steps of the generation to optimize the AST and/or the IR.

- We have designed Shader Shaker so that it's really easy to support new output shader languages. Currently, we only support output to HLSL and GLSL, but new languages could be easily supported.

17.9   Conclusion

This technique and its user-semantic linking algorithm brings a new ways of creating shaders. It provides a new way to manage the complexity and combinatory complexity. Each feature can be developped independently, depending only on the choice of semantics. Shader Shaker, our implementation, is distributed as open source software [Fishing Cactus 15].

Bibliography

[Engel 08a] Wolfgang Engel. "Shader Workflow." *Diary of a Graphics Programmer*, http://diaryofagraphicsprogrammer.blogspot.pt/2008/09/shader-workflow.html, September 10, 2008.

[Engel 08b] Wolfgang Engel. "Shader Workflow—Why Shader Generators are Bad." *Diary of a Graphics Programmer*, http://diaryofagraphicsprogrammer.blogspot.pt/2008/09/shader-workflow-why-shader-generators.html, September 21, 2008.

[Epic Games Inc. 15] Epic Games Inc. "Materials." *Unreal Engine 4 Documentation*, https://docs.unrealengine.com/latest/INT/Engine/Rendering/Materials/index.html, 2015.

[Ericson 08] Christer Ericson. "Graphical Shader Systems Are Bad." http://realtimecollisiondetection.net/blog/?p=73, August 2, 2008.

[Fishing Cactus 15] Fishing Cactus. "Shader Shaker." https://github.com/ FishingCactus/ShaderShaker2, 2015.

[Frykholm 11] Niklas Frykholm. "Platform Specific Resources." http://www. altdev.co/2011/12/22/platform-specific-resources/, December 22, 2011.

[Hargreaves 04] Shawn Hargreaves. "Generating Shaders from HLSL Fragments." http://www.shawnhargreaves.com/hlsl_fragments/hlsl_fragments. html, 2004.

[Holmér 15] Joachim 'Acegikmo' Holmér. "Shader Forge." http://acegikmo.com/ shaderforge/, accesssed April, 2015.

[Jones 10] Tim Jones. "Introducing StitchUp: 'Generating Shaders from HLSL Shader Fragments' Implemented in XNA 4.0." http://timjones.tw/blog/ archive/2010/11/13/introducing-stitchup-generating-shaders-from-hlsl -shader-fragments, November 13, 2010.

[Kime 08] Shaun Kime. "Shader Permuations." http://shaunkime.wordpress. com/2008/06/25/shader-permutation/, June 25, 2008.

[LLVM 15] LLVM. "The LLVM Compiler Infrastructure." http://llvm.org/, 2015.

[Pranckevičius 10a] Aras Pranckevičius. "Compiling HLSL into GLSL in 2010." http://aras-p.info/blog/2010/05/21/compiling-hlsl-into-glsl-in-2010/, May 21, 2010.

[Pranckevičius 10b] Aras Pranckevičius. "GLSL Optimizer." http://aras-p.info/ blog/2010/09/29/glsl-optimizer/, September 29, 2010.

[Pranckevičius 12] Aras Pranckevičius. "Cross Platform Shaders in 2012." http: //aras-p.info/blog/2012/10/01/cross-platform-shaders-in-2012/, October 1, 2012.

[Pranckevičius 14a] Aras Pranckevičius. "Cross Platform Shaders in 2014." http: //aras-p.info/blog/2014/03/28/cross-platform-shaders-in-2014/, March 28, 2014.

[Pranckevičius 14b] Aras Pranckevičius. "Shader Compilation in Unity 4.5." http://aras-p.info/blog/2014/05/05/shader-compilation-in-unity-4-dot-5/, May 5, 2014.

[Pranckevičius 15] Aras Pranckevičius. "GLSL Optimizer." *GitHub Repository*, https://github.com/aras-p/glsl-optimizer, 2015.

[Trapp and Döllner 07] Matthias Trapp and Jürgen Döllner. "Automated Combination of Real-Time Shader Programs." In *Proceedings of Eurographics 2007*, edited by P. Cignoni and J. Sochor, pp. 53–56. Eurographics, Aire-la-Ville, Switzerland: Eurographics Association, 2007.

[Väänänen 13] Pekka Väänänen. "Generating GLSL Shaders from Mako Templates." http://www.lofibucket.com/articles/mako_glsl_templates.html, October 28, 2013.

[Wikipedia 15a] Wikipedia. "A* Search Algorithm." http://en.wikipedia.org/wiki/A*_search_algorithm, 2015.

[Wikipedia 15b] Wikipedia. "Template Method Pattern." http://en.wikipedia.org/wiki/Template_method_pattern, 2015.

[Yeung 12] Simon Yeung. "Shader Generator." http://www.altdev.co/2012/08/01/shader-generator/, August 1, 2012.

18

ANGLE: Bringing OpenGL ES to the Desktop

Shannon Woods, Nicolas Capens,
Jamie Madill, and Geoff Lang

18.1 Introduction

The Almost Native Graphics Layer Engine (ANGLE) is a portable, open source, hardware-accelerated implementation of OpenGL ES 2.0 used by software like Google Chrome to allow application-level code to target a single 3D API, yet execute on platforms where native OpenGL ES support may not be present. As of this writing, ANGLE's OpenGL ES 3.0 implementation is under active development. Applications may choose among ANGLE's multiple rendering backends at runtime, targeting systems with varying levels of support. Eventually, ANGLE will target multiple operating systems.

ANGLE's original development was sponsored by Google for browser support of WebGL on Windows systems, which may not have reliable native OpenGL drivers. ANGLE is currently used in several browsers, including Google Chrome and Mozilla Firefox. Initially, ANGLE provided only an OpenGL ES 2.0 implementation, using Direct3D 9 as its rendering backend. D3D9 was a good initial target since it's supported in Windows systems running XP or newer for a very large range of deployed hardware.

Since that time, WebGL has been evolving, and ANGLE has evolved along with it. The WebGL community has drafted new extensions against the current WebGL specification, as well as draft specifications for WebGL 2.0. Some of the features contained within these, such as sRGB textures, pixel buffer objects, and 3D textures, go beyond the feature set available to ANGLE in Direct3D 9. For this reason, it was clear that we would need to use a more modern version of Direct3D to support these features on Windows systems, which led us to begin work on a Direct3D 11 rendering backend.

While we use the Direct3D 11 API in our implementation, we target the 10_0 feature level. A feature level in D3D groups a set of limitations and capabilities; see the D3D11 programming guide for more information [MSDN 14c]. All the features of OpenGL ES 2.0, most of the extensions we expose via OpenGL ES 2.0 contexts, and even most of the features of OpenGL ES 3.0 are available within 10_0. A few features of OpenGL ES 3.0, however, are only available in hardware at the 10_1 or 11_0 feature levels; we'll cover those in more detail later in the chapter.

We chose to implement the Direct3D 11 backend as an addition, not as a replacement, for the original renderer; runtime renderer selection allows the application to support new features when the hardware is available and fall back to previous feature sets on older hardware. The abstraction necessary to allow multiple backends to be easily swapped in and out would come with an additional benefit: it would be relatively easy to add further backends in the future.

Koch and Capens [Koch and Capens 12] have discussed some of prior ANGLE challenges in creating a conformant implementation of OpenGL ES 2.0 using Direct3D 9. Recreating this implementation using Direct3D 11 presented challenges of its own; while we found that the newer API reduced implementation complexity in some areas, it raised it in others. We'll discuss some of these differences below. We'll then discuss ANGLE's shader translator in Section 18.3, give some case studies of implementing OpenGL ES 3.0 features in Section 18.4, and discuss the future directions of ANGLE in Section 18.5. We close off with recommended practices for application developers in Section 18.6.

18.2   Direct3D 11

Of the API differences we encountered while implementing ANGLE's new Direct3D 11 backend, some were relatively minor. In the case of fragment coordinates, for example, Direct3D 11 more closely aligns with OpenGL ES and related APIs, in that pixel centers are now considered to be at half-pixel locations—i.e., $(0.5, 0.5)$—just as they are in OpenGL. This eliminates the need for half-pixel offsets to be applied to fragment coordinates as in our Direct3D 9 implementation. There are quite a few places, however, where Direct3D 11 differs from both Direct3D 9 and OpenGL, requiring ANGLE to find new workarounds for this rendering backend.

18.2.1   Primitives

Direct3D 9's available set of primitive types for draw calls is more limited than OpenGL's, and Direct3D 11's is reduced slightly further by removing triangle fans. ANGLE enables `GL_TRIANGLE_FAN` by rewriting the application-provided index buffer to express the same polygons as a list of discrete triangles. This is a similar tactic to the one we employed to support `GL_LINE_LOOP` in Direct3D 9 (and which is still necessary in Direct3D 11), although the modification required to index buffers for line loops is considerably simpler—we need only repeat the initial point to close the line loop.

Direct3D 11 also removes support for large points, commonly used for rendering point sprites. While point lists themselves are still supported, the size of points is no longer configurable. This is a less trivial problem for ANGLE to solve. Thankfully, Direct3D 11 also introduces geometry shaders, which allow us to expand each point into a billboarded quad, achieving the same effect without CPU overhead.

18.2.2 Texture Formats

One small change from Direct3D 9 to Direct3D 11 that provides a significant benefit to ANGLE is the addition of native support for RGBA formats. While Direct3D 9 had very limited support for texture and screen formats outside of BGRA, Direct3D 11 provides a wide range of supported formats, including RGBA. This reduces the amount of pixel-by-pixel copying and channel swizzling that ANGLE needs to do to get textures from user space to the GPU. Direct3D 11 does lose a couple of formats used by OpenGL ES, though: native support for luminance and luminance alpha textures is dropped, requiring ANGLE to support them by storing to RGBA textures. Compressed texture formats, specified by `ANGLE_texture_compression_dxt`, and immutable textures, as defined in `EXT_texture_storage`, continue to be supported as they were for Direct3D 9 [Koch and Capens 12].

18.2.3 Vertex Buffers

One of the most significant differences between Direct3D 9 and Direct3D 11 from the perspective of ANGLE is a change in the way that vertex and index buffers are declared. In Direct3D 9, it's necessary to specify whether a buffer will be used to store vertex or index data at creation time. OpenGL has no such restriction—it's perfectly valid for an application to generate a buffer, fill it with data, bind it for use as a vertex buffer in one draw call, and then rebind it as an index buffer for a subsequent draw call. In our Direct3D 9 implementation, this meant that we would need to cache the vertex data CPU-side until draw time, at which point we could create vertex and index buffers based on the current bindings.

Additionally, Direct3D 9 supports a much more limited set of vertex element types than OpenGL ES 2.0, which contributes significantly to the complexity of our implementation for that API and can influence performance, as we must interpret and convert application-provided vertex data on the CPU before uploading. Additionally, our Direct3D 9 implementation unpacks interleaved vertex data to avoid conversions on unused data in any given draw. For more information, refer to Koch and Capens's discussion of vertex data [Koch and Capens 12].

Direct3D 11 removes these restrictions to some degree, albeit with some caveats. It uses a single buffer class instead of specializations for index and vertex buffers. Additionally, Direct3D 11 provides native support for all OpenGL ES vertex formats. This frees ANGLE from its prior duty of expanding, converting, and/or de-interleaving application-provided vertex data in many cases; instead, we can forward this data directly to the GPU without manipulation.

One major exception to the automatic vertex format support in Direct3D 11 is unnormalized integer data. While supported in Direct3D 11, integer attributes are not automatically converted to floating points when sent to a vertex shader that accepts floating point inputs. This issue becomes moot in GLSL ES 3.00, which does provide nonfloat vertex attribute types, but *all* vertex data, regardless of how it is provided to the API, is accessed via floats in GLSL ES 1.00 shaders. ANGLE's initial Direct3D 11 implementation addressed this by converting vertex attributes with the CPU before upload. This imposed the same performance overhead that we'd seen in our Direct3D 9 implementation—but we could do better. We will discuss our solution in Section 18.3.7.

One other caveat about Direct3D 11's buffer handling became apparent after we deployed our initial implementation. While Direct3D 11 allows us to bind a vertex buffer as both a source for vertex and index data, some hardware would use the bind flags we provided as a hint for how the buffers should be stored and processed. When we were initially flagging all buffers with both `D3D11_BIND_VERTEX_BUFFER` and `D3D11_BIND_INDEX_BUFFER`, there was a clear performance penalty for some hardware and some drivers. To avoid dual-flagged buffers, we instead store application-provided vertex data in staging buffers until draw time. At draw time, we know if the buffer is being used for index or vertex data, and we can copy the data to an appropriately flagged buffer object. We found this extra copy overhead was preferable to the performance drag introduced by dual-flagging buffers.

What also caught us by surprise is that for Direct3D 11, a −1 in the index buffer (corresponding to 65535 or 0xFFFF for a 16-bit index format) is always interpreted as a triangle strip cut, also known as a primitive restart. In OpenGL ES 2.0 and Direct3D 9, this is a valid index value, so we were seeing geometric anomalies using the same index buffer data with Direct3D 11. We worked around it by promoting buffers that contain this index value to 32 bits.

18.2.4 Moving Forward

For the most part, Direct3D 11 provides an opportunity for ANGLE to support new features and improve performance. Old features that required emulation on Direct3D 9 can often utilize hardware features exposed by the newer API to keep the extra work on the GPU. Perhaps an even more interesting observation is that adding a Direct3D 11 backend caused us to start abstracting things in a way that opened the door for even more rendering backends in the future. This will turn ANGLE into a dependable implementation of OpenGL ES across multiple operating systems and graphics API generations. We'll discuss this vision and the architectural implications in more detail in Section 18.5.

18.3 Shader Translation

Shaders play a major role in modern graphics APIs, and their complexity makes translating between them challenging. Early on in ANGLE's development, it was decided that we should only translate between high-level shading languages and not attempt to compile them down to assembly shaders. This was largely motivated by the availability of Microsoft's HLSL compiler and the fact that unlike Direct3D 9, from Direct3D 10 onward there would no longer be assembly-level shader support. Source-to-source translation was also what Chrome needed for validating WebGL's variant of GLSL ES and translating it into OpenGL ES's GLSL or desktop GLSL and for applying security measures or driver bug workarounds.

This decision turned out to be a double-edged sword. The Direct3D 9 assembly shading language has many quirks and restrictions, and the HLSL compiler knows how to deal with those adequately, most of the time. This saved us from duplicating that effort, and we did not have to deal with optimizations. However, any shortcomings in the HLSL compiler turned out to be a bigger problem to us than to someone directly targeting Direct3D. That's because when a developer encounters an issue with HLSL, he or she will simply rewrite the shader, and the application that gets shipped will work on all the platforms it targets (often using precompiled shaders). With ANGLE, it's unacceptable to expect developers to adjust their shaders just because this one implementation on this one platform has a certain issue, no matter how understandable the limitation and no matter how easy it is to work around. So the ANGLE team had to identify problematic patterns and apply their workarounds as part of the ESSL-to-HLSL shader translator. We found out about most of the issues the hard way from bug reports, as there is no systematic way to discover them. We'll highlight some of the most challenging issues later in this section, but first we'll provide an overview of the translator's architecture and design.

18.3.1 Source-to-Source Translation

The general approach for source-to-source translation is to parse the input string(s) and build an abstract syntax tree (AST) intermediate representation, and then traverse the AST to systematically construct the output string. An example of how some code is parsed and represented as an AST is illustrated in Figure 18.1.

ANGLE's shader translator was founded on 3Dlab's open source GLSL compiler framework [3Dlabs 05]. Out of the box, this framework only supported desktop GLSL version 1.10, but its parser is generated by the Bison tool, which

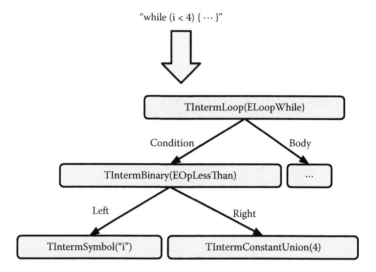

Figure 18.1. Example of parsing a string into an abstract syntax tree.

makes it relatively easy to update the grammar. The GLSL ES specification conveniently lists the entire grammar in its appendix. Also, 3DLab's code was clearly intended for assembly or binary output, but the AST traverser architecture is nicely object-oriented to allow for alternative implementations. The biggest change that was required for outputting a high-level language was to not just perform an implementation-dependent action before and after traversing a tree node's children (dubbed `PreVisit` and `PostVisit`), but also in between them (`InVisit`). This allows for the instance to put commas in between a list of arguments, or semicolons in between a sequence of statements.

We also defined new AST node types to preserve information from the GLSL source code that would not have been required for assembly output, for instance, predeclared functions. While traversing the AST to output the body of the HLSL code, we also keep track of information that should be added to the top. This gets written to the header stream and later prepended to the body. Examples of things that have to be in the header include intrinsic function definitions, which we'll cover later, and structure constructors. In GLSL, structures have an implicit constructor function that has the same name as the structure and takes the field types as parameters. This allows us to create nameless instantiations in the middle of an expression. HLSL does not support this directly. Instead, structures can only be initialized at declaration using an initializer list (similar to C). Therefore, we explicitly generate functions that act as a constructor by declaring and initializing a local variable of the required structure type and returning it.

When we commenced the work to support OpenGL ES 3.0, an architectural decision had to be made on how to deal with multiple input languages. Either we duplicated a large portion of the translator, or we somehow had to support both (significantly different) specifications while minimizing the entanglement. The latter turned out to be feasible through two elegant modifications. First, the lexer, which provides the parser with tokens from the input string, was adjusted to ensure that new keywords in ESSL 3.00 would still be recognized as identifier names for ESSL 1.00 input. Likewise, some keywords of ESSL 3.00 were already reserved for ESSL 1.00 and thus would generate an error or not depending on the specified shader version. To avoid cluttering the lexer specification itself, these decisions are delegated to a few functions that will return the proper token type.

The second major change to support ESSL 3.00 was made to the symbol table. The symbol table is essentially a map used by the parser to store previously encountered variable, structure, or function names and their corresponding types. This also includes predefined intrinsic function names, which greatly differ between ESSL 1.00 and 3.00. The symbol table has multiple layers to deal with variables that are redefined at a different scope or become unavailable by going out of scope. This led us to implement the difference between ESSL 1.00's and 3.00's intrinsics by defining a persistent symbol table layer specific to each specification, and a shared one for common intrinsics. When looking up an identifier for ESSL 3.00 input, we would first look for it in its own layer, skip the ESSL 1.00 layer, then check the common layer, and afterward look into the scoped layers for user-defined identifiers.

For the HLSL backend, no changes had to be made to deal with the two input specifications differently. That's because at this level the GLSL code is fully validated, so we just have to generate any HLSL code that properly implements each AST node, regardless of which version it originated from. ESSL 1.00 intermediate code can be translated into either Shader Model 3.0 or Shader Model 4.0 HLSL, which needed few changes (except for texture intrinsics, discussed below), while ESSL 3.00 constructs demand Shader Model 4.0 features, which we're targeting anyway for OpenGL ES 3.0, so the translator doesn't explicitly have to differentiate between anything at this level.

18.3.2 Shader Debugging

One of the added advantages of source-to-source compilation is that ANGLE's output is relatively easy to debug. Most shader constructs translate in a predictable way, and you can debug your application with Direct3D debugging tools. To assist with this, several features of ANGLE and Chrome help expose its implementation. First, Chrome can be launched with the `--gpu-startup-dialog` command line flag. This halts its execution right after creating the GPU process. This allows you to attach a debugger or other analysis tool to it before

```
var debugShaders = gl.getExtension('WEBGL_debug_shaders');
var hlsl = debugShaders.getTranslatedShaderSource(myShader);
```

Listing 18.1. WEBGL_debug_shaders extension usage.

continuing (which is especially useful when you've set your WebGL application as the startup page) or use **--new-window yoursite.com**. For HLSL compilation issues, you can set a breakpoint at `HLSLCompiler::compileToBinary()` (function name subject to change).

You can also retrieve the HLSL code from within WebGL through the WEBGL_debug_shaders extension, as in Listing 18.1. Note that the format returned by this extension is implementation specific.

You may notice that the original variable names have been replaced by hardly legible _webgl_<hexadecimal> names. This circumvents bugs in drivers that can't handle long variable names, but makes the HLSL difficult to debug. To disable this workaround, you can use Chrome's **--disable-glsl-translation** flag. Note that this merely disables Chrome's ESSL-to-ESSL translation, meant only for validation and driver workaround purposes, not ANGLE's ESSL-to-HLSL translation. This may change in the future as more of the validation becomes ANGLE's responsibility and duplicate translation is avoided. Even with the aforementioned flag, some variable names may have been modified to account for differences in scoping rules between GLSL and HLSL.

18.3.3 Semantic Differences

Source-to-source translation meant that many workarounds could be handled with some string manipulation. But what if the actual core semantics of the languages differ? This was encountered when it turned out that the ternary operator (e.g., `x = q ? a : b;`) evaluates differently between GLSL and HLSL. GLSL conforms to the C semantic specification by only evaluating the expression corresponding with the condition, while HLSL evaluates both sides before selecting the correct result. Similarly, the || and && operators have short-circuiting behaviors in GLSL but not HLSL.

We actually did find a way to deal with this through mostly string operations. For each expression containing a ternary operator, we'd create a new temporary variable in HLSL to hold the ternary operator's result and outputted an `if...else` construct to evaluate only the desired result. Because ternary operators can be nested, we handle this substitution in a separate AST traverser, which can be called recursively, before the original statement, which contained the short-circuiting operators, is outputted with the corresponding temporary variables replacing the short-circuiting operators.

More recently, we've started dealing with these differences at the AST level itself instead of at the string output level. When a short-circuiting operator is encountered, we replace it with a temporary variable node and move the node representing the short-circuiting operator itself up through the tree before the most recent statement and turn it into an `if...else` node. When the child nodes are visited and they themselves contain short-circuiting operators, the same process takes place. So this approach takes advantage of the naturally recursive nature of AST traversal. This doesn't work at the string level because that would require inserting code into part of the string that has already been written.

18.3.4 Intrinsics Implementation and Emulation

Shading languages provide a large part of their built-in functionality that isn't basic arithmetic or flow control constructs through intrinsic functions. Examples include `min()`, `max()`, trigonometric functions, and, most notably, texture sampling operations. Intrinsic functions use the syntax of a function call but are compiled into just one or very few assembly instructions. For ESSL-to-HLSL translation, we had to implement intrinsics that don't have a direct equivalent as actual functions. This is fine because functions typically get inlined, so this typically doesn't have a performance impact compared to a native OpenGL implementation.

ANGLE implements all ESSL texture-sampling intrinsics as functions in HLSL. For ESSL 1.00, this was only a handful of intrinsics, so for each of them we had a handwritten HLSL equivalent. When Direct3D 11 and ESSL 3.00 support was added, there were so many variations of the intrinsics that this became impractical. For example, the ESSL 3.00 specification defines a `gsampler` virtual type to signify `sampler`, `isampler`, and `usampler` types, and most of these texture intrinsics also optionally take a `bias` parameter, resulting in six variants in HLSL for just a single definition in the specification (and there are several dozen definitions). To make this more manageable, we switched to generating the necessary HLSL functions on the fly. Also, to avoid code duplication for predeclaring them in the symbol table, we defined our own `gsampler` type, which causes the function declaration to be expanded into the three actual variants.

While most ESSL 3.00 texture intrinsics have close relatives in HLSL, we were surprised to find that HLSL has no support whatsoever for unnormalized integer format cube maps. Of course, one might also question why ESSL offers support for a feature for which no significant use case was found to make it a feature of HLSL. Whichever stance is taken, we were stuck having to pass the conformance tests for a feature for which there's fundamentally no support in Direct3D 11. The solution was to treat these cube maps as a six-element array texture and to manually compute which face of the cube should be sampled from. Fortunately, because unnormalized integers can't be filtered in any meaningful way and thus only point sampling is defined, we didn't have to deal with finding the closest neighboring texels (potentially across multiple faces)! In any case, it was an interesting exercise in software rendering on the GPU, and we expect to encounter more occurrences like this in the future as graphics APIs become more low level and the operations become more granular and software controlled.

18.3.5 HLSL Compiler Issues

Source-to-source compilation saved us from writing a compiler backend but made us very dependent on Microsoft's HLSL compiler. Bugs and intrinsic limitations require our constant attention and intricate workarounds. Early on, we discovered that for Direct3D 9, loops with more than 254 iterations would fail to compile. While most common uses of WebGL and OpenGL ES 2.0 don't require loops with more iterations, the Khronos conformance test suite includes shaders with 512 iterations to create references to compare trigonometric operations against! So, to obtain conformance certification, we needed a workaround. The solution was to split these loops into multiple loops each with a duplicated body that processes 254 or fewer iterations. Fortunately, the OpenGL ES 2.0 specification limits loops to have statically determinable iteration counts with a single iterator variable which cannot be modified within the loop. We also had to be careful to ensure that a `break;` statement in a prior (split) loop would cause subsequent loops to be skipped. Note that Direct3D 9's assembly instructions are limited to 255 iterations due to its encoding format (an 8-bit field for the iteration count), so a similar solution of splitting the loop would be required at the assembly level. It's just a low-level limitation the HLSL compiler doesn't abstract away at the high-level language.

Similarly, we hit several issues related to balancing the optimization level—not really to achieve better performance (we found that it has little effect, probably due to driver-level reoptimization), but to ensure that the optimizations try to keep the number of instructions and registers within the limits, while not making it take too long to compile. Chrome kills the GPU process after 10 seconds of no progress to prevent attacks where your system would be made unresponsive. Some optimization levels of the HLSL compiler appear to be very aggressive and take a long time to complete. Some shaders even appear to cause the compiler to get stuck in an infinite loop. These optimizations are probably aimed at being used for offline compilation only. Still, we need some optimization to get relatively poorly written ESSL shaders to fit the resource limits.

One particularly challenging issue is that of avoiding differential operations on discontinuous execution paths. This includes explicit differential operations like `dFdx` and `dFdy`, but also implicit ones for texture-sampling intrinsics to determine the mipmap level. The way these gradients are computed is based on how pixels are processed in 2×2 pixel quads in parallel and the value of the variable in question is compared (subtracted) between the neighboring pixels. This works as long as the code path executed by each pixel in the quad is the same. Any divergence caused by taking different branches may cause differentiated variables to not have meaningful values for some of the pixels, and thus there's an undefined discontinuity in the differentiation. GLSL deals with this by simply stating that the result is undefined, while for HLSL it causes a compilation error. You can either use a texture-sampling intrinsic with an explicitly specified LOD value or "flatten" the branches that contain texture sampling intrinsics. *Flattening* means that all pixels execute all code blocks and the desired results are selected afterward. Until recently, there was no control over the HLSL compiler's flattening behavior, and results depended on the presence of texture-sampling intrinsics, and the optimization levels. Nowadays, it can be controlled with the `[flatten]` attribute, but for ANGLE it is hard to determine for which branches it is needed. At the time of writing, we instead generate `Lod0` texture-sampling functions that always sample from the top-level mipmap, which is valid since GLSL defines the derivatives to be undefined.

The HLSL compiler continues to be a source of various issues, most of which are fairly small and affect few users. Ultimately, ANGLE has different design goals than those of applications that target Direct3D directly, which is mostly games with statically compiled shaders or shaders known to compile without issues for a certain HLSL compiler version and optimization flags. Still, we manage to isolate the user from these issues as much as possible, making ANGLE the de facto robust and conformant OpenGL ES implementation on Windows. In the future, we may have to resort to performing most optimizations at the AST level ourselves and outputting only very basic HLSL statements closely corresponding with assembly instructions.

18.3.6 Driver Bugs

We also encountered shader-related issues deeper into the graphics stack. A number of them are related to robustness. Some graphics drivers would, for example, attempt to compile shaders with arrays much larger than 4096 elements, even though that's a limit for many register resources in Direct3D 11, and they would end up choking on it. In the best case, it just exceeds the 10-second time limit of Chrome and the tab gets killed, but in the worst case the user-mode graphics driver crashes and the entire screen goes black until the driver resets itself. To prevent this, we had to limit the size of arrays within ANGLE. We settled on 65,536 for now because optimizations may cause shaders with such a large array to still fit within the actual resources, although it is low enough to avoid the crashes.

One specific driver bug was caused by wrong optimization of `if...else` statements on one brand of graphics cards, and only within vertex shaders. Values of a variable that could only be computed in one branch would pop up in the other branch. This was worked around by rewriting things as `if(x) {} if(!x) {}`. Avoiding re-evaluation of `x` and dealing with one or more `else if` statements makes this nontrivial. Although issues like these are eventually addressed by the graphics card vendors, it takes a while for these fixes to be deployed to all users, so thus far we've always left these kinds of workarounds enabled.

Driver bugs are even less under our control than HLSL compiler issues, but hopefully graphics APIs will continue to become more low level so that eventually we get access to the bare instructions and data. Just like on a CPU, the behavior of elementary operations is very tightly defined and verifiable so that compilers can generate code that produces dependable results.

18.3.7 Dynamic Shaders

Because ANGLE can only generate full HLSL programs after we know the signatures between the vertex and pixel stages, we cannot immediately call the Direct3D compiler at GL compile time. Moreover, we also might modify our shaders at draw time. For ESSL 1.00 shaders, which treat all vertex inputs as floating point, we insert conversion code to transform unnormalized integer vertex attributes in the shader preamble.

ANGLE is not the only program to do this kind of draw-time optimization. A common complaint from application developers is that draw calls sometimes perform very slowly due to dynamic shader re-compilation [AMD 14]. A future design direction for ANGLE, when targeting a more modern API, is to perform the vertex conversion in a separate shader pass, which would then be linked with another compiled shader.

18.4 Implementing ES3 on Feature Level 10

18.4.1 Lessons Learned

The degree of similarity or difference between GLES 3 and Direct3D 11 varies significantly depending on the graphics feature in question. ANGLE's task of implementing GLES 3 on top of Direct3D 11 feature level 10 ranged in difficulty accordingly. We might describe some aspects of our translation as "squashing a dog into a cat suit, and asking it to meow." In other cases, the implementation came naturally. Often the most challenging workarounds come from corner cases, the little sneaky cases, instead of the most common usage. In this section, we'll discuss three examples of some conflicting limitations and corner cases: uniform buffers, transform feedback, and pixel buffer objects.

In the future we might choose a simpler, more flexible approach. Instead of mapping one high-level feature onto another high-level feature, we might improve our lives by assembling the high-level features from simple compute shader components. ANGLE's stars align with the direction of many modern APIs, such as the recently announced (as of this writing) Direct3D 12 [McMullen 14], Apple's Metal [Apple 14], and AMD's Mantle [AMD 14]; with these modern APIs, ANGLE could use the features we discuss in this section as compute shaders.

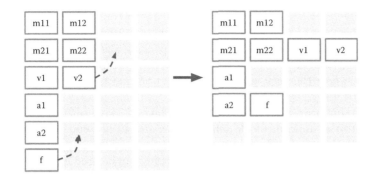

Figure 18.2. Example HLSL packing of a simple uniform block.

18.4.2 Uniform Buffers

Uniform buffer objects (UBOs) are a marquee feature of OpenGL ES3. UBOs give applications the ability to upload blocks of uniform data as typed, mappable buffer objects. UBOs are particularly useful for applications, such as skinning, that deal with large arrays of bone and joint matrices. Moreover, UBOs are a more complex part of the ESSL 3.00 specification. This complexity is due partially to the intricate packing and unpacking rules for getting data out of the buffer to the active vertex or fragment shader.

Here's a simple UBO with four members:

```
uniform sampleBlock
{
    mat2 m;
    vec2 v;
    float a[2];
    float f;
};
```

The GL API defines three layouts for unpacking data from UBOs to the shader. We treat the *packed* and *shared* layouts identically; in both, the details are left to the GL implementation. The *std140* layout, however, is defined precisely by the GL specification. Because it's an application, you can choose the simplicity of the standardized layout or the benefit of a memory-saving packed layout. With a GL implementation, you must at the very least support the std140 layout.

UBOs map relatively closely to Direct3D 11's concept of *constant buffers* [MSDN 14d]. We chose to implement UBOs on top of constant buffers and offer the memory-saving benefits of the packed layout, while maintaining the necessary std140 layout. In both cases, good performance is also a requirement.

Unsurprisingly, HLSL's default unpacking scheme for constant buffers differs from the std140 layout; thus, we have two competing requirements.

The (somewhat undocumented) HLSL unpacking algorithm reads subsequent variables from the empty space left over from unpacking prior variables. See Figure 18.2, where the `vec2` is folded into the prior `mat2`, and the `float` is folded into the prior array.

Thus, to support both std140 and packed layouts, we insert invisible padding variables into the uniform block definition for std140 layouts. We leave packed blocks as the default HLSL definition. This works well, except for the case of nested structures. Nested structures, because they can be used in both std140 and other layouts, require us to create two internal struct definitions: one definition with the extra std140 padding and one without.[1] Nested structures also prevent us from using HLSL's register offset specifiers to specify the unpacking scheme.

While our implementation offers a choice between space and generality, both with good performance, it suffers from complexity. A future direction is to skip the specialized API for constant buffers entirely; we could opt to bind our UBOs as structured buffers and unpack the data manually in the shader preamble. Using a more modern feature level in Direct3D, or MANTLE or Metal, would give us access to the necessary tools.

18.4.3 Transform Feedback

GLES 3 adds a method for the application to capture the vertex data stream's output from the vertex shader stage. GLES calls this operation transform feedback, while Direct3D 11 has a very analogous operation called *Stream output* [MSDN 14e]. In both, the application can even skip rasterization completely. Vertex stream capture has a few notable use cases; inspecting vertex outputs for debugging is much easier by capturing streams directly. GPGPU applications, such as particle systems, often need to transform vertex data (particle position, velocity, etc.) in their update step.

Direct3D's stream output has many similarities, and some notable differences—particularly notable in their limitations on the number of active capture buffers. Under feature level 10, our low-specification feature set, we are limited to writing a single four-component vector output per stream-output buffer[2]. Feature level 10 also imposes a limit of no more than four Stream-Output buffers per draw call. These limits, fortunately enough, exactly match the minimum/maximum values in the GLES 3 Specification, Table 6.24 [Lipchak 13].

In the future, under more flexible APIs, we could implement GL's transform feedback from more general shaders. Instead of mapping to the high-level stream output, we could implement stream output in a compute shader kernel. This

---

[1]We also end up with two additional `struct` permutations to handle unpacking row-major and column-major matrices from nested `structs`.

[2]Note that the stream-output buffer at slot zero has a larger upper bound.

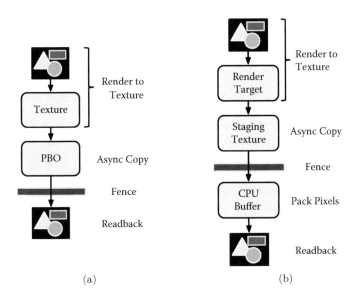

(a)   (b)

Figure 18.3. Asynchronous readback with PBOs: (a) Simple GL implementation. (b) ANGLE–Direct3D 11 implementation.

simple shader approach would fit naturally into a MANTLE/Metal-like API, or even with a higher feature level in Direct3D 11.

18.4.4 Pixel Pack Buffers

Pixel pack and unpack buffers, collectively known as *pixel buffer objects* (PBOs), round out the new data copying operations in GLES 3. Of particular interest to us are pack buffers, which are buffer objects that receive pixel data from a texture object. A primary use case for pack buffers is reading back texture data asynchronously. The application first triggers the pixel copy operation to the pack buffer without blocking the application layer. Next, it creates a fence sync object (see Section 5.2 of the OpenGL ES 3 specification [Lipchak 13]) to detect when the GPU is finished. The application then reads back the pixel data, while spending minimal time blocked waiting for the GPU. Figure 18.3(a) gives an example of asynchronous readback.

PBOs map to Direct3D 11's notion of staging resources [MSDN 14b]. Staging resources act as CPU-accessible memory; they proxy data to and from the GPU. They are not orthogonal; Direct3D places several limitations on staging (and also nonstaging) resources, making life for our PBO implementation a bit tougher.

First, Direct3D 11 does not allow direct copies between texture and buffer resources. Thus, when we implement a copy from a texture to a buffer, we can't rely on Direct3D 11's `CopyResource` methods. Another option might be stream output, as we described in Section 18.4.3, to capture texture data into a buffer using a vertex shader. Direct3D's constraints on stream output notably lack support for some data types, making this quite challenging. Compute shaders also offer a promising and elegant solution. Since we are limited to supporting Shader Model 4 as a minimum, we unfortunately couldn't rely on compute shaders in all cases.

More problems arise from the different requirements GL and Direct3D 11 both enforce on the data packing after the asynchronous copy step. GL gives a set of fine-grained pack parameters, which control how the pixel data packs into the pack buffer (see Table 4.4 of the OpenGL ES 3 specification [Lipchak 13]). Direct3D 11, on the other hand, packs pixels row by row with a gap at the end of each row, specified by a stride [MSDN 14a].

The intended use of staging buffers and pack buffers is to copy from CPU to GPU memory; this similarity makes the use of staging buffers a suitable starting point. The differences in details lead us to choose a simple, nonoptimal implementation. After copying back to the staging texture, we do an extra CPU-side packing step that requests the data, usually via a call to `glMapBufferRange`. We run the GL packing algorithm, resolving the GL pack parameters with the Direct3D 11 offsets, into a CPU memory buffer. This process is illustrated in Figure 18.3(b). The net result cleanly dresses up Direct3D in a GL suit, at the cost of a bit of extra work.

A compute shader could lead to a simple, preferable implementation; running the packing algorithm on the GPU give more work to the GPU. On feature level 11 or other modern APIs, such as Metal or MANTLE, we could make better use of compute shaders.

18.5   Future Directions: Moving to New Platforms

Since early 2014, the ANGLE team has been redesigning ANGLE to cover a broader scope and to provide a conformant and fast OpenGL ES 2/3 and EGL implementation across as many platforms as possible.

18.5.1   Creating a Cross-Platform OpenGL ES Driver

The last year has seen the announcements of at least three new major graphics APIs, most of them tied to specific hardware or platforms. The new APIs are typically very low level, attempting to abstract very little of the hardware, and are a great opportunity for graphics engines to write specialized code for targeted devices. For writing simple applications and games, this can be a big burden; ANGLE hopes to alleviate this by being able to provide a common API that can translate to the lower-level APIs without a significant performance impact. See Figure 18.4 for a high-level diagram of an application's interaction with ANGLE and the native graphics API.

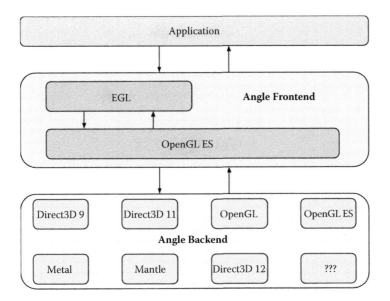

Figure 18.4. ANGLE–application interaction.

18.5.2   An Extensible Architecture

To easily support multiple rendering backends, ANGLE needed an architecture that did as much work as possible before sending work to the native renderer. The library has been split into three distinct layers to create the simplest possible interface that a new renderer must implement. See Figure 18.5 for a high-level diagram of ANGLE's architecture.

Layers.   The layers are the following:

1. The *entry point/validation* layer exports all of the EGL and OpenGL ES entry point functions and handles validation of all paramters. All values passed to the layers below this are assumed to be valid.

2. The *object layer* contains C++ representations of all EGL and OpenGL ES objects and models their interactions. Each object contains a reference to a native implementation for forwarding actions to the native graphics API.

3. The *renderer layer* provides the implementation of the EGL and GL objects in the native graphics API; the interfaces are simplified to only *action* calls such as drawing, clearing, setting buffer data, or reading framebuffer data. All queries and validation are handled by the layers above.

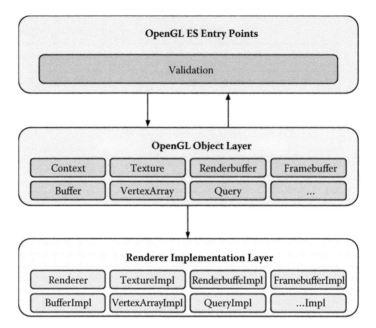

Figure 18.5. ANGLE architecture.

```
class BufferImpl
{
  public:
    virtual void setData(size_t size, void *data,
                         GLenum usage) = 0;
    virtual void setSubData(size_t offset, size_t size,
                            void *data) = 0;
    virtual void *map(GLenum access) = 0;
    virtual void unmap() = 0;
};
```

Listing 18.2. The `Buffer` interface.

The buffer object. A simple example of a renderer layer object that requires a native implementation is the OpenGL ES 3.0 `Buffer` (see Listing 18.2). ANGLE's Direct3D 9 implementation simply stores the supplied memory in CPU-side memory until the first use of the `Buffer` in a draw call when the data is uploaded to a `IDirect3DVertexBuffer9` or `IDirect3DIndexBuffer9`. The Direct3D 11 implementation stores the data in a `ID3D11Buffer` with the `D3D11_USAGE_STAGING` flag and will copy the buffer data lazily to one of several specialized buffers for use as an index buffer, vertex buffer, transform feedback buffer, or pixel buffer.

```
class Renderer
{
  public:
    virtual BufferImpl *createBuffer() = 0;
    virtual TextureImpl *createTexture() = 0;
    ...

    virtual void drawArrays(const gl::State &state, GLenum mode,
                            size_t first, size_t count) = 0;
    ...
    virtual void clear(const gl::State &state,
                       GLbitfield mask) = 0;
    ...
};
```

Listing 18.3. A snippet of the `Renderer` interface.

```
const char *ex = eglQueryString(EGL_NO_DISPLAY, EGL_EXTENSIONS);
if (strstr(ex, "EGL_ANGLE_platform_angle")     != NULL &&
    strstr(ex, "EGL_ANGLE_platform_angle_d3d") != NULL)
{
    EGLint renderer = EGL_PLATFORM_ANGLE_TYPE_D3D11_ANGLE;
    const EGLint attribs[] =
    {
        EGL_PLATFORM_ANGLE_TYPE_ANGLE, renderer,
        EGL_NONE,
    };
    display = eglGetPlatformDisplayEXT(EGL_PLATFORM_ANGLE_ANGLE,
                                       nativeDisplay, attribs);
}
```

Listing 18.4. Example ANGLE `Renderer` selection.

The renderer object. The `Renderer` object is the main interface between the object layer and the renderer layer. It handles the creation of all the native implementation objects and preforms the main actions, such as drawing, clearing, or blitting. See Listing 18.3 for a snippet of the `Renderer` interface.

Runtime renderer selection. Specific renderers can be selected in EGL by using the `EGL_ANGLE_platform_angle` extension. Each renderer implemented by ANGLE has an `enum` that can be passed to `eglGetDisplayEXT` or a default `enum` that can be used to allow ANGLE to select the best renderer for the specific platform it is running on. See Listing 18.4 for an example of selecting the Direct3D 11 renderer at runtime.

18.5.3 The Next Step: Creating an OpenGL Renderer

The first non-Direct3D renderer to be implemented by the ANGLE team will use desktop OpenGL. This will allow the project to quickly expand to other desktop platforms and allow users to write OpenGL ES applications that run on all mobile and desktop platforms.

Despite the ANGLE project originally being created to work around the poor quality of OpenGL drivers on the Windows desktop, the quality has improved enough over the last five years that offering an OpenGL renderer is viable. With having the Direct3D renderer fallback, ANGLE will be able to offer OpenGL renderers on driver versions that are known to be stable and fast with less CPU overhead than a Direct3D renderer.

Dealing with the enormous number of permutations of client version and extension availability in desktop OpenGL will be a complicated aspect of implementing an OpenGL renderer. Loading function pointers or using texture format enumerations may involve checking a client version and up to three extensions. For example, creating a framebuffer object could be done via `glGenFramebuffers`, `glGenFramebuffersEXT`, `glGenFramebuffersARB`, or `glGenFramebuffersOES` (when passing through to OpenGL ES), depending on the platform.

Driver bugs are notoriously common in OpenGL drivers, and working around them will be necessary. In order to promise a conformant OpenGL ES implementation, ANGLE will have to maintain a database of specific combinations of driver versions, video card models, and platform versions that have known conformance issues and attempt to work around these issues by avoiding the issue or manipulating inputs or outputs. In the worst case, when a driver bug cannot be hidden, EGL offers the `EGL_CONFORMANT` configuration field to warn the user that there are issues that cannot be fixed.

18.6   Recommended Practices

ANGLE is an important implementation of OpenGL ES for desktops and powers the majority of WebGL usage. So it pays off to try to take a few of its preferred and less preferred rendering practices into account.

- Avoid line loops and triangle fans. Instead try using line lists and triangle lists.

- Wide lines are not supported. Many native OpenGL implementations also don't support them, because there's no consensus on how to deal with corner cases (pun intended). Implement wide lines using triangles.

- Avoid having an index value of 0xFFFF in a 16-bit index buffer. Configure your tool chain to create triangle strips with a maximum index of 65534.

- Keep geometry that uses different vertex formats in separate buffers.

- Avoid using luminance and luminance-alpha texture formats. Try to use four-channel texture formats instead.

- Make use of the `EXT_texture_storage` extension (only applies to desktop applications).

- Avoid using texture-sampling intrinsics within control flow constructs (e.g., `if`, `else`, `switch`). Instead, sample the texture outside of these constructs.

- Test your WebGL application with early releases of Chrome (Beta, Dev, and Canary). It's the best way to catch bugs early, fix them, and create a conformance test for it so it will never affect your users.

Bibliography

[3Dlabs 05] 3Dlabs. "GLSL Demos and Source Code from the 3Dlabs OpenGL 2." http://mew.cx/glsl/, 2005.

[AMD 14] AMD. "AMD's Revolutionary Mantle." http://www.amd.com/en-us/innovations/software-technologies/mantle#overview, 2014.

[Apple 14] Apple. "Metal Programming Guide." *Apple Developer*, https://developer.apple.com/library/prerelease/ios/documentation/Miscellaneous/Conceptual/MTLProgGuide/, 2014.

[Koch and Capens 12] Daniel Koch and Nicolas Capens. "The ANGLE Project: Implementing OpenGL ES 2.0 on Direct3D." In *OpenGL Insights*, edited by Patrick Cozzi and Christophe Riccio, pp. 543–570. Boca Raton, FL: CRC Press, 2012.

[Lipchak 13] Benjamin Lipchak. "OpenGL ES Version 3.0.3." *Khronos Group*, http://www.khronos.org/registry/gles/specs/3.0/es_spec_3.0.3.pdf, 2013.

[McMullen 14] Max McMullen. "Direct3D 12 API Preview." *Channel 9*, http://channel9.msdn.com/Events/Build/2014/3-564, April 2, 2014.

[MSDN 14a] MSDN. "D3D11_MAPPED_SUBRESOURCE Structure." *Windows Dev Center*, http://msdn.microsoft.com/en-us/library/windows/desktop/ff476182(v=vs.85).aspx, 2014.

[MSDN 14b] MSDN. "D3D11_USAGE Enumeration." *Windows Dev Center*, http://msdn.microsoft.com/en-us/library/windows/desktop/ff476259(v=vs.85).aspx, 2014.

[MSDN 14c] MSDN. "Direct3D Feature Levels." *Windows Dev Center*, http://msdn.microsoft.com/en-us/library/windows/desktop/ff476876(v=vs.85).aspx, 2014.

[MSDN 14d] MSDN. "How to: Create a Constant Buffer." *Windows Dev Center*, http://msdn.microsoft.com/en-us/library/windows/desktop/ff476 896(v=vs.85).aspx, 2014.

[MSDN 14e] MSDN. "Stream-Output Stage." *Windows Dev Center*, http://msdn.microsoft.com/en-us/library/windows/desktop/bb205121(v=vs.85) .aspx, 2014.

19

Interactive Cinematic Particles
Homam Bahnassi and Wessam Bahnassi

19.1   Introduction

In this chapter, we describe a new real-time particle simulation method that works
by capturing simulation results from Digital Content Creation (DCC) tools and
then replaying them in real time on the GPU at a low cost while maintaining the
flexibility of adding interactive elements to those simulations.

This technique we call *Interactive Cinematic Particles* (ICP) has been applied
successfully in the game *Hyper Void*, which runs at 60 FPS on the Playstation
3 console. Figure 19.1 shows one of the enemies in the game modeled using a
large number of particles. The enemy moves and attacks the player interactively
while retaining the cinematic animation aspects by conveying an angry liquid
face designed and simulated using Autodesk Softimage's ICE environment.

19.2   Background

In a lot of games—including new AAA titles on the latest generation of gaming consoles—particles have been limited in their uses (mainly to represent fire,
explosions, and smoke). While there has been quite some investment in the ren-

Figure 19.1. An enemy from *Hyper Void* modeled using a large number of particles.

dering and display techniques of these particles to make them look realistic, their simulation techniques remain rather simplistic and limited. One possible source of this limitation is due to the tools used to design those particle simulations— which in themselves shaped a mindset that confines using particles to smoke and explosion effects only. The result is that there is much unexplored potential in this freeform method of visualization.

Interestingly, one does not have to look too far to see the state-of-the-art tools for authoring particle simulations. Major DCC tools have long offered advanced simulation capabilities and a rich library of operators to drive simulations in the way the artist envisions. Admittedly, some of these operators can be quite expensive to evaluate at runtime in a game scenario, which is one reason why DCC tools are capable of introducing more interesting results. The question here is, how can we leverage the powerful simulation authoring capabilities of those DCC tools and port their results to real-time scenarios? We bring up ICP as a step toward this goal.

Please note that the focus of this chapter is on the simulation aspect rather than the rendering aspect, which is a different area of study in 3D particle effects.

19.3   Challenges and Previous Work

In the following we highlight some of the research areas that have contributed toward this highly demanded aspect of 3D game rendering.

19.3.1   Particle Simulations on the GPU

The GPU's capability to execute general computations has attracted developers for solving particle simulation on the GPU instead of the CPU [Drone 07, Thomas 14]. As a result, games are able to simulate higher particle counts with more complex operators. However, with the performance boost, the tools for authoring simulations for games are still limited.

19.3.2   Solving Fluids in Games

Solving physical and specifically fluid simulations in games has been the focus of the industry in the recent years [Stam 03, Hegeman et al. 06]. With the impressive and realistic results of these solvers, they are still not applicable on a large scale due to the high memory and performance costs. In addition to that, they are still limited when it comes to creating fantasy simulation scenes due to the limitations of authoring tools in game engines. DCC tools offer higher flexibility when combining different operators and solvers (including fluid solvers), which allows artists to apply any art style to the effects. (See the example in Figure 19.2.)

Figure 19.2. Fluid smoke simulated in real time [Macklin et al. 14].

19.3.3 Dedicated Particle Editors for Games

There are very few particles editors dedicated for games [PopcornFX 15, Fork 15]. The main advantage of these tools is providing better authoring tools than most of the out-of-the-box particle editors in game engines. Also, they provide more simulation operators, allowing artists to create more interesting effects. However, editors are still not as powerful as DCC tools and artists need to learn new tools. The particle editors also require integration in the game editor, especially for in-house engines. Performance is heavily affected by the optimization of the simulation operators provided by the middleware tool and the complexity of the effect (operator count, particle count, etc.).

With all the advancement in particle simulation, we can summarize the main challenges in three main points:

- performance,

- artist friendly workflow,

- cinematic quality operators.

19.3.4 Streaming Presimulated Data per Frame

While not particularly built for particle simulations, the work of Gneiting was used to drive geometric animations exported frame by frame in the game *Ryze* developed by Crytek [Gneiting 14]. The feature was driven by the need to achieve next-generation mesh animations. Some of the concepts in [Gneiting 14] are similar and useable in the system outlined in this chapter. However, that technique does not include any support for real-time interactivity.

19.4   Interactive Cinematic Particles (ICP) System Outline

The ICP system handles particle simulations in a similar way to how a modern game handles animations for a character. In this example, the character has a bank of animation clips authored by animators; those clips are loaded at runtime and are played back and blended together according to character actions. Furthermore, additional procedural animation operators can be executed on the final pose to add detail (e.g., head-tracking, breathing, etc.).

The ICP system works in a similar way. First, particle simulation clips are exported from a DCC tool. Those clips are loaded or streamed at game runtime and are selectively blended and processed according to interactive game logic. Runtime operators can additionally be applied to the blended simulation to add further detail. The final output is the location, rotation, size, color, etc. of each particle each frame. This information is then used to render the particle system using any rendering technique needed to achieve the final look.

There are three main aspects to ICP:

1. Data authoring workflow: This aspect covers the process of designing and exporting particle simulation clips out of the DCC tool.

2. Offline build process: The data exported from DCC tools is passed through a build process that transforms it into a representation suitable for runtime streaming and playback on the GPU. This involves a GPU-friendly compression scheme that reduces disk size for storing the simulation clips as well as reducing runtime memory requirements.

3. Runtime execution: This describes how to load and execute the particle simulation clips efficiently on the GPU. With this building block, a system is designed to take those clips and process them in the context of a larger graph that can apply further operators to support interactivity and response to real-time conditions. The implementation of some operators used in *Hyper Void* is described (e.g., blend, local shatter, and deformation to bullets).

The high-level flowchart in Figure 19.3 explains the pipeline.

19.5   Data Authoring Workflow

The goal of the data authoring workflow is to start from the concept of an interactive particle simulation and to break it down into elements that can be represented by one or more particle simulation clips. Then, each of those clips is

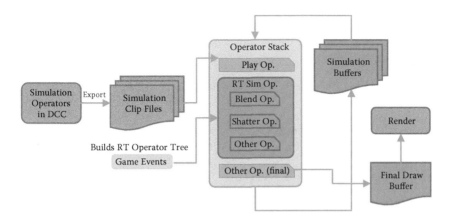

Figure 19.3. Interactive Cinematic Particles pipeline.

authored and exported using some intermediary file format that will be further processed to prepare it for runtime execution.

This section will delve into the details of each of the above mentioned steps. A case study from our game *Hyper Void* will be used as an example.

19.5.1 Authoring Interactive Particle Simulations

Adding interactivity to an offline-authored particle simulation requires considering how this simulation is to be used in the game. Here is a simple example scenario: A water flood starts by a break in a barrier, then water continues to pour in for a time determined by varying game conditions, and finally the flood stops and the water stream reduces to drips before it completely stops. In this example, three major components can be identified:

1. an intro clip (flood breaking in),

2. a looping section (water pouring),

3. an outro clip (water drying out).

When these three simulation clips are made available to the game, the game can then play the intro once, then loop on the looping section until the event to stop the flood is triggered, at which time the outro clip is played once.

Breaking down a particle simulation depends on the user story behind the effect. Since it is impossible to cover all user story possibilities, here are a few questions that can be asked to determine a good simulation breakdown:

1. Does the effect have interactivity elements to it?

2. What parts of the effect need to be done via authored simulation clips versus being achieved using runtime operators? (Real-time operators will be covered later.)

3. For an interactive effect, what are the possible states in which it can end up?

4. How do these states transition between each other? Are special transition clips needed, or would a simple runtime cross-blend work?

5. Does the effect have any looping parts?

Based on the answers to these questions, it is possible to plan and identify what parts need to be authored and how they should be authored. Later, this plan is used to put the effect together in the game engine.

With this information, artists can now use whatever DCC tool they see fit to author those simulation clips. They can use all available features in the tool in the way with which they are familiar.

19.5.2 Exporting Simulation Clips

Once simulation clips are authored, they must be exported to a file format for the game engine build process to handle.

DCC tools offer the capability to store particle simulations in *cache files*. Those caches are used to accelerate simulation playback and scrubbing through time. But, they can also be parsed by the game engine build process to extract the simulation state every frame, provided that the file format specification is well documented.

When caching particle simulations, DCC tools are capable of storing many simulation attributes per particle. This includes basic data such as ID, position, rotation, color, and velocity as well as more-specific data such as age, heat, and glow.

It is important to note that the data attributes stored will have a big impact on the cache file size. Remember that this data is multiplied per particle per simulation frame. Thus, it is of big importance to plan ahead about what attributes are needed for the runtime effect and to only store those in the files.

19.5.3 Case Study

In the case of *Hyper Void*, effects were authored using Softimage ICE. ICE is a multi-threaded visual programming language designed for creating cinematic effects. (See Figure 19.4.)

The tool was liberally used in the same manner as in full motion-picture production. Simulation clips were cached to disk using the `.icecache` file format,

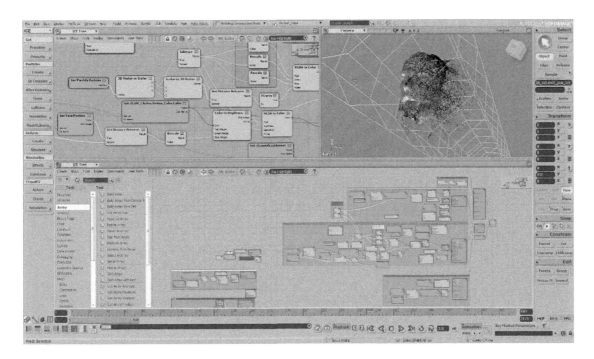

Figure 19.4. ICE visual programming language graphs.

which is the built-in format for caching particles in Softimage. There are numerous advantages to using this file format. First, it is readily available and its specifications are documented. Second, it is capable of storing any selected set of particle attributes (e.g., ID, position, color, and velocity) to save disk space as well as time spent processing those files in the game engine build process.

Another great advantage is the ability to import the simulation cached files back to Softimage and reassemble the effect the same way it is going to be assembled in the game, using the Cache Manager (shown in Figure 19.5). In Softimage, imported simulation caches are edited similar to how video clips are edited in a nonlinear video editing software. Artists can re-time, loop, and mix multiple simulations together and see the final result in the 3D viewport. (See Figure 19.6.) This allows artists to experiment with different breakdowns for the effect before building the final logic in the game.

To streamline the process of breaking down simulation states, exporting packages, and importing them in the game engine and/or DCC tool, a set of tools were implemented. These include tools for defining different states of the effect, batch-exporting simulation clips with proper settings, and importing previously exported simulation clips. (See Figure 19.7.)

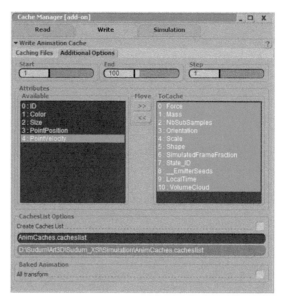

Figure 19.5. The Cache Manager allows picking which attributes to store in a file cache.

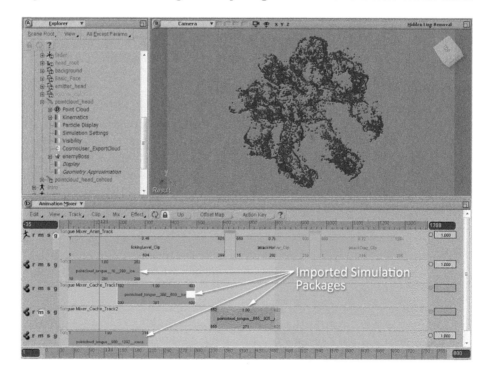

Figure 19.6. Imported simulation cache files edited as clips.

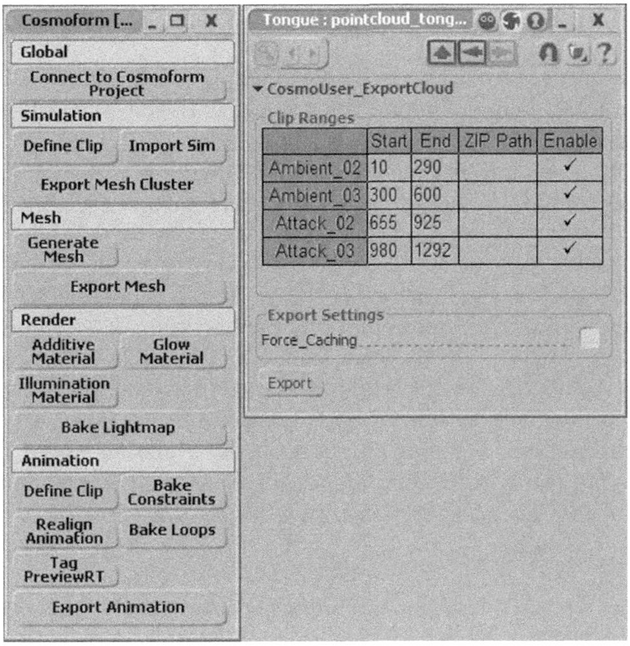

Figure 19.7. Tool for defining simulation clips and batch-exporting them.

19.6 Offline Build Process

The particle simulation clips generated from the DCC tool contain all the simulation information at full precision. This raw representation will result in large clip sizes on disk. For example, consider an exported clip of 300 frames made of 100,000 particles. Each particle contains the following:

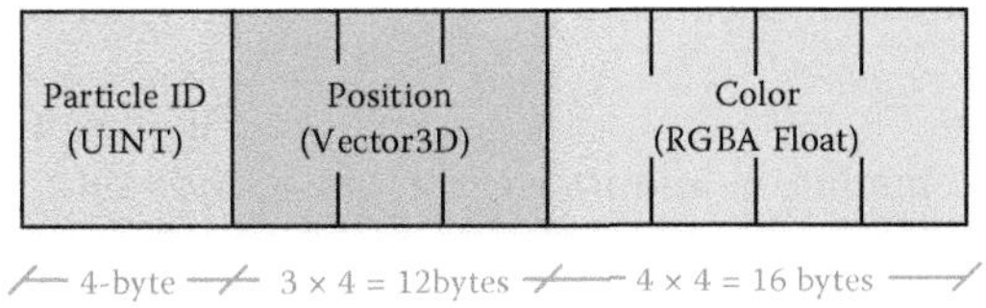

1. Particle ID: 4-byte integer.

2. Position: 3D vector of 32-bit floats.

3. Color: 4D vector of 32-bit floats.

The resulting disk size for the above clip would be roughly 915.5 MB. Even streaming such a file at runtime to play at 30 FPS would be problematic for disk access (reading ca. 90 MB per second). Therefore, it is important to compress these clips for efficient runtime access.

19.6.1   Data Compression

Data compression is an art by itself. Leveraging on the nature of compressed data is key to achieve good compression rates. We do not advocate for a specific compression scheme. Instead, it is advisable that this part of the ICP system gets reconsidered for every project's needs. The following is a list of considerations that should help guide the decision for a certain compression scheme for a project:

1. The playback mode used at runtime: If clips are to be played back from their first frame and onward without seeking, then it is possible to avoid storing any intermediate key frames and rely only on frame-to-frame differences.

2. The range of data variation: Difference encoding works best if the variation in data values falls within a limited range. For example, a particle effect in which particles are moving generally at a similar speed could be re-expressed in terms of initial position, direction, and speed. Since the speed is not varying between particles, then higher compression can be utilized on the speed term.

3. How much data loss is acceptable: Particle effects usually involve large numbers of particles. The detailed location and state of each particle might not be that noticeable as long as the overall effect maintains its general shape and properties. It is thus possible to accept a window of error for each individual particle.

4. Amount and frequency of animation detail: If the animation of the particle effect does not involve a lot of detail, then it is possible to drop frames entirely and regenerate them at runtime as the interpolation between two more-distant frames. For example, it might be acceptable to export the simulation clip at 15 FPS but play it back at 60 FPS in runtime, using smooth interpolation between frames to maintain the same timing.

5. Processing power budgeted for the ICP system: The nature of the processor executing the simulation and its capabilities can dictate how elaborate the compression scheme can be. GPUs can efficiently process disjoint data, whereas CPUs can be a better option for schemes like LZ4.

19.6.2   Case Study

Since *Hyper Void* had to run on the older Playstation 3 console, the technical capabilities of the hardware had a big impact on the choice of compression scheme for the game's particle simulation clips.

The particle effects in the game needed only two pieces of information: position and color. Other properties were constant and thus needed not be stored for every particle every frame (e.g., size, orientation, glow amount, and illumination). Thus, the files exported from the DCC tool included only the following information: ID, position, and color.

The particle ID was needed by the `.icecache` file representation because the particles are not always guaranteed to be listed in the same order across all frames of the simulation clip. In the build process, those IDs are only used to identify the particle throughout the `.icecache`. The output of the build process is an ordered list of particles for every frame. The ordering does not change across frames; therefore, storing the IDs was not necessary in the final output.

Compressing position is the interesting part. The particle effects in *Hyper Void* did not have a large variation in movement speed between particles. Moreover, simulation clips needed only to play forward without seeking. Thus, difference encoding over position was chosen. The first frame of the clip records the initial absolute 3D position of each particle as three 16-bit floating point values. Each subsequent frame is expressed as the difference against its predecessor. Then, the difference values for all particles within a single frame are normalized to $[0, 1]$, and each value is stored as a single 8-bit integer $[0, 255]$. The frame stores the numbers needed to denormalize the difference values during decompression. In conclusion, the first frame consumes 6 bytes per particle, while subsequent frames consume only 3 bytes per particle for storing position information.

The last piece of data remaining is color information. After determining that the position consumes 3 bytes per particle, it was highly desired to reserve only 1 byte for color information, leading to a total of 4 bytes per particle. To achieve this, a color palette of 256 entries was used. The color palette is generated from all colors across the entire simulation clip. It is also possible to generate a palette for each frame, but the particle effects in *Hyper Void* did not have a lot of variety across frames, hence a single color palette for the entire simulation clip was quite sufficient. Each particle searches for the palette entry closest to its color and takes the palette entry ID.

The final output format thus is as follows:

1. Color palette: made of 256 entries of 4-channels; each channel is 1-byte.

2. First frame: 8 bytes per particle (6 bytes for position, 1 byte for color, and the final byte was left unused).

3. All other frames: 4 bytes per particle (3 bytes for position and 1 byte for color), as in the following graph:

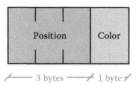

Back to the example of the 300 frames simulation clip with 100,000 particles, the new compressed size will come close to 115 MB, down from 915.5 MB of uncompressed data (streaming at ca. 11 MB per second). The size can further be cut in half should the simulation clip be processed in 15 FPS instead of 30 FPS (by dropping every other frame and interpolating it at runtime), thus resulting in streaming at ca. 5.5 MB per second. This is yet without any additional compression schemes such as LZ4. (See Table 19.1.)

19.7   Runtime Execution

In this section, the runtime aspects of the ICP system are described. With the particle simulation clips exported and compressed, the only part remaining is to stream clip data at runtime and incorporate it into the simulator that will generate the final particle simulation state at every frame ready for rendering.

19.7.1   Streaming Particle Simulation Clips

With the clip's runtime data format fully specified, the runtime must stream and decode the exported data. Again, there are a number of decisions to be made depending on the game's needs.

One major consideration is CPU access. If the particle effect must interact with other game entities that are simulated on the CPU, then the data must be made available to the CPU. However, it is advisable that such interactions are carried on the GPU instead since the processing involves possibly thousands of particles.

The case study compression scheme described in the previous section allowed streaming of the compressed particle data directly to VRAM resident textures.

Data Layout (100,000 particles)	Particle Size	Average Frame Size	Average Data Rate
ICE Cache (30 FPS)	32 bytes	3 MB	90 MB/s
Hyper Void (30 FPS)	4 bytes	0.38 MB	11.4 MB/s
Hyper Void (15 FPS interpolated to 30 FPS)	4 bytes	0.38 MB	5.7 MB/s

Table 19.1. Data size and streaming data rate comparison.

The CPU did not do any work besides driving the memory flow from the simulation clip file to VRAM. All the details of decoding and interpolating frames to update the state of the particle effect were done on the GPU using pixel shaders. The streaming code reads the first frame and instructs the GPU to use it as a key frame. Then, it reads subsequent frames as time advances, while keeping a look-ahead buffer of some size. This was possible because the clips were only meant to be played from start to finish without seeking.

19.7.2   Decoding Frames

In *Hyper Void*, the textures receiving the streamed clip data were as follows:

1. Color palette: A 1D texture of 256 texels in ARGB8 format.

2. Key frame: A 2D texture with powers-of-two dimensions aiming for a square aspect ratio where possible. The total number of texels in this texture must be equal to or greater than the total number of particles in the effect. The format is ARGB16.

3. Difference frame: Same as the key-frame texture except that the format is ARGB8.

The data streamed to all these textures was pre-swizzled in the offline build process so that the GPU could access these textures with optimal performance.

The last resource needed in the decoder is the *state render target texture*. This is a double-buffered texture that will hold the state of all particles in the effect. The goal of the decoding process is to fill this texture. Once this texture is updated, it can be used for actually rendering the particle effect on screen.

This texture is of the same dimensions as the key-frame and difference-frame textures mentioned above, but its format is RGBA32F because it will hold decompressed 3D positions.

The graph in Figure 19.8 illustrates how the data flows for a single particle simulation clip.

The high-level decoding process proceeds as follows:

1. Upon opening the clip file, read the palette texture.

2. Read the first frame texture.

3. Directly populate the double-buffered state texture with contents from the first frame texture. Only one of the buffers (the current) needs to be populated.

   By now, the first frame has been decoded and the particle effect can be rendered from the contents of the current state texture.

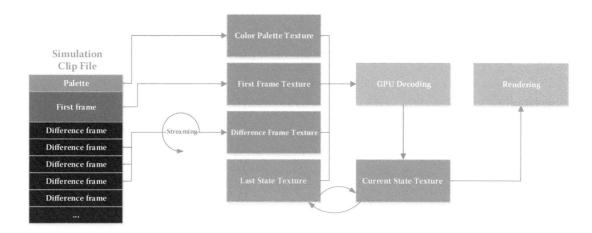

Figure 19.8. Data flow for a single particle simulation clip.

4. Time advances by a certain amount (t), and the updated clip time now falls in the frame after the current one.[1]

5. The double-buffered state texture is flipped, and what was "current" will be used as input to update the new "current."

6. A difference frame is streamed into the difference texture.

7. The GPU uses both the input state texture and the difference texture to compute the new state texture according to the following formula:

$$\texttt{newPos} = \texttt{oldPos} + \texttt{decode}(\texttt{posDifference}),$$

where `decode()` is a function that denormalizes the compressed position difference values as described in Section 19.6.2.

8. The color index is carried over from the difference texture to the state texture. Only at render time is this color index looked up from the color palette.

19.7.3 Particle Effect Graph

So far, the system is able to stream-in and playback a single particle simulation clip exported from a DCC tool in which an artist has authored the particle effect to his desire. The only remaining part of the system is to add interactivity.

---

[1]To keep the system description simple, assume no interpolation between particle simulation frames for now. Section 19.8.1 will show the additional operations needed to support smooth playback.

Interactivity means that the effect played back in runtime is capable of responding to interactions ultimately instigated by player actions.

Perhaps the most basic shape of responding to interactivity is the ability to play a certain particle simulation clip in response to a certain player action. However, a sudden switch between clips breaks continuity and is rejected aesthetically in most cases. Thus, the ability to *blend* between two different clips is required. Additionally, various particle operators could be executed at runtime to further modify the final effect in interesting and interactive ways. Those will be described in Section 19.7.4.

Taking clip playback as a basic building block, it is possible to include it under a larger framework that can hold multiple clips, play them back, blend between them, and do various effects as well according to game conditions.

In *Hyper Void*, clip playback logic was encompassed in what we call "Goal-Source," and the framework under which various clips can exist is called "Simulation." Those entities were exposed in the engine's logic builder, allowing the game designer to take full control of which clips to play, as well as when and how to blend between them. (See Figure 19.9.)

Underneath, the framework code keeps track of clip playback, as well as doing further processing after the active clips update their state. For example, the blend operator takes the final state of two different clips and simply does a linear interpolation between them to a separate render target texture that will be used for rendering.

19.7.4 Procedural Operators

Depending on the project's needs, further procedural operators could be added to the framework and exposed for triggering by game design. For *Hyper Void*, major enemy bosses were expressed using particle effects that shape up in monstrous forms and attack the player. To serve this purpose, a number of special procedural operators were added. The following list shows some of those operators:

1. Full shatter: When the enemy is destroyed, all of its particles are shattered away in random directions from a central point. To implement this, the framework takes the state texture and pushes each particle in a direction determined by a random value (originating from a noise texture). Additionally, it fades away the particle color with time.

2. Local shatter: The player can explode a bomb near the enemy boss, taking off a portion of its surface. The boss can heal again and restore the missing portion.

   The framework keeps track of explosion spheres. For each explosion sphere, all particles that fall in that sphere at a certain frame are marked to be affected by the local shatter logic, which pushes the marked particles away

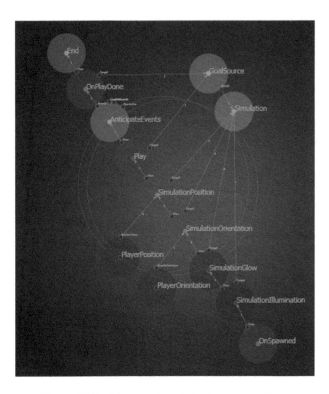

Figure 19.9. The graph tool in the game editor.

from the sphere's center. The push amount goes from 0 to the maximum then back to 0 when restoration is done.

3. Deformation to bullets: The framework sends bullet information to the GPU simulation update shader, which evaluates if a particle falls close to a bullet and pushes that particle away from the bullet until the bullet passes by a certain amount. The final effect is as if the particles forming the enemy boss are being disturbed by the player's bullets but regain formation when the bullets pass by.

19.7.5 Rendering

The final output of the entire system is a texture holding each particle's location. Other properties may come in more textures as well (such as color). It is up to the game to decide what to show using these locations and properties.

For *Hyper Void*, the textures were fed into a simple vertex shader that transformed each particle to the clip space and then handed it to the hardware for point-sprite expansion. The result was a very efficient rendering system capable of handling hundreds of thousands of particles in a few milliseconds. The game even had to draw the same particle effect more than once in a frame due to multiple passes being needed for some postprocess effects. Still, even the Playstation 3 was capable of handling the entire operation in less than 3.5 ms of GPU time.

19.8 Additional Notes

19.8.1 Variable Time Step

The decoding process in Section 19.7.2 accumulated full decoded frames, which resulted in playback at discreet time steps without possible interpolation between frames. To support variable time steps, one additional parameter is needed in the formula used to update the new position:

$$\texttt{newPos} = \texttt{oldPos} + \texttt{decode}(\texttt{posDifference}) \times \texttt{timeRatio},$$

where $\texttt{timeRatio}$ is a weight $[0, 1]$ determined from the time step and the clip's playback speed. This way, only a portion of the next frame is accumulated to the state at each system tick. The accumulated amount is proportional to how much time has passed since the last system tick. It is necessary to ensure that the decoded frame is fully accumulated before moving to the next one.

19.8.2 Preloading Clip Files

In addition to large bosses in *Hyper Void*, some smaller enemies where also modeled using ICP. However, they only had a few thousand particles and rather short clips, but multiple enemies could appear together. In that case, reading the clip data for each enemy put unnecessary stress on disk access. Thus, an additional feature was added to allow reading the entire clip file to memory first, and the rest of the ICP system would read from this in-memory file instead of reading from disk.

The implementation details of the two notes above should be easy to figure out and are left as an exercise to the reader.

19.9 Conclusion

The Interactive Cinematic Particles (ICP) system is a full pipeline that supports authoring particle effects using DCC tools, compressing them and loading them at runtime, and simulating those effects while adding interactivity to the simulation using procedural operators. The system was developed and used in the game *Hyper Void*, which shipped at a constant 60 FPS on multiple platforms including old-generation consoles.

19.10   Acknowledgment

We would like to thank Nicolas Lopez for his help and time reviewing this chapter.

Bibliography

[Drone 07] Shannon Drone. "Real-Time Particle Systems on the GPU in Dynamic Environments." In *ACM SIGGRAPH 2007 Courses*, pp. 80–96. New York: ACM, 2007.

[Fork 15] Fork Particle: Effects editor and particle system middleware, http://www.forkparticle.com/, 2015.

[Gneiting 14] Axel Gneiting. "Realtime Geometry Caches." In *ACM SIGGRAPH 2014 Talks*, article no. 49. New York: ACM, 2014.

[Hegeman et al. 06] Kyle Hegeman, Nathan A. Carr, and Gavin S. P. Miller. "Particle-Based Fluid Simulation on the GPU." In *Computational Science— ICCS 2006*, Lecture Notes in Computer Science vol. 3994, pp. 228–235. Berlin: Springer, 2006.

[Macklin et al. 14] Miles Macklin, Matthias Müller, Nuttapong Chentanez, and Tae-Yong Kim. "Unified Particle Physics for Real-Time Applications." *ACM Transactions on Graphics (TOG): Proceedings of ACM SIGGRAPH 2014* 33:4 (2014), article no. 153.

[PopcornFX 15] PopcornFX: Real-time particle FX solution, https://www.popcornfx.com/, 2015.

[Stam 03] Jos Stam. "Real-Time Fluid Dynamics for Games." Paper presented at Game Developers Conference, San Jose, CA, March 4–8, 2003.

[Thomas 14] Gareth Thomas. "Compute-Based GPU Particle Systems." Paper presented at Game Developers Conference, San Francisco, CA, March 17–21, 2014.

20

Real-Time BC6H Compression on GPU

Krzysztof Narkowicz

20.1 Introduction

BC6H texture compression is a lossy block compression designed for compressing high-dynamic range (HDR) images; it is also widely supported by modern GPUs. It drastically decreases memory usage and improves runtime performance, as it also decreases required GPU bandwidth.

Real-time HDR compression is needed in certain applications—e.g., when HDR data is generated at runtime or when offline compression is too slow. It is usually desirable for real-time compression to entirely bypass the CPU and run the compression algorithm on the GPU. This way, resource expensive CPU-GPU synchronization is avoided and data transfer between CPU and GPU is not required at all.

This chapter describes a simple real-time BC6H compression algorithm, one which can be implemented on GPU entirely.

20.1.1 Real-Time Environment Map Compression

A typical BC6H compression application is HDR environment maps, commonly used in physically-based lighting. Open-world games often require separate environment maps for every location, time of day, or weather condition. The resulting combinatorial explosion of possibilities makes it impractical to generate and store them offline. In those cases games have to generate environment maps dynamically. Some games use simplified scene representation to render a single global environment map every frame [Courrèges 15]. This environment map is attached to the camera and used for all reflections. Another possible option is to store G-buffer data for every environment map and dynamically relight it when lighting conditions change [McAuley 15].

Generating dynamic environment maps is not limited to open world games only. It also allows dynamic scenes to be lit—procedurally generated scenes, scenes containing geometry destruction, or ones containing dynamic object movement.

Furthermore, when using dynamic environment map generation, only the environment maps in the viewer's proximity have to be kept in memory. This allows a greater density of environment maps and better lighting quality. Environment maps are pre-convolved for a given single point—usually the center of capture. Lighting quality degrades further from that center because of the changing filter shape, occlusion, and limited resolution [Pesce 15]. The simplest way to alleviate those artifacts is to increase the number of environment maps by generating them at runtime.

20.1.2   BC6H Alternatives

Before BC6H was introduced, HDR images were usually stored in BC3 compressed textures with special encoding. These encodings could also be used to compress in real time as suitable BC3 compression algorithms exist [Waveren 06]. Such encodings either separate chrominance and luminance and store luminance in two channels (LogLuv, YCoCg) or store normalized color and some kind of multiplier (RGBE, RGBM, RGBD, RGBK) [Guertault 13]. The compression ratio is on a par with BC6H and runtime performance is usually better for LDR formats. However, those approaches will result in inferior image quality, as the mentioned methods result in various encoding and compression artifacts. Encoding only individual channels causes a hue shift, while encoding all the channels together increases luminance errors. BC3 compression was designed for LDR images, where small value changes resulting from compression are acceptable. In the case of encoded HDR data, the consequence of such small changes can be magnitude differences in the decoded results. Finally, current hardware does not support native texture filtering for these kinds of encodings, so either additional filtering artifacts will appear or manual texture filtering is required.

20.2   BC6H Details

BC6H block compression was introduced together with Direct3D 11. It is designed for compressing signed and unsigned HDR images with 16-bit half-precision float for each color channel. The alpha channel is not supported, and sampling alpha always returns 1. BC6H has an 6:1 compression ratio and stores the texture data in separate 4×4 texel blocks. Every block is compressed separately. It is convenient for native GPU decompression, as the required blocks can be located and decompressed without the need to process other data. The basic idea is the same as for BC1, BC2, or BC3. Two endpoints and 16 indices are stored per block. A line segment in RGB space is defined by endpoints, and indices define

Bits	Value
[0;4]	Header – 0x03
[5;14]	First endpoint red channel
[15;24]	First endpoint green channel
[25;34]	First endpoint blue channel
[35;44]	Second endpoint red channel
[45;54]	Second endpoint blue channel
[55;64]	Second endpoint green channel
[65;67]	First index without MSB
[68;71]	Second index
[72;75]	Third index
. . .	. . .
[124;127]	Last index

Table 20.1. Mode 11 block details [MSDN n.d.].

a location of every texel on this segment. The entire format features 14 different compression modes with different tradeoffs between endpoint, index precision, and palette size. Additionally, some modes use endpoint delta encoding and partitioning. Delta encoding stores the first endpoint more precisely, and instead of storing the second endpoint, it stores the delta between endpoints. Partitioning allows defining two line segments per block and storing four endpoints in total. Using one of 32 predefined partitions, texels are assigned to one of the two segments.

BC6H was designed to alleviate compression quality issues of BC1, BC2, and BC3: "green shift" and limited color palette per block. "Green shift" is caused by different endpoint channel precision. BC1 uses 5:6:5 precision—this is why many grayscale colors cannot be represented and are shifted toward green (e.g., 5:6:5 encodes the grayscale color RGB 15:15:15 as RGB 8:12:8). In order to prevent a hue shift, BC6H encodes every channel with the same precision. Another prominent compression issue occurs when a block contains a large color variation—a variation that cannot be well approximated by a single segment in RGB space. In order to fix this, BC6H has introduced compression modes with two independent endpoint pairs.

20.2.1 Mode 11

The proposed real-time compression algorithm uses only mode 11. This specific mode was chosen because it is simple, universal, and, in most cases, has the best quality-to-performance ratio. Mode 11 does not use partitioning or delta encoding. It uses two endpoints and 16 indices per 4×4 block (see Table 20.1). Endpoints are stored as half-precision floats, which are quantized to 10-bit integers by dropping last 6 bits and rescaling. Indices are stored as 4-bit integers indexed into a palette endpoint interpolation weight table (Table 20.2).

Index	0	1	2	3	4	5	6	7	8	9	10	11	12	13	14	15
Weight	0	4	9	13	17	21	26	30	34	38	43	47	51	55	60	64

Table 20.2. Index interpolation weight table.

Weight 0 corresponds to the first endpoint and weight 64 to the second endpoint. The values in between are calculated by interpolating quantized integers and converting the results to half-precision floats. They are interpolated as 16-bit integers instead of as floats, thus allowing efficient hardware implementation. Due to IEEE floating point specification, this method actually works reasonably well, as the integer representation of a float is a piecewise linear approximation of its base-2 logarithm [Dawson 12]. In this case, interpolation does not have to handle special cases because BC6H does not support NAN or infinities.

There is one final twist. The MSB (most significant bit) of the first index (the upper-left texel in the current block) is not stored at all. It is implicitly assumed to be zero, and the compressor has to ensure this property by swapping endpoints if the first index is too large.

20.3 Compression Algorithm

The compression algorithm consists of two steps:

1. Compute two endpoints per block.

2. Compute indices for every texel located in this block.

20.3.1 Endpoints

The classic endpoint algorithm for real-time BC1 compression computes a color-space bounding box of the block's texels and uses its minimum and maximum values as endpoints [Waveren 06]. This algorithm is very fast, as it requires only 16 minimum and 16 maximum instructions. J. M. P. van Waveren additionally decreases the size of the calculated bounding box by 1/16th. In most cases, this lowers the encoding error because most colors will be located inside the new bounding box, but it also tends to cause visible blocky artifacts when colors in a block are clustered near the edges of the bounding box. To solve this, it is better to refine the bounding box by rebuilding it without the outliers—minimum and maximum RGB values. The resulting bounding box decreases encoding error and removes mentioned artifacts (Figure 20.1).

The final step of the endpoint calculation algorithm is to convert the resulting endpoints to half-precision floats and quantize them to 10-bit integers. The presented algorithm does not form an optimal palette, but it is a good and fast approximation.

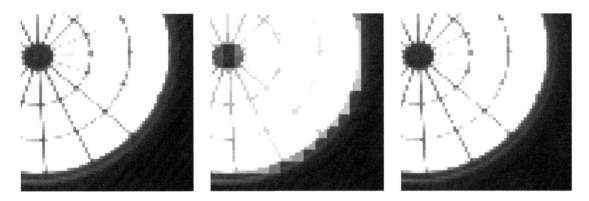

Figure 20.1. Endpoint algorithm: reference (left), compressed using bounding box inset (center), and compressed using bounding box refine (right).

20.3.2 Indices

Index computation requires picking the closest color from a palette that consists of 16 interpolated colors located on the segment between endpoints. A straightforward approach is to compute the squared distance between the texel's color and each of the palette entries and to choose the one that is closest to the texel's color. Due to a relatively large palette, this approach is not practical for real-time compression. A faster approach is to project the texel's color on a segment between the endpoints and pick the nearest palette entry. Unfortunately, endpoint interpolation weights are not evenly distributed (see Table 20.2). The first and last indices have the smallest range of best weights, and the remaining indices have similar ranges. A simple approximation is to fit the equation for smallest error—which is the same as solving the equation for the first and last bucket:

$$\text{index}_i = \text{Clamp}\left[\left(\frac{\text{texelPos}_i - \text{endpointPos}_0}{\text{endpointPos}_1 - \text{endpointPos}_0}\right) \times \frac{14}{15} + \frac{1}{30}, 0, 15\right].$$

The above equation wrongly assumes that the distance between middle indices is equal, but in practice this error is negligible. The final step is to swap endpoints if the MSB of the first index is set, as it is assumed to be zero and, thus, is not stored.

20.3.3 Implementation

The algorithm can be entirely implemented using a pixel shader, but if required, it could also be implemented using a compute shader or CPU code.

In the case of pixel shader implementation in DirectX 11, two resources are required: temporary intermediate `R32G32B32A32_UInt` render target and the destination BC6H texture. The first step is to bind that temporary render target and output compressed blocks from the pixel shader. The render target should be 16 times smaller than the source texture, so one texel corresponds to one BC6H block (16 source texels). The final step is to copy the results from the temporary render target to the destination BC6H texture using the `CopyResource` function.

To achieve optimal performance, the algorithm requires a native float to half conversion instructions, which are available in Shader Model 5. Additionally, it is preferable to avoid integer operations altogether (especially 32-bit divides and multiplies), as they are very costly on modern GPUs. For example, the popular Graphics Core Next (GCN) architecture does not natively support integer division, and it has to be emulated with multiple instructions [Persson 14]. The floating point number consists of a 24-bit integer (1-bit sign and 23-bit mantissa) and an 8-bit exponent. The algorithm uses only 16-bit integers, so all of the calculations can be done using floating point numbers without any loss of precision. Fetching a source 4×4 texel block can be done efficiently using 12 gather instructions instead of sampling a texture 16 times, as the alpha channel is ignored. Finally, `CopyResource` can be skipped entirely, when using low-level APIs that support resource aliasing of different formats.

The HLSL code in Listing 20.1 shows an implementation of the presented algorithm.

```
float Quantize( float x )
{
    return ( f32tof16( x ) << 10 ) / ( 0x7bff + 1.0f );
}

float3 Quantize( float3 x )
{
    return ( f32tof16( x ) << 10 ) / ( 0x7bff + 1.0f );
}

uint ComputeIndex( float texelPos, float endpoint0Pos,
                   float endpoint1Pos )
{
    float endpointDelta = endpoint1Pos - endpoint0Pos;
    float r = ( texelPos - endpoint0Pos ) / endpointDelta;
    return clamp( r * 14.933f + 0.0333f + 0.5f, 0.0f, 15.0f );
}

// Compute endpoints (min/max RGB bbox).
float3 blockMin = texels[0];
float3 blockMax = texels[0];
for ( uint i = 1; i < 16; ++i )
{
    blockMin = min( blockMin, texels[i] );
    blockMax = max( blockMax, texels[i] );
}

// Refine endpoints.
float3 refinedBlockMin = blockMax;
float3 refinedBlockMax = blockMin;
for ( uint i = 0; i < 16; ++i )
{
```

```
        refinedBlockMin = min( refinedBlockMin,
            texels[i] == blockMin ? refinedBlockMin : texels[i] );
        refinedBlockMax = max( refinedBlockMax,
            texels[i] == blockMax ? refinedBlockMax : texels[i] );
    }

    float3 deltaMax = ( blockMax - blockMin ) * ( 1.0f / 16.0f );
    blockMin += min( refinedBlockMin - blockMin, deltaMax );
    blockMax -= min( blockMax - refinedBlockMax, deltaMax );

    float3 blockDir = blockMax - blockMin;
    blockDir = blockDir / ( blockDir.x + blockDir.y + blockDir.z );

    float3 endpoint0    = Quantize( blockMin );
    float3 endpoint1    = Quantize( blockMax );
    float endpoint0Pos = f32tof16( dot( blockMin, blockDir ) );
    float endpoint1Pos = f32tof16( dot( blockMax, blockDir ) );

    // Check if endpoint swap is required.
    float texelPos = f32tof16( dot( texels[0], blockDir ) );
    indices[0] = ComputeIndex( texelPos, endpoint0Pos,
    endpoint1Pos );
    if ( indices[0] > 7 )
    {
        Swap( endpoint0Pos, endpoint1Pos );
        Swap( endpoint0, endpoint1 );
        indices[0] = 15 - indices[0];
    }

    // Compute indices.
    for ( uint j = 1; j < 16; ++j )
    {
        float texelPos = f32tof16( dot( texels[j], blockDir ) );
        indices[j] = ComputeIndex( texelPos, endpoint0Pos,
                                   endpoint1Pos );
    }
```

Listing 20.1. BCH6 compression algorithm.

20.4 Results

The proposed algorithm was compared with two offline BC6H compressors: Intel's BCH6 CPU-based compressor and the DirectXTex BC6H GPU-based compressor.

20.4.1 Quality

Root mean square error (RMSE) was used for measuring quality. RMSE is a generic measure of signal distortion, where lower values are better:

$$RMSE = \sqrt{\frac{1}{3n}\sum_{i=1}^{n}\left[(\hat{r}_i - r_i)^2 + (\hat{g}_i - g)^2 + (\hat{b}_i - b_i)^2\right]}.$$

Based on the results shown in Table 20.3, the proposed algorithm has similar quality to Intel's "veryfast" preset. Intel's "veryfast" has a smaller error

	Proposed Algorithm	Intel BC6H "veryfast"	Intel BC6H "basic"	Intel BC6H "veryslow"	DirectXTex BC6H
Atrium	0.122	0.112	0.1	0.099	0.084
Backyard	0.032	0.027	0.024	0.024	0.025
Desk	0.992	1.198	0.984	0.975	0.829
Memorial	0.25	0.278	0.241	0.237	0.216
Yucca	0.086	0.083	0.065	0.064	0.063
Average	0.296	0.340	0.283	0.280	0.243
Average of relative errors	22%	22%	10%	7%	0%

Table 20.3. Quality comparison (RMSE).

for images with a low RMSE, where 10-bit mode 11 quantization becomes a limiting factor. This is due to the delta encoding that is implemented even in the "veryfast" preset. For harder-to-compress images ("desk" and "memorial"), however, the proposed algorithm has error similar to Intel's "basic" preset. (See Figure 20.2.)

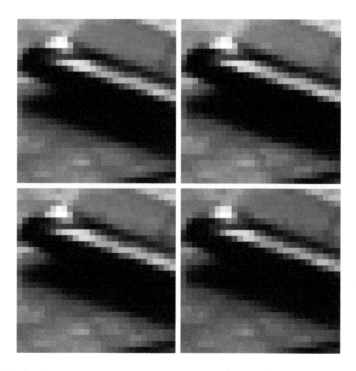

Figure 20.2. Quality comparison of "desk": original (top left), proposed algorithm (top right), Intel "veryfast" (bottom left), and Intel "basic" (bottom right).

	Image Size	Proposed Algorithm	DirectXTex BC6H
Atrium	760×1016	0.094 ms	1230 ms
Backyard	768×1024	0.095 ms	1240 ms
Desk	644×872	0.074 ms	860 ms
Memorial	512×768	0.057 ms	840 ms
Yucca	1296×972	0.143 ms	1730 ms
Average		7957.8 MP/s	0.6 MP/s

Table 20.4. Performance comparison.

20.4.2 Performance

Performance was measured using AMD PerfStudio. Results were verified by comparing timings obtained from DirectX performance queries. Tests were run on AMD Radeon R9 270 (mid-range GPU). The timings presented in Table 20.4 do not include `CopyResource` time, so the measured times should be increased by ~15% for APIs that require a redundant copy in order to modify the destination BC6H texture.

A standard $256 \times 256 \times 6$ environment map with a full mipmap chain has almost the same number of texels as the "Desk" image, which can be compressed in about 0.07 ms on the mentioned GPU. This performance level is fast enough to compress dynamically generated environment maps or other content without a noticeable impact on performance.

20.5 Possible Extensions

A straightforward way to enhance quality is to use other compression modes. There are two possibilities:

1. to add delta encoding,

2. to use partitioning.

20.5.1 Delta Encoding

The first possible approach is to add modes 12, 13, and 14. These modes extend mode 11 with delta encoding by storing the first endpoint in higher precision (respectively 11, 12, and 16 bits) and storing the delta instead of a second endpoint in the unused bits (respectively 9, 8, and 4 bits). Delta encoding implementation is not too resource expensive. Its impact on quality is also limited, as in the best case delta encoding cancels the 10-bit quantization artifacts.

The delta encoding algorithm starts by computing the endpoints using the proposed endpoint algorithm. Endpoints are encoded with various formats, and the encoding precision is compared in order to select the best mode. Next, the indices are computed with the same algorithm as for mode 11. Finally, the appropriate block is encoded in a rather non-obvious way. First, 10 bits of the first endpoint are stored just as in mode 11. Next, the bits are stored together with the delta instead of the second endpoint. Both have their bits reversed.

20.5.2 Partitioning

The second approach is to add mode 10 (supporting partitioning). Partitioning adds a second palette (endpoint pair). This greatly improves the worst-case result—when colors in a block cannot be well approximated by a single segment in RGB space. Unfortunately, it is slow due to a large search space.

The partitioning algorithm starts with the selection of the best partition. This requires calculating all possible endpoints for partitions. There are 32 possible partition sets, so it means computing 32 combinations of endpoints. The partition with the smallest sum of bounding-box volumes is selected. Indices are computed just as for mode 11. Finally, the block is encoded using the computed endpoints, indices, and selected partition index.

20.6   Conclusion

The presented algorithm allows real-time BC6H compression on GPU with quality similar to fast offline solution presets. The quality can be improved further by using other compression modes—at the cost of lower performance. The algorithm proved to be efficient enough in the terms of both quality and performance for compressing runtime generated environment maps in *Shadow Warrior 2*—a game by Flying Wild Hog. The full source code for a simple application that implements the presented algorithm and the HDR images used for the tests can be found in the book's supplemental materials or on GitHub (https://github.com/knarkowicz/GPURealTimeBC6H).

20.7   Acknowledgments

Big thanks for proofreading to Przemysław Witkowski, Bartłomiej Wronski, Michał Iwanicki, and Artur Maksara.

Bibliography

[Courrèges 15] Adrian Courrèges. "GTA V—Graphics Study." http://www.adriancourreges.com/blog/2015/11/02/gta-v-graphics-study, November 2, 2015.

[Dawson 12] Bruce Dawson. "Stupid Float Tricks." https://randomascii.wordpress.com/2012/01/23/stupid-float-tricks-2/, January 23, 2012.

[Guertault 13] Julien Guertault. "Gamma Correct and HDR Rendering in a 32 Bits Buffer." http://lousodrome.net/blog/light/2013/05/26/gamma-correct-and-hdr-rendering-in-a-32-bits-buffer/, May 26, 2013.

[McAuley 15] Stephen McAuley. "Rendering the World of Far Cry 4." Presented at Game Developers Conference, San Francisco, CA, March 2–6, 2015.

[MSDN n.d.] MSDN. "BC6H Format." https://msdn.microsoft.com/en-us/library/windows/desktop/hh308952, no date.

[Persson 14] Emil Persson. "Low-level Shader Optimization for Next-Gen and DX11." Presented at Game Developers Conference, San Francisco, CA, March 17–21, 2014.

[Pesce 15] Angelo Pesce. "Being More Wrong: Parallax Corrected Environment Maps." http://c0de517e.blogspot.com/2015/03/being-more-wrong-parallax-corrected.html, March 28, 2015.

[Waveren 06] J. M. P. van Waveren. "Real-Time DXT Compression." http://mrelusive.com/publications/papers/Real-Time-Dxt-Compression.pdf, 2006.

21

A 3D Visualization Tool Used for Test Automation in the Forza Series

Gustavo Bastos Nunes

21.1 Introduction

Physics engines usually rely on a collision mesh that is hand-crafted by artists. This meshes may have holes, bad normals, or other wrong data that might cause weird behavior at runtime. Testing those wrong behaviors manually has an extremely high cost in regards to manual testing. One small hole or bad normal can cause a character or vehicle to behave in a completely wrong manner, and those bugs are seldom reproduced because it might depend on many variables such as engine time step, character speed, and angle.

Finding issues like open edges in a mesh is not a complex problem in the polygon mesh processing area, and this feature is available in some 3D content creation packages. However, topology-wise for non-closed meshes, there is no difference from a boundary of a mesh and a hole. Therefore, visualizing what is by design and what is a bug requires filtering and semantic analysis of such a given mesh, which is simply impractical at those tools, particularly for multiscale collision meshes. Thus, this yields a myriad of hard-to-find bugs.

This chapter will introduce a 3D visualization tool that automatically analyzes a mesh for bad holes and normal data and gives the manual tester an easy semantic view of what are likely to be bugs and what is by-design data. It will also go through a quick review of the algorithmic implementation of topics in polygon mesh processing such as mesh traversal, half-edge acceleration data structures, detection of holes, open edges, and other issues. This tool was used during the entire production cycle of *Forza Motorsport 5* and *Forza: Horizon 2* by Turn 10 Studios and Playground Games. At previous releases of the *Forza* series, without this tool, the test team used to spend several hundred hours manual-testing the game to find collision mesh issues and finished without a guarantee that there were none, since it was basically a brute-force approach. With this tool, an entire mesh of a track can now be analyzed and all collision bugs can be found in less than 500 milliseconds. Moreover, this provides us the trust that we are shipping the game with collision meshes in a perfect state.

21.2 Collision Mesh Issues

The tool was originally crafted to detect only holes at the collision mesh; later on it was expanded to also detect flipped/skewed normal and malformed triangles. Those are the main issues that causes problems with the physics engine at runtime.

21.2.1 Holes

Holes in the collision mesh was a great problem to us. Big holes were usually not a problem because they end up being caught by the testers and their behaviors are typically very deterministic and clear: e.g., the car goes through a wall that it is not supposed to or it falls through the world. Although it was not fast to detect those issues and sometimes it was costly, they wind up being detected and fixed. The real problems were the small/tiny holes where it would cause the car to behave oddly and in a non-natural way; such a bug would only reproduce with a specific car, in a specific speed, and if hit at a specific angle. Moreover, when the bug was filed, it usually only had a video with the odd behavior happening at that specific part of the track, so the artist that would be responsible to fix it usually would not know what specific triangle was causing that. Figures 21.1 and 21.2 show a tiny hole being detected by the tool.

21.2.2 Wrong Normals

Normals in the collision mesh are responsible for determining the force that is applied to the car at each particular vertex. Thus, if a particular piece of road is flat, the normal at those vertices should be straight up. If the normal was flipped, the user would see the car being dragged into the ground. As with small holes, a single skewed or flipped normal could cause a completely wrong behavior at runtime, and it may also be very hard to detect by only reproducing in very specific scenarios. In this chapter I will call a *flipped normal* any normal where the angle with the Y-up vector is greater than 90°. A flipped normal is always a wrong normal; however, we can have by-design skewed normals, which is how we simulate the physics effects of the tires hitting the rumble strips. Therefore, it is particular hard to detect when a skewed normal is by design or not.

Artists do not usually author the normals by hand; they are created by the 3D digital content creation tool. The reason why the normals get skewed or flipped

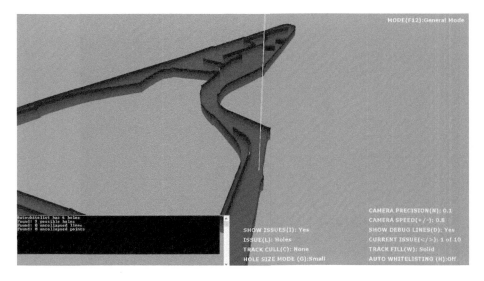

Figure 21.1. A small hole highlighted by the tool in green.

Figure 21.2. Same hole from Figure 21.1 on a very close-up view.

is because they might weld vertices and create really small triangles. Those small triangles together yield precision issues on the calculation of normals by the 3D DCC tool, and the collision mesh ends up with bad normals. Figure 21.3 shows a flipped normal detected by the tool. Note how every normal is following a good

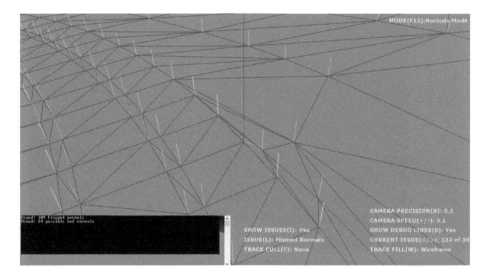

Figure 21.3. A flipped normal flagged by the tool in red.

pattern of being aligned with the Y-up vector while the flagged normal clearly disturbs this pattern.

21.2.3 Malformed Triangles

Triangles that are malformed, such as triangles that are lines (i.e., two vertices are collinear) or triangles where the three vertices are the same, are also detected by the tool. Usually they are not sources of very bad behaviors like holes or bad normals, but they are definitely wrong data that should not be there to begin with.

21.3 Detecting the Issues

This section will cover the details of building the data structure needed to query and traverse the mesh and how we detect each of the issues described in the previous section.

21.3.1 Building the Data Structure

To be able to detect holes, we need to add the mesh to an easy queryable data structure. We used a half-edge data structure [Mäntylä 88, pp. 161–174; Kettner 99]. Half-edge data structures are easy to implement and are able to represent arbitrary orientable 2-manifold polygonal meshes with no complex edges or vertices.

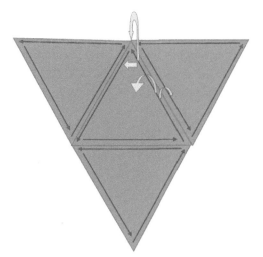

Figure 21.4. Half-edges in red and its references in yellow to the face, vertex, next half-edge, and opposite half-edge.

The data structure is stored in such a way that each triangle face has three half-edges in the same winding order and each of those edges references the next half-edge, the opposite half edge of its neighbor face, and a vertex like it is shown in Figure 21.4. The members of our mesh are detailed in the following pseudocode snippet:

```
class Mesh
{
    List<Face> faces; //List of all faces of this mesh.
}

class HalfEdge
{
    Face face; //Reference to the face this half-edge belongs to.
    HalfEdge next; //Reference to the next half-edge.
    HalfEdge opposite; //Reference to the opposite half-edge.
    Vertex v; //Reference to the tail vertex of this half-edge.
}

class Face
{
    HalfEdge edge; //Reference to one half-edge of this face.
    Vertex v1, v2, v3; //Reference to the three vertices of this face.
}
class Vertex
{
    Vector3 Position; //Position of the vertex.
    Vector3 Normal; //Normal of the vertex.
}
```

By parsing the vertex and index buffer of a mesh and filling into a data structured like the above one, it is really easy to start doing queries on the mesh. For instance, the following snippet finds all neighboring faces of a given face:

```
List<Face> GetNeighbors(Face face)
{
    List<Face> neighbors = new List<Face>();

    if (face.edge.opposite != null)
    {
        neighbors.Add(face.edge.opposite.face);
    }
    if (face.edge.next.opposite != null)
    {
        neighbors.Add(face.edge.next.opposite.face);
    }
    if (face.edge.next.next.opposite != null)
    {
        neighbors.Add(face.edge.next.next.opposite.face);
    }

    return neighbors;
}
```

For more information on half-edge data structures, we suggest the following references to the reader: [McGuire 00, Botsch et al. 10].

21.3.2   Detecting Holes

After storing the mesh in the half-edge data structure, we iterate on the mesh by first looking for holes. To do that, we treat the mesh as if it is an undirected graph where each triangle face is a node and each triangle edge is an edge of the graph. This is illustrated in Figure 21.5.

Next, we conduct a breadth-first search (BFS) looking for any half-edge that does not have an opposite half-edge; this would be an open edge as shown on Figure 21.5. Any open edge is always part of a hole, and we store this open edge on a list of open edges. This process is shown in the following pseudo-code snippet:

```
List<Hole> FindHoles()
{
    //All open edges.
    List<HalfEdgeIdxs> holesEdges = new List<HalfEdgeIdxs>();

    //List of holes to return.
    List<Hole> meshHoleList = new List<Hole>();

    //A set that contains all visited faces.
    Hashset<Face> visitedFaces = new Hashset<Face>();
    //Start by visiting the first face of the mesh.
    Face currFace = meshFacesList[0];
    //A set that contains the non-visited faces.
    HashSet<Face> allFacesHashSet
```

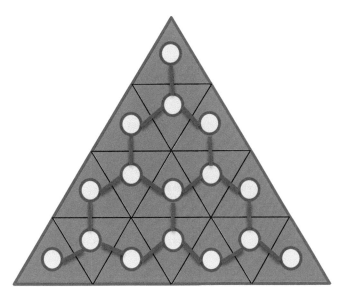

Figure 21.5. Each face is a node, and each triangle edge is an edge of the undirected graph. All the red edges are open edges.

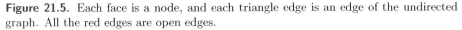

```
                = new HashSet<Face>(meshFacesList);

//Initialize the BFS queue.
Queue<Face> bfsQueue = new Queue<Face>();
bfsQueue.Enqueue(currFace);
visitedFaces.Add(currFace);
//Only quit if we have visited all faces
while (bfsQueue.Count > 0 || visitedFaces.Count
                          != meshFacesList.Count)
{
    //If the BFS queue is empty and we are still in the
    //loop, it means that this mesh is a disjoint mesh;
    //we leave this set and go to the next set by
    //re-feeding the queue.
    if (bfsQueue.Count == 0)
    {
        Face face = allFacesHashSet.Next();
        visitedFaces.Add(face);
        bfsQueue.Enqueue(face);
    }
    //Remove from the queue and from the non-visited faces.
    currFace = bfsQueue.Dequeue();
    allFacesHashSet.Remove(currFace);

    //Visit the neighbors of the face.
    List<Face> neighbors = currFace.GetNeighbors();
    foreach (Face neighbor in neighbors)
    {
        if (!visitedFaces.ContainsKey(neighbor))
        {
            visitedFaces.Add(neighbor, true);
            bfsQueue.Enqueue(neighbor);
```

```
        }
    }
    //If the number of neighbors of this face is 3,
    //it has no open edges; continue.
    if (neighbors.Count == 3)
    {
            continue;
    }

    HalfEdge currHalfEdge = currFace.Edge;
    int i = 0;
    //This face has open edges; loop through the edges of
    //the face and add to the open edges list.
    while (i < 3)
    {
            if (currHalfEdge.Opposite == null)
            {   //Add the half edge to the hole;
                //V1 and V2 are the indices of the vertices
                //on the vertex buffer.
                HalfEdgeIdxs holeEdge
                    = new HalfEdgeIdxs(currHalfEdge.V1,
                                       currHalfEdge.V2);

                holesEdges.Add(holeEdge);
            }

            currHalfEdge = currHalfEdge.Next;
            i++;
    }
}
    //If there are no open edges, return an empty hole list.
    if (holesEdges.Count == 0)
    {
        return meshHoleList;//No holes.
    }
    //Method continues in the next code snippet.
```

The last step is to create a hole based on the open edge information. To do that, we get the first open edge from the list, and let the vertices of this edge be V1 and V2. Next, we assign the open edge to a hole and remove that edge from the open edge list. Also, we mark V1 as the first vertex of the hole; this is the vertex where the hole has to end when the hole cycle is completed. In other words, there must be an edge on the mesh with vertices (Vn, V1) that completes this hole. Now, we loop through all the open edges to find an edge where the first vertex is V2; this is the next edge of our hole, and we add it to the hole and remove it from the list of open edges. We continue this search until we find the edge (Vn, V1); this edge completes the hole, and we move on to the next hole. The loop finishes when there are no more edges in the open edges list. The following snippet illustrates this last step:

```
//Get the first open edge and add it to a new hole.
HalfEdgeIdxs currEdge = holesEdges[0];
Hole hole = new Hole();
hole.HoleHalfEdges.Add(currEdge);
//Mark the first vertex of the hole.
```

```
int firstVertexOfHole = currEdge.V1;
//Remove the open edge added to the hole from the list of open edges.
holesEdges.Remove(currEdge);
while (true)
{
    //Find the next edge of this hole, where the first vertex is
    //equal to the second one of the current edge.
    HalfEdgeIdxs currEdgeNext = holesEdges.Find(x => x.V1
                                                == currEdge.V2);
    //Add the found edge to the hole and remove it from the list
    //of open edges.
    hole.HoleHalfEdges.Add(currEdgeNext);
    holesEdges.Remove(currEdgeNext);

    //Test if we found the edge that ends the hole cycle.
    if (currEdgeNext.V2 == firstVertexOfHole)
    {
        meshHoleList.Add(hole);
        //No more open edges; finish loop; all holes found.
        if (holesEdges.Count == 0) break;

        //If there are still open edges, get the next one from
        //the list and start a new hole.
        currEdge = holesEdges[0];
        holesEdges.Remove(currEdge);
        firstVertexOfHole = currEdge.V1;
        hole = new Hole();
        hole.HoleHalfEdges.Add(currEdge.GetName(), currEdge);
    }
    else
    {
        //If we did not find the end of the hole, just go to
        //the next edge.
        currEdge = currEdgeNext;
    }
}
//Return the mesh list with all holes.
return meshHoleList;
}
```

This algorithm identifies mesh boundaries as a hole, which is explained in the next subsection.

21.3.3 Hole Classification

Topology-wise, for an open mesh, there is no difference between a hole and a boundary of a mesh. This can be easily visualized by making a sector of a circle with a piece of paper and building a cone with this circle, leaving the bottom of the cone open. The bottom of the cone is a hole in the mesh, but it is also the boundary of it. By flattening the cone and making it a circle again, you can again visualize that there is no topology difference between a boundary and a hole; see Figure 21.6.

In our collision meshes there are a great number of boundaries that are by design, and flagging them all as possible issues to be filtered out by the tester would generate too much noise and false positives, making the usage of the tool

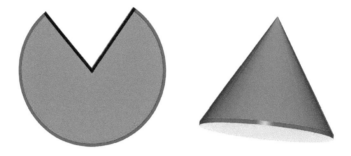

Figure 21.6. The boundary of our flattened cone is highlighted in red (left). The cone is assembled with its hole/boundary highlighted in red (right).

unpractical. To address this issue, we came up with two rules to whitelist holes that are highly likely to be by design. First, our collision meshes have very high vertical walls to prevent cars from falling out of the world, and the vast majority of the by-design boundaries are at the tops of those walls. We usually do not care about issues on the collision mesh that are very high; thus, we whitelist any hole that is found above the upper half of the mesh. The second rule that we use to whitelist is when holes are very big. Our collision mesh contains barriers along the track that have big boundaries, which are all by design; the intent of the second rule is to whitelist those barriers. Whitelisting based on a large hole size has proven to be safe; of course, we could have a giant hole in the track that is indeed a bug, but those are easily and quickly found by playing the build normally. Moreover, the user can also remove the whitelisting and let all holes appear and give a quick inspection by flying above the track.

21.3.4 Detecting Bad Normals

As mentioned in Section 21.2.2, there are two kinds of bad normals: flipped normals and skewed normals. Flipped normals (see Figure 21.3) are straightforward to detect. We loop through all the normals of the collision mesh and mark as flipped any normal that satisfies the following equation:

$$\mathbf{n} \cdot \hat{\mathbf{y}} < \mathbf{0},$$

where $\hat{\mathbf{y}}$ is the unit Y-up vector. Skewed normals are more complicated because we can have those kind of normals by design; see Figure 21.7. However, the ones that are actual bugs come from defects in the crafted mesh, usually very small triangles. The first approach we have tried to identify those is to simply flag triangles with small areas. This did not work well because a normal is influenced by the entire one-ring neighborhood of a vertex and looking locally at only one triangle produced too many incorrect results.

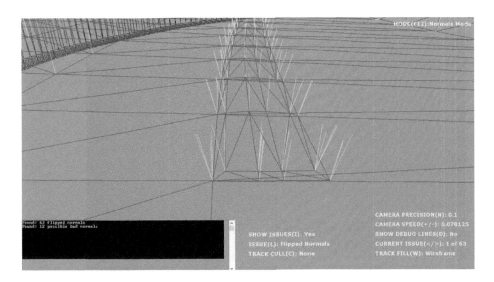

Figure 21.7. By-design skewed normals to simulate the effect of bumpy surfaces on the tires.

Later we arrived on a heuristic that works quite well for our meshes to detect those bad skewed normal. Our normals are exported with a 64-bit precision, and in the tool we recalculate the normal with the following non-weighted formula:

$$\text{normalize}\left(\sum_{i=0}^{k} n_i\right),$$

where k is the number of faces in the one-ring neighborhood of a vertex and n_i is the face normal of each triangle. We calculate this formula with 32-bit precision. After this, we have two set of normals: the original one with 64-bit precision and the calculated one with 32-bit precision. We then compare the two normals of each set; if their directions differ more than a specific threshold, it is highly likely that there are bad skewed normals in that area of the mesh and we flag it. This was done to simulate the behavior of the exporter in order to make a meaningful comparison and catch less false positives.

This method has proven to be a good heuristic; however, it can still cause false positives sometimes. When looking at those issues, we ask the testers to pay attention to the area around the flagged vertex and to see if all normals are following a well-behaved pattern. The threshold for comparing the two sets of normals is predefined for the user, but it can be modified at runtime in case some weird physics behavior is still happening in the area and the tool is not flagging anything. As the threshold gets smaller, there will be more false positives flagged.

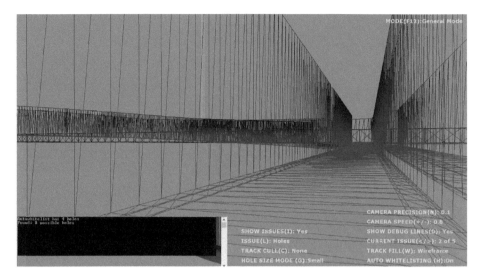

Figure 21.8. For the same small hole from Figure 21.2, the user can easily find it with the help of the green lines.

21.3.5 Detecting Malformed Triangles

Malformed triangles are simple to detect. When traversing the mesh to fill the half-edge data structure, we look at the triangle data and see if any triangles have vertices set in the same coordinates or if the three vertices are collinear. Those issues are flagged by the tool.

21.4 Visualization

Our visualization scheme has proven to be simple and effective. Usually the users of the tool are not very technical, and when designing the tool, we took into consideration that visualizing the issues should be very straightforward. The tool has basically two modes. The *general mode* is used to display holes and malformed triangles, and the *normal mode* is used to display flipped and skewed normals. In each mode, the user selects the type of issue that he wants to visualize (i.e., holes) and all of them are highlighted. The user can then loop through them by using the keyboard arrows, and while he is looping, a set of green lines that goes from each of the highlighted vertices to very high up in the Y-axis appears. Those green lines are extremely useful to actually find where in the mesh the issue appears; see Figure 21.8.

21.5 Navigation

As mentioned in the previous section, the users of the tool are not very technical, and our navigation system should be as easy as possible for a first-time user to learn. For multiscale environments, 3D content creation packages usually use some sort of an arc-ball camera scheme to navigate in the scene. Although artists are usually pretty comfortable with such schemes, regular users may find it hard and nonintuitive at the beginning. The ideal navigation scheme for the testers would be a first-person shooter style, which they would find very familiar. The biggest problem for such a scheme in a multiscale environment is the velocity of the camera; sometimes the user wants it to be very fast to traverse a long distance, and other times one may need it to be very slow to take a closer look at a very small hole. To solve this velocity issue, we tried automated approaches similar to [Trindade et. al 11], where a dynamic cubemap is generated to calculate the distance between the camera and surrounding objects and to automatically adjust the speed based on the distance. This approach worked to some extent, but there were still very bad cases where the camera was going too slow or too fast, which caused frustration to the user.

After testing some possible navigation approaches, we found one that was the best cost benefit in terms of usability and learning curve for our environment. The camera starts at a default speed and the user can increase its speed linearly with subtle moves on the mouse wheel. Yet, quicker moves in the wheel will make it increase exponentially (doubling each time), and a threshold controls the lower and upper speed limit. We also have a shortcut bound to a hotkey for snapping directly to a particular selected issue. Although this is not a scheme used in first-person shooter games, we found that after a few sessions the user can use this scheme quickly and precisely.

21.6 Workflow

The workflow in the studio begins with the artist crafting content source files, then the track will be built with its collision mesh and every other piece of content into binaries that are ready to be read by the game at runtime. After the build finishes, the tracks sits on an escrow folder waiting to be promoted by a test pass; if every test criteria passes, the track is promoted and others in the studio will see it in the build. At the beginning we had a separate export process for the collision mesh from the 3D content creation package to a format that our tool would read. However, this caused too many synchronization-related issues. Sometimes the export process would fail and new collision files would not be created, and testers would do an entire test pass in an old mesh. Moreover, the export script had to always be updated if artists try to use different source files for the collision mesh; if the export process did not get an update, testers would also be testing a wrong collision mesh. To solve this problem, we got rid of the export process and made the tool read the same binary file that is read by the physics engine at runtime.

The tool also has a couple of nice features that improve testers' and artists' workflows when filing and fixing bugs. Whenever an issue is highlighted, the user can press a hotkey to output the coordinates of the issue in the 3D content creation package space. Thus, when fixing the bug, the artist knows the exact coordinates where the hole is. Also, every time the tester presses "print screen" while in the tool, a screenshot will automatically be saved in a user folder with the type and the number of the issue, which makes it easier for the tester to navigate to the tool, take screenshots with the coordinates of every bug, and later file them all.

21.7 Conclusion

This chapter presented a 3D visualization tool for detecting collision mesh issues. This tool was used in production, and we were able to save hundreds of manual testing hours during development by using it. Our goal is not only to provide a solution to this particular problem but also to hopefully inspire the readers to use computer graphics techniques to solve problems in other domains, as it was shown with our testing problem.

21.8 Acknowledgments

Thanks to Zach Hooper for constantly providing feedback in the development of this tool and to Daniel Adent for the support on publishing this. Special thanks to my wife and family for all their help and to my friend F. F. Marmot.

Bibliography

[Botsch et al. 10] Mario Botsch, Leif Kobbelt, Mark Pauly, Pierre Alliez, and Bruno Levy. *Polygon Mesh Processing*. Natick, MA: A K Peters/CRC Press, 2010.

[Kettner 99] Lutz Kettner. "Using Generic Programming for Designing a Data Structure for Polyhedral Surfaces." *Computational Geometry* 13.1 (1999), 65–90.

[Mäntylä 88] Martti Mäntylä. *An Introduction to Solid Modeling*. New York: W. H. Freeman, 1988.

[McGuire 00] Max McGuire. "The Half-Edge Data Structure." http://www.flipcode.com/articles/articlehalfedgepf.shtml, 2000.

[Trindade et al. 11] Daniel R.Trindade and Alberto B. Raposo. "Improving 3D Navigation in Multiscale Environments Using Cubemap-Based Techniques." In *Proceedings of the 2011 ACM Symposium on Applied Computing*, pp. 1215–1221. New York: ACM, 2011.

22

Semi-Static Load Balancing for Low-Latency Ray Tracing on Heterogeneous Multiple GPUs
Takahiro Harada

22.1   Introduction

Ray tracing is used to render a realistic image but the drawback is its high computational cost. Although there are studies accelerating ray tracing using the GPU, even with the latest GPU, we cannot get a satisfactory rendering speed. An obvious way to accelerate it further is to use more than one GPU. To exploit the computational power of multiple GPUs, the work has to be distributed in a way so that it minimizes the idle time of GPUs. There are studies on load balancing CPUs, but they are not directly applicable to multiple GPUs because of the difference of the architectures, as discussed in Section 22.2.

If we could restrict the target platform as GPUs with the same compute capability, the problem is simpler. However, there are more and more PCs with multiple GPUs with different compute capabilities (e.g., a PC with an integrated GPU on a CPU and a discrete GPU). Also, when we build a PC with multiple discrete GPUs, it is easier to get different-generation GPUs than GPUs with the same specification, or the same compute capability. Therefore, if we develop a ray tracing system that works well on multiple GPUs with nonuniform compute capabilities, there are more PCs that benefit from the method comparing to a ray tracing system developed only for GPUs with a uniform compute capability.

If we restrict ourselves to a system with multiple GPUs of the same specification, we could use alternate frame rendering [Advanced Micro Devices, Inc. 16]. However, an issue of the method is latency; it does not improve the latency to render a single frame. There are many applications that prefer a low-latency rendering. They include games and other interactive applications. Also, the rise of the head-mounted display is another strong push of a low-latency rendering.

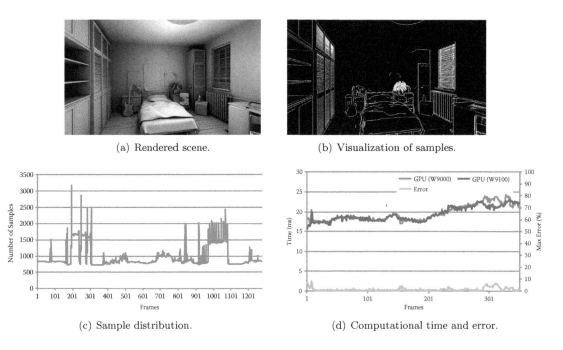

(a) Rendered scene.   (b) Visualization of samples.

(c) Sample distribution.   (d) Computational time and error.

Figure 22.1. (a) Ray traced scene on AMD FirePro W9000 and W9100 GPUs. (b) Visualization of the number of samples per pixel (black = 1, white = 5). The depth buffer of the scene is first rendered using OpenGL. Then, an edge detection algorithm computes this image, which is an input for a primary ray generation kernel generating more samples at pixels containing geometry edges. (c) Histogram of the number of samples of (b) for each vertical scanline. (d) Computational time on two GPUs and maximum deviation of computational time under a camera motion. Average error is 1.2%.

The goal of this chapter is to develop a low-latency ray tracing system for multiple GPUs with nonuniform compute powers. To realize this goal, we propose a semi-static load balancing method that uses rendering statistics of the previous frame to compute work distribution for the next frame. The proposed method does not assume uniform sampling density on the framebuffer, thus it is applicable for a problem with an irregular sampling pattern as shown in Figure 22.1. The method is not only applicable for the multi-GPU environment, but it can be used to distribute compute work load on GPUs and a CPU as we show in Section 22.4.

22.2   Load Balancing Methods

22.2.1   Frame Distribution

Frame distribution, also known as alternate frame rendering, is often used to utilize multiple GPUs for a raster graphics for interactive application [Advanced

Micro Devices, Inc. 16]. Although it performs well when all the GPUs in a system have the same compute capability, it results in underutilization of GPUs unless we use the same GPUs. When n GPUs are used, a GPU should spend $n \times t$ for computation of a single frame to have zero idle time where t is the time to display a single frame. Therefore, the latency of interaction is high; it takes time to propagate a user input to all the GPUs. Thus, alternate frame rendering is not suited for many GPUs with different compute capabilities.

22.2.2 Work Distribution

Data distribution, also known as sort last rendering, splits input geometry into small chunks each of which is processed on a node (when GPUs are used, a node is a GPU). Although it reduces the rendering time for each GPU, it is not straightforward to use for global illumination in which rays bounce. Moreover, the computation time is view dependent, thus it is difficult to get a uniform computation time for all the nodes. It also requires transferring screen-sized images with depth, which results in large network traffic. Therefore, it is not suited for rendering running at an interactive speed.

Pixel distribution, also known as sort first rendering, splits the screen into cells, and rendering a cell is distributed on nodes as work. If the works are distributed proportional to the compute capability of the nodes, all the nodes remain active and therefore we maximize the computation power of all nodes. This is often the choice to distribute work on multiple CPUs [Heirich and Arvo 98]. We also employ pixel distribution for work distribution, although the preferable work size is different for GPUs than for CPUs.

22.2.3 Work Size

CPUs prefer small work size for pixel distribution because it allows the system to adjust the workload on each node, which results in a uniform computation time on all nodes. However, when GPUs are used for computation, we also need to take the architectural difference into consideration. A GPU prefers a large or wide computation because of its architecture optimized for very wide computation. If a work size is small, it cannot fill the entire GPU, which results in underutilization of the GPU. Thus, we want to make the work as large as possible when GPUs are used as compute nodes. However, load balancing becomes more difficult if we make the work size larger and the number of works smaller, as it easily causes starvation of a GPU. The optimal strategy for our case is to generate m works for m GPUs and to adjust the work size so that computation times on GPUs are exactly the same. This is challenging for ray tracing in which the computation time for a pixel is not uniform. We realize this by collecting GPU performance statistics and adjust the work size for each GPU over the frames.

Cosenza et al. studied a load balancing method utilizing frame coherency, but they assume the same compute capability for processors [Cosenza et al. 08]. The method only splits or merges a work, thus it cannot perform precise load balancing unless using small leaves. Therefore, it is not well suited as a load balancing strategy for multiple compute devices. Another similar work to ours is work by Moloney et al., who studied load balancing on multiple GPUs for volume rendering [Moloney et al. 07]. However, they assume uniform compute capabilities and uniform distribution of samples. They also assume that the computational cost for each ray can be estimated. As none of those applies to ray tracing, their method cannot be used for our purpose.

22.3   Semi-Static Load Balancing

A frame rendering starts with a master thread splitting the framebuffer into m areas using the algorithm described below, where m is the number of GPUs. Once the framebuffer assignment is sent to slaves, parallel rendering starts. Each GPU executes the following steps:

1. Generate samples (primary rays) for the assigned area.

2. Ray trace at sample location to compute radiance.

3. Send the framebuffer and work statistics to the master.

Note that master-slave communication is done only twice (send jobs, receive results) in a frame computation.

At the first frame, we do not have any knowledge about workload nor compute capabilities of the GPUs. Thus, an even split is used for the frame. After rendering frame t, compute device i reports the area of processed framebuffer s_i^t, the number of samples processed n_i^t, and the computation time for the work t_i^t. That information is used to compute the optimal framebuffer split for frame $t+1$.

The algorithm first estimates processing speed $p_i^t = n_i^t/t_i^t$ (number of processed samples per second) for each compute device. Then, it computes the ideal time $T = N^t/\sum p_i^t$ to finish the work with the perfect load balancing, where $N^t = \sum n_i^t$ is the total number of samples processed at t. With these values, we can estimate the number of samples we need to assign for compute device i at frame $t+1$ as $n_i'^{t+1} = Tp_i^t$.

If the sample distribution is uniform on the screen, we could assign area $s_i'^{t+1} = Sn_i'^{t+1}/N$ for compute device i, where $S = \sum s_i^t$. However, as we do not assume the uniform distribution over the frame, we need to compute the area of the framebuffer that contains $n_i'^{t+1}$ samples for compute device i. The procedure to compute area s_i^{t+1} is illustrated in Figure 22.2 in which we assume that there are four GPUs. GPU i processed the assigned area s_i^t at frame t and reported that there are n_i^t samples in the area (Figure 22.2(a)). A histogram of sample

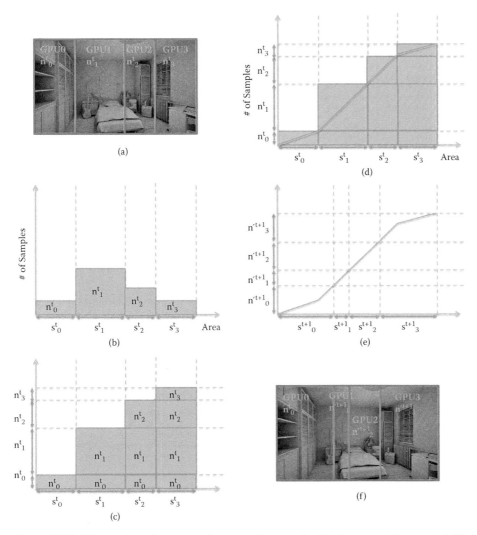

Figure 22.2. Illustration of computation steps for sample distribution at frame $t+1$ (f) using the information reported at frame t (a).

distribution at frame t is built from these values (Figure 22.2(b)). Samples n_i^t are stacked up, as shown in Figure 22.2(c), to draw lines as shown in Figure 22.2(d). These lines are built to look up the number of samples at a given area. For example, we can find that there are n_0^t samples at s_0^t, and $n_0^t + n_1^t$ samples at $s_0^t + s_1^t$. When building the lines, we ignored the distribution of samples in s_i^t and assumed the uniform distribution. After building them, we search for s_i^{t+1} corresponding to $n_i'^{t+1}$ by the binary search.

Since we linearize the sample distribution at area processed at each GPU, there is no guarantee that the computed work distribution is perfect. Therefore, we gradually move the distribution to the computed distribution by interpolating the split of t and $t+1$ as $n_i''^{t+1} = (1-\alpha)n_i^t + \alpha n_i'^{t+1}$, where α is the only parameter for the proposed method. We set $\alpha = 0.4$ for computation of Figures 22.1 and 22.3 and $\alpha = 0.2$ for Figure 22.4, which has a higher variation in the sample density.

22.4   Results and Discussion

The proposed method is implemented in a OpenCL ray tracer. Experiments are performed using three combinations of compute devices: AMD FirePro W9000 GPU + AMD FirePro W9100 GPU, Intel Core i7-2760QM CPU + AMD Radeon HD 6760m GPU, and four AMD FirePro W9000 GPUs. The framebuffer is split vertically for all the test cases. The method can be used with rendering pipelines with any sampling strategies, but here we show example usages of it with two rendering pipelines.

The first test rendering pipeline is similar to [Mitchell 87] but implemented as a hybrid of rasterization and ray tracing. It first fills the depth buffer using OpenGL, and it is used to compute a sample density map, as shown in Figure 22.1(b). The primary ray generation kernel for ray tracing reads the map and decides the number of samples per pixel. In our test case, we generate five samples for a pixel containing edges of geometry to reduce geometric aliasing, and one for the other pixels. Ambient occlusion is progressively calculated at 1280×720 resolution with two shadow rays per sample per frame. This is a challenging case for the proposed method because it has high variation in the number of samples in the direction of the split axis, as shown in Figure 22.1(b). We interactively control the camera for all the test cases to evaluate the robustness of the method for a dynamic environment. Sample distribution changes as the camera moves. This is the reason why the computational times and work distribution reported in Figures 22.1 and 22.3 have ups and downs. We can see that the method successfully keeps the computational time on different compute devices almost the same. Figures 22.3(d) and (e) show that the analysis of the work load distribution on the framebuffer is good. The same number of pixels would have been assigned for GPUs if we ignored the sample distribution. It however splits the framebuffer into works with different framebuffer area to achieve load balancing. The averages of the maximum deviations of computational time are 1.4, 0.9, 1.8, 2.9, and 2.1% for Figures 22.3(a), (b), (c), (d), and (e), respectively.

The other test rendering pipeline uses a foveated sampling pattern [Guenter et al. 12]. The sampling pattern we prepared in advance has higher sampling density at the center of the screen, and density decreases as the distance of the pixel from the center increases (Figure 22.4(a)). Sample density is less than one

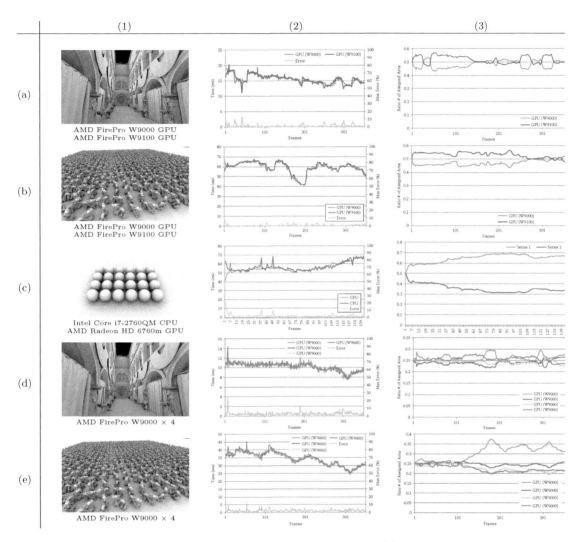

Figure 22.3. (1) Test scene and compute devices used for testing. (2) Computation time over frames. (3) Ratio of the number of processed pixels.

per pixel for sparse area. Primary rays are generated according to the pattern, and direct illumination is computed. We can see that the method keeps the computation time on four GPUs almost the same (Figure 22.4).

The method is also applicable to load balancing on multiple machines. In the example shown in Figure 22.5, the framebuffer is split into three areas each of which are processed by each machine, and each machine split the area further to distribute the computation on installed GPUs.

(a) Sample pattern.

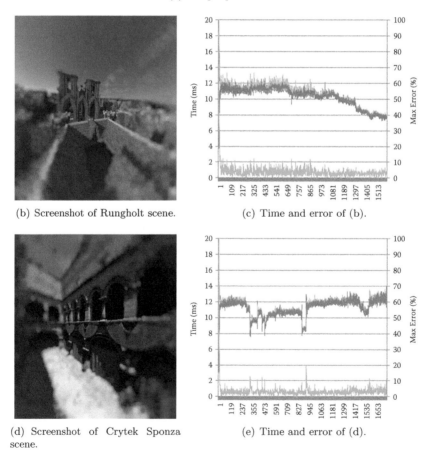

(b) Screenshot of Rungholt scene.   (c) Time and error of (b).

(d) Screenshot of Crytek Sponza scene.   (e) Time and error of (d).

Figure 22.4. Foveated rendering on four AMD FirePro W900 GPUs. Samples are only created at white pixels in (a).

Figure 22.5. Bedroom scene rendered using three machines connected via 10-Gb Ethernet. The frame is split horizontally to distribute the work for machines. In each machine, the frame is split vertically on GPUs. We used $4 \times$ AMD Radeon HD 7970, $2 \times$ AMD Radeon HD 6970, and $1 \times$ AMD Radeon HD 6850.

22.5   Acknowledgments

We thank Syoyo Fujita for help in implementing the foveated rendering. We thank David Vacek and David Tousek for Bedroom, Frank Meinl and Crytek for Crytek Sponza, Stanford for Dragon, and kescha for Rungholt.

Bibliography

[Advanced Micro Devices, Inc. 16] Advanced Micro Devices, Inc. "AMD Radeon Dual Graphics." http://www.amd.com/en-us/innovations/software-technologies/dual-graphics, 2016.

[Cosenza et al. 08] Biagio Cosenza, Gennaro Cordasco, Rosario De Chiara, Ugo Erra, and Vittorio Scarano. "On Estimating the Effectiveness of Temporal and Spatial Coherence in Parallel Ray Tracing." In *Eurographics Italian Chapter Conference*, pp. 97–104. Aire-la-Ville, Switzerland: Eurographics Association, 2008.

[Guenter et al. 12] Brian Guenter, Mark Finch, Steven Drucker, Desney Tan, and John Snyder. "Foveated 3D Graphics." *ACM Trans. Graph.* 31:6 (2012), 164:1–164:10.

[Heirich and Arvo 98] Alan Heirich and James Arvo. "A Competitive Analysis of Load Balancing Strategies for Parallel Ray Tracing." *J. Supercomput.* 12:1-2 (1998), 57–68.

[Mitchell 87] Don P. Mitchell. "Generating Antialiased Images at Low Sampling Densities." *SIGGRAPH Comput. Graph.* 21:4 (1987), 65–72.

[Moloney et al. 07] Brendan Moloney, Daniel Weiskopf, Torsten Möller, and Magnus Strengert. "Scalable Sort-First Parallel Direct Volume Rendering with Dynamic Load Balancing." In *Proceedings of the 7th Eurographics Conference on Parallel Graphics and Visualization*, pp. 45–52. Aire-la-Ville, Switzerland: Eurographics Association, 2007.

About the Contributors

Rémi Arnaud has worked on some of the most advanced real-time graphics systems. First at Thomson Training & Simulation, he designed a real-time visual system (Space Magic) for training purposes. Then at Silicon Graphics, he was part of the famous Iris Performer team working on the largest Infinite Reality systems. Then at Intrinsic Graphics, he worked on the Sony GsCube prototype system, which led to working at Sony Computer Entertainment R&D on the Playstation 3 SDK. He was at Intel working on gaming technology for the Larrabee and now is at AMD where CPUs and GPUs are finally working closely together thanks to him. He has been a witness of 3D technology making its way from multi-million-dollar systems to mainstream over the years. He is convinced 3D can be tamed and, once domesticated, make its way out of the niche into everyone's lives for the better.

Homam Bahnassi is a lead technical artist with over a decade of computer graphics experience supported by a strong and wide multi-disciplined engineering background (i.e., software, robotics, and civil engineering). He has developed and published new techniques for accomplishing challenging visual effects on game consoles—some of which were embraced by the industry, like Mega Particles. For many years, he has designed and developed workflows and tools in different game engines such as Frostbite, Unreal, and Dead Space Engine, including the engine that he developed with his brother Wessam. His experience was effective in optimizing production pipelines of several AAA projects.

Wessam Bahnassi is a software engineer and an architect (that is, for buildings not software). This combination drives Wessam's passion for 3D engine design. He has written and optimized a variety of engines throughout a decade of game development. Together with his brother Homam, they recently shipped their own company's first game, *Hyper Void*, which is a live showcase of shaders and GPU techniques (some of which are featured in previous *GPU Pro* volumes and in this volume). The game runs on PlaystationVR at natively rendered 120 FPS at 1440p.

Nicolas Capens is a member of Google's Chrome GPU team and a contributor to Android graphics tools. He is passionate about making 3D graphics more widely available and less restricted. His work on the ANGLE project helped create reliable WebGL support for Chrome on Windows. As the lead developer of SwiftShader, he enabled WebGL on systems with blacklisted GPUs or drivers. Through innovative multi-threading, wide vectorization, and dynamic code specialization, he continues to drive the convergence between CPU and GPU capabilities. Nicolas received his MSciEng degree in computer science from Ghent University in 2007.

Bartosz Chodorowski started his programming journey in the mid-1990s when he played around with Schneider CPC6128, a German clone of Amstrad CPC. Then he switched to PCs and has been programming mostly in Pascal, Delphi, C, C++, and Perl. He graduated from Wrocław University of Technology with a master's degree in computer science in 2012. He is a Linux and open source enthusiast, a gamer, and, above everything, a game programmer. He was Lead Programmer at Madman Theory Games for over a year, working on a hack-and-slash mobile/PC game. Currently, He works as Engine Programmer at Flying Wild Hog. He also co-runs a game and middleware company, Blossom Games.

Daniel Collin is a senior software engineer at EA DICE, where he for the past 5 years he spent most of his time doing CPU and memory optimizations, tricky low-level debugging, and implementing various culling systems. He is passionate about making code faster and simpler in a field that moves rapidly.

Patrick Cozzi is coauthor of *3D Engine Design for Virtual Globes* (2011), coeditor of *OpenGL Insights* (2012), and editor of *WebGL Insights* (2015). At Analytical Graphics, Inc., he leads the graphics development of Cesium, an open source WebGL virtual globe. He teaches "GPU Programming and Architecture" at the University of Pennsylvania, where he received a master's degree in computer science.

Michael Delva always thought he would be a sports teacher until he realized after his studies that his way was in programming. He learned C++ by himself, and he created his own company to develop and sell a basketball video and statistical analysis software, until he had to end this great period four years later. Then, he worked for a few years at NeuroTV, where he participated in the development of real-time 3D solutions and interactive applications for the broadcast industry. He is now happy to be able to mix his passion for programming and video games at Fishing Cactus, where he works as an engine/gameplay programmer.

Vladimir Egorov is a lead programmer at Mail.Ru Games LLC. He currently works on the *Skyforge* MMORPG. Before that, he had shipped *Allods Online*, *Heroes of Might and Magic 5*, *Blitzkrieg 2*, and other titles. He is now responsible for the entire client application architecture, from the auto-update system to the rendering engine.

Pascal Gautron received his PhD from the University of Rennes, France, for his work on interactive global illumination. He is now a senior scientist at Technicolor Research & Innovation. His major fields of interest are global illumination, rendering of participating media, and interactive navigation in large environments. He also contributes to high-quality rendering and real-time previsualization of post-production assets for the Moving Picture Company.

Holger Gruen ventured into creating real-time 3D technology over 20 years ago writing fast software rasterizers. Since then he has worked for games middleware vendors, game developers, simulation companies, and independent hardware vendors in various engineering roles. In his current role as a developer technology engineer at NVIDIA, he works with games developers to get the best out of NVIDIA's GPUs.

Julien Hamaide is an experienced programmer and technical director of Fishing Cactus. His main interest is sharing his accumulated knowledge with his team while learning more every day. Previously senior and lead programmer in a scrumm-based team at 10Tacle Studio Belgium, he decided to launch Fishing Cactus with Bruno Urbain and Ramses Ladlani. Always looking to increase overall knowledge, he contributed five articles to the *Game Programming Gems* series, one to *AI Programming Wisdom 4*, and one to *Game Engine Gems 2*. He also presented two lectures at the GDC 2008 and 2009. Owning an engineering degree in electricity and signal processing, he has a complete scientific background. By working in small studios, he had the chance to work on lots of different topics, running from low-level console programming to AI passing through multithreading.

Takahiro Harada is a researcher and the architect of a GPU global illumination renderer called Firerender at AMD. He developed Forward+ and the GPU rigid body simulation solver that is used as a base of Bullet 3.0. Before joining AMD, he engaged in research and development on real-time physics simulation on PC and game consoles at Havok. Before coming to the industry, he was in academia as an assistant professor at the University of Tokyo, where he also earned his PhD in engineering.

Benjamín Hernández earned a PhD in Computer Science from Instituto Tecnológico y de Estudios Superiores Monterrey, Campus Estado de México, under the supervision of Isaac Rudomin. He recently joined the faculty at Instituto Tecnológico y de Estudios Superiores Monterrey, Campus Ciudad de México. He has published several papers in the field of computer animation, crowd behavior, GPGPU programming, and virtual reality for art applications. His research interests include animation of virtual characters, procedural generation of crowds, rendering of complex scenes, and interaction design for mobile devices.

Stephen Hill is a 3D technical lead at Ubisoft Montreal, where for the past 6 years he has been single-mindedly focused on graphics R&D for the Splinter Cell series (Conviction and Chaos Theory). For him, real-time rendering in games is the perfect storm of artistic and technical creativity, low-level optimization, and pure showing off, all within a fast-paced field.

Meng-Cheng Huang is currently a PhD candidate in computer graphics at the Institute of Software, Chinese Academy of Sciences. His research interests include real-time rendering, GPGPU, interactive user interface and Internet-based computer vision.

Matthew Johnson is a software engineer at Advanced Micro Devices, Inc., with over 13 years of experience in the computer industry. He wrote his first game as a hobby in Z80 assembly language for the TI-86 graphic calculator. Today, he is a member of the DirectX 11 driver team and actively involved in developing software for future GPUs. Matthew currently lives in Orlando, Florida, with his lovely wife.

Ramses Ladlani is lead engine programmer at Fishing Cactus, the video game company he co-founded in 2008 with three former colleagues from 10tacle Studios Belgium (a.k.a. Elsewhere Entertainment). When he is not working on the next feature of Mojito, Fishing Cactus's in-house cross-platform engine, he can be found playing rugby or learning his new role as a father. He received his master's degree in computer engineering from Université Libre de Bruxelles.

Geoff Lang is a software engineer at Google on the Chrome graphics team. He is currently working on bringing ANGLE and OpenGL ES to as many platforms as possible to make the lives of graphics developers easier. In his spare time, he creates indie video games.

Jamie Madill works on Google Chrome's GPU team to help Chrome's OpenGL backend work uniformly across every device and API, via ANGLE. His background is in simulation and rendering, with which he still tinkers in his spare time. He graduated with a master's degree in computer science from Carleton University in 2012.

Sergey Makeev is the technical director at Mail.Ru Games LLC, where he is currently working on the next-generation MMORPG *Skyforge*. One of his main work duties is to design and develop a proprietary game engine to reach maximum graphics quality on a wide variety of PC configurations. Before joining Mail.Ru Games LLC, he worked on several console games (Xbox 360, Xbox, PS3) at 1C Games and Akella. He also worked as a consultant for a variety of Russian game-development companies.

Dzmitry Malyshau is a game engine developer at JVL Labs Inc. He was born and grew up in Belarus, graduated in applied math and computer science, and later migrated to Canada to work on interactive touch-screen games. Aside from experimenting with different rendering pipelines, he is actively researching compression techniques, networking security, and artificial intelligence problems.

Jean-Eudes Marvie is a Senior Scientist at Technicolor Research & Innovation. He received an MSc degree from the University of Rennes 1 and a MEng degree from the National Institute of Applied Sciences in 2001. He was awarded a PhD in computer graphics by INRIA in 2004. His research interests are real-time rendering, large models visualization and generation, procedural modeling and rendering, distributed applications dedicated to interactive visualization, rendering on large displays, and virtual reality. He is currently leading a team of 10 researchers, applying these techniques to the field of interactive previsualization for cinema production at Moving Picture Company and also to interactive applications on set-top boxes at Technicolor Digital Delivery Group. He previously applied some of these techniques for real-time visual effects on live broadcast systems for Grass Valley.

Stephen McAuley is a graphics programmer at Bizarre Creations, where he has worked on titles such as *Project Gotham Racing 4*, *The Club*, and *Boom Boom Rocket*. He graduated with a first-class honors degree in mathematics from Queens' College, University of Cambridge, in 2005 and undertook Part III of the Mathematical Tripos before starting work in the games industry. He enjoys participating in the demo scene, which originally sparked his interest in real-time computer graphics.

Krzysztof Narkowicz worked for more than 10 years as an engine programmer with a very strong focus on graphics. Currently he is the Lead Engine Programmer at Flying Wild Hog. He loves working with artists, coding graphics, and coding "close to metal."

Gustavo Bastos Nunes is a graphics engineer in the Engine team at Microsoft Turn 10 Studios. He received his BSc in computer engineering and MSc in computer graphics from Pontifícia Universidade Católica do Rio de Janeiro, Brazil. He has several articles published in the computer graphics field. He is passionate about everything real-time graphics related. Gustavo was part of the teams that shipped Microsoft Office 2013, Xbox One, *Forza Motorsport 5*, *Forza Horizon 2*, and *Forza Motorsport 6*.

Tony Parisi is an entrepreneur and career CTO/architect. He has developed international standards and protocols, created noteworthy software products, and started and sold technology companies. He may be best known for his work as a pioneer of 3D standards for the web. He co-created VRML and X3D, ISO standards for networked 3D graphics that were awesome but a bit ahead of their time. He is currently a partner in a stealth online gaming startup and has a consulting practice developing social games, virtual worlds, and location-based services for San Francisco Bay Area clients.

Eric Penner is a rendering engineer at Electronic Arts and a research associate at the Hotchkiss Brain Institute Imaging Informatics lab at the University of Calgary. He holds a MSc degree from the University of Calgary, Alberta, where he worked on GPU-accelerated medical volume rendering algorithms. Eric's MSc work is being commercialized by Calgary Scientific Inc. At Electronic Arts Eric has filled the roles of lead programmer on a Creative R&D team focused on cutting edge rendering and new forms of controller free interaction, as well as rendering engineer on the NHL series of games. Prior to working at Electronic Arts, Eric was a rendering engineer on the Advanced Technology group at Radical Entertainment and worked on the popular games *Prototype* and *Scarface*.

Donald Revie graduated from the University of Abertay with a BSc (Hons) in computer games technology before joining Cohort Studios in late 2006. He worked on Cohort's Praetorian Tech platform from its inception, designing and implementing much of its renderer and core scene representation. He also worked individually and with others to develop shaders and graphics techniques across many of the company's projects. Since leaving Cohort Studios in early 2011 he has been continuing to refine his ideas on engine architecture and pursuing his wider interests in game design and writing.

Fabrice Robinet works for MontageJS on seamlessly integrating 3D content on the web. He is also the COLLADA Working Group Chair at Khronos and lead for glTF (graphics library transmission format). Prior to joining the MontageJS team, he worked as an engineer at Apple where he co-created the Scene Kit framework.

Isaac Rudomin earned a PhD in computer science from the University of Pennsylvania in 1990, with a dissertation "Simulating Cloth using a Mixed Geometrical-Physical Method," under the guidance of Norman I. Badler. He joined the faculty at Instituto Tecnológico y de Estudios Superiores Monterrey, Campus Estado de México, in 1990 and from that date on he has been active in teaching and research. He is interested in many areas of computer graphics and has published a number of papers. Lately his research has an emphasis in human and crowd modeling, simulation, and rendering.

Peter Sikachev graduated from Lomonosov Moscow State University in 2009, majoring in applied mathematics and computer science. He started his career game development in 2011 at Mail.Ru Games as a graphics programmer. He contributed to a range of rendering features of the *Skyforge* next-generation MMORPG. In 2013 he joined Eidos Montreal as a research-and-development graphics programmer. He helped ship *Thief* and *Rise of the Tomb Raider* and contributed to *Deus Ex: Universe*. Peter has been an author of multiple entries in the *GPU Pro* series and a speaker at ACM SIGGRAPH courses. He now holds a senior graphics programmer position at Rockstar Toronto.

Gaël Sourimant is a researcher at Technicolor Research & Innovation. He received his PhD in computer vision from the French University of Rennes 1 in 2007. After working on 3D reconstruction and rendering for 3DTV at the INRIA lab, his research interests now focus on real-time rendering, image processing, and procedural geometry modeling.

Wojciech Sterna has been an avid programmer since 2002. He started with simple programs made in Delphi but quickly moved towards C++, games, and graphics programming. From that time on, he has continuously (co-)worked (mostly) on private game projects. In 2011 he graduated with a Bachelor's degree in computer science from Wrocław University of Technology, writing a thesis on software rendering using CUDA. This led him to a three-month internship as a DevTech Engineer Intern at NVIDIA London's office. He had a short stint in Sweden, studying computer graphics for six months. Since that time he has worked professionally mostly on engine/rendering development at Madman Theory Games in Wrocław and most recently at Flying Wild Hog in Warsaw. He also co-runs a game and middleware company, Blossom Games.

Steven Tovey is a graphics coder in the Core Technologies Team at Bizarre Creations, where he is currently chained to a PS3 working on *Blur* (and another couple of unannounced titles). Prior to joining the Bizarre crew, he enjoyed stints at both Juice Games and Slitherine Software, where he worked on a bunch of different stuff, some of which glimpsed the light of day. He regrettably holds a first class honors degree in computer games technology, which basically means he's stuck doing this forever.

Shannon Woods is the project lead for ANGLE at Google. Prior to her current work, she explored other corners of the 3D graphics world, developing software for game portability and real-time distributed simulation. She is a graduate of the University of Maryland and enjoys close specification analysis, music, and teapots.

Jason Zink is a senior engineer and software developer currently working in the automotive industry. He holds a bachelor's degree in electrical engineering and a master's degree in computer science. He has received a Microsoft MVP award for XNA/DirectX for the past four years running. Jason is also an active writer, coauthoring the book *Practical Rendering and Computation with Direct3D 11* (2011) and the online book *Programming Vertex, Geometry, and Pixel Shaders* (2008–2011), and he has contributed to the *ShaderX* series, the *Game Programming Gems* series, and the GameDev.net collection. He also actively maintains and develops the open source rendering framework Hieroglyph 3 (http://hieroglyph3.codeplex.com/) and can be found on the GameDev.net forums as "Jason Z," where he maintains a regularly updated developer journal.